FOCUS ON SUCCESS

The new edition

Ausgabe Wirtschaft

Michael Benford

David Clarke

Michael Macfarlane

Cornelsen

Focus on Success – The new edition: Ausgabe Wirtschaft wurde geplant und entwickelt von der Redaktion Moderne Fremdsprachen des Cornelsen Verlags, Berlin.

Verfasser:	Michael Benford, Bochum; David Clarke, Witten; Michael Macfarlane, Oxford
Berater/innen:	Rolf Bastian, Wetzlar; Philipp Fehrenbach, Nürtingen; Inge Schenkel, Friedrichshafen; Klaus Schlichtling, Oldenburg; Elke Uthoff, Osnabrück; Sibylle Vogel, Erfurt; Sybille Weiß, Mönchengladbach; Kathrin Wendling, Kamenz
Projektleitung:	Jim Austin
Verlagsredaktion:	Andreas Goebel; Kari-ann Seamark
Außenredaktion:	Christine House
Redaktionelle Mitarbeit:	Leah Holroyd, Laura Spratling, Lauren Chexal, Yovana Gruissem, Udo Diekmann, Fiona Mitchell, Edda Vorrath-Wiesenthal, Fritz Preuss (Wörterverzeichnisse)
Bildredaktion:	Jürgen Frey, Gertha Maly
Layout und technische Umsetzung:	Petra Eberhard Grafik Design, Berlin
Umschlaggestaltung:	werkstatt für gebrauchsgrafik, Berlin
Illustrationen:	Marcin Nowakowski, Mariusz Zabdyr, Oxford Designers & Illustrators

Erhältlich sind auch:

Workbook	978-3-06-020277-5
Handreichungen für den Unterricht mit CD-ROM und Audio-CDs	978-3-06-020276-8
Vocabulary Practice Book	978-3-06-020284-3

www.cornelsen.de

1. Auflage, 2. Druck 2011

Alle Drucke dieser Auflage sind inhaltlich unverändert und können im Unterricht nebeneinander verwendet werden.

Druck: CS-Druck CornelsenStürtz, Berlin

ISBN 978-3-06-020275-1

Inhalt gedruckt auf säurefreiem Papier aus nachhaltiger Forstwirtschaft.

VORWORT

Liebe Lehrerinnen und Lehrer,

Focus on Success – The new edition: Ausgabe Wirtschaft ist konzipiert für Lernende an Fachoberschulen und Berufskollegs. Es setzt Englischkenntnisse auf dem Niveau des mittleren Abschlusses voraus und bereitet auf die neuesten Prüfungen zur Erlangung der Fachhochschulreife vor. Das Lehrwerk führt zur Stufe B2 des Gemeinsamen europäischen Referenzrahmens.

Focus on Success – The new edition: Ausgabe Wirtschaft ist ein komplett neu erarbeitetes Lehrwerk und bietet neue, interessante Texte, aktuelle Themen und einen auf die Lehrpläne und Prüfungen abgestimmten Aufgabenapparat. Die bewährte Struktur wurde beibehalten: Auf den *Refresher Course* folgen 12 *Main Course*-Units, die einheitlich aufgebaut sind:

> *Focus:* Der Einstieg ins Thema – bildgesteuert, anregend und motivierend.

> Text A (*Personal perspectives*) betrachtet das Thema der Unit aus einer persönlichen Perspektive.

> Text B (*The bigger picture*) behandelt die gleichen Aspekte in ihrer Wechselwirkung mit Gesellschaft, Politik und Umwelt.

> *Business options* bieten Zusatzmaterialien zur Erweiterung und individuellen Schwerpunktsetzung aus einem wirtschaftlichen Blickwinkel.

Die Übungen, die auf die Texte folgen, schulen eine Vielzahl von *Skills* und trainieren darüber hinaus alle Aufgabentypen, die in den Abschlussprüfungen vorkommen.

Die Grammatik befindet sich am Ende jeder Unit in einem *Grammar checkpoint*.

Die 12 *Business Topics* im Anhang decken unterschiedliche Aspekte des heutigen Wirtschaftslebens ab. Dabei spielen *Business English*, Geschäftskorrespondenz und handlungsorientierte Aufgaben eine wichtige Rolle.

Der Anhang bietet neben einer *Grammar summary* umfangreiche Wörterverzeichnisse und einen Leitfaden zu Lernstrategien.

Liebe Schülerinnen und Schüler,

Focus on Success – The new edition: Ausgabe Wirtschaft ist Ihr neuer Begleiter auf dem Weg zur Fachhochschulreife. Verschaffen Sie sich einen kurzen Überblick über das Buch, und Sie werden darin alles finden, was Sie für einen erfolgreichen Englischunterricht benötigen.

Sie möchten ...

> Ihre Grundkenntnisse aufpolieren, um für die Arbeit mit längeren Texten besser gerüstet zu sein?
Kein Problem, der *Refresher Course* bringt Grammatik und Wortschatz wieder auf Vordermann – in sechs Units, jeweils anhand eines interessanten Magazinartikels.

> eine grammatische Form nachschlagen?
Dann schauen Sie einfach hinten in der *Grammar summary* oder der Liste der *Irregular verbs* nach.

> Tipps und Hilfen für den Umgang mit schwierigen Texten und kniffligen Aufgaben bekommen?
Dann werden Sie in dem Teil *Skills* im Anhang fündig – hier finden Sie zahlreiche Tipps, die Ihnen helfen, das Lernen effektiver zu gestalten.

> Vokabeln so lernen, dass Sie sie nicht gleich wieder vergessen?
In der *Unit word list* im Anhang ist der Lerneffekt gleich doppelt: Neben der deutschen Übersetzung lernen Sie auch Wörter mit gleicher oder gegensätzlicher Bedeutung, kurze und bündige Umschreibungen usw.

> Ihren Grundwortschatz wiederholen?
Die *Basic word list* bietet Ihnen alle wichtigen Wörter – thematisch geordnet, damit Sie nicht nur einzelne Wörter, sondern ganze Wortfelder auffrischen können.

Viel Spaß und Erfolg mit dem Buch!

Autoren und Redaktion

CONTENTS

Refresher Course

Main Course

Business Topics

Appendix

A

Free-time activities

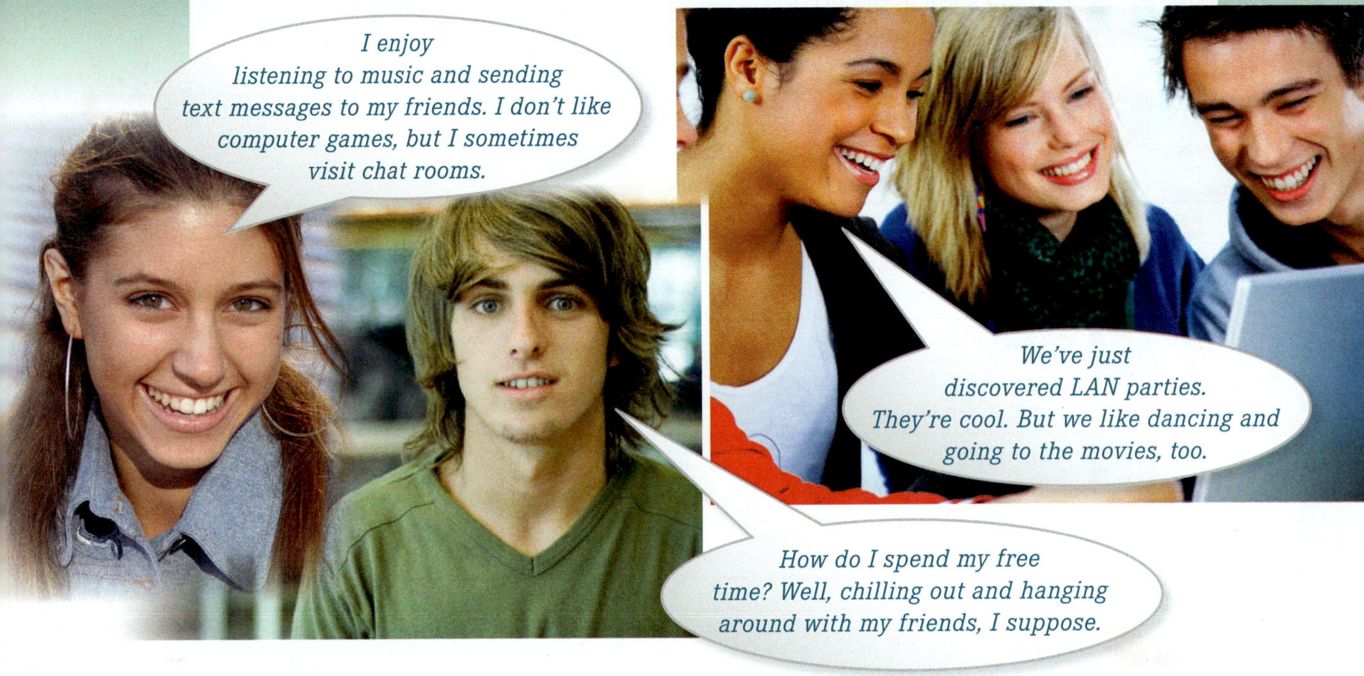

1 TALKING ABOUT YOURSELF

How do you spend your free time? Just chilling out, or doing something more active like sport? Use the language in the speech bubbles and the ideas in the box to talk about what you do.

chilling out | clubbing | dancing | doing sport | fishing | going to LAN parties | going to the movies | hanging around with friends | listening to music | making/mixing music | playing computer/video games | playing online poker | reading | riding | sending text messages / images with a mobile | shopping | surfing the net | phoning friends | visiting chat rooms | watching TV/DVDs

2 CARRYING OUT A SURVEY

A Ask other people what they like – or don't like – doing in their free time.

What's your favourite free-time activity?
What do you like doing most, ... or ...?
Which (activity) do you prefer, ... or ...?
Do you enjoy reading / doing a sport / ...?
Do you belong to a sports club?
How much time do you spend playing computer games / ... every day/week?

B Now carry out a survey. Which are the three most popular activities in your class?

According to the media, young people today spend too much of their free time just sitting in front of televisions or computers. But is this true? We asked four young people to describe their free-time activities. Read what they had to say.

DANA ***I spend most of my free time working for the Red Cross.*** *I really feel that I'm doing something worthwhile, not just sitting in front of the box! This week we're working with the homeless. That may not sound like fun, but I get a lot out of it. My brother Lee says I should enjoy life while I'm young, but he doesn't know what he's talking about. I'm sure that I'm having more fun than he is at the moment!*

LUCY ***Free time? Are you joking?*** *I work three evenings a week and all day Saturday too – I don't have much time for anything else. And then there's my mum. She says I can only have a job if my schoolwork doesn't suffer. So when I get home after work I usually do my homework and go to bed. When I go out, I enjoy looking round the shops with my friends. But that doesn't happen very often, I'm afraid.*

RAVI ***I'm playing in the first team of my football club*** *this season, so that takes up most of my free time. We train twice a week, you see, and then I usually have matches at the weekend. When I'm not playing football, I hang around with my friends or just chill out. I really like clubbing, but that's difficult in the football season. The coach expects us to keep fit and I don't want him to take me off the team.*

SAM ***What do I do in my free time?*** *Well, I enjoy playing computer games most, I suppose, but I don't like the violent stuff. I prefer the games that test your skill against other players. I often network with other players online or go to LAN parties. They're really cool. I make a lot of new friends that way. At the moment, we're planning a big international LAN party. People are coming to it from all over the place.*

3 LOOKING AT THE TEXT

Join the beginnings (1–6) to the endings (a–f) to make sentences about the texts.

1 An international LAN party could
2 The four people all have
3 One of the four people doesn't have
4 Dana's voluntary work with the Red Cross
5 Competitive computer games have the
6 Some parents say that part-time jobs

a can have a bad effect on schoolwork.
b makes her feel good about herself.
c much free time because she has a job.
d advantage of bringing people together.
e be a great way to make new friends.
f very different interests.

4 WORKING WITH WORDS

A Find words/expressions in the texts above to fit the definitions.

DANA
1 adjective: useful, valuable
2 people without a permanent home
3 certain

RAVI
4 noun: time of year during which something happens
5 noun: competitive game
6 verb: relax by doing nothing

LUCY
7 opposite of 'being serious'
8 verb: become worse
9 another expression for 'I'm sorry to say'

SAM
10 verb: like one thing more than another
11 noun: ability to do sth
12 verb: English for German *vernetzen*

B **Complete the sentences with six of the words/expressions from exercise A. They are not necessarily in the same order. Sometimes you must change the form.**

1 My team has an important ... today.
2 A lot of employers say social ... are as important as qualifications.
3 Can you call back later, please? ... Ms Barton is in a meeting at the moment.
4 When parents work too hard, family life always ...
5 DVDs are OK, I suppose, but I ... to see films at the cinema.
6 Can't you do something ... instead of just watching TV all the time?
7 Petrol prices always go up during the holiday ...
8 You're ...! You don't really expect me to work all weekend, do you?

C **Say who or what the circled words refer to in the texts.**

EXAMPLE > I don't want him to take me off the team. (*Ravi*)
> *'Him' refers to Ravi's football coach.*

1 ... but I get a lot out of it. (*Dana*)
2 ... he doesn't know what he's talking about. (*Dana*)
3 I usually have matches at the weekend. (*Ravi*)
4 The coach expects us to keep fit. (*Ravi*)
5 She says I can only have a job if ... (*Lucy*)
6 But that doesn't happen very often, I'm afraid. (*Lucy*)
7 They're really cool. (*Sam*)
8 At the moment, we're planning a big international LAN party. (*Sam*)

5 LOOKING AT GRAMMAR: SUBJECT AND OBJECT PRONOUNS

Subjektform	Objektform
I	me
you	you
he/she/it	him/her/it
we	us
you	you
they	them

A **Replace the underlined words with suitable subject pronouns.**

1 John and Ann often go cycling at the weekend.
2 Does Jack belong to a sports club?
3 Sharon spends too much time in chat rooms.
4 Paul scored the goal from a distance of 30 metres.

B **Now use object pronouns.**

5 A lot of people enjoy going to LAN parties.
6 I'm lucky. My parents pay for my mobile.
7 Jack phones Sharon five or six times a day.
8 We meet Joshua in town every Friday.

6 LOOKING AT GRAMMAR: SIMPLE PRESENT

Form

Lucy and her friends ***enjoy*** *shopping.* *Sam* ***plays*** *computer games.*	wie der Infinitiv, außer in der 3. Person Singular (*he, she, it*), die auf *-s* endet
Lucy ***wishes*** *she had more free time.* *Ravi* ***tries*** *to keep fit.* *Dana* ***has*** *more fun than her brother* ***does.***	Besonderheiten der 3. Person Singular: > endet das Verb auf *-ch, -sh, -s, -x*, folgt *-es* > endet das Verb auf Konsonant + *-y*, wird die Endung zu *-ies* Sonderformen: *do* – ***does,*** *go* – ***goes,*** *have* – ***has,*** *be* – ***am/are/is***
I ***do not / don't want*** *to lose my place on the first team.* *Sam* ***does not / doesn't like*** *violent games.*	**Verneinung:** *do not / don't* bzw. *does not / doesn't* (3. Person)
How ***do*** *you* ***spend*** *your free time?* ***Does*** *Lucy* ***work*** *on Saturdays?*	**Fragen:** *do* bzw. *does*

Gebrauch

I'm still at school and I also ***have*** *a job.* *Sam often* ***goes*** *to LAN parties.*	für Dauerzustände und wiederholte, oft regelmäßige Ereignisse bzw. Handlungen

> Das *simple present* steht häufig mit den folgenden Zeitangaben:
- *always, often, sometimes, rarely/seldom* (selten), *never*
- *generally* (im Allgemeinen), *normally, regularly, usually* (gewöhnlich)
- *every day/week/month/..., every morning/afternoon/...*
- *on Mondays/Tuesdays/...*
- *on weekdays / during the week, at weekends / the weekend / ...*

> Kurze Adverbien der Häufigkeit wie *often, never* usw. stehen unmittelbar vor dem Vollverb.
Lucy ***never*** *goes out during the week.*

A Put the verbs into the correct form of the simple present. Be careful about negatives and questions.

1 My mate Josh ...1 (*spend*) a lot of time playing online poker, but he ...2 (*not play*) for money.

2 A ...1 (*Lucy/meet*) her friends in town every day?
B No, of course she ...2 (*not meet*) them every day. She usually ...3 (*meet*) them on Tuesdays and Fridays, I ...4 (*think*).

3 A ...1 (*you/watch*) much TV?
B Well, I ...2 (*not watch*) TV at all during the week, but I ...3 (*enjoy*) watching a good film at weekends.

4 I ...1 (*belong*) to a football club but I ...2 (*not play*) in the first team because I just ...3 (*not have*) the time to train twice a week.

5 A What ...1 (*Frank/do*) in his free time? ...2 (*you/know*)?
B He ...3 (*play*) the drums in a rock band and so he ...4 (*not do*) anything else really.

6 Girls ...1 (*not surf*) the net as much as boys. ...2 (*you/think*) that ...3 (*be*) the reason why girls' marks ...4 (*be*) often better than boys' marks at school?

B **Work with a partner. Use the ideas below and the activities on page 6 to tell your partner what you normally/often/sometimes/never/… do or don't do and when.**

argue with my parents/brother/sister | catch the bus | come home late | do homework | email friends | get up | go clubbing/dancing/shopping | go to school / to the cinema / to the pub / to bed | leave for school / leave the house

EXAMPLES
> I **usually go** to bed at about 11 o'clock **on weekdays**.
> My mate and I **often go** to LAN parties **at the weekend**.
> I **don't watch / never watch** TV **during the week**.

C **Now ask your partner about what he/she does or does not do. Add other activities if you wish.**

EXAMPLES
> **When** do you leave for school?
> **How often** do you work?
> **Where** do you go shopping?
> **Do** you **go** to LAN parties?

D **Report back to the class. Say what your partner does and when.**

Bernd usually goes clubbing on Saturdays.

Kathrin and her sister often play computer games.

7 LOOKING AT GRAMMAR: PRESENT PROGRESSIVE

Form	
I am / I'm playing *in the first team this season.* *At the moment, we* ***are / we're planning*** *a LAN party.*	*am / is / are* + *-ing*-Form des Vollverbs
When I ***am / I'm not working****, I'm sleeping.* *You* ***are / You're not*** *just* ***sitting*** *in front of the box.*	**Verneinung:** *not* unmittelbar nach *am / is / are*
Are you *helping homeless people, Dana?* ***Is Ravi*** *training at the moment?*	**Fragen:** Austausch von Subjekt und *am / is / are*
Gebrauch	
I ***am working*** *at a supermarket.* *We* ***are helping*** *homeless people.*	für Situationen und Ereignisse, die im Moment des Sprechens bzw. Schreibens tatsächlich im Gange sind

> Das *present progressive* steht häufig mit den folgenden Zeitangaben:
at present, at the moment, currently, now
> Normalerweise haben folgende Verben keine Verlaufsform:
be, believe, dislike, hate, know, like, love, mean, notice, see, seem, think (= meinen), *understand, want, wish*

A Put the verbs into the correct form of the present progressive.

1 The players ... (*have*) a shower at the moment.
2 Wait a minute, please. I ... (*talk*) to a customer.
3 Dana ...[1] (*not work*) with old people. She ...[2] (*help*) the homeless at present.
4 A What ...[1] (*you/do*), Sam? B I ...[2] (*try*) to organize a LAN party.
5 A Why ...[1] (*Lucy/cry*)? B She ...[2] (*not cry*). She has a cold, that's all.
6 A Can you two help me, please? B Can't it wait? We ... (*serve*) meals.
7 Jack ...[1] (*not ride*) an ordinary bike. He ...[2] (*use*) an exercise bike.
8 Lucy's mum is very angry. Lucy ... (*work*) so many hours at the moment that she doesn't have time for her schoolwork.

B Use the present progressive to ask each other questions with *what* and *who*.

EXAMPLES
> What is Tom doing/practising?
> Who is practising penalties?
> Tom is (practising penalties).

cycle to the shops | do keep-fit exercises | get money from a cash machine | meet friends at the pub | play poker | practise penalties | surf the internet | take the dog for a walk | try on some shoes | wash the car

1 Tom

2 Mary + Julie

3 Brian + Sam

4 Tracey

5 Dick + Ella

6 Josh + Becky

7 Kate

8 Lee + Vera

9 Helen

10 Janna

8 MANAGING SITUATIONS

Sie möchten jemandem auf Englisch sagen, dass ...

1 ... Peter Drexler nicht mehr für Ihren Club spielt. Jetzt spielt er irgendwo in Norddeutschland, aber seinen neuen Club kennen Sie nicht.
2 ... Sie sich für Online-Poker interessieren und viel Freizeit damit verbringen.
3 ... Markus mit einem Freund gerade ein Computerprogramm schreibt.
4 ... Jasmin in der Woche meist zu Hause bleibt, da sie viel für die Schule tun muss.
5 ... Sie zurzeit Geld sparen, da Sie ein Auto kaufen wollen.
6 ... Sie einen neuen Job bei einer Pizzeria haben, Ihre Eltern aber wegen der Schule dagegen sind.
7 ... Ihr Bruder im Moment zu viel Zeit vor dem Fernseher verbringt.
8 ... die meisten Leute gar keine Freizeitbeschäftigung ausüben.

Girls fight for their rights

1 3

'Title IX' is a law that bans sex discrimination in US public schools[1]. One requirement of this law is that girls must have exactly the same chance to do sports as boys. The result? Girls have to join boys' teams if there are not enough girls to make up a team of their own. Read on to find out more.

Last March, Ashley Moore, 18, faced an awesome challenge[2]. She walked on to a wrestling mat to fight against her school's biggest wrestling rival. As he looked at her with hard, unblinking[3] eyes, Ashley felt a shiver of fear. Was she crazy? She was about to wrestle a hulk of a guy[4].

Four minutes later, however, Ashley walked off the mat a winner - and the hulk left on a stretcher. "He was big and strong, but he was slow," says Ashley of Edison High School, Richmond, Virginia. "He always tried the same hold. Then I took his arm and twisted it behind his back. When I did that, I pulled his back muscles. I didn't want to injure him. That's not what wrestling is about."

Ashley Moore is one of a growing number of American high school girls who play on boys' sports teams. While that can be tough, fighting stereotypes can be even tougher. But Ashley and girls like her are showing week after week that girls can compete against boys - and win.

Ashley had to fight hard to earn the respect of her male teammates. At the first training session, they greeted her with funny looks and nasty jokes. "Some of my teammates didn't say a word. They just looked at me," says Ashley. "Other boys said stuff like 'Hi sweetie, the volleyball team's next door. Aren't you at the wrong training session?'"

But Ashley didn't listen to the jokes and set to work - and soon she really impressed her teammates. "When they couldn't beat me in training," she says, "they soon backed off."

However, Ashley, who is called Xena after the TV warrior princess by her fans, doesn't want guys to back off. In fact, when she's on the mat, she wants to be their equal in every way.

1 **public school (AE) = state school (BE)** *staatliche Schule*
2 **awesome challenge** *überwältigende Herausforderung*
3 **unblinking** *unbewegt*
4 **hulk of a guy** *Kerl wie ein Baum*

1 LOOKING AT THE TEXT

Read the speech bubbles and the list of people in the box. Then decide who said each statement.

a female ice-hockey player ǀ a first aider ǀ Ashley ǀ Ashley's mother ǀ Ashley's opponent ǀ one of Ashley's fans ǀ one of Ashley's teammates ǀ the wrestling coach at Edison High

1 *At first I said Ashley should do something, well, more 'feminine'. But now I'm so proud of her!*

2 *I had to take her because of Title IX. There's no girls' wrestling team at Edison High, you see.*

3 *I thought, "No problem, she's just a girl", but she taught me a lesson. I won't be able to wrestle again this season.*

4 *Ashley doesn't look like Xena, but she's our warrior princess. We never miss a match.*

5 *Ashley's hard to beat – very fast, very clever. We're all glad she's on the team now.*

6 *Ashley's right. I had problems at the beginning too, but after a couple of games the boys accepted me.*

7 *My partner said, "Let's go and get the girl off the mat." Then we realized it was the boy.*

8 *Well, I watch a lot of wrestling on TV with my dad. I thought, "Why not?"*

2 WORKING WITH WORDS

A Find words in the text and introduction that fit the definitions below.

1 verb: synonym for '(to) forbid' (*introduction*)
2 adjective: opposite of 'private' (*introduction*)
3 adverb: synonym for 'precisely' (*introduction*)
4 verb: synonym for '(to) put together' (*introduction*)
5 adjective: 'difficult or frightening' (*ll. 1–4*)
6 adjective: synonym for 'mad' (*ll. 1–4*)
7 noun: opposite of 'loser' (*ll. 5–10*)
8 adjective: opposite of 'weak' (*ll. 5–10*)
9 adjective: synonym for 'increasing' (*ll. 11–18*)
10 adjective: synonym for 'very difficult' (*ll. 11–18*)
11 noun: 'member of the same team' (*ll. 19–25*)
12 adjective: opposite of 'nice', 'pleasant' (*ll. 19–25*)

B Now write six sentences of your own about sport, using words you found in exercise A.

C Copy the table and fill in the missing forms from the text.

	Verb	*Noun*
1	…	*ban*
2	*(to) discriminate*	…
3	*(to) require*	…
4	*(to) challenge*	…
5	*(to) rival*	…
6	…	*wrestler*
7	*(to) win*	…
8	…	*injury*
9	…	*competition*
10	…	*impression*

D Complete the sentences using words from the table on page 13. Sometimes you must change the form.

1 Many EU countries have a ... on smoking in pubs.
2 It is harder for women to play sport because there is so much ... against them.
3 Ashley took part in an important wrestling ... in Charlotteville yesterday.
4 Ashley's biggest ... has challenged her to fight him again when he's fit.
5 When she beat them in training, Ashley's skill ... her teammates.
6 A lot of people were surprised when Ashley left the mat as the ...

3 LOOKING AT GRAMMAR: SIMPLE PAST

Form

*Ashley **walked** off the mat a winner.* *I **took** his arm and twisted it behind his back.*	**regelmäßig:** Infinitiv + *-ed* **unregelmäßig:** Sonderform, siehe S. 300
*Some of my teammates **didn't say** a word.*	**Verneinung:** *did not / didn't* + Infinitiv
***Did I win** just because I'm a girl?*	**Fragen:** *did* + Subjekt + Infinitiv

Gebrauch

*Ashley **faced** an awesome challenge last March.* *This big guy **backed off** at a match last week.*	für Handlungen/Situationen, die in der Vergangenheit abgeschlossen wurden

Signalwörter

yesterday, the day before yesterday
two / three / ... days / weeks / months / years ago
last week / month / year / summer / Christmas / ...
the week / month before last
in 1973 / 2007 / ...
at that time / in those days
when he / she was a child / at school / ...

1 4 **A Complete the report with the simple past forms of the verbs in the box. Then listen to the CD to check your answers.**

agree | give | grow up | hear | kick | live | not be | not do | not even have | not go | promise | talk

Otis Shipley ...[1] in the poorest part of Perryton, a small town in Texas. He ...[2] with his mother and four brothers and sisters. Otis didn't know his father and sometimes the family ...[3] enough money to buy food. But Otis had one thing going for him: his skill as a football player. Nobody could run as fast as Otis and nobody ...[4] the ball as far as Otis.

It ...[5] long before Duane Tyler, the football coach at Robert E. Lee High School in Abilene, ...[6] about Otis's phenomenal talent. Tyler went to Perryton and ...[7] to Mrs Shipley. He ...[8] her that she would have money, a nice house and a future for her children. How could she say no? Mrs Shipley soon ...[9] to move to Abilene.

And Otis didn't disappoint her. Although he ...[10] anything except play football and often ...[11] to his classes, his teachers still ...[12] him very good grades.

B **This is a page from Ellie Brown's weekly planner. Use the simple past to say what Ellie and her friends did last week. Add any further details if necessary.**

EXAMPLES
> Ellie rang Ben and Annie about tennis at lunchtime on Monday.
> Ben and Annie had a phone call from Ellie about tennis on Monday.

MARCH

14	Monday	*lunchtime: ring Ben & Annie (tennis)* *evening: do ironing!!*
15	Tuesday	*8:00 a.m. take bike to Apex Bikes* *3:15 p.m. hairdresser's* ✕ *on way home: bank, pay garage bill*
16	Wednesday	*late afternoon: pick up bike (Apex)*
17	Thursday	*5:30 p.m. meet Mandy, Annie (Virgin Media) buy birthday present (Sam)*
18	Friday	*6–8 p.m. training, swimming competition* *9:30 p.m.–11:00 p.m. record film, BBC2*
19	Saturday	*10 a.m. meet Mandy (power walking, Mousehold Heath)*
20	Sunday	*visit Kate (hospital, Ward 4)* *GET BOOK – NO FRUIT, NO FLOWERS!!*

C **Work with a partner. Use the words in the box and the simple past to ask your partner what he or she did *yesterday / last night / last weekend / last summer / last Christmas / ….* Swap roles at least once.**

go riding/camping/dancing/swimming/shopping/… | go to a disco / the gym / the leisure centre / the movies / a party / the pub / … | go on holiday / a trip / a cycle tour to … | go on a date | meet sb | play basketball/cards/ computer games / football / …

EXAMPLES
> Did you go to the pub last Friday?
> Yes, I did. / No, I didn't. I went to a party at Paula's.

> What did you do last weekend?
> We went shopping on Saturday, but I stayed at home on Sunday.

4 MANAGING SITUATIONS

Sie möchten jemandem auf Englisch sagen, dass …

1 … Ihr Fußballverein gestern den Pokal gegen eine holländische Mannschaft gewonnen hat.
2 … es Donnerstag Abend kein Training gab, da der Trainer krank war.
3 … Sie und Ihr Bruder am Sonntag eine 60-km-Radtour gemacht haben.
4 … Sie vor zwei Monaten Golf ausprobiert haben, aber das Spiel äußerst langweilig fanden.
5 … Sie und Ihre Familie letztes Jahr einen Campingurlaub in Italien gemacht haben.
6 … Ihr Kanuverein letzten Samstag eine tolle Saisonabschlussfeier (*end-of-season party*) hatte.

You are what you eat

BEFORE YOU READ

1 5 **What do you think the text might be about?**

A case study: **Maddy Johnson's double life**

A lot of people eat too much food or spend too much time sitting in front of the TV. That's OK because if they eat less and do more exercise, they can become healthy. But some people have a genuine problem. They have a compulsive eating disorder like anorexia[1] or bulimia[2]. Read on to find out more ...

Maddy Johnson is charming, attractive and successful. She's popular, too - at school, in her part-time job and in her community. Everybody loves Maddy. But the reality is different. Maddy is leading a double life - the public one and a secret one that nobody sees. Maddy is ill. She suffers from bulimia.

The poster outside the fast-food restaurant showed a double-decker cheeseburger with an XXL packet of fries, two little tubs of sauce and a big can of coke. 'Today's Special!' it screamed. 'Buy two cheeseburgers and get free fries!'

Maddy looked at the poster and had that familiar, tingling feeling. It was like sex. "No!" she said to herself. "Just walk away! You don't want it! You don't need it!" But that was the problem, wasn't it? Maddy couldn't 'just walk away'. It was as if she had lost control over her own body.

Maddy went into the restaurant and bought two cheeseburgers with free fries. She walked to an empty table and sat down with her back to the room. She didn't want people to see how she stuffed the burgers greedily into her mouth. In no time, she was back at the counter. She ordered a dessert: an XL tub of ice cream with caramel sauce and two cream donuts. The guy behind the counter looked at her. "Hungry, are we?" he said with a cheeky grin. "He knows," thought Maddy. She wanted to sink through the floor.

Maddy finished her meal and went into the toilets. The tingling had stopped, but she hated herself. She felt dirty and so guilty. She went into a cubicle, bent over the toilet pan and threw up.

When she came out of the cubicle, a woman was washing her hands. "Are you all right?" she asked. "That sounded ... Well, I couldn't help hearing. I'm so sorry." The woman offered Maddy a card. 'Ellen Anderson, National Association for Eating Disorders', it said. It gave the number of a free hotline and Ellen's email address. "Will you let me help you?" Ellen asked. Maddy looked at her. "It's OK," she said. "What do you mean 'help me'? I'm fine. Really. I just felt sick, that's all. I don't need ... Well, I mean, ..." "You don't have to explain, dear. I've been down that road as well. I *know*. You just can't beat this illness alone. Please ring that number, day or night."

1 anorexia: refusal to eat for fear of putting on weight *Magersucht*
2 bulimia: addiction to food and vomiting to lose weight *Ess-Brech-Sucht*

1 LOOKING AT THE TEXT

A Do the following tasks.

1 Compare Maddy's public and secret lives.
2 Describe how Maddy felt a) outside the restaurant and b) when she went into the toilets.
3 Find evidence to show that Maddy felt embarrassed and ashamed of herself in the restaurant.
4 Describe Maddy's reaction to Ellen Anderson's offer of help. What does it tell us about Maddy's attitude to her illness?
5 Explain how we know that Ellen Anderson really understood Maddy's problem.

B Read the speech bubbles and say which opinion about eating disorders you agree or disagree with most. Give reasons for your choice.

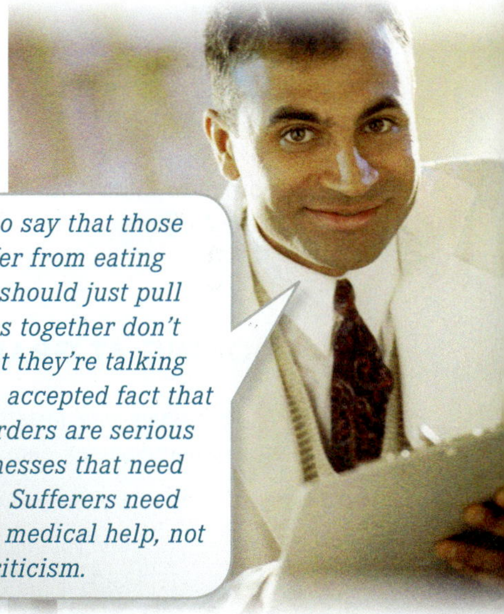

2 WORKING WITH WORDS

A Read the introduction and the case study again. Complete the table with the missing verbs.

verb + noun / noun phrase					
1	*(to) eat*	*too much food*	*6*	*(to) ...*	*free fries*
2	*(to) ...*	*an eating disorder*	*7*	*(to) ...*	*food into one's mouth*
3	*(to) ...*	*a double life*	*8*	*(to) ...*	*a dessert*
4	*(to) ...*	*from bulimia*	*9*	*(to) ...*	*a meal*
5	*(to) ...*	*a cheeseburger*	*10*	*(to) ...*	*an illness*

B Complete the sentences with verbs from exercise A. Make sure the verbs are in the right form.

1 I'm sure Alice can ... bulimia if she gets help from a doctor.
2 I always ... too much chocolate at Easter.
3 Two years ago Sally was very thin because she ... anorexia.
4 At this restaurant you ... a free dessert with every meal.
5 George must be hungry – he is ... that cake into his mouth!
6 I ... chicken but the waiter brought me fish.

C Replace the underlined words with a synonym from the introduction and text. They are in the same order.

1 Many burger bars attract customers with special offers. *A lot of*
2 People who drink too much alcohol get drunk.
3 Do you have a real reason for not doing any exercise today?
4 The difficulty is that 'natural food' is too expensive for most people.
5 Everybody knows that good-looking people have an easier life.
6 I live in a mixed neighbourhood with people from all over the place.
7 The truth of most people's lives is far from what you see in TV ads.
8 The driver of the car was so angry that she shouted at me.
9 The film was really disgusting. Afterwards I was sick.
10 It is almost impossible to overcome an eating disorder without help.

3 WRITING

Imagine you are Maddy. Use your answers from exercise 1 A to write an email to Ellen Anderson asking for her help.

Email

Hi Ellen

Thanks for giving me your email address. I think you are right – yes, I have a problem and I just don't know what to do about it. I feel so …

4 LOOKING AT GRAMMAR: POSSESSIVE ADJECTIVES

> *Possessive adjectives* zeigen an, wem irgendetwas gehört. Sie stehen – wie andere Adjektive – unmittelbar vor dem Nomen.

I	*Maddy is **my** sister.*	
you	*Can you tell me **your** name, please?*	
he	*What is **his** job?*	
she	*Is Joshua **her** brother?*	
it	*Wales is in the UK. **Its** capital is Cardiff.*	⚠ ***it's** = it is*
we	*There are 1,500 students at **our** school.*	
you	*Please open **your** books at page 23.*	
they	***Their** home is in London.*	⚠ ***there** = da, dort*

Complete these sentences with the English equivalent of the words in brackets.

1 What's *your name* (*dein Name*), please?
2 He's walking home because ... (*sein Rad*) is broken.
3 Maddy is writing ... (*ihrer Freundin*) an email.
4 Unfortunately the students have to buy ... (*ihre Bücher*) themselves.
5 The trainer asked me for ... (*meinem Gewicht*).
6 This table is too small for ... (*unsere Gruppe*).
7 The doctor thinks ... (*ihre Krankheit*) is curable.
8 You shouldn't give ... (*Ihren Kindern*) so much fatty food.
9 (*Ihr Name*) ... is Madison, but she calls herself 'Maddy'.
10 Look at that poor bird. What's the matter with ... (*seinem Bein*)?

5 LOOKING AT GRAMMAR: COUNTABLE AND UNCOUNTABLE NOUNS

Maddy ordered ***a dessert****. She had* ***an ice cream*** *and* ***two donuts****.*	*dessert, ice cream, donuts* usw. = zählbare Nomen (Pluralform möglich, können mit Zahlwörtern oder *a/an* verwendet werden)
I'd like ***cheese*** *and* ***mayonnaise*** *on my burger, please.*	*cheese, mayonnaise* usw. = nicht zählbare Nomen (keine Pluralform, keine Verwendung mit Zahlwörtern oder *a/an*)
Oliver had ***two cups of tea, a plate of ham and eggs*** *and* ***a bowl of corn pops*** *for breakfast.*	bei nicht zählbaren Nomen: Pluralbildung durch Hinzufügen eines zählbaren Nomens wie *two cups of …, a plate of …, a bowl of …*
Research *shows that bulimia is a serious illness. Ellen gave Maddy* ***some advice*** *about bulimia. Two recent* ***pieces of news*** *showed that exercise is very important.*	nicht zählbare Sammelbegriffe: *luggage, furniture, hardware/software* sowie *advice, evidence, information, knowledge, news* und *research* stehen mit Verben im Singular; Pluralbildung mit *pieces of …* (formell) bzw. *bits of …* (weniger formell)

⚠ Beachten Sie, dass wir die Nomen *people* und *police* nur im Plural verwenden können. Wollen wir sie im Singular gebrauchen, benutzen wir ***person*** für *people* und ***police officer*** für *police*.

> *The* ***people*** *in the café* ***were*** *drinking coffee. Only* ***one person was*** *drinking wine.*
> ***A police officer*** *said that* ***the police were*** *on their way.*

A In your exercise book, draw a table for countable and uncountable nouns like the one below. Put the nouns in box A into the correct column.

B Give the plural form of the countable nouns. Add a suitable countable expression from box B to the uncountables so that you can use them in the plural.

A

box | bread | bus | car | cheese | child | chocolate | coffee | evidence | family | fish | glass | house | kiss | knife | life | meat | mustard | news | oil | paint | water | woman | yoghurt

B

bars/pieces of | bits/pieces of | bottles/glasses of | cans/tins of | cups of | loaves/slices of | tubs of | tubes/jars of

Countable		Uncountable	
Singular	Plural	Base form	Qualified form
box	*boxes*	*bread*	*loaves/slices of bread*

C Now write five sentences using some of the expressions from exercise B. Be careful with singular/plural verbs.

6 LOOKING AT GRAMMAR: UNSPECIFIED QUANTITIES

> ***Some, any*** **und ihre Zusammensetzungen**

Please add ***some*** *salt to the potatoes.*	**bejahte Aussagen:** *some*
We don't have ***any*** *butter. Use olive oil.* *Did you put* ***any*** *salt on the potatoes?*	**verneinte Aussagen** und **Fragen:** *any*
May I have ***some*** *salt, please?* *Can I get you* ***some*** *orange juice, Maddy?*	**Bitten** und **Angebote,** die wahrscheinlich mit ja beantwortet werden: *some*
There is ***something*** *wrong with the toaster.* *I didn't see* ***anybody*** *I knew at the pub.* *Have you seen the cookbook* ***anywhere****?*	Zusammensetzungen von *some/any* werden genauso verwendet

A Complete the sentences with *some* or *any*.

1 Do you have *any* mustard, please?
2 We don't need ... bread.
3 There is ... butter in the kitchen.
4 It was awful. ... men had too much to drink and started a fight.
5 Would you like ...1 more fries? You can have ...2 of mine. I don't want ...3 more.
6 The party was a bit boring because there wasn't ... music.
7 Don't forget to buy ...1 drinking chocolate or we won't have ...2 for breakfast.
8 We can't invite ...1 more people to the party. We don't have ...2 room.

B Complete the sentences with *somebody/anybody*, *something/anything* or *somewhere/anywhere*.

1 A Listen! I think there's *somebody*1 at the door.
B I didn't hear *anything*2. I don't think there's ...3 there.
2 I can't find the shopping list. Have you seen it ...1? It must be here ...2
3 A Did you buy ...1 to drink?
B Well, I bought some mineral water, but I expect you'd like ...2 stronger.
4 I need ...1 to help with the barbecue on Saturday. Can you think of ...2 we could ask?
5 We need some more coke. If you're not doing ..., could you go and buy some?
6 Do you know ... who can mix cocktails, Janna?

> ***Much, many, a lot of*** **und** ***plenty of***

We don't need ***many steaks.*** *How* ***many tomatoes*** *do we need?* *I don't use* ***much salt*** *in my cooking.* *How* ***much butter*** *do we have?*	**verneinte Aussagen** und **Fragen:** *many* mit zählbaren und *much* mit nicht zählbaren Nomen
A lot of/Lots of children *are too fat.* *Maddy eats* ***a lot of food*** *and then she makes herself sick.*	**bejahte Aussagen:** *a lot of* oder *lots of* (weniger formell) bei zählbaren und nicht zählbaren Nomen
Drink ***as much water*** *as you like.* *We bought far* ***too many steaks.***	Beachten Sie: *much/many* nach *as, how, so, too* und *very* auch in bejahten Aussagen
There's ***plenty of bread*** *in the freezer.*	„viel" in der Bedeutung „mehr als genug": *plenty of* statt *a lot of / lots of*

C Complete the sentences with *much, many, a lot of* or *plenty of*.

1 There weren't *many*[1] people at the supermarket. I think *a lot of*[2] people are away on holiday at the moment.

2 A Hurry up! We don't have ...[1] time.
B Don't panic. We have ...[2] time. The shops don't close until 10 o'clock.
A Really? I thought they closed ...[3] earlier than that.

3 A How ...[1] people are coming to the barbecue on Saturday?
B Not ...[2]. Six, I think.
A Only six? Why on earth did you buy so ...[3] meat then?

4 You needn't go shopping. We have ...[1] food in the freezer and we won't need ...[2] drink. ...[3] people are driving.

5 ...[1] women work in supermarkets but not ...[2] of them have a top job.

6 A John eats ...[1] chocolate, doesn't he?
B Yes. He eats far too ...[2] sweets and he shouldn't drink so ...[3] coke, either.

> *(A) little, (a) few*

*Add **a little water** if necessary.* (ein wenig) *Jake has **little interest** in food.* (nur wenig)	**nicht zählbare Nomen:** *(a) little*
*You need **a few carrots**, too.* (ein paar) ***Few cooks** are as good as she is.* (nur wenig)	**zählbare Nomen:** *(a) few*

D Complete the sentences with *(a) little* or *(a) few*.

1 A Can I give you *a few*[1] more fries?
B No, thanks, but I'd like *a little*[2] more bread, please.

2 A Why did you buy so much beer?
B Because we only have ... cans in the fridge.

3 A Nobody gets fat at Brenda's parties. You only get ...[1] bread.
B Be fair. Last time we got ...[2] bits of cheese, too.

4 A Most doctors say that you should only use ...[1] salt.
B Sure, but only ...[2] doctors follow their own advice.

5 A There's ...[1] point in saying anything. The boss never listens to us.
B I know, but I have ...[2] questions I want to ask him.

6 A Shops can open on Sundays in the UK but only ...[1] do so.
B That's understandable. People want ...[2] time off.

7 MANAGING SITUATIONS

Sie möchten jemandem auf Englisch sagen, dass ...

1 ... Sie eine gute Nachricht haben. Die Polizei hat das Kind gefunden.
2 ... Sie nur wenig Zeit haben, da Sie noch viel Arbeit zu erledigen haben.
3 ... die medizinischen Beweise eindeutig (*conclusive*) sind. Essstörungen sind eine psychische Erkrankung. Viele junge Mädchen leiden unter Essstörungen.
4 ... Sie auf der Party viel Fisch und Käse aber nur wenig Fleisch anbieten wollen.
5 ... viel zu viele Leute Fast Food essen, weil sie keine Zeit haben, etwas gesundes zu kochen.
6 ... es dieses Jahr so viel Obst gibt, dass die Bauern nur wenig Geld verdienen. Viele lassen das Obst an den Bäumen.

D

Time out

Many young people now choose to spend some time abroad after they leave school. Holly Morris wants to do exactly that – but she can't decide where to go. So she writes an email to a magazine, asking for help with her problem.

Hi Jala

I hope other readers will help me with my problem. It's like this: I'm leaving school next July and then I'm taking time out, six months or so, to spend time abroad. I'd really like to go somewhere like Brazil or maybe India that I won't have a chance to see again. But my parents, who are going to help me financially, are totally against these 'exotic destinations'. They want me to go to a rich English-speaking country like Australia or Canada.

As I am going to work some of the time, they say it'll be easier for me to find a 'proper job' there and 'people are more like us'. But what's the point in going somewhere like that? I want to see new places and meet new people. But what can I do? My dad says that there's no way that he's going to pay for me to get myself killed!

Do you or your readers have any bright ideas?

Holly Morris

OK, Holly, so you're going to pay for some of your time out as you go – but how? Are you going to pick fruit or work in a bar, for example? If so, your dad's absolutely right. You can forget places like South America and India – and safety really is a problem, especially for girls. Please believe this, Holly, or I can see that you're going to have a lot of very nasty surprises.

1 LISTENING

1 6 **Work with a partner. Complete the email with suitable words. Then listen to the CD to check your answers.**

Hi

Look, this may sound totally uncool, Holly, but I *agree*[1] with your dad. You will find it very …[2] to find a job in a country like Brazil, where millions of people are out of …[3]. And even if you do find one, what are you going to do about language difficulties? Or do you …[4] Portuguese? Come on! Let's get real!

Here's my advice. Go to a richer, English-speaking …[5] like the USA or Australia, where you speak the …[6] and will be able to find a job. Please remember that you won't just want to earn enough for your ordinary living expenses, either. You'll also want to save some …[7] to travel around while you're there. Otherwise, what's the …[8] in going?

Now, here's a tip. You will find it very difficult to organize a trip like this yourself. You need expert …[9]. As a first step, why not visit a …[10] like bunac.org and …[11] the country you want to go to, America, for example? There you will find all the information, advice and job offers you need.

Good …[12], Holly, and have lots of fun!

Casey

2 LOOKING AT THE TEXTS

A Draw a table like the one below in your exercise book. Then complete it with information from the emails.

Holly	Holly's parents	Jala + Casey
– is leaving school in July	*– are going to help financially*	*– agree with Holly's parents*

B Holly is telling a friend about her plans. Use information from your table to complete the conversation.

3 WORKING WITH WORDS

Complete the sentences with words from the emails. They are not necessarily in the same order.

1 So many tourists go to 'exotic ...' that they are no longer exotic.
2 You won't have any language ... because everyone in Australia speaks English.
3 The USA is the biggest English-speaking ... in the world.
4 My dad wants me to get a '... job', but how? I'm only here for a month or so.
5 Spending time ... can be a great way to find out about life in another country.
6 We had a nasty ... when we got home. Somebody had broken into the house.
7 You can pick ..., but you will not earn very much money.
8 Holly will have to work some of the time to pay her living ...
9 How can she find a job in Canada? Do you have any ... ideas?
10 If you've never worked in Brazil before, you should get expert ... before you leave.

4 LOOKING AT GRAMMAR: FUTURE

> Das *will future*

Form

You ***will be able to*** *find a job in the USA.*	*will* + Infinitiv für alle Personen
I ***will not / won't have*** *a chance to go there again.*	**Verneinung**: *not* unmittelbar nach *will* ⚠ Kurzform: *won't*
Will Holly *be safer in the USA?*	**Fragen**: Austausch von Subjekt und *will*

Gebrauch

I think you ***will have*** *problems finding a job.* *I* ***won't have*** *a chance to go there again.* *I hope Holly* ***will follow*** *Jala's advice.*	Vorhersagen/Vermutungen/Hoffnungen über die Zukunft
I've missed my bus. – Don't worry. ***I'll give*** *you a lift.*	spontane Entscheidungen
Will *you* ***help*** *me complete this form, please?*	Bitten

> Das *going to future*

Form

My parents ***are going to help*** *me.*	*am/is/are going to* + Infinitiv
We ***are/'re not going to help*** *you get yourself killed!*	**Verneinung**: *not* unmittelbar nach *am/is/are*
Are you *going to work in a bar, for example?*	**Fragen**: Austausch von Subjekt und *am/is/are*

Gebrauch

Holly ***is going to take*** *time out in the USA.*	Absichten und Pläne
I can see that you ***are going to have*** *a lot of nasty surprises.*	unmittelbar bevorstehende Ereignisse, für die es schon Anzeichen gibt

A Use the correct form of the *will* or *going to* future.

1 I'm sure Holly *will enjoy* (*enjoy*) her time out in Georgia.
2 Holly's parents ... (*visit*) her in the USA.
3 The weatherman on TV thinks it ... (*rain*) tomorrow.
4 Watch out! Can't you see that child ... (*run*) across the road?
5 Is it true? ... (*Casey/help*) Holly find a job?
6 We ... (*do*) our best, but I don't think your visa ... (*be*) ready by Friday.
7 Let me know what flight you're on and I ... (*meet*) you at the airport, OK?
8 Hey, Dad, ... (*you/help*) me with my luggage, please?

> Das *present progressive* und *simple present* mit zukünftiger Bedeutung

I ***am leaving*** *school* ***next July.*** *Holly* ***is flying*** *to Atlanta* ***at 7:30 this evening.***	für Termine und fest geplante Vorhaben, mit Zeitangabe
Holly's plane ***takes off*** *at 10:30 tomorrow.* *The film* ***starts*** *at 8 o'clock on Sundays.*	für Flugpläne, Fahrpläne usw. für Kinoprogramme usw.

B Make sentences with the *going to* future or the present progressive. Only use the present progressive when there is an adverb of future time. Add any missing words.

EXAMPLES
> several school-leavers | take time out | Australia
> *Several school-leavers* ***are going to take*** *time out in Australia.*

> I | fly | Cologne next Saturday
> *I* ***am flying*** *to Cologne next Saturday.*

1 we + meet | 7 or 7:30 tomorrow?
2 we | get a job | pay for our holiday
3 you + come | Holly's farewell party | Friday?
4 Casey + work | the USA?
5 I | start work | six | and I | finish | two | next week
6 A What are your plans for the summer?
  B we | look for | a job on a farm in France
7 they + sell | their car | internet?
8 we | not have | holiday | next summer | | we | stay at home

C Put the verbs into the correct form: *will* future, *going to* future, present progressive or simple present.

1 A What time ...[1] (*you/go*) into town tomorrow, Ann?
  B Well, I ...[2] (*meet*) Ellie in the pub at 7. Jack and Sarah ...[3] (*come*), too. Why don't you come? I'm sure they ...[4] (*be*) really pleased to see you again.
  A Great. I ...[5] (*definitely* + *be*) there. It ...[6] (*be*) nice to see Jack and Sarah again.

2 A Is it true that Holly ...[1] (*not come*) back home at the end of her time out?
  B Who told you that? She ...[2] (*come*) home in August and then she ...[3] (*start*) college in October.

3 A The TV programme ...[1] (*start*) at 8:15 so I want to get the bus that ...[2] (*leave*) at 7:50.
  B But that bus ...[3] (*not get to*) Oak Street until about 8:10. We ...[4] (*only* + *have*) five minutes to walk home. Let's take the bus that ...[5] (*go*) at 7:30.

4 A We ...[1] (*not go*) away on holiday at all next summer. We ...[2] (*spend*) the whole time at home.
  B Good idea. They say we ...[3] (*have*) a very hot summer. I'm sure you ...[4] (*be*) much more comfortable at home.
  A True - and we ...[5] (*save*) a lot of money, too!

5 MANAGING SITUATIONS

Sie möchten jemandem auf Englisch sagen, dass ...

1 ... es morgen sonnig sein soll.
2 ... Ihre Schwester am 10. Juli in die USA fliegt, um ihren Job in New Orleans anzufangen.
3 ... Ihre Eltern Sie während Ihrer Zeit im Ausland finanziell unterstützen werden.
4 ... Sie wissen wollen, ob Tom vorhat, eine neue Stelle zu suchen.
5 ... Mary bestimmt ein Jahr in Australien verbringen wird.
6 ... Sie am Donnerstag nicht zu Hause sind, da Sie am Mittwoch in den Urlaub nach Italien fliegen.

Shopping

Shopping online certainly has its advantages: no parking problems, no queues, no pushy sales staff, no carrying shopping home. Plus credit cards make it so easy to pay – too easy, perhaps. Read on to find out what that can mean.

Sharon Miller's virtual world of online shopping

Clothes and fashion are important to me. When I was a child, my mum had mail-order catalogues. I liked to look at them and make long lists of the clothes I wanted. Of course, my mum didn't buy them. She couldn't. She didn't have the money.

When I got older, I started buying my own clothes. I spent happy hours at the bargain counters of big department stores in Manchester. Then, when I was 16, I discovered a 'nearly-new' shop in King Street. My first purchase there was a fabulous blouse in the latest fashion colours for just £30.

After that, I went there every week. The clothes were cheaper than in ordinary shops and often much better quality. You see, a lot of rich, fashion-conscious women sometimes wear really expensive clothes only once. And I wanted to be like those women. I wanted the coolest and smartest and most fashionable clothes, you know, exclusive Italian designer labels like Versace, Armani and Gucci – and I wanted my wardrobe to be full of them.

When I was 18, I discovered the thrill of eBay. I always thought eBay was just for techno freaks, but how wrong I was! Once I bought a lovely Armani cocktail dress in pure silk for just £4.99!

Soon I was doing all my shopping online – not just on eBay, but at top designer sites as well. But I spent more money than I had – much, much more money. With a credit card, it was so easy. I just clicked the mouse – click, click, click into the virtual shopping trolley. But in the meantime I've run up debts of over £4,500. And they aren't virtual, they're real.

1 LOOKING AT THE TEXT

Choose the right answer to complete the statements.

1 Sharon discovered her interest in clothes by ...
  a visiting exclusive boutiques.
  b looking through mail-order catalogues.
  c searching for special offers.

2 At first, Sharon bought her clothes at ...
  a bargain counters in big stores.
  b second-hand shops.
  c exclusive designer boutiques.

3 When she was 16, Sharon ...
  a heard about bargains on eBay.
  b bought fashionable clothes from rich women.
  c found a nearly-new shop in Manchester.

4 Sharon wanted to be like ...
  a her friends who wore the latest fashions.
  b smart women who wore expensive clothes just once.
  c the other customers at the nearly-new shop.

5 Sharon thought that eBay was ...
  a only for techno freaks.
  b an internet auction site that sold everything.
  c an online clothes shop.

6 On eBay, Sharon once bought a ...
  a blouse in the latest fashion colours.
  b wardrobe full of designer clothes.
  c silk cocktail dress.

7 Soon Sharon was doing all her clothes shopping ...
  a in online shops and on eBay.
  b on eBay.
  c in ordinary shops.

8 Sharon got into debt because she ...
  a used a credit card.
  b spent much more money than she had.
  c did a lot of online shopping.

2 WORKING WITH WORDS

A Link the nouns in the box on the left with a noun from the box on the right to form compounds.

1 bargain	5 designer	9 shopping
2 cocktail	6 fashion	10 techno
3 credit	7 mail-order	
4 department	8 sales	

card | catalogue | colour | counter | dress | freak | label | staff | store | trolley

B Complete the sentences with the English equivalent of the German words or phrases in brackets. Be careful to use the correct form.

1 There are many ...[1] (*Vorteil*) in shopping online. ...[2] (*Inzwischen*) more and more people have ...[3] (*entdecken*) how easy shopping from home is.
2 Many people prefer to order goods from a ...[1] (*Versandhauskatalog*) because they don't like ...[2] (*aufdringlich*) sales assistants.
3 ...[1] (*modebewusst*) women don't like to wear the same ...[2] (*Kleidungsstück*) too often.
4 It's a crime to ... (*Schulden zusammenkommen lassen*) that you know you won't be able to pay.
5 I didn't ...[1] (*ausgeben*) much at the supermarket yesterday. In fact, I didn't even use a ...[2] (*Einkaufswagen*) as I only needed two things.
6 Clothes at the new boutique are not as ...[1] (*teuer*) as at the ...[2] (*Warenhaus*) next door.

C First read the five golden rules. Then complete them with words from the box.

The Five Golden Rules

1 Know how much ...[1] you have. Be ...[2] and **never** just 'hope for the best'.
2 Buying for ...[1] is **always** much, much cheaper than buying ...[2].
3 Be very sceptical about ...[1]. In the end, nothing is ...[2].
4 If you ignore ...[1], it doesn't go away. It just gets worse - and ...[2].
5 Keep in touch with your ...[1]. Describe your problem honestly and say how you plan to ...[2] the debt.

cash | creditors | debt | free | free offers | money | on credit | realistic | repay | worse

3 LOOKING AT GRAMMAR: ADJECTIVES AND ADVERBS

*Sharon spent **happy** hours in boutiques.* *Shopping online is **quick** and **convenient**.*	Adjektive beschreiben Nomen Stellung: entweder unmittelbar vor dem Nomen oder nach einer Form von *be/become*
*Think about your needs **honestly**.* *All the clothes in this shop are **nearly** new.*	Adverbien beschreiben Verben oder Adjektive
*Sharon ran up debts **quickly**.*	Form: weitaus die meisten Adverbien enden auf *-ly*
*We must do two things **fast**.*	wichtige unregelmäßige Adverbien: *good – **well**, fast – **fast**, hard – **hard***
*Sharon **looks awful** in that dress.*	*(to) feel, (to) look, (to) sound, (to) taste* stehen mit Adjektiven

Choose the correct form of the underlined words to complete this text.

The man walked into the phone shop and went over to the display of mobile phones. He walked slow/slowly[1] along the rows of elegant/elegantly[2] phones, stopping occasional/occasionally[3] to look at a phone more close/closely[4]. But he couldn't look at them proper/properly[5]. They were all fixed firm/firmly[6] in anti-theft pads with little red lights that glowed bright/brightly[7].

An assistant came over. "Can I help you at all?" she asked polite/politely[8]. "Sure," said the man. "I need a new phone. This one looks good/well[9]." "The 6131? Well, you can't go wrong there. It's a very reliable/reliably[10] model." "Yes, but it's not cheap/cheaply[11], is it?" "You're right there," said the assistant. She smiled pleasant/pleasantly[12] at the customer. "But it's fantastic/fantastically[13] good value for money, you know. It's got every possible/possibly[14] modern feature. Let me show you." The assistant switched off the alarm and removed the phone careful/carefully[15] from its pad. "This way, please, sir," she said.

4 LOOKING AT GRAMMAR: POSITION OF ADVERBS

Satzadverbien	
Of course, *Mum didn't buy the clothes.*	**Satzanfang:** *(un)fortunately, actually, in fact, (un)luckily, maybe, perhaps, naturally, obviously*
Art und Weise	
Think about your needs ***honestly.***	**Satzende**
Ort und Zeit	
The shop is ***in King Street.*** *Mum comes home* ***at 6 o'clock.*** *The train leaves* ***Manchester at 10:30.*** *Ashley was* ***great in the match last night.***	**Satzende:** Reihenfolge bei mehreren Adverbien: Ort – Zeit Art und Weise – Ort – Zeit
Häufigkeit	
We ***often*** *go shopping in King Street.* *Sharon is* ***sometimes*** *irresponsible.* *We go shopping* ***every Saturday.*** *We only go shopping* ***once a week.***	**Satzmitte:** unbestimmte Häufigkeit – vor Vollverben, nach *be* **Satzende:** bestimmte Häufigkeit sowie zusammengesetzte Häufigkeitsangaben wie *from time to time, (every) now and then*

A Say where you would put the adverbs of frequency: position A or B.

1 Retailers A say B that shoplifting is getting worse. (*often*)
2 Tough punishment A stops a shoplifter B. (*seldom*)
3 Modern technology is A catching more and more shoplifters B. (*every year*)
4 Some shoplifters are so clever that they A get caught B. (*never*)
5 Other shoppers A see people shoplifting B. (*now and then*)
6 But they don't A do B anything about it. (*usually*)

B Rewrite the sentences with the adverbs in the correct position.

1 The coat was in the sale. (*luckily*)
2 Before buying on credit, you should think about your financial situation. (*realistically*)
3 Fashionable women wear expensive clothes only once. (*sometimes*)
4 I am very tired after doing the shopping. (*always*)
5 Sharon visits the eBay site. (*several times a week*)
6 I didn't buy anything because the shop assistant spoke to me. (*rudely*)
7 The Brad Pitt film is on TV this evening. (*at 9:30, on Channel 4*)
8 I think you acted very well – congratulations! (*in the play, last night*)

5 MANAGING SITUATIONS

Sie möchten jemandem auf Englisch sagen, dass ...

1 ... nächste Woche ein neues Kaufhaus in der Stadt eröffnet.
2 ... viele Produkte online billiger sind.
3 ... man leicht Schulden macht, wenn man immer online kauft.
4 ... riesige Supermärkte viele kleinere Geschäfte ruinieren (*ruin*).
5 ... Sie versuchen so oft wie möglich in kleineren Geschäften einzukaufen.
6 ... Stadtzentren in der Zukunft ganz anders aussehen werden.

Ready for a job?

Have you ever thought of working in your spare time? If so, this questionnaire will help you to find out if you're ready to take on a part-time job as well as school.

1 DOING A QUESTIONNAIRE

Do the questionnaire by choosing the answer for each question that fits you best. Use the table opposite to work out your score and then read what your score means.

1 *Why do you want a part-time job?*

A I've just seen a really cool new MP3 player and I have to buy it!
B I want to earn some money so I don't have to keep asking my parents to buy stuff for me.
C To get some work experience – I think it will help me find a good job when I leave college.

2 *How much time do you spend doing your homework?*

A Some nights I stay up late working, some nights I watch TV instead.
B I usually spend an hour every evening working. That way I get all my work done and have time for other things.
C Sometimes I get home from school and start watching a DVD or texting my friends and forget all about my homework.

3 *How often do you do out-of-school activities?*

A I do loads of stuff after school – I'm always busy!
B I'm quite lazy. When I get home from school, I just want to sit and watch TV.
C I go to one or two after-school clubs but I'm free most evenings.

4 *How much time do you plan to spend doing your part-time job?*

A My schoolwork and my social life are important, so maybe 15 hours a week.
B As much as I can! Just think of all the money ...
C That depends on what job I get.

5 *Are you ever late for school?*

A I always get to school on time – with my homework ready to be handed in.
B If my mum didn't wake me up every morning, I'd probably never get out of bed.
C I've missed the bus a couple of times, but I usually get to school on time.

6 *How well do you work with other people?*

A I hate being told what to do.
B I work quite well in a group. But sometimes I just sit back and let the others do the work.
C I like meeting new people and I'm always happy to help someone out.

Scoring

Question	Answer	Points
1	A	2
	B	4
	C	6
2	A	4
	B	6
	C	2

Question	Answer	Points
3	A	2
	B	4
	C	6
4	A	6
	B	2
	C	4

Question	Answer	Points
5	A	6
	B	2
	C	4
6	A	2
	B	4
	C	6

What your score means

29-36 Congratulations! You are organized, motivated and have a really positive attitude to work – all things that employers think are really important! Getting a part-time job should be no problem for you.

21-28 You seem to be ready for a part-time job. Just make sure you don't do too much – leave enough time for doing your schoolwork and having fun.

12-20 You're not ready for a part-time job yet. You should learn to organize your time better. Forget about looking for a job and concentrate on getting your schoolwork done on time! You need to be more sensible with money too.

2 LISTENING

1 8 **Reporter Clare Harris is interviewing careers adviser Bob Jackson. Work with a partner. Read the interview and try to fill the gaps with suitable words. The words are all linked to the theme of school and work. Then listen to the CD to check your answers.**

CLARE Good morning, Bob, and thanks for seeing me.

BOB Don't mention it.

CLARE Over the last few years, more and more teenagers have taken a part-time ...[1] while they're still at school. But is that a good thing? Shouldn't they concentrate on their ...[2]?

BOB Well, Clare, that depends on the person. Some people do part-time work and do well at ...[3] too. But others find schoolwork more difficult and might need more time for it.

CLARE But some people don't have a choice, do they? Lots of young people say they have to work just to get by – they have to earn ...[4] to buy the things they need.

BOB I'm not sure that's true, Clare. What do they need the money for? For food or for a new mobile phone? But you're right, part-time ...[5] among the over-16s has increased a lot since the 1990s and, in most cases, I think that's a good thing.

CLARE Really? But don't young people nowadays have much more stress in their lives because they have jobs?

BOB No, not really. People have been working their way through school for generations. Many people think it's right that students help to ...[6] for their education.

CLARE Sure, I understand that. But I still think people who have to work while they're at school are at a disadvantage.

BOB Well, most American ...[7] are looking for someone with experience. They think working while you're at school helps young people to learn important job-related skills.

CLARE Oh, come on, Bob! Filling supermarket shelves and cooking burgers are skills, are they?

BOB That's not what I meant. I'm talking about real ...[8] that are important for all jobs. Things like getting to work on time – I mean, if you can't organize your ...[9] then you're not ready to work yet. Part-time jobs teach you how to work well with other ...[10] too.

3 LOOKING AT THE TEXT

Do the following tasks.

1 List three objections that Clare has to school students taking part-time jobs.
2 Say why Bob is sceptical about Clare's point that some young people have to take a job just to live.
3 Explain why American employers think that working your way through school or college is an advantage.
4 Describe the misunderstanding that Clare and Bob have about 'job-related skills'.

4 WORKING WITH WORDS

A Find the English equivalents of these German phrases in the interview in exercise 2. They are in the same order.

1 Keine Ursache!
2 darauf ankommen
3 über die Runden kommen
4 recht haben
5 Wirklich?
6 eigentlich nicht
7 Ich bitte dich!
8 nicht so weit sein

B Use two of the English words or expressions you found in exercise A to complete these cartoons.

C Complete Susan Barton's description of her job with words from the box.

afternoons | brochures | busy | careless | customers | interesting | main job | parents | pay | part-time | plenty | work

Hi. My name's Susan Barton and I'm 17. I'm still at school, but I have a ...[1] job at a travel agency in the town centre. I ...[2] there for three hours on Wednesday, Thursday and Friday ...[3], and four hours on Saturday mornings, from 8:30 to 12:30. That makes 13 hours in all, which my ...[4] say is more than enough.
My ...[5] is to make sure that there are always enough ...[6] in the racks, and that they are all correctly sorted. That doesn't sound much, but in fact there's ...[7] to do. Some people are so ...[8]. They often look at brochures and then put them back in the wrong rack – if they put them back at all, that is! Now that I have been there for a few months, I also sometimes help the assistants to deal with ...[9] and answer the phone when we're ...[10]. As I like people, I find that more ...[11] than just looking after brochures, of course. And the ...[12] is good – £5.50 an hour! I certainly can't complain about that, can I?

5 SPEAKING

A Work with a partner. Take it in turns to ask each other questions about your part-time jobs. Use the language below to help you.

Do you have a part-time job?	*Yes, I do. / No, I don't.*
What do you do?	*I'm a bartender/cashier/shelf-stacker/waiter/...* *I give private tuition.* *I help in an old people's home / at a filling station / ...*
How long have you had it?	*I've had it for (+* Zeitraum: *six weeks, three months).* *I've had it since (+* Zeitpunkt: *last February, summer 2008).*

B Now discuss someone you know who has a part-time job.

Does ... have a job?	
What does he/she do?	*He's/She's a ...*
How long has he/she had it?	

6 LOOKING AT GRAMMAR: PRESENT PERFECT

Form

Your boss ***has asked*** *you to clean the floor.* *A lot of students* ***have taken*** *part-time jobs.*	*have/has* + 3. Form **regelmäßig:** *have/has* + 3. Form auf *-ed* **unregelmäßig:** *have/has* + unregelmäßige 3. Form: siehe S. 300
Ellie ***has not / hasn't found*** *a job yet.*	**Verneinung:** *not* unmittelbar hinter *have/has*
Have you *answered the questions honestly?*	**Fragen:** Austausch von Subjekt und *have/has*

Gebrauch

I can't come to work. I ***have hurt*** *my hand.* *Jane isn't here. She****'s gone*** *to the bank.*	ohne Zeitangabe für Situationen/Ereignisse, die noch andauern oder deren Auswirkungen noch in der Gegenwart spürbar sind
Have *you* ***ever been*** *to the USA, Holly?* ***I've never had*** *a part-time job.* *Casey* ***hasn't answered*** *my email* ***yet.*** *Part-time work among the over-16s* ***has increased*** *a lot* ***since the 1990s.*** *Maddy* ***hasn't stopped*** *eating* ***all day.***	mit Zeitangaben für die ganze Zeit bis jetzt wie *ever* (jemals), *never, yet, still, for* (+ Zeitraum), *since* (+ Zeitpunkt)
Ellie ***has just found*** *a job at a boutique.* ***I've been*** *to the cinema a lot* ***recently.***	mit Zeitangaben für die (aller)letzte Zeit wie *just, recently*

⚠ Beachten Sie die Stellung der Adverbien:
The film has ***just*** *started.*
The bus has ***already*** *left.*
I have ***never*** *been to New York.*
They ***(still)*** *have* ***not*** *finished the job* ***yet.*** ⚠ (immer) noch nicht

A Put the verbs into the correct form of the present perfect. Be careful about negatives and questions.

1 The students *have already arrived*[1] (*already* + *arrive*). In fact, they ...[2] (*already* + *be*) here for an hour.
2 The mechanic ...[1] (*repair*) the car and he ...[2] (*wash*) it as well.
3 The men ...[1] (*not start*) work yet. ...[2] (*you/tell*) them what to do yet?
4 I ...[1] (*not see*) Ben since yesterday. I hope he ...[2] (*not take*) the day off again.
5 The boss ...[1] (*ask*) me twice if we ...[2] (*finish*) this job yet.
6 I ...[1] (*not be*) here long. I ...[2] (*only* + *live*) in Atlanta for two weeks.
7 ...[1] (*Benny/clean*) the floor yet? I ...[2] (*ask*) him to do it several times.
8 ...[1] (*you/meet*) our new part-timer yet? He ...[2] (*just* + *start*) here.

B Complete the sentences with *for* (period of time: *for two years*) or *since* (point in time: *since 3 o'clock*).

1 I haven't watched TV ... last weekend.
2 I haven't seen Sharon ... months.
3 Have you seen Carey ... she got back from Georgia?
4 Jack hasn't spent any time with his family ... years.
5 Amy has worked here ever ... we opened.
6 Holly has worked here ... a month now.
7 I haven't seen Ann ... she started her part-time job.
8 Kenny has only lived in England ... a few weeks.

C Look at the pictures. Use the present perfect to say what has *just* happened.

1 finish
The film *has just finished*.

2 leave
Mum and Dad ... for work.

3 send
Ed ... a text message.

4 switch on
Susan ...

5 clean
The boys ...

6 begin
The news ...

7 MANAGING SITUATIONS

Sie möchten jemandem auf Englisch sagen, dass ...

1 ... Sie seit sechs Monaten einen Nachmittagsjob haben.
2 ... Sie gerade eine E-Mail geschrieben haben.
3 ... Holly nie für Geld gearbeitet hat.
4 ... Familie Carter seit zwei Jahren in Deutschland wohnt.
5 ... Sie seit drei Wochen in einem Computergeschäft arbeiten.
6 ... ein Freund gerade angerufen hat, um Ihnen seine Ankunftszeit (*time of arrival*) zu sagen.

1

Main Course

City lights

FOCUS

1 Read the quotation. Explain how this statement could be true.

'The strange thing about New York City is that you feel as though you've been there before, even if you've never set foot in the US.' Simon Gage, Introduction to *Out Around New York*

2 Look at photos A–F and match them to places 1–6.

1 Brooklyn Bridge
2 Central Park
3 Grand Central Terminal
4 the Chrysler Building
5 the Empire State Building
6 the Statue of Liberty

A

B

C

D

E

F

3 Work with a partner. Think of films that show some of these places. Use the ideas below to help you talk about the films.

A	*I think the Empire State Building*	*features appears*	*in King Kong.*
B	*Oh, you mean that (famous)*	*scene, sequence,*	*don't you? The one where King Kong climbs to the top and catches planes in his hand.*

4 Say which place in New York you would most like to visit and why. Use the list from exercise 2 or your own ideas.

A Personal perspectives

BEFORE YOU READ

A Compare and contrast the two photos opposite. Use the language below to help you.

One photo shows a country scene, whereas the other one ...		
In the picture on the right,	*there are a lot of* *we can see lots of*	*cars, while in the ...*

B Scan the emails quickly and find out who they are to and from.

Lesen schwieriger Texte: S. 196

1 LOOKING AT THE TEXTS

A Read the emails and do these activities.

Lesen schwieriger Texte: S. 196

1 Put emails A–D in order from 1 to 4.
2 Name the places in the photos. Match the writer and reader of the emails to the photos.
3 Find the state of Oregon and the city of New York on the map at the back of the book. Say roughly how far Ricky and his family travelled when they moved.
4 Put the following events in the order that they happened.
  a Ricky meets Lucy.
  b The family move to their new apartment.
  c Ricky goes to a party with his new friend.
  d Ricky and his family travel to New York.
  e The family look for a place to live.
  f The family move into a hotel.
  g The family see Manhattan from the top of the Empire State Building.

B Say what you think.

1 Compare the endings of the emails.
2 Work out what is probably happening with Ricky and Lucy.
3 What are your views on this kind of change in this particular situation?

C Compare urban and rural life.

1 Imagine a New York family moving to Silver Creek. Say how they might feel about their new home. Use these phrases and adjectives to help you.

Compared with NY, life here is much more ...
The people are a lot less ...

calm | enjoyable | exciting | fast | friendly | fun | gentle | intense | interesting | noisy | pleasant | quiet | relaxed | slow

2 Say if you would prefer to live in New York or in Silver Creek. Use phrases like these.

Personally, I would prefer to live in ...	
I think life there would be (much) more ...	*than life in ...*
I don't think life there would be as ...	*as life in ...*

1 9

A

Dear Sue

I still miss you as much as ever – more, in fact! I've been checking out flight prices on the internet, and they're less expensive than I thought. Pretty soon, I promise, I'll be back in Silver Creek with you.

I still can't get used to this city. It's just too fast, too loud. The people too. Out on the street, they seem like they're always power-walking – except when they stop to yell at each other! Yesterday, we went up the Empire State Building, and the view was really something. The downtown Manhattan skyline just blows you away.

Must run. We're going to check out some places to live.

Lots of love
Ricky

B

Dear Sue

Well, I'm starting to like New York a lot more than before. They say it's the most exciting place in the world, and maybe it really is. Music, sport, movie theaters, festivals – you name it, New York's got it!

I start at John F Kennedy High next week, and that's scary. But I met a girl called Lucy in the elevator – she lives two floors down – and we got talking. Turns out Lucy's at JFK, and she's going to be a senior too. She's going to introduce me to everyone, and that's great.

There's a lot more to tell you, but I have to stop now. I'm going to a party with Lucy.

Best wishes
Ricky

C

Dear Sue

Sorry I didn't write last week, but life was busy. We finally got our new apartment, and last week we moved in.

It's much smaller than our old place, but I guess that's because there's no space to waste in this city. (After all, it's the city of skyscrapers, isn't it?) Anyway, it's big enough, and we've got great views of Central Park. It's huge, it's green and it's right in the middle of Manhattan. Amazing.

I'm beginning to get to know NY now, and it's OK. But it would be a whole lot better if you could be here too.

Love
Ricky

D

Dear Sue

I still can't believe what's happening. A week ago, I was still in the best place in Oregon, with the best girl in the world.

And now what? The forest and waterfalls are gone, and I'm stuck in this non-stop nightmare of noise. Even up here on the 17th floor of our hotel, you still hear the traffic 24-7. What were Mom and Dad thinking of, coming to work in New York?

All I want is to get back home to see you. I miss you more than anything in the world. Write soon.

I love you so much! XXX
Ricky

(438 words)

2 WORKING WITH WORDS

A Explain the words and expressions from their context.

1 ... the view was **really something**. (*email A, line 12*)
2 The downtown Manhattan skyline just **blows you away**. (*email A, line 13*)
3 ... – **you name it**, and it's here. (*email B, line 6*)
4 ... you still hear the traffic **24-7**. (*email D, line 6*)

B Find words and phrases in the emails that mean the same as the following.

Email A	Email B	Email C	Email D
1 shout	4 frightening	6 suppose	9 never-ending
2 city-centre (adjective)	5 lift	7 exactly	10 day and night, all week
3 have a look at		8 much	

C Now use some of the words from exercise B to complete these sentences.

1 We have a ... apartment ... opposite the new shopping mall.
2 I once got stuck in the ... of a skyscraper – it was really ...
3 I ... we could ... the new art exhibition tonight – we have no other plans.

3 BUILDING SKILLS: LISTENING

1 10 **A Listen for general understanding. Listen to Part 1 and complete the statements.**

> Das Hörverständnis üben S. 199

1 The speakers are probably ...
a New York City tourist guides.
b tourists in New York.
c presenters on a TV travel programme.

2 The speakers are talking about ...
a how to get to New York.
b what to see and do in New York.
c what to eat in New York.

1 11 **B Listen for detail. Listen to Part 2 and take notes. Copy the table on the right. Then cross out the things that are not suggested and write down times for those that are.**

Suggestion	*Time needed*
~~*the Chrysler Building*~~	...
the Empire State Building	*1 hr*
Times Square	...
Broadway	...
Central Park	...
helicopter ride	...
the Statue of Liberty	...
the Staten Island Ferry	...

4 WRITING

Write Sue's reply to Ricky's last email.

1 Start with your greeting:
Dear ...
2 Paragraph 1: Refer to Ricky's email, and say how you felt when you received it.
Well, I got your email. And when I read it, I have to say I felt ...
3 Paragraph 2: Say how you feel about the relationship and what has happened to it.
Thinking about our relationship now, it seems to me that ...
4 Paragraph 3: Say what you think should happen now.
I'll tell you what I think should happen now. I think ...
5 Use one of Ricky's endings.

B The bigger picture

BEFORE YOU READ

A Look at the map. Do these activities.

1 Try to match the six famous places shown in Focus to numbers 1-6 on the map.

2 Say how a) a German immigrant in 1900 and b) a German tourist today might reach the centre of New York.

B The main title of the text on page 40 is 'A Bite of the Big Apple'. Say what you think the text might be about.

C Look at the sub-headings. Which of the following could the text be from?

an encyclopedia entry on New York

a novel about life in New York

a tourist guidebook about New York

1 12

A Bite of the Big Apple

Coming to New York

When you come from the airport on a sunny day, the distant towers of Manhattan shine magically. Closer, as you cross the river, the great skyline still takes your breath away, even though you know it from a thousand films.

As you begin exploring 'the Big Apple', you soon realize that it is many cities in one. For a start, New York is far more than Manhattan. Famous though this is, it is only one of five boroughs. There are also the Bronx, Brooklyn, Queens and Staten Island. Together, they cover the shores and islands of the Hudson and East Rivers and New York Bay.

Every borough has a different look and feel to it, and within each there are neighbourhoods, all with their own characteristics and sense of community.

The melting pot

Much of the city's variety comes from its many cultural and ethnic traditions. In the 19th century, the city drew millions of Irish, German, Italian, Jewish and other immigrants from Europe. And since then the waves of immigration have never stopped. After World War II, they came from Latin America and the Caribbean, and then from eastern Europe and Asia. In fact, 36% of today's New Yorkers were born abroad.

New York has also always attracted Americans from all over the country - people who want to make it in the big city.

The effects are everywhere. There are street festivals for everything from Chinese New Year to St Patrick's Day. In Queens, for example, you will hear a hundred different languages. As for food, you will find every dish under the sun in New York City.

The city that never sleeps

By the late nineteenth century, Manhattan was becoming quite crowded. With typical energy, New York began to use the newly-invented steel-frame construction to build streets to the sky. The skyscraper was born.

This energy is famous and has made New York the city that never sleeps. It has also made it a world leader in many areas, including finance, fashion, advertising, media and the arts. And, of course, NYC is the shopping capital of the world!

However, there have been hard times, too. The worst was in the 1970s. Drugs and crime were taking over, taxpayers were moving out and the city was nearly bankrupt. But, as always, the city came back stronger than ever.

The terrorist attacks of 9/11 of course brought more hard times, and another bad period of business failure and unemployment followed. The huge new 'Freedom Tower' will soon replace the former World Trade Center as a symbol of the city's recovery. (443 words)

1 LOOKING AT THE TEXT

A Copy the mind map and add to it from the text, the map and what you know.

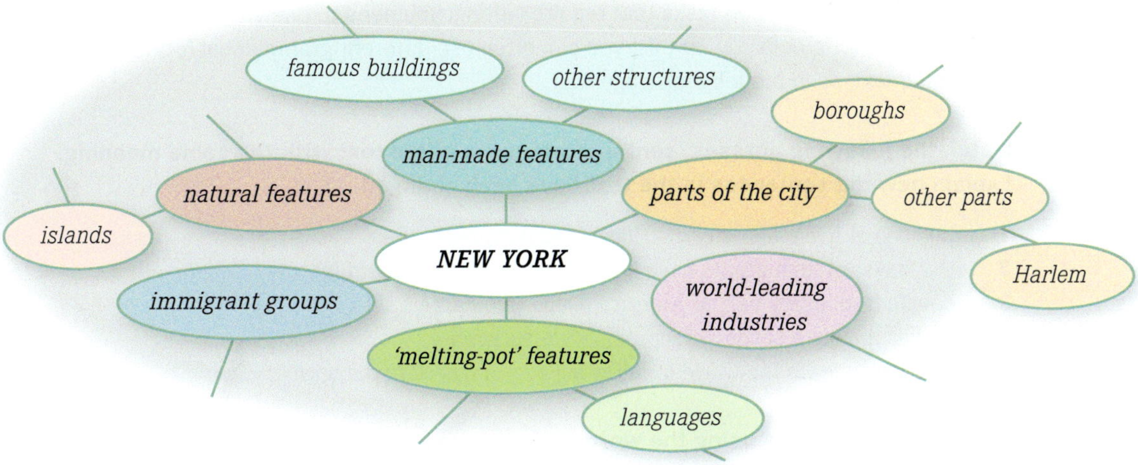

B Complete the sentence beginnings 1–6 by adding a sentence part from the first box and an ending from the second.

> Lesen schwieriger Texte: S. 196

1 Manhattan is the most famous part of New York, ...
2 The city has many cultural traditions ...
3 It has always attracted not just people from around the world, ...
4 When construction with steel became possible, ...
5 Through its huge energy, ...
6 Even though New York has had bad times,

... this soon led to the birth of ...
... because of the non-stop ...
... but also people from ...
... but it is only one of ...
... the city now leads the world ...
... it has always recovered and ...

... become even stronger than before.
... every part of America itself.
... in many aspects of life.
... the skyscraper in crowded Manhattan.
... the five city boroughs.
... waves of immigrants.

C Write out the sentences from exercise B as a short summary. Start like this:

Manhattan is the most famous part of New York, but it is only one of the ...

2 WORKING WITH WORDS

Copy and complete the table with a) words from the text and b) other words that you know. (Check your dictionary if necessary.)

Verb	Noun	Adjective
differ	difference	...
immigrate	...	
...	attraction	...
...	...	sleepy
...	...	leading
...	...	informative
strengthen	...	...

> **TIP**
> When you collect words like this, you get two, three or even more words for the price of one.

3 BUILDING SKILLS: USING YOUR OWN WORDS

> TIP

When you do comprehension tasks that require writing, you need to use your own words as much as possible. To help you do this, you can often use different grammatical forms of the words in the text, as in the table on page 41.

A Match the following phrases/sentences to parts of the text with the same meaning. Explain how the sentences in the text have been changed.

1. ... just one of five major city districts. (*2nd paragraph*)
2. ... the waves of immigrants have been non-stop. (*4th paragraph*)
3. ... people from every part of America itself. (*5th paragraph*)
4. This was the birth of the skyscraper. (*7th paragraph*)
5. The city now leads the world in many aspects of life. (*8th paragraph*)

B Rewrite the sentences using the words in brackets in the correct form – see exercise 2.

1. One great attraction to visitors is the city's huge energy. (*attract*) *One thing that greatly ...*
2. Many parts of NY differ amazingly. (*difference*) *There are amazing ...*
3. NY leads the financial centres of the world. (*leading*) *NY is the ...*
4. This book has a lot of information about NY's history. (*informative*) *This book is ...*
5. Over the last two centuries, large numbers of people have continued to immigrate to America. (*immigration*) *Over the last two centuries, large-scale ...*

4 PLANNING A VISIT

A Work with a partner. You have won a competition, and the prize is a two-day visit to New York for you and a friend or partner. Follow these steps to plan your visit.

1. Make a list of all the things that you would both like to see and do. You can look back through the Unit for ideas. (Don't worry about money: there's nothing to pay!)

I'd really like to ...	*I've always wanted to ...*

2. Decide how much time you think you need for each thing on your list.

We'll probably need about (one) hour to ...	*It'll definitely take us at least ...*

3. If you have too much for a two-day visit, decide which things not to do/see and why.

It'll be better to ...	*It'll be more interesting ...*
It'll take too long to ...	*There isn't enough time to ...*
So I'd prefer to ...	*I'd rather ...*

4. Work out a timetable for your visit.

First, let's ...	*Then, we can ...*

B Together, report your plans to the class. Try to use these words and phrases.

On the (first) day, we're going to ... | In the (afternoon), ... | First of all, ... | Then ... | Next, ... | After that, ... | Afterwards, ... | Finally, ...

C Business options

Now everyone can go to the Big Apple

Mass tourism is not profitable just because a location is attractive. It also has to be easily accessible, have good infrastructure, enough cheap and up-market accommodation and a wide range of entertainment for all ages at affordable prices. New York has all of these features but, in the 1990s, it was not realizing its full potential because of its infamous crime rate. New York was plagued by beggars and vandals. When Rudy Giuliani became Mayor in 1993, he was already famous for his fight against organized crime and with the help of a new police chief, Bill Bratton, Giuliani cleaned up the streets of New York. His policies were tough and controversial but the city is now a safer place and Giuliani was elected for a second term as mayor in 1997. Despite 9/11, tourists still flock to New York in increasing numbers and contribute to its economic success. (149 words)

1

Airfare:
Return trip
Düsseldorf to New York/JFK
1–6 July 2008
€206.00

2

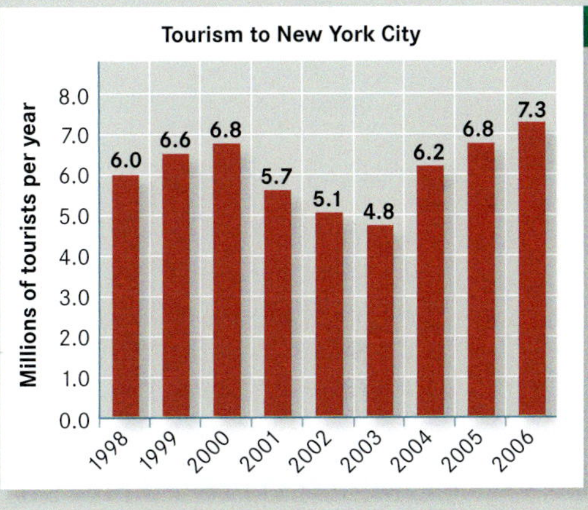

3

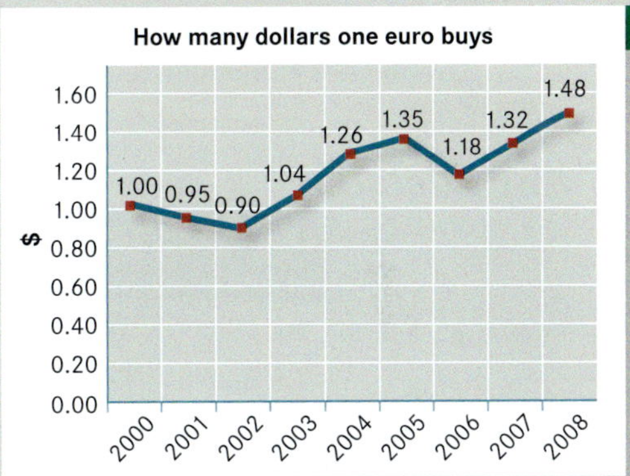

4

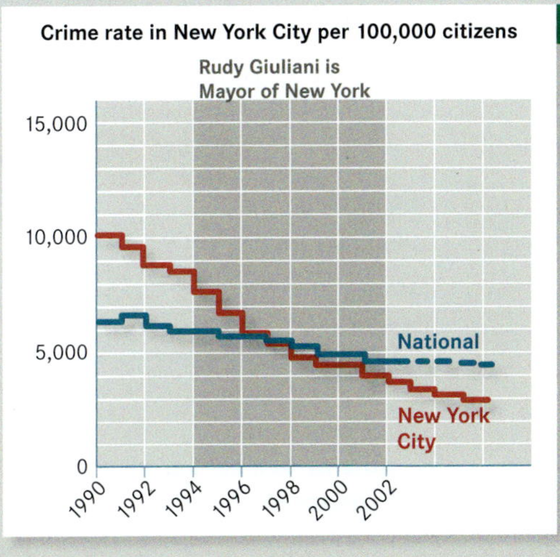

1 LOOKING AT THE TEXT

Explain what is meant by easily accessible, infrastructure and accommodation. Research examples of these features in New York.

2 LOOKING AT THE GRAPHS

A Look at figures 1–4 and then explain the following statements.

1. New York is very popular with European tourists.
2. People feel safer on the streets of New York now.
3. 9/11 had a temporary impact on tourism.

B Choose one of the three graphs and describe recent developments. The verbs in the box may help you.

to rise (rose, risen) | to climb | to fall (fell, fallen) | to bottom out at | to peak at

D Grammar checkpoint

1 COMPARISON OF ADJECTIVES

> Grammar summary S. 223

A **Work with a partner. Choose a city from below and find it on the map at the back of your book. Do not tell your partner the name of your city!**

City	Approx population	City	Approx population	City	Approx population
New York	8.0 million	Houston	2.0 million	Seattle	570,000
Los Angeles	4.0 million	Phoenix	1.4 million	Washington D.C.	560,000
Chicago	3.0 million	San Francisco	750,000	Miami	380,000

B **Give your partner some clues about your city. Which one is it? Can he/she guess?**

A It's bigger than ..., but it isn't as big as ...
B That means you're talking about either ... or ...
A And it's farther south than ..., but it isn't as far south as ...
B Well, in that case, you mean ..., don't you?
A That's right. Now it's your turn. | No, sorry. You'd better try again.

2 COMPARATIVES AND SUPERLATIVES

> Grammar summary S. 223

A **Look at *Top Holiday* magazine's survey of New York bus tours. Then read the junior reporter's comments and correct his five mistakes.**

Tour details

	Length of tour	Cost	Departures
Big Apple Tours	2hr 50min	$25.00	Every 30 minutes
City Sights	1hr 50min	$22.00	Every hour
Central Experience	2hr 40min	$30.00	Every two hours

Visitors' opinions

	How interesting?	How helpful?	Value for money
Big Apple Tours	*****	**	****
City Sights	**	*	**
Central Experience	****	***	***

City offers the shortest tour of the three companies. At $22.00, the tour is cheaper than Big Apple's but more expensive than Central's. With departures every hour, it provides the least frequent service of all. Visitors feel that the tour itself is more interesting than Big Apple's and less interesting than Central's. They also say that the company is the most helpful of the three. Overall, they feel that the City tour is better value for money than the Central tour.

B **Now write a similar paragraph to compare Big Apple Tours with City Sights and Central Experience.**

2 Advertising

FOCUS

1 **Advertising never leaves us alone. Where have you seen or heard advertisements in the last 24 hours? What sorts of advertising were they?**

brochures | classified, full-page or panel adverts in magazines/newspapers | leaflets | online pop-up/banner ads | posters | product placements (in TV programmes or films) | radio/TV commercials | sponsorship advertising (on football shirts, etc.)

A

B

C

D

E

F

2 **What do you think of the adverts above? Use adjectives like these.**

annoying | boring | clever | disgusting | funny | glamorous | shocking | silly | strange

3 **The aims of advertising vary – for example, to present products, promote brands or to make the public think. What do the adverts above do?**

A Personal perspectives

BEFORE YOU READ

Look at the photo and the title of the magazine article. Say which of the following you think it is not about, and why.
a) Places to go on holiday, b) planning for a happy old age or c) finding a great career.

1 13

DREAM destinations

Every week, DO IT! magazine's Ben Starr talks to young people in great jobs who have great futures. This week, Ben meets Lisa Scott at the fast-growing advertising agency *iMAGE iMPACT*.

BEN *Lisa, what brought you to iMAGE iMPACT's online advertising team?*

LISA *Well, while I was studying ICT at college, I designed a website for the volleyball team I played for. We were doing well in the national league, so we had lots of hits on the site. We also had a sponsor - SportStyle. They got their name on our shirts, and we got financial help. Then I added a simple game to the website. Visitors to our website pressed number keys to make a player jump and return the ball. Of course, SportStyle's name was on the player's shirt. They loved the whole website - and we got extra money.*

BEN *What happened then?*

LISA *After college, I became a freelance web-site developer, but I wanted something more. One day, I was looking at job ads on the internet when I saw that 'something'. iMAGE iMPACT were expanding their online team, and they wanted someone like me.*

BEN *So you applied for the job. And I guess the interview went well.*

LISA *Yes, and the volleyball website also helped, of course, so here I am. We're still only a small group in the Creative Design Department, but online advertising is the part of the whole business that's now growing the fastest.*

BEN *Where does Creative Design fit in?*

LISA *Well, let's start at the beginning. A potential client needs a campaign for a new product and invites several agencies, including us, to 'pitch' for the contract. One of our account managers visits the client to discuss their needs and then becomes the bridge between the client and us. Together, we and the account manager work out the key campaign concept. Then we, the 'creatives', produce the magic words and images that will sell the product.*

BEN *Let's say you win the pitch. What happens then?*

LISA *We get the green light to develop the concept into a full campaign. That's when the media planners also become very important. They're the people who decide exactly what media to use when, and how much. We could launch the campaign with a first run of TV commercials, for example, followed by online advertising.*

BEN *And what are you working on at the moment?*

LISA *Right now, I'm having real fun with a campaign for a new online travel agency. I'm using characters from the TV commercials to create a travel game that takes you on journeys to dream destinations right round the world.*

BEN *Well, thank you, Lisa. It's clear that this job really suits you - it's your own dream destination!*

(457 words)

1 LOOKING AT THE TEXT

A Read the text carefully. Choose the best answer or answers.

1 *SportStyle* loved ...
   a the finished website that Lisa produced.
   b playing games with website visitors.
   c Lisa's game and having their name on the player's shirt.

2 *iMAGE iMPACT* wanted a designer ...
   a to join their online team.
   b to produce innovative magazine adverts.
   c who could create an online advertising team.

3 Business at *iMAGE iMPACT* is ...
   a declining slightly.
   b fairly stable.
   c growing.

4 Lisa is now ...
   a developing a new online travel game.
   b travelling to destinations that she has always dreamed about.
   c doing her dream job.

B This flow chart shows how an advertising campaign is set up. Copy and complete it with information from the text. Use the simple present, and leave out unnecessary words, e.g. *a, an, the*.

STEP 1	→	*STEP 2*	→	*STEP 3*	→	*STEP 4*	→	*STEP 5*	→	*STEP 6*	→	*STEP 7*
Potential client invites agencies to pitch.		...		...		...		...		...		*Agency launches campaign.*

C Which of these typical agency jobs – if any – might be right for you? Why? Discuss with a partner using the words and phrases below.

account manager | creative | IT support staff member | media booker (booking commercial slots, e.g. TV) | media planner | PA (personal assistant) to a senior manager

(I think) I'd find *I'd (probably) find*	*being a (creative)* *the job of (account manager)*	*(very) enjoyable.* *(quite) stressful.*
That's (probably) because *(I think) that's due to the fact that*	*I (don't) like ...* *I'm (quite/not very) good at ...*	

2 BUILDING SKILLS: DESCRIBING A PROCESS

Look back to exercise 1B. Now write a summary of the process in full sentences. Use these connectors.

First (of all), ... | Then ... | Next, ... | After that, ... | Following that, ... | Finally, ...

3 WORKING WITH WORDS

A **Copy and complete the table.**

B **Complete the *iMAGE iMPACT* advert that Lisa saw. Use words from the table.**

	Verb	Noun (thing)	Noun (person)
1	...	design	...
2	...	development	...
3	...	interview	...
4	...	management	...
5	sponsor	sponsorship	...
6	supply	supply	...

http://www.

iMAGE iMPACT is a fast-developing, London-based advertising agency. We are expanding our online team and urgently require an innovative ...[1].
Please visit our website at www.imageimpact.co.uk for further information and an application form, or call Human Resources ...[2] Helen Troy on 020-1946583. The closing date for applications is 28th February, and we expect to ...[3] candidates between 10th and 14th March. All shortlisted candidates will be asked to ...[4] examples of their work.

4 CULTURE CHECK: FORMS OF ADDRESS

Email

Dear Ms Scott,
Thank you for your application for the new position in our online team. I am pleased to invite you for an interview on 12 March at 2 p.m. Please confirm that you are able to attend on this date and bring some recent examples of your work with you.
I look forward to meeting you.
Best wishes,
Mandy Carr

Email

Dear Lisa,
I am very pleased to offer you the position in our online team. Please reply by 28 March to confirm whether you would like to accept the post. Then we can organize contracts, etc.
I look forward to working with you!
Best regards,
Mandy Carr
P.S. Please do call me Mandy – we are pretty informal here!

Read the correspondence between Mandy Carr and Lisa Scott. Decide the following:

1 When and why were these emails written?
2 What rules does the writer follow? Who can/cannot suggest using first names?
3 In the same situations in Germany, what forms of address would people use?

> INFO

1 *Mr*, *Mrs* and *Ms* are the usual formal titles used when dealing with clients, customers and senior colleagues. *Ms* is used for all women, whether they are married or not.
2 In many companies, staff use first names with each other, even between junior and senior staff. This may seem very informal, but it is not and has nothing like the closeness of the German 'du'.
3 As in Germany, changing from formal style to first names must come from the senior person, e.g. here, from Mandy Carr to Lisa Scott.

5 SPEAKING

Discuss things that you should and should not do before and during an interview.

B The bigger picture

BEFORE YOU READ

A **Where does this text come from?**

B **Look at the heading. Say what you understand by the word 'Forum'.**

http://www.

1 14

FOCUS Forum

JOIN TODAY'S DISCUSSION: 'We're swimming in a sea of advertising'

Rob, London, UK

Dear FOCUS Forum
It's more true to say that we're drowning in a sea of advertising! And what's so terrible is that it tries to control our minds.
We just have to ignore all the thousands of adverts around us as much as we can. For example, when commercial breaks come on, it's time to make coffee. Even better, I often record programmes and my DVD recorder automatically cuts the commercials.

Lucy, Melbourne, Australia

Dear FOCUS Forum
Rob is far too negative. We live in a very rich society that offers lots of choices. And advertising tells us about those choices. Think of it as a public information service! Personally, I also love ads. They're lively and fun. So lighten up, Rob!

Julia, Seattle, United States

Dear FOCUS Forum
Like Rob I hate living in a sea of advertising, but I know that we can't escape from the advertisers so easily. Just think of the branded entertainment on our screens. With all that product placement, programmes like House Wars are really extended commercials! For example, the competing families always go to the same store for their building supplies.
And then there's online viral advertising, too. This often comes as a game, and it passes from friend to friend by email. And then the product appears on every screen. It spreads around the world like a virus.
'Word of mouth' agencies that pay people to talk up a product at parties or in online chatroom discussions are just another sort of viral advertising.
So while I really dislike traditional advertising, I prefer it to the new methods. At least you know it when you see it, and you can always change channel or turn the page. Viral advertising is often harder to recognize.

Peter, Johannesburg, South Africa

Dear FOCUS Forum
Unlike Julia, I think viral advertising is good because it's cheaper than traditional forms of advertising. I must admit, I do worry about those billions of dollars that traditional advertisers spend. What's more, advertising makes us buy more than we need, so we're using global resources more wastefully than ever. We should spend the money on something more useful – more hospitals, for example.

Sally, Toronto, Canada

Dear FOCUS Forum
Poor Peter! He just doesn't understand. Advertising adds a bit to costs, but it helps keep the whole global economy going. Without it, sales drop, companies collapse, jobs disappear, the economy fails, and we all go back to the Middle Ages! Is that what we want? Are we mad enough to do that?

(409 words)

1 LOOKING AT THE TEXT

A Read for information.

1 List four different forms of advertising that are mentioned in the text.
2 Which are traditional 'hard sell' methods and which more modern 'soft sell' techniques?

B Use the information from the forum to decide which person made each comment. Read the speech bubbles 1-5 and match them to the photographs A–E.

1 *I enjoy watching ads on TV! And I often buy things that I see in adverts.*

2 *Yes, advertising makes products a bit more expensive, but we would have so many problems without it.*

3 *People don't understand how much advertising there is around them – it's everywhere. We just can't escape from it!*

4 *I don't let advertising influence me. I do everything I can to avoid it. People should make their own choices.*

5 *What about the impact on the environment? Just think of all the raw materials that are used up to produce the things we buy.*

A Rob, 17

B Lucy, 15

C Julia, 20

D Peter, 18

E Sally, 20

C Explain one point of disagreement between each pair.

Use these connectors in your answers.

| but | whereas | while | By contrast | However | On the other hand |

1 Rob and Lucy   2 Rob and Julia   3 Julia and Peter   4 Peter and Sally

EXAMPLE *Rob says that there is far too much ..., while Lucy feels that advertising ...*

D Say what you think.

1 Name some adverts that you like or dislike and say why.
I love/hate that new advert for ... because ...

2 In FOCUS Forum there are five different opinions on advertising. Which do you agree/disagree with? Use these phrases:
I totally/partly agree/disagree with ... when he/she says/suggests that ...
Personally, I think that ... is exaggerating.
It seems to me that ... is giving a one-sided view.
In my opinion, ... has got it about right.

2 LISTENING

1 15 **A Listen for general understanding. Listen to Part 1 and answer the questions.**

1 Where are these people?
2 What industry does the guest work in?
3 Why is she here?
4 Who are the other people in the room?

1 16 **B Listen for detail. Listen to Part 2 and do the tasks.**

1 Note what AIDA stands for.
2 Use your notes to say why the ad is a good example of AIDA.

3 BUILDING SKILLS: ANALYZING CHARTS

A Match the chart types a–c to their names 1–3.

> Interpretation von Grafiken, Diagrammen und Tabellen S. 209

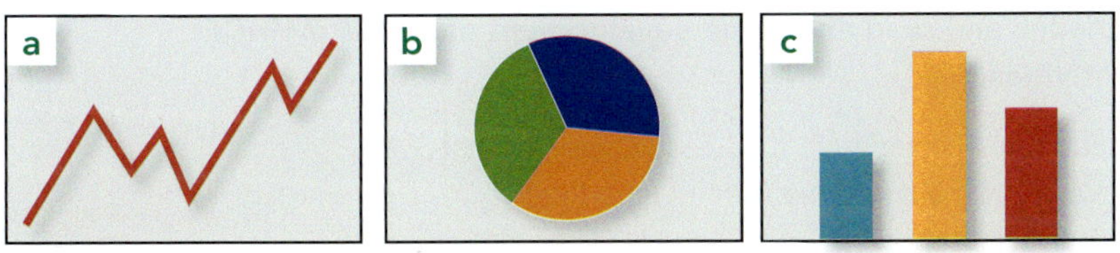

1 bar chart
2 line graph
3 pie chart

> **TIP**
> Charts show statistical information in a way that is easy to understand. When you give presentations, try to use suitable charts to support your explanations.

B Here are some useful words for describing graphs and statistics. Use them to describe what is happening in A–F.

verb +	*adverb*
rise	*rapidly*
increase	*sharply*
grow	*steadily*
fall	*gradually*
decrease	*slowly*
decline	*slightly*

adjective +	*noun*
rapid	*rise*
sharp	*increase*
steady	*growth*
gradual	*fall*
slow	*decrease*
slight	*decline*

verb +	*adjective*
be	*flat*
remain	*steady*

Sales

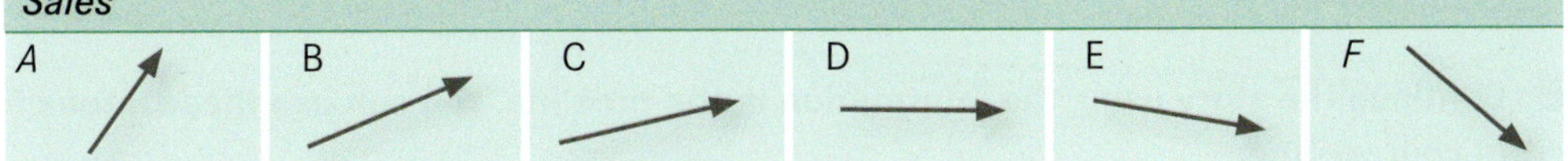

EXAMPLES *In A, sales increased sharply.*
In A, there was a rapid rise in sales.

C Read and do the activities.

Tony Lee, *iMAGE iMPACT*'s Finance Director, is describing some company sales trends.

1 Look at the chart, read what Tony Lee says, and decide whether he is talking about total sales or TV sales.

2 Say which five years he is talking about.

In the first year of this period, sales were flat, but in the next year they increased steadily, and in the year after that, they rose slightly again. However, in the following year, sales were flat again, and in the final year of the period they fell very sharply.

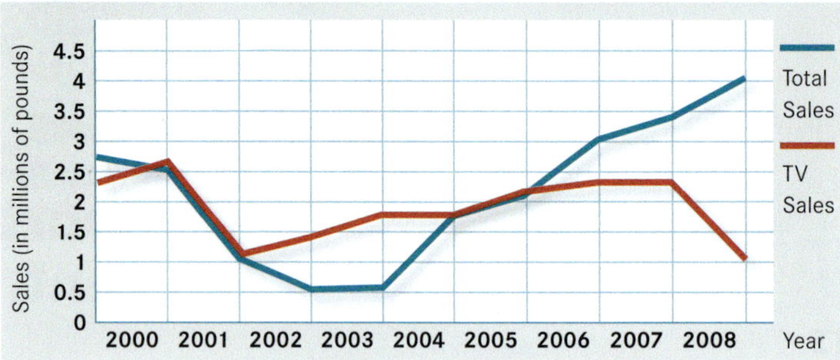

4 WRITING

A Look at the timeline and read about the development of *iMAGE iMPACT*. Then do the activities.

1 Find information that comes from the above chart for *Total Sales*.

2 Compare the style of the notes and the full text. Find:
- > words that the full text adds;
- > full forms of the abbreviations that are used in the notes.

iMAGE iMPACT Timeline	
2000	Mandy Carr & Tony Lee build up new agency – small office, SE London; worldwide dot-com crash begins > immediate problems.
2001	Crash hits global advertising industry v hard. ***iMAGE iMPACT*** nearly goes bankrupt.
2004	Company recovers, M&T decide to start online advertising & hire new staff to help.
2006	Online team win several important contracts. ***ii*** moves to bigger offices.
2007	***ii*** wins 2 important advertising industry awards > new clients & business.
2008	Further expansion of online advertising. Most other areas also grow, but not TV.

The development of *iMAGE iMPACT*

While Mandy Carr and Tony Lee were building up their new agency in a small office in South-East London in 2000, the worldwide dot-com crash began. This led to immediate problems. Sales declined steadily that year. Then, in 2001, the dot-com crash hit the global advertising industry very hard. Sales fell extremely ...

B Continue the story using the information in the timeline. You can use these intensifiers in your writing.

quite | fairly | very | extremely

C Business options

4 2 Google knows what you want ...

Soon after starting up in 1998, Google rapidly became the most used search engine because its founders, Larry Page and Sergey Brin, gave users what they were looking for without graphics, animations and flashing banners. By 2000, however, Google still had no really big source of revenue, so it started selling simple, targeted advertising. Its revenues soared and it has never looked back.

Try this experiment with the Google email program. Write yourself an email using some key words, such as 'holiday', 'hotel', 'beach' and 'Spain', and send it to yourself. When you get it back, open it and look at the part of the screen outside the email box. You'll see adverts for holidays and hotels in Spain. Google uses context-sensitive advertising – a program scans your text input and considers your location, your internet connection and even the time of day. The program then draws a profile of you as a user and matches this with a huge database of adverts waiting to be used. All of this is done in milliseconds. If you then click on one of the adverts, the company that placed it will be charged a fee for the click-through.

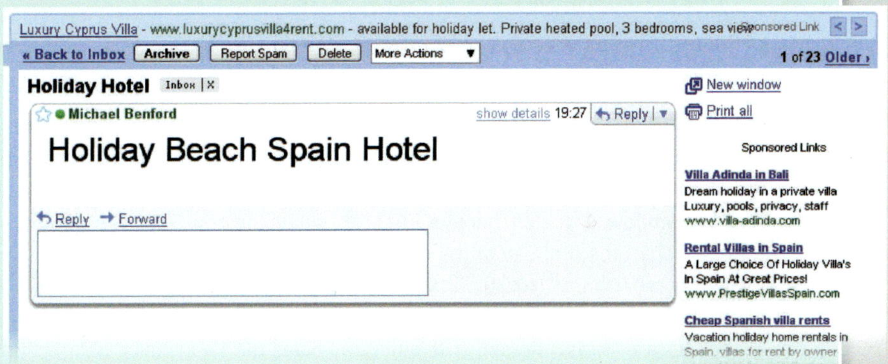

Just how much one click costs is partly decided using an auction-based system. This is how it works. Let's say you're an advertiser and you want your advert to be at or near the top of the list, so you make a high bid for each click-through. You would normally expect the highest bid to win the auction and go to the top but Google is different. Firstly, it has a special 'second-price auction system'; the winner only pays one cent more than the next highest bidder. In this way, advertisers are encouraged to bid high but don't lose out if their bid is much higher than the rest. Secondly, Google places the company with the largest advertising budget – and which therefore generates the most advertising revenue – at the top of the list, even if it bid less for each click-through. (336 words)

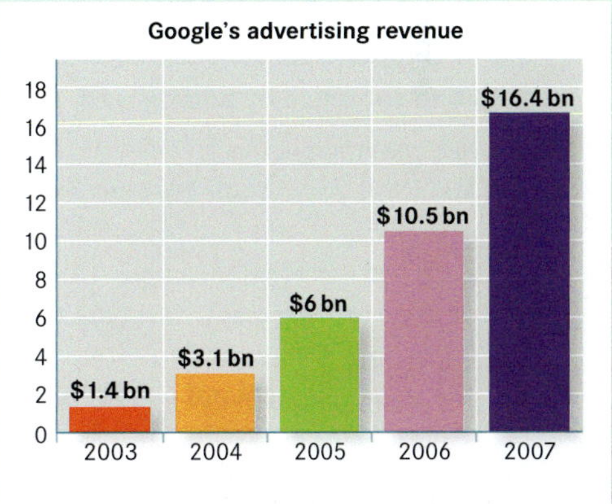

LOOKING AT THE TEXT

A Finish the following sentences.

1 Google is popular because it doesn't use ...
2 Google's program matches ...
3 An advertiser pays a click-though fee when ...
4 You normally win an auction if ...

B Explain how Google advertises. Use the words from the box to help you.

Google | scan | input | match with | database | price of a click-through | determine | special type of auction | place in the list | depend | revenue generated | advertising budget

D Grammar checkpoint

1 PAST PROGRESSIVE

> Grammar summary S. 213

At 6 p.m. everybody at *iMAGE iMPACT* was still working. Use the past progressive to say what they were doing. Add any missing words.

1 Lisa Scott (*test*) | new online game | SkyTravel.com.
Lisa Scott was testing her new online game for SkyTravel.com.
2 Mandy Carr (*prepare*) business plan | next year.
3 Tony Lee and his assistant (*study*) | latest sales figures.
4 Media planners (*discuss*) | new campaign.
5 Carrie, the senior account executive, (*call*) | client | America.

2 PAST PROGRESSIVE AND SIMPLE PAST

> Grammar summary S. 213

Fill in the gaps with the past progressive or simple past. (Use the past progressive when both tenses are possible.)

Lisa has worked very long hours for months now, without any holidays.Yesterday, for example, she *was still working*[1] (*still work*) at 7.00, and she *finally finished*[2] (*finally finish*) at nearly 7.30.

While she ...[3] (*walk*) past an electrical store on her way to the bus stop, something on the TV screens in the window ...[4] (*catch*) her eye. They ...[5] (*show*) the new SkyTravel commercial! Then she ...[6] (*remember*): this ...[7] (*be*) the first day of the campaign.

At home, Lisa ...[8] (*put*) a curry in the microwave and ...[9] (*turn on*) the TV. She ...[10] (*see*) the commercial again. The people in it ...[11] (*have*) a wonderful time on a golden beach under a blue sky. 'And why not me, too?' Lisa ...[12] (*ask*) herself. The company owes me two weeks' holiday!'

While she ...[13] (*eat*) her curry, Lisa ...[14] (*log on*) to SkyTravel. She ...[15] (*get*) really excited when she ...[16] (*find*) cheap holidays available in Ibiza. Two minutes later, she ...[17] (*talk*) on the phone to her friend Alice about dates. Later, she ...[18] (*think*), 'Our commercial must be pretty good: it even worked on me!'

3 RELATIVE CLAUSES

> Grammar summary S. 224

Form complete sentences by putting together one line from 1–5 and one from a–e. Make them into one sentence by adding *who*, *which* or *that*.

1 Rob (*be*) the person
Rob is the person who tries to ignore and avoid advertising.
2 Lucy and Sally (*be*) the ones
3 Viral advertising (*be*) a new type of advertising
4 Rob (*use*) a DVD recorder
5 There (*be*) programmes like *House Wars*

a It (*cut*) the commercials.
b They clearly (*support*) advertising.
c They (*be*) really just long commercials.
~~d He (*try*) to ignore and avoid advertising.~~
e It (*work*) by spreading from person to person, often by email.

4 RELATIVE CLAUSES AND CONTACT CLAUSES

> Grammar summary S. 224

Copy and complete the slogans. Add *who*, *which* or *that* where necessary. If not, write *X*.

1 STARWAYS – a film *X* you'll never forget
2 AIR-WISE – the people ... get you there
3 HOME GYM – for a personal trainer ... you can trust
4 PRO-VIT – the vitamins ... doctors recommend
5 LOOKS – for fashion ... won't break the bank
6 RANGER XF – the car ... the whole world's waiting for
7 SAT-PAK – the satnav system ... beats them all

3

Main Course

Media madness

FOCUS

> **TIP**
> Word fields and networks are great ways of collecting and learning new vocabulary.

1 Think about the ways you keep in contact with the world.

A Copy and complete the network with the ideas below.

B Say which of these ways of communicating you use most and least. Say why.

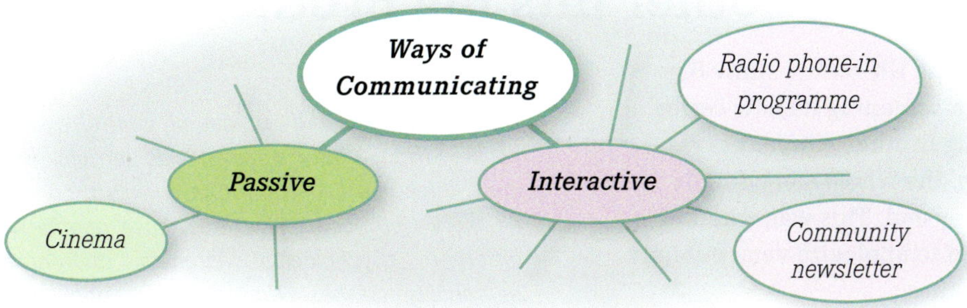

Blog

Celebrity magazine

Face-to-face contact

Mobile phone

Newspaper

Social networking site

Television

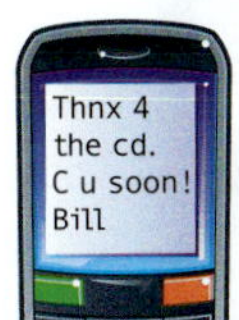

Text message

2 Decide how you would react in these situations.

1 Hurricane Zoe has just hit Florida. Your cousin is on holiday there, so you want to find out the latest news - and fast. How?

2 Your school is organizing a public event to raise money for the charity 'Children in Need'. Which forms of communication could help, and how?

3 For a presentation about refugees in the EU, you want to understand the background better. Which forms of communication might help most - or would you go to the library?

4 You suddenly realize that you missed the last Spiderman film when it was on at the local multiplex! What can you do about it?

5 You want to chat with a friend. What might you do?

6 You want to meet new people. What could you do?

A Personal perspectives

BEFORE YOU READ

A **Explain what you understand by 'reality TV'.**

B **Give examples of reality TV programmes in Germany at the moment, and say what you like/dislike about them.**

1 17

http://www.

THE BIRMINGHAM HERALD

Big Bother hits Big Brother

The long-running UK reality show Big Brother began screening its new series – Celebrity Big Brother – in January. But yesterday, the whole story finally came to a sorry end. This was when BB's producers had to apologize very publicly for their mistakes.

As usual, the series brought together a group of people – this time they were all well-known celebrities – in the Big Brother House. And, as usual, TV cameras followed every action and every word, and then the most 'entertaining' parts went out to millions of viewers. Every week they voted by phone or text to throw out the least popular member of the group.

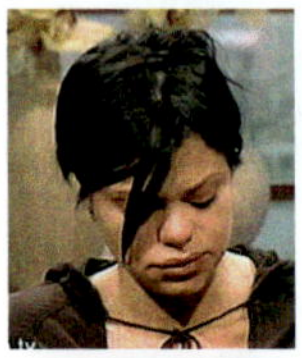

The trouble began when Jade Goody (and others) launched into a series of racist attacks on the Indian Bollywood actress Shilpa Shetty. Thousands of viewers complained, and the popular press quickly joined the protest. Soon, Goody could no longer stay: millions of the audience had voted her out.

Then the press attacked the programme makers. After all, they had encouraged and exploited the situation. Before long, the BB series was no longer able to continue.

(179 words)

Readers' comments

The programmes did get out of control and the abuse Shilpa Shetty suffered was terrible. But I don't think you can blame the show's producers. Reality TV producers have to choose people with different psychological profiles to create personality clashes. That produces popular TV, which brings the advertisers and the big profits.

If we really disagree with these shows, we needn't watch them, need we? After all, they can't survive without an audience. The problem is that so many people are addicted to these shows and simply can't turn them off. Lisa Sanchez (92 words)

Why do people agree to appear on programmes like Big Brother? They know the world will see them in embarrassing or stressful situations. I suppose some of them want to test themselves or win the big prize, but I think lots of them just want their 'fifteen minutes of fame'. As for celebrities like Jade Goody and Shilpa Shetty, perhaps they want to keep themselves in the public eye and have fifteen more minutes of fame. Mark Romano (76 words)

I wonder about the psychology of reality TV viewers. What makes us want to watch these shows? With Big Brother, I suppose we enjoy seeing people behaving badly towards each other. And on other reality TV programmes the contestants have to do really painful and grotesque tests. It seems that we actually enjoy watching people suffer. Are these shows making us all a little mad?

Perhaps we aren't very different from the Romans – they loved watching people die for sport.
Jean O'Hanlon (81 words)

1 LOOKING AT THE TEXT

A Put statements a–f in the correct order to summarize the newspaper article.

a And as usual, the viewers voted one of these people out every week.
b The press also attacked the producers for encouraging the situation and forced the whole series to stop.
c But then, one of the *Big Brother* housemates began to make racist remarks against another housemate.
d Yesterday, the producers of TV's *Big Brother* had to apologize to the public.
e This brought huge protests from viewers and the press, and the viewers quickly voted the abusive housemate out.
f During the latest *Big Brother* series, cameras filmed the lives of a group of people in the BB House in the usual way.

B Pick out the readers' points on the weakness of human nature.

One reader says that ... *Another reader notes that ...* *A third reader suggests that ...*

C Say what you think.

1 Why do you think people appear on reality TV shows?
2 Would you agree to appear on any of the German reality TV shows? Give reasons.

2 WORKING WITH WORDS

A Collect opposites. You can use your dictionary if you need to.

1 The words in the box below are all from page 56. Copy the table and complete columns 1-3 with opposite forms.

able | agree | appear | behave | encourage | popular | understand | usual

1	*2*	*3*	*4*
un~	*dis~*	*mis~*	*in~ il~ ir~ im~*

2 Now add some more words that you already know to columns 1-3.
3 Put the opposites of these words in column 4.

accurate | complete | correct | legal | legible | logical | moral | perfect | possible | regular | relevant | responsible

4 What do you notice about all the opposites with the forms *il~* and *ir~*?
5 Add more words to column 4.

B Use the adjectives above or their opposites to complete the following sentences.

1 Jade Goody became very ... because of her racist attacks on Shilpa Shetty.
2 A lot of people felt that the producers were ... because they let the situation develop.
3 Following the press attacks, *Big Brother* was ... to continue.
4 Goody later apologized for her behaviour, but she said she was not a racist, and she believed that people had ... her.
5 A lot of people were pleased that BB had ... from the TV screen.
6 But, after a year with no *Big Brother*, the TV producers finally decided that, with some changes, it would be ... to bring it back.

3 LISTENING AND SPEAKING

1 18 **A Listen for general understanding. Listen to Part 1 and answer the questions.**

1 Why is Dave able to drive this evening? (Give two reasons.)
2 How many people are going out together?
3 Where are they going to go?
4 What are Steve and Claire going to find out?
5 What are they going to have to eat?

1 19 **B Listen for detail. Listen to Part 2 and complete the notes.**

1 First, look at the list of film genres and give examples of each.

action comedy | action movie | comedy | documentary | road movie | romantic comedy | satire | sci-fi movie | spy movie

2 Copy Steve's notes and listen to Part 2 to complete columns 1 and 2.
3 Listen to Part 2 again to complete column 3.

Film title	*Genre*	*Evening showing times*		
		early	*mid-evening*	*late*
Pirates of the Caribbean	...	...	...	...
Journey to the ...	...	...	...	...
One ...	...	...	...	...

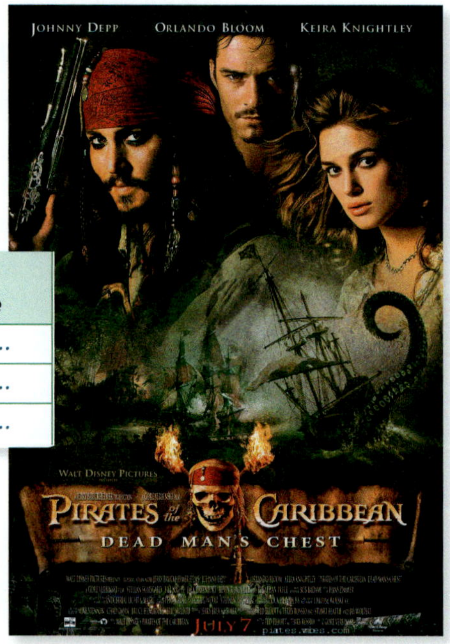

4 List some more film genres. Then give examples of films in these genres that you have enjoyed and explain why.

C Do the following role-play.

1 Work in groups of four and choose a role each.
2 Put forward your point of view. Use some of these phrases.

Roles

Debbie > File 1, page 192
Dave > File 6, page 192
Claire > File 11, page 194
Steve > File 8, page 194

I (don't) think we should / ought to ... *I think we'd better (not) ...*	*We can/could ... first, and then ...* *We might (not) be able to ...*	*I wish we could ...* *It's a pity we can't ...* *Whatever we do, we must(n't) ...*

3 Report your group's decisions to the class.
4 Compare different groups' plans. Has everyone made the same decisions? If not, try to say why not.

B The bigger picture

BEFORE YOU READ

A **What information about yourself would you be happy to put on a social networking site (e.g. MySpace)?**

B **What sort of details would you not want to put on the internet? Give reasons.**

1 20

Great medium, but what about your message?

Jenny has tried several different drugs, has two piercings and also a butterfly tattoo on her arm. She earns $23,000 a year, and hasn't seen her parents for two years. I know her address, but they don't.

Altogether, I know a lot about Jenny, although I've never met her and probably never will. This is strange really. A few years ago, I'm sure hardly anyone in her circle of friends knew as much about her as I, a complete stranger, do today.

Not that this is unusual. Millions of people share very personal details with others on social networking sites such as MySpace. Everyone knows the dangers to children if they put personal information on the internet. But what about the dangers to the rest of us? Should adults not be careful too?

The US National Association of Colleges and Employers recently discovered that 27% of employers search Google and other sites such as MySpace for profiles of their job applicants. And they may find information that those applicants do not want them to have.

On the face of it, the difference between behaviour online and offline makes no sense. In their ordinary lives, people do not easily give strangers personal details such as their phone number or date of birth. It is simply not sensible. Why then do the same people offer these things freely when they go on the internet? It is because both the social network providers and the users know that they need to give quite a lot of information in order to make the system work. After all, it is hard for people to start communicating if they know very little about each other. The trouble is that when private information gets out there, it can become very public, and it may also remain out there forever.

We are starting to hear about people who have lost jobs or college places because of things they said about themselves online. And it is not just jobs and college places at risk. Many people are worried that social networking sites could also be used by identity thieves. As for chatrooms, you can never be absolutely sure who you're talking to, and this can be dangerous. Perhaps we should think more carefully about the risks we run when we share information online.

Some students in the USA now have to take a 1st-semester class in social networking so that they clearly understand the risks. Internet researcher Steve Jones of the University of Illinois goes further. He says, 'If you put something on MySpace or Facebook, ask yourself whether you'd be comfortable shouting it out at a family reunion. If the answer is no, then don't put it up.' (449 words)

Heavily abridged and adapted from *Things you wouldn't tell your mother, Alison George, New Scientist 16/09/06 p. 50*

1 LOOKING AT THE TEXT

A Scan the text for these numbers. Then read further and explain what the numbers refer to in the text.

$23,000   27%   1st

B Copy and complete the statements. As far as possible, use your own words.

1 It is sad for Jenny's parents that ...
2 We all know that children should not put personal information on the internet, but adults should ...
3 Employers often search the internet in order to ...
4 People do not usually give personal information to people they have just met, so it is strange that ...
5 A good general rule is that you should only put information on the internet that ...

C Use words from the text to complete this summary.

Large numbers of people use social ...[1] sites like MySpace to share their ...[2] details. They often share information online that they would never share ...[3]. The more information they give, the easier it is to begin ...[4] with similar people. This is the system the social networking ...[5] have created. And if this private information becomes ...[6], people could lose their job or their place at university. ...[7] thieves are another danger. There is also a risk that when you talk to someone in an internet ...[8], they might be lying about who they are.

D Say what you think.

What are the dangers of meeting people through the internet? What should you do to make sure that you stay safe?

2 WORKING WITH WORDS

A Match the words from each box to form word pairs and expressions from the text.

personal / job / date of / social / circle of / family	applicant / birth / details / friends / networking / reunion

B Use word pairs from exercise A to complete the following sentences.

1 All my cousins are coming to our ... next month.
2 We're asking all the ... to come for interviews on March 28th.
3 ... websites like MySpace and Facebook are becoming more and more popular.
4 Susie is at a different party every weekend! She has a very large ...
5 People's ... can be very useful for identity thieves. Make sure that you keep yours safe!

C Match the sentence halves to make statements. Pay attention to the prepositions.

1 I haven't used MySpace	a at risk if they use internet chatrooms.
2 Edward knows a lot	b with someone I don't know.
3 I never share my personal details	c for two years.
4 Identity thieves are a danger	d to anyone who uses networking sites.
5 Young people are	e about computers.

D Read this information about online abbreviations. Then look at the discussion from an online chatroom and complete it with abbreviations from the list.

When people are talking to each other in a chatroom, they often use abbreviations because they can type them more quickly and easily. For example, they write **u** instead of 'you', **r** instead of 'are' and **2** instead of 'to'. Words are often reduced to their phonetic components, so 'someone' could become **sum1**. Phrases can also be shortened to the first letter of each word. Here are some common abbreviated phrases that you might see used online:

AFK – away from (the) keyboard
ATM – at the moment
BTW – by the way
FYI – for your information
IMO – in my opinion
LOL – laughing out loud
OTT – over the top
PLS – please
TBH – to be honest
THX – thanks
TMI – too much information
TTYL – talk to you later

http://www.

***fun* chat**

Alex: What r u doing?
Ben: Homework …[1] but I've nearly finished.
Chris: Homework? I bet ur on MySpace really.
Ben: No Chris, I don't have a MySpace page.
Alex: I have a MySpace page but …[2] I don't use it very often.
Daisy: Can sum1 …[3] tell me what MySpace is?
Chris: …[4]! I don't believe it! U must be joking!
Ben: Don't be so …[5],Chris. Not every1 wants 2 spend their life on the internet. Right, Daisy?
Alex: Daisy? R u there?
Daisy: Sorry, I was …[6]. Back now.
Ben: Well, I've finished my work now so I'm going out. …[7] every1.

3 BUILDING SKILLS: MEDIATION

> Mediation S. 210

Write a two-paragraph article about social networking sites in German for your school newspaper.

1 For paragraph 1, collect information from text B on page 59 about:
- what they are;
- examples of sites;
- how new members get started.

2 For paragraph 2, collect information about the possible dangers of these sites.

4 SPEAKING

Work with a partner. Talk about your own experiences with social networking sites.

1 Ask each other questions about the sites you have heard of and what you think of them.
2 If you are a member of a networking site, explain why you use it and whether you have had any bad experiences with the site.

5 SPEAKING

Say which of the points in the text the cartoon illustrates.

"What shall I do? She wants to meet for coffee."

6 CULTURE CHECK: NETIQUETTE

Many young people in English-speaking countries like Britain and America use internet forums to have discussions online. These forums allow English speakers from around the world to talk about a wide range of topics, from politics and religion, to music and computer games.
English speakers are careful to sound polite in a face-to-face conversation and this is just as important in an online discussion. Most forums have their own rules but here are some general points on how to behave in an internet forum.

> Keep to the point - only write about the topic that is being discussed.
> Don't write everything in CAPITAL LETTERS. This is considered 'shouting' and is difficult to read. If you want to emphasize a word, you can use **bold** or underline it.
> Use capital letters for names, places and so on - otherwise you will seem lazy.
> Check your spelling and grammar and avoid using too many abbreviations, as other people may not understand them.
> Be polite to other users and do not be rude about them or their ideas.
> Use normal punctuation - don't write '!!!!' or '????' to emphasize a point, this is just unnecessary.

Read this discussion and say which users are not showing good 'netiquette' and why.

http://www.

forum

we should do more to protect children who use the internet!!!! my brother jack is only 8 and i don't think he should go online. what do you think???? David

SHUT UP. That's STUPID. Kids can have so much FUN online. If you don't like the internet, why are you here? Ed

I think David is rite, we hav 2 b careful that kids don't spend 2 much time online. There r lots of things they can do instead of sittin in front of a computer all day! Georgia

PLS can we talk about something else? Did any1 c the football match on TV last night? Ben

Ben, if you want to talk about that, you can find a football forum. I think it's important to talk about this - if children use the internet, we need to make sure that they are safe. Laura

C Business options

When is a phone not just a phone? – When it's a mobile …

Mobiles have so many functions nowadays that they can no longer be seen as just for making telephone calls. Mobiles are now so useful that we often feel 'lost' without them. We check them continuously; we can see who's calling us; we can refuse a call if we don't like the person calling; we can recognize friends by their ring tones; we can have almost real-time communication by using text messages; the police can locate a mobile to within a few metres by tracing the signal; we use them to plan our day, find our way, contact friends, wake up in the morning, remember important appointments, get information about sports results and fashion tips. In short, mobiles are a 'must-have' item and a great commercial success. (126 words)

1 DISCUSSION

Discuss the following questions.

1 What functions of a mobile phone are listed in the text? Can you think of any others? Put the functions in order of priority and then compare your list in a group discussion.
2 Do you feel 'lost' without a mobile? Explain why or why not.
3 What extra functions would you like mobiles to have and why?
4 Can you think of any disadvantages of a mobile?

2 MOBILE PHONE DEBT

Look at this posting in a chat room for teenagers. What advice would you give? Begin your answer with *If I were you, I'd / I wouldn't …* The ideas in the box below may help you.

http://www.teenagerhelp.com

Junebaby08 Please … I just need some advice …
I got this really cool new mobile from my parents for my 18th birthday. They said I was old enough to be responsible and my gran told me she would put some money towards the bill every month. So of course I downloaded a personal ring tone and voted on 'Pop Idol' – about 10 times for that little guy who came second! I was on holiday in Mallorca and so I checked my mailbox to hear messages from my new boyfriend and I also sent him some really funny pix of the holiday. Then I got the bill! It's £296.23! I can't tell my parents, my gran, nobody! Please tell me what I can do to get out of this debt! ☹

write to the phone company | change to a pay-as-you-go phone | change your contract | change your provider | take legal advice | pay back the money in instalments | deactivate the mailbox | never send an MMS | stop downloading ring tones | never take part in competitions | keep your phone calls short

D Grammar checkpoint

1 MODAL VERBS

> Grammar summary S. 216

A **Your school is planning a fundraising event. Write full sentences to make suggestions for the event.**

EXAMPLES *All of us should put up posters around town.*
Somebody ought to invite the TV news to film us.

I *We* *Somebody* *One of us* *Some of us* *All of us*	*can* *could* *should* *ought to* *must*	*put up posters around town.* *invite the TV News to film us.* *get an interview on local radio.* *ask local shops to sell tickets for us.* *put a special page on the school website.* *ask all the local bands to come and play.* *hire a bouncy castle for the children.* *have a barbecue and sell soft drinks.* *organize a car park for visitors.*

B **Think about how you can stay in touch with the world. Talk about good ways and ways that do not seem so good.**

EXAMPLES *I could go on the internet to do research for school projects.*
I shouldn't call friends on my mobile so much.

Use these ideas.

call friends on my mobile | email my friends | go on the internet to do research for school projects | read celebrity magazines | send friends text messages | watch TV during the week

2 *MUST, MUST NOT AND NEED NOT*

> Grammar summary S. 216

Complete the exchanges with *must*, *must not* and *need not*.

1 A My sister's getting her exam results today, so I .... get home and call her.
B You .... wait till then. You can use my mobile to call her.

2 A We .... tell anybody about what has happened.
B I agree. Sarah .... never hear about it, or she'll be really angry!

3 A Quick, turn on the TV! I .... miss the news.
B But you've already heard the news on the radio, so surely you .... watch it as well!

4 A .... I really pay over the internet? It doesn't feel safe.
B You .... worry: it's a secure website. And in fact, you .... pay this way, or they won't send you the goods!

5 A Come on! Hurry! We .... miss the big film, and that means we .... be at the cinema by 3.30.
B But we .... watch it then because they're showing the film again at 6.00. So stop panicking!

On the move

FOCUS

1 Talk about the cartoons.

Today, we are free to travel where we want and when we want. Or are we? What do these cartoons say about various forms of transport?

"The salesman said that this was the ideal car for life in the fast lane."

"The flight is only 99p ... but it will be another £120 if you want to sit inside the plane!"

2 Think about it.

To what extent do these British and American cartoons also show the reality of travel in Germany?

3 Talk about your own travel experiences. Use words from the box.

1 Have you ever had any bad experiences while travelling at home or abroad? What happened? How did you feel?
2 What about good experiences? What happened? How did you feel?

amazed | angry | annoyed | anxious | delighted | depressed | disappointed | embarrassed | excited | exhausted | frightened | frustrated | nervous | pleased | relaxed | shocked | surprised | terrified | upset | worried

A Personal perspectives

BEFORE YOU READ

1 22 **Look at the photo. How do you think the people in this traffic jam probably feel?**

TONY ASH green campaigner

Twenty years ago, there were 22 million cars on Britain's roads. Now there are over 30 million. And soon there will be 40 million if we don't take urgent action. Think of the pollution, and the environmental and health damage from the exhaust fumes. The world's choking to death on its tailbacks and gridlocks. And when you look up and down a traffic jam, 90% of those cars contain one driver and no passengers. It's mad, and it has to stop!

LAURA SMITH government transport minister

More roads aren't the answer. If we build one to reduce congestion on another, what happens? In five years, they're both congested. So, if we try to build our way out of road chaos, we will just build our way into more road chaos. As for public transport, this is improving, but it's a long and expensive job. And much of the money has to come from drivers, so the cost of driving can only increase. What we need is a better balance. People who must drive should be able to drive efficiently. Others must change to public transport. If that happens, life will be much better for everyone and CO_2 emissions will be much lower.

RUTH ROSS working mother

I'm a working mum, and I have to drive. If public transport could get me everywhere I need to go, I'd use it. But can it get me to the nursery after work to pick up my little girl? And to the supermarket or the dry-cleaner's? No. There isn't enough of it, and it's also far too expensive. Plus we pay a fortune to drive our cars! Surely, if the government spent all our road and fuel taxes on more and cheaper public transport, things would be better.

WAYNE SIMPSON office worker

OK, so I spend too much time in tailbacks, but I wouldn't give up my car even if you paid me. It says who I am. It means freedom and flexibility. I can go where I want when I want. It also means privacy. I've got my own space, and I can listen to the music I like. Cars give people the freedom to live and work where they want.

(412 words)

1 LOOKING AT THE TEXTS

A Make notes from the texts.

Give five reasons why the drivers do not want to change to public transport.

B Say what you think.

You and your partner live in the suburbs, and you both drive to work in the city centre.

1 Discuss the options below to save money. Talk about the pros and cons, e.g. costs, savings, flexibility, time and impact on the environment.

2 Decide what to do. Give reasons for your choice.

> Drive to work with friends/colleagues (= car sharing).
> Sell one or both cars and use public transport.
> Sell both cars; use bikes to get to work. Use public transport or hire a car for longer trips.

2 WORKING WITH WORDS

Find idiomatic expressions in Tony Ash's comments to complete the following sentences.

1 With everyone trying to leave the city, there was soon total ... on every road: nothing could move for hours!
2 Just look at the ... from that truck: emissions like that are illegal! (*word pair*)
3 If we don't take action to cut emissions, the world will ... (*idiom*)
4 After the accident, there was a ten-mile ... on the motorway.

3 LISTENING

1 23 **A Think about it.**

Distance and travel are the themes of many songs. Can you think of any? Brainstorm some ideas with a partner.

B Listen to the song *Route 66*. Route 66 is the famous road that runs through seven American states. Listen for general understanding and answer these questions.

1 Do you think that the singer likes travelling on Route 66? Why/Why not?
2 In which direction across the USA does the song travel?

C Listen for detail. Look at the map below, listen again and answer these questions.

1 Where does Route 66 start and finish? Identify cities A and E on the map.
2 What are the names of towns/cities B, C and D?
3 How long does the song say the road is?
4 Which city does the singer describe as pretty?

D Say what you think.

What differences are there between the image of travel in the song *Route 66* and the real situation that most commuters experience every day? Think about cartoon 1 on page 65.

4 BUILDING SKILLS: INTERPRETING CARTOONS

> **TIP**
> Some cartoons are just visual jokes, but most deliver a serious message. When you prepare a presentation (see page 206), look out for cartoons that could help present a key point. This could make your presentation much more fun and memorable!

> Interpretation von Bildern und Karikaturen S. 207

A **With a partner, briefly talk about what is happening in the cartoon.**

B **Now use the 'D-A-C method' (Describing, Analyzing and Commenting) to discuss the cartoon in more detail.**

1 First look at sentence beginnings a–e and decide if they are used for describing, analyzing or commenting on the cartoon.

a This is something we know from personal experience. For example, we see that ...
b There is a smaller mountain ...
c The cartoonist is trying to show that SUVs ...
d The message behind the cartoon is that the number of SUV sales is falling because gas prices are ...
e The SUV is driving off ...

2 Now complete the ideas in a–e and add them to the outline below.

1 **Describing**
The cartoon shows a steep mountain with a vertical cliff down one side ...
2 **Analyzing**
The steep mountain is in fact a line graph labelled gas prices, and the SUV represents ...
3 **Commenting**
In my opinion, the cartoonist is quite right ..., but I also think ...

C **Now use this method to write about another cartoon.**

1 Choose one of the cartoons on page 65 and write your own analysis using the ideas above and phrases from the appendix, page 208.
2 Work with your partner again to discuss and improve your writing.

B The bigger picture

BEFORE YOU READ

If you were the German minister for transport, how would you try to reduce a) traffic congestion and b) vehicle emissions?

1 24

Satellite road pricing is on the way

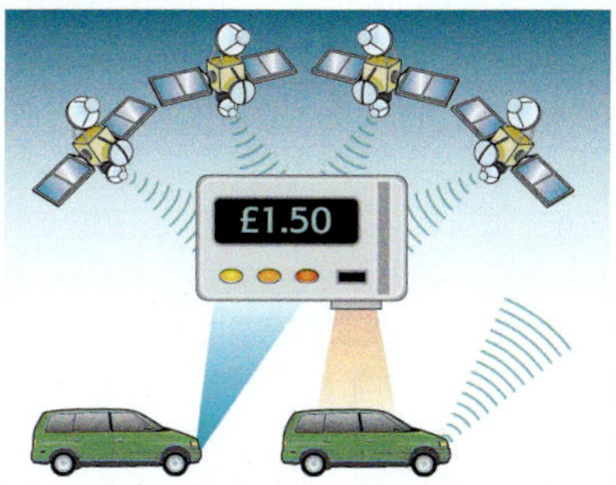

Transport Minister Laura Smith has given new details of our future road tax system: road pricing.

If you drive in a road-pricing zone, you are charged according to where, when and how far you drive. On a quiet road in the country at night you will pay just 2p per mile. However, on a busy main road in the rush hour you can expect to pay £1.34 per mile. 'Unless we do this,' Smith says, 'there will be national gridlock by 2020.'

The technology is quite similar to the 'satnav' (satellite navigation) systems in many modern cars. In each case, satellites and a 'black box' in the vehicle communicate to record location, time and distance travelled. Your bill will arrive monthly.

For some people, this means a 'Big Brother' society, and they hate the idea. 'But,' Smith argues, 'as long as you've nothing to hide from the police, what's the problem?' Road hauliers say that the cost will destroy their businesses, but Smith believes that costs will balance - provided that hauliers avoid rush hour on the busiest roads. City commuters say their lives will be impossible. However, Smith says that people will turn to public transport and car sharing. 'Road use will become more efficient, and we estimate that traffic congestion will fall by 50%.' (214 words)

1 25

THE ROAD TO ZERO EMISSIONS

Fuel prices have increased hugely, and CO_2 emissions have to decrease hugely. At last, car owners and environmentalists want the same thing - a car that does not 'cost the earth' to run. Engineers using several different technologies are racing to provide that car.

Some city dwellers are choosing electric vehicles like the tiny, zero-emission 'G-Wiz'. Joanna Page, actress, Londoner and G-Wiz owner, says: 'We've saved a small fortune in petrol.' Costing 40p (50 cents) to charge at night, it has a range of 80 kilometres. 'That's enough to drive round town all day.' The problem? The electricity comes from a traditional power station.

Hybrid petrol-electric vehicles like Toyota's best-selling Prius cleverly turn energy from the car's movement into electricity. The electric motor then supports the petrol engine, for example on hills. The technology is complicated and expensive, but these cars give something like petrol-engine performance with much greater fuel efficiency.

Long in development, zero-emission fuel-cell technology finally entered commercial car production in 2008. The Honda FCX Clarity is the result. It combines hydrogen and oxygen to produce power - and the only waste is water. Amazing. But remember: we still have to manufacture the hydrogen. If, though, we can do this with renewable energy sources one day, we will finally have an environmentally friendly car with low running costs. (217 words)

1 LOOKING AT THE TEXTS

A Do these tasks.

1 Read the first article and work out how much it will cost to drive ten miles on a main road into London at 8.00 a.m. on a Monday.
2 Calculate the future charge for driving ten miles on a country road at 8 p.m. on a Sunday evening.
3 Describe what today's car navigation technology and the road pricing technology of the future have in common.
4 Find the cost of a 40-kilometre journey in a G-Wiz.
5 Explain why, eventually, fuel cell technology will probably win against hybrid technology.
6 Describe what environmental problem both electric cars and cars powered by fuel cells have at the moment. Then state a possible solution to this problem.

B Say what you think.

Dad – why can't we have a proper car?

2 WORKING WITH WORDS

A There are several word pairs in the texts. Find partner words for 1–8.

Text 1			*Text 2*		
1	*Paragraph 1:*	*... tax*	*5*	*Paragraph 1:*	*... prices*
2	*Paragraph 1:*	*road ...*	*6*	*Paragraph 1:*	*... emissions*
3	*Paragraph 2:*	*... road*	*7*	*Paragraph 4:*	*... production*
4	*Paragraph 4:*	*traffic ...*	*8*	*Paragraph 4:*	*... sources*

B The same words can have other partners. Find more using the words in the box.

country | diesel | electricity | haulier | income | jam | lights | oil | power | side

> TIP

Use this technique to help collect and learn vocabulary efficiently.
Use your dictionary to add partner words.

3 SPEAKING

A Follow these steps to prepare a role-play.

1 Read the following information about congestion charging.

London started congestion charging several years ago, and many other cities want to do the same. All vehicles (except public transport, taxis and 'green' cars like the G-Wiz) have to pay a daily charge if they enter the city centre. The aim is to reduce congestion as much as possible.

Positive results:

a) 30% congestion reduction in the central zone;
b) bus travel up by 38%;
c) 65% of charges go towards better public transport.

Negative results:

a) much more traffic now on roads around the zone: new areas of congestion;
b) reduced sales for 65% of small businesses in and close to the zone: many have considered moving away;
c) a lot of anger among people negatively affected.

Source: Times Online, Oct 29, 2006: Focus: How to get gridlock Britain moving again

2 As a class, choose a city near you which could benefit from congestion charging.

3 Imagine you are at a meeting on congestion charging. Work in groups of four and choose a role each.

Roles

Businessperson > File 9, page 194

City councillor > File 5, page 192

Road commuter > File 2, page 192

Government transport official > File 12, page 194

B Do the role-play.

1 Put forward your point of view and try to persuade the others. Use these phrases:
If we do/don't ..., ... will/won't ...
Provided ...
As long as ...
Unless ...

2 Agree what to do.

3 Compare your decision with the other groups. Take a class vote to choose the best one.

4 CULTURE CHECK: APPROPRIATE GREETINGS

At the congestion charging meeting some people know each other and some do not. Choose which greetings are appropriate in the following situations.

Situation 1

City councillor Jean Hayes and businessperson Bob Hill are not close friends, but they have met quite often before at meetings.
Which greeting might Jean Hayes use? How might Bob Hill reply?

HAYES
- a Hi, Bob. How's it going?
- b Hello, Bob. How are you?
- c Hello, Bob. How do you do?

HILL
- a How are you?
- b Not bad.
- c Very well, thank you. And you?

Situation 2

Jean Hayes is formally introducing Bob Hill to government minister Nick Redding.
How should he reply? How might she continue?

HAYES Mr Redding, this is Mr Hill.

REDDING How do you do?*

HILL
- a Fine, thank you. How do you do?
- b I'm fine, thanks. How are things going?
- c How do you do?

REDDING
- a Not bad, thanks. And you?
- b It's nice to meet you.
- c How fantastic to meet you!

* The greeting "How do you do?" is now becoming a little old-fashioned, but it is still used in some very formal situations.

5 DISCUSSION

> Diskussionen führen S. 210

In small groups, discuss the possible effects of an oil crisis.

Imagine a major oil and gas crisis during the winter. Both oil and gas are almost completely unavailable and extremely expensive. How would a crisis like this affect you personally? How might it affect the whole community? Use phrases like these:

If we had a crisis like that,	*it might*	*mean ...ing ...*
If something like that happened,	*it could*	*make me / us ...*

C Business options

Containerization – a booming industry

1 Up until the 1950s ships had large holds under the deck for their cargoes, which dockers loaded on board by hand. The goods, which were in cartons, crates, barrels, bales or boxes, were lowered into the hold of the ship in nets or on pallets by crane. This procedure was called breaking bulk and was labour-intensive, time-consuming and expensive. It also had many disadvantages including mistakes, damage and theft. In 1956 dockers at the port of New York charged $5.86 per ton to load or unload a ship and would often take up to a week to do so.

2 Everything changed when, in 1956, Malcom McLean, the owner of a trucking company in the US state of North Carolina, introduced the first container ship, a converted oil tanker, which sailed from the port of Newark, New Jersey to the port of Houston, Texas. Using containerization it only cost 16 cents per ton to load a ship. A further advantage was added security because the container was sealed at the factory and only opened by the customer. Whisky was one of the first products to be transported in containers.

3 By the 1970s, despite great opposition from the unions to containerization, further revolutionary changes had taken place. Containers were of a standard size (40 feet long) and could be transported cheaply by road, rail, air or sea to almost any location in the world. They were loaded and unloaded mechanically using huge cranes and gantries on land. Warehouses were no longer so important because containers could be left outside in all weathers. City ports (e.g. New York, San Francisco, London and Liverpool) became obsolete because container terminals needed space, not labour, and new ports in cheaper rural areas grew (e.g. Felixstowe in the UK or Seattle in the US). Low transport costs meant that goods could be sourced virtually anywhere and East and South-East Asia could become the workplace of the world. (320 words)

1 LOOKING AT THE TEXT

Match three of the following five headings to the paragraphs of the text.

A Whisky sold internationally
B Inefficient working practices
C Containerization stops city expansion
D Transportation in the global village
E A great step forwards

2 DISCUSSION

Discuss the following questions.

1 Why do you think the unions were opposed to containerization?
2 Do you think this was a good development and why? Think about the effects it had on the industry, the workforce and the surrounding areas.
3 What other areas of business can you think of where similar big changes have happened?

D Grammar checkpoint

1 *IF*-SENTENCES TYPE 1

> Grammar summary S. 220

A Tomas, a student in London, has to travel to Paris. Use the table to help him decide how to get there. Use *if*-sentences type 1 and add information from the table where required.

Travel between London and Paris

	Cost	Time
By plane	£122 return	1 hr 20 min (+ about 3 hours travel/waiting time)
By train & Eurostar	£159 return	2 hr 30 min
By car & ferry	£135 return	about 9 hr

TOMAS What's the best way to get to Paris?
YOU If you *go*[1] (*go*) by plane, it *will be*[2] (*be*) cheaper than by train or ferry.
TOMAS Will it be faster to fly too?
YOU Well, yes and no. If you …[3] (*count*) just the flight time, it …[4] (*take*) less time.
TOMAS So why do you say 'yes and no'?
YOU Because it …[5] (*take*) longer if you …[6] (*also allow*) time for travel to and from the airport.
TOMAS Really? So if I …[7] (*travel*) by plane, how much …[8] (*it/cost*) and how long …[9] (*it/take*)?
YOU It …[10] (*cost*) …[11], and it …[12] (*take*) about …[13] altogether.
TOMAS What about the train? How long …[14] (*it/take*) if I …[15] (*go*) by train?
YOU Just …[16] from the UK straight to Paris. But then there's also the cheaper ferry option. If you …[17] (*take*) your car, it …[18] (*cost*) …[19]. Of course, the journey time is longer – about …[20].
TOMAS Well, I like ships and the sea, so perhaps I'll take the ferry. Thanks for your help.

B Work with a partner. Practise the dialogue together.

2 *IF*-SENTENCES TYPE 2

> Grammar summary S. 220

A Make *If*-sentences type 2 with the verbs in the right forms and the correct punctuation.

1 Wayne Simpson: the government (*build*) more roads | we (*not have*) road congestion | And | we (*not have*) congestion | everybody (*be able to*) get around faster
If the government built more roads, we would not have congestion. And if we did not have congestion, everybody would be able to get around faster.
2 Tony Ash: car drivers (*carry*) more passengers | traffic jams (*disappear*) | And | traffic jams (*disappear*) | everybody (*be*) much healthier
3 Ruth Ross: transport services (*become*) cheaper | more people (*use*) them | And | more people (*use*) them | they (*expand)* and (*get*) better
4 Laura Smith: the government (*do)* nothing about transport | the situation (*go*) from bad to worse | And | that (*happen*) | the government (*lose*) the next election

B Imagine you are in London and in the following situations. Look at the table in exercise 1A again, and make statements using *If*-sentences type 2.

1 You need your car for a holiday in France.
  a How would you go?
  If I needed my car for …, I would go by …
  b Cost?
  If I went by …, it …

2 You have to get to Paris urgently.
  a How would you travel?
  b Time?

3 You need to connect with a flight from Paris to Tokyo.
  a How would you go?
  b Cost and time?

5

Green enough?

FOCUS

1 Compare the past and the present.

Thinking about the environment ...

> how are things worse now than, say, 50 years ago?

> could some things actually be better now than 50 years ago?

2 Work with a partner. Discuss some Hollywood views of the future.

a Look at pictures 1–4 and match them to titles a–d.

2

a Waterworld
b 28 Days Later
c The Day after Tomorrow
d Armageddon

1

4

3

b All of these films imagine future disasters. Are the disasters a) natural, b) man-made or c) a mixture of both?

c Briefly discuss what each film is about. The following words may be helpful.

asteroid | catastrophe | destruction | disaster | epidemic | flood | hurricane | ice age | tsunami

A *Armageddon is set in the (near/distant) future, and it's about (an asteroid which is going to hit Earth).*

B *That's right. And they have to (find a way of stopping it).*

A Personal perspectives

BEFORE YOU READ

A **Look at the pictures and say what is happening in each.**

B **Read the title of the text. Try to link the pictures to the title.**

Going green: the final report

By Julie Price

A

B

C

D

We started our 'green year' exactly twelve months ago – on January 1st last year. Now, we have finished, and it is time to look back on the experience.

Like a lot of people, Paul and I had already made ourselves a little greener. For example, we had started recycling more carefully, and we had fitted low-energy light bulbs around the house.

But last year was a very different matter, and this is how it all began. As a journalist, I had written an article in December called *How to save the planet*. My boss had then asked me to turn my fine words into action for a year – and write monthly progress reports. Oh, dear! My boss is a woman you do not refuse.

Fortunately, Paul agreed, and so our new way of life began. First, we simply turned down the heating. That was not too difficult: we just suggested that visiting friends should wear sweaters! And we immediately started saving both energy and money.

We also considered changing to alternative energy sources. Should we put a wind turbine on the roof perhaps? No. Wind strength in a city crowded with buildings is too weak and unreliable. Well, then, what about solar power? Surely even under grey north European skies we could meet many of our energy needs. Well, yes, but the cost was far too high. In the end, we spent our limited budget on more roof insulation. This simple, sensible step has already paid for itself.

After we had done this, we faced our first hard decision. We loved our car, but we decided it had to go. Once we had finally sold it, things slowly got easier. After all, we live in a city, so we could walk, cycle and use public transport. Sometimes it took longer, but we learned to allow extra time. As for the money we got from selling the car, we decided to use it to finish double-glazing the house. (We had done most of the house previously but had run out of cash.)

The other difficult thing was the summer holiday. We had always loved going somewhere warm and exotic, especially India, but last year no. Instead, we took the train to Wales and had a walking holiday. We got wet but very fit, and we also discovered beautiful places we had never heard of in our own country. And, by avoiding those flights, we saved two tonnes of CO_2 emissions – the amount that two average cars produce in a whole year!

What about the future? Well, we're used to our new lifestyle now, and we aim to continue. The only thing is this: somehow we *must* find a way to travel the world again.

(454 words)

1 LOOKING AT THE TEXT

A Read the text quickly to match pictures A–D to different paragraphs.

B Copy and complete the tables using information from the text.

Timeline
December, the year before last
January 1st last year
Today, a year later

→

Events
1 JP wrote 'How to save the planet'.
2 …

Actions taken last year
1 Turned down …
2 …
3 …
4 …

→

Benefits mentioned in the text
1 Saved energy & …
2 …

Actions not taken
1 Put a …
2 …

→

Reasons mentioned
1 …

Plans/Hopes for the future
1 …
2 …

C Use your notes to give a spoken summary. You can use these ideas.

In December the year before last, Julie Price wrote …, and her boss then … And so, on January …, … Today, a year …, …
Julie and her husband took a number of actions last year. First of all, they …, and this immediately saved energy and … Then they … They also … Finally, they …
There were other actions that they considered but did not take. For one thing, they thought about putting a …, but they … because … For another, they wondered about …, but …
As for the future, they plan to … However, they really want to …

D Write an email in German.

> Mediation S. 210

A German friend asks for your advice on quick ways to save energy and money on heating her home. Write an email to her in German, suggesting two things she should do and two she should not. Use the information in the text to explain your advice.

E Say what you think.

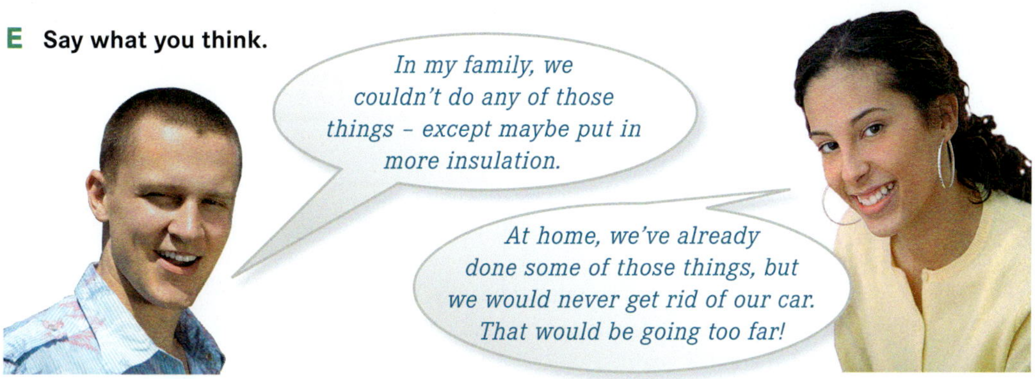

2 WORKING WITH WORDS

A Find words or expressions in the text that have similar meanings to these expressions.

1 every month (*lines 15-20*)
2 at once (*lines 20-25*)
3 finally (*lines 26-41*)
4 got used to (*lines 43-56*)
5 before that (*lines 43-56*)
6 particularly (*lines 57-69*)
7 quantity (*lines 57-69*)
8 way of life (*lines 70-74*)

B Rewrite the sentences with the words and phrases from the box below and your own words.

1 We started our 'green year' on January 1st last year.
2 My boss had asked me to write monthly progress reports.
3 We suggested that visiting friends should wear sweaters.
4 We also considered changing energy sources.
5 We learned to allow extra time.

advised | every month | got used to | in addition | was the start of

> **TIP**
> When you use information from a text to write a comment or summary, you need to change the original words and phrases as much as possible. But be careful: changing a word might mean you need to change other parts of the sentence too, like the word order.

C Read the dictionary section below on phrasal verbs with the verb *turn*. Then do the following tasks.

1 Complete the following sentences from the text with the correct phrasal verbs.
 a My boss had then asked me to ... my fine words ... action for a year.
 b First, we simply ... ... the heating.

2 Complete the following with phrasal verbs from the dictionary section.
 a Every month last year, a lot of readers used to ... ... page 8 to read Julie Price's latest monthly report on her green year.
 b Her husband Paul was very interested in her project, and the many difficult changes to their way of life did not ... him ...
 c They quickly learned to ... ... all lights and appliances that they were not using.
 d They also used to ... ... the hot water system for fewer hours a day.
 e They were quite worried about going on holiday to Wales, but everything ... ... very well, and they loved their time there.
 f One cloudy day, they walked about two kilometres along a valley, and then ... ... the road and climbed a steep mountain path.
 g They nearly ... ... when it started raining heavily, but they kept going and came to a beautiful lake – just as the sun started shining again!

turn back to go back in the same direction as you came: *The weather became so bad that they had to turn back.*
turn sb/sth down to refuse an offer or request, or the person that makes it: *Why did you turn that job down? · He asked her to marry him, but she turned him down.*
turn off sth to leave one road and and go on another: *We turn off the motorway at junction 10.*
turn (sb) off to lose or make sb lose interest; to make sb feel bored or disgusted: *Men with beards turn me off.*
turn sth off to move the switch, etc. on a piece of machinery, etc. to stop it working: *He turned the TV off.*
turn sth on to move the switch, etc. on a piece of machinery, etc. to start it working: *Turn the lights on!*
turn out (to be sth) to be sth in the end: *The weather turned out fine. · The house that they had promised us turned out to be a tiny flat.*
turn to sth to find a page in a book: *Turn to page 45.*

B The bigger picture

BEFORE YOU READ

A Look at the two halves of the picture and describe each in turn.

B Say whether they seem to show versions of the past, present or future.

GLOBAL Times January 2, 2060

News from the future 1

Yesterday, entering the 2060s, we heard the news we desperately did not want to hear. Around the world, the airwaves were full of it: we have passed the figure of 560 parts per million of CO_2 in the Earth's atmosphere, twice the level it was before the Industrial Revolution. More importantly, 99% of scientists agree that it is also the point of no return for climate change. We have just passed the last red danger light at high speed.

What will happen now? The answer is: a lot. Here in Europe, summers will get hotter and hotter and winters ever wetter. Sudden violent storms will become more and more common. And we are the lucky ones. In other parts of the world, life has already become impossible because of climate change. Hurricanes are forcing people away from Central America and the USA's south-eastern coasts. In Asia, cyclones are doing the same from China to India. Africa's deserts are expanding fast. Thousands are dying. Millions more are refugees. These regions are falling into chaos.

Moreover, the Greenland and Antarctic ice sheets are melting and sea levels are rising a centimetre a year. Many low-lying islands have disappeared, and soon great coastal cities from Shanghai to Alexandria to New York will drown.

Scientists were warning the world about this 60 years ago. If people had acted quickly back then, they would have prevented today's disasters. But they did nothing. Why? (238 words)

GLOBAL Times January 2, 2060

News from the future 2

Yesterday, entering the 2060s, we heard the news we were hoping for. Champagne has become a rare luxury these days, but people happily paid €1,000 for a bottle to celebrate. For the world has again held atmospheric CO_2 at 450 ppm. Moreover, the level will fall slightly this year – even though the world economy will continue growing by 4%.

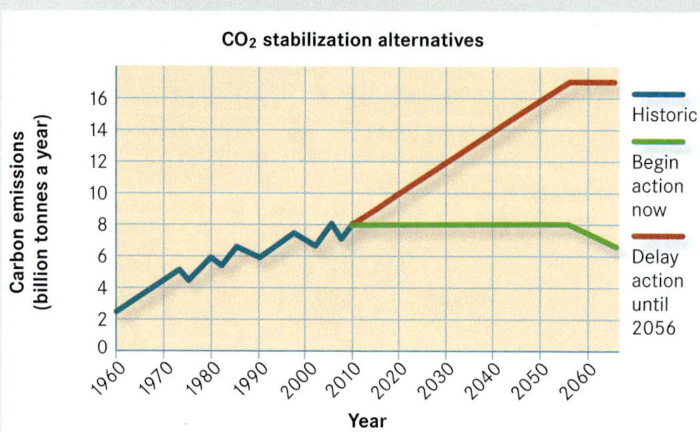

There are many reasons for this success, and here are just a few. First, we have reduced our use of oil, gas and coal by nearly 80% over the last 50 years, and it is these fossil fuels that produce most of the CO_2 emissions. We have replaced them with various alternative forms of energy, including 'renewables' such as solar, wind, tidal and hydroelectric power. There is also fuel cell technology. Today this runs the world's three billion vehicles, and it produces no CO_2 at all – nor any other sort of pollution. Then there is nuclear fusion, the safe, cheap nuclear technology that EU members first began developing 80 years ago.

These and other changes have happened thanks to the strength and vision of our grandparents' generation. Their governments understood the need to fight global warming. If they had not started – and continued – the fight to control CO_2 emissions then, severe climate change would have begun by now. Our world would have fallen into chaos if those wise leaders had not been there. Today we owe them a big thank you as we emerge from human history's greatest crisis.

(248 words)

1 LOOKING AT THE TEXTS

A Read the texts quickly to match them to the two halves of the picture on page 79.

B Read the first text carefully. Choose the best answer or answers.

1 The writer tells us that before the Industrial Revolution ...
   a there was half as much CO_2 in the atmosphere as in 2060.
   b there was twice as much atmospheric CO_2 then as in 2060.
   c there were about 280 ppm of CO_2 in the Earth's atmosphere.

2 According to the author, writing in 2060 about climate change, ...
   a the effects are bad in Europe but much worse in other places.
   b it has become impossible to live in many regions such as Europe.
   c storms have forced people to leave their homes in Europe.

3 The writer believes that it would have been possible to stop climate change in the early 21st century, but ...
   a people then did not do anything about it.
   b people back then did something but it was too little and too late.
   c people in those days did not know why they needed to do anything.

C Read the second text carefully and then write a letter in German to *Wissenschaft Heute*. Explain what we must do to make the world safe for our grandchildren in 2060 and beyond.

> Mediation S. 210

2 WORKING WITH WORDS

A Use fractions and percentages from the box to complete the statements.

a fifth (1/5) | half (1/2) | three-fifths (3/5) | 20 % | 60 % | 100 %

1 According to the first report, CO_2 levels before the Industrial Revolution used to be ... of the 2060 figure of 560 ppm. In other words, they have risen by ... %.

2 Turning to the second report, we can say that if the pre-industrial CO_2 level was 280 ppm, then that was about ... of the 2060 figure of 450 ppm that this report notes. That is to say, the level of CO_2 shows an increase of roughly ... %.

3 The second report goes on to say that today's use of fossil fuels is roughly ... of the 2010 total, i.e. the use of fossil fuels now is only about ... % of what it was.

B Practise saying fractions and percentages. Read out the statements in exercise A.

3 LISTENING

2 5 **A Listen for general understanding. Listen once and say whether the statements are true or false.**

1 The speakers are on either a radio or a TV show.
2 The guest writes for a magazine called *Science Now*.
3 Dr Parry is talking about CO_2 emissions around the world.
4 He believes that the whole world must immediately start reducing emissions.
5 If the world does what Dr Parry says, he believes that we will save ourselves from the worst possibilities of climate change.

B **Listen for detail. Copy the chart, listen again and complete it.**

C **Make statements about the chart. Use fractions and percentages.**

In the period to 2020, emissions have to ...

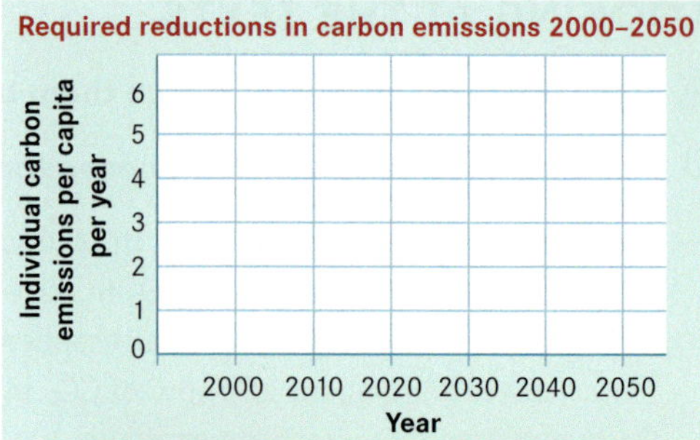

4 BUILDING SKILLS: SUMMARIZING

> TIP

Summary writing is a very useful skill: it makes you focus on the essential information in a text. Looking carefully at the structure of a text will help you to write a well-structured summary.

A **Read the summary of *News from the future 1* and compare it with the original.**

1 Note examples of rephrasing.
2 Find examples of new connectors to link ideas together.
3 Compare the lengths of the original and the summary.

(Yesterday, entering the 2060s, we heard the news we desperately did not want to hear.) (Around the world, the airwaves were full of it:) we have passed the figure of 560 parts per million of CO_2 in the Earth's atmosphere, twice the level it was before the Industrial Revolution. (More importantly, 99% of scientists agree that) it is also the point of no return for climate change. (We have just passed the last red danger light at high speed.)

(What will happen now? The answer is: a lot.) Here in Europe, summers will get hotter and hotter and winters ever wetter. Sudden violent storms will become more and more common. And we are the lucky ones. In other parts of the world, life has already become impossible because of climate change. (Hurricanes are forcing people away from Central America and ...) Thousands are dying. Millions more are refugees. (These regions are falling into chaos.)

Moreover, the (Greenland and Antarctic) ice sheets are melting and sea levels are rising (a centimetre a year). Many low-lying islands have disappeared, and soon great coastal cities (from Shanghai to ...) will drown.

Scientists were warning the world about this 60 years ago. If people had acted quickly back then, they would have prevented today's disasters. (But they did nothing. Why?) (238 words)

Unnecessary anecdote
Unnecessary supporting figure & source of opinion
Simile
Rhetorical question
Unnecessary examples
Repetition
Unnecessary names
Unnecessary supporting figure & examples
Rhetorical finish

Summary

Now, in 2060, CO_2 in our planet's atmosphere has risen above 560 parts per million. This is 100% higher than it was before the Industrial Revolution, and it means climate change is out of control.

In Europe, we will see hotter summers, wetter winters and more violent, stormy weather. Things are even worse in other regions. There, life has already become very difficult because of climate change. Millions of people have become refugees, and many are dying.

The Earth's ice is melting, and sea levels are rising. Low-lying islands have flooded and soon so will important coastal cities.

If the world had responded to scientists' warnings 60 years ago, these catastrophes would have been avoided. (115 words)

B **Now write a summary of *News from the future 2*. It should be between a third and half of the original length.**

> Zusammenfassung S. 204

C Business options

Renewable and non-renewable energy

Gone are the days when energy was plentiful and cheap. Although fossil fuels still account for approximately 85% of the world's energy consumption, global warming means the race is on to replace them with renewable, environmentally friendly sources. So far wind and solar power have proved to be the most promising and commercially viable alternatives to conventional sources. Experts believe that wind power has the potential to provide five times the current total amount of energy used globally and they think it would be a good future source of energy.

Wind farms are now being built offshore (e.g. the London Array Wind Farm, 1,000 MW) or in deserts (e.g. the Horse Hollow Wind Energy Center, Texas, 735.5 MW). Solar power plants are also being built in sunny areas, for example, in Serpa, Portugal (11 MW), where the solar panels are two metres above the ground, so cattle can graze beneath them, or the Waldpolenz Solar Park in Germany (40 MW), which will be as big as 200 football pitches. Kenya currently has the largest number of solar power systems per capita.

Some see the answer to our energy problems in nuclear energy and biofuels but both have major disadvantages in the long term, including waste disposal and the use of farm land.

(212 words)

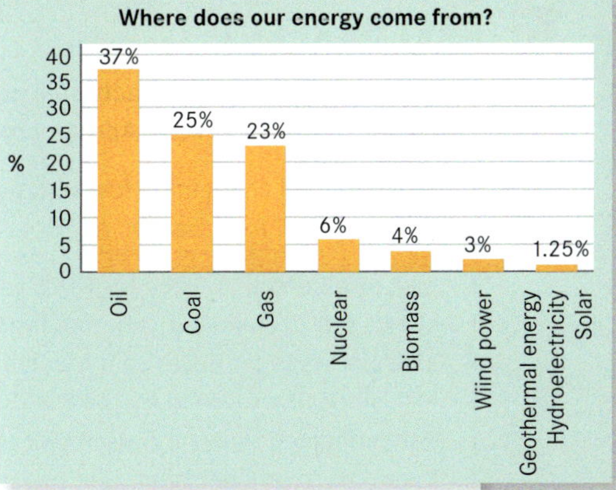

TALKING ABOUT ENERGY

biofuels – liquid fuels, e.g. ethanol, biodiesel made from biomass
biogas – methane gas from waste
biomass – wood, manure, crops (e.g. sugar cane, sugar beet, wheat, corn)
carbon footprint – how much CO_2 is produced by a human activity
fossil fuels – oil, coal, natural gas from dead plants and animals millions of years old
geothermal energy – energy from the heat under the earth's crust
hydro – to do with water (rivers, waves, tides)
offshore – in the sea
watt – a unit of energy
kW = kilowatt – one thousand watts
MW = megawatt – one million (10^6) watts
GW = gigawatt – one billion (10^9) watts

1 LOOKING AT THE TEXT

Answer the following questions.

1 Explain what damage is done by fossil fuels.
2 What are the conventional sources of energy?
3 Which alternative source of energy mentioned is expected to become more popular and why?

2 GROUP WORK

Two wind farms and two solar power plants are mentioned in the text. In groups find more information about one of them and present your results to the class.

3 OPINION

Think about the following questions.

1 Why do we need to reduce our carbon footprint? Write 80–100 words. Think about developments such as global warming, rising sea levels and rising food prices.
2 If you could change how your country uses energy, what would you do and why?

D Grammar checkpoint

1 PAST PERFECT

> Grammar summary S. 214

Make one sentence from each pair of sentences using the expression in brackets. Put one clause in the past perfect. Add a comma if necessary.

1 Julie and Paul changed to low-energy light bulbs. She wrote 'How to save the planet'. (*before*)
Julie and Paul had changed to low-energy light bulbs before she wrote 'How to save the planet'.

2 Julie produced this piece for the *Daily News*. She and Paul also started recycling. (*before*)
3 Life began to change much, much more dramatically. She wrote about saving the planet. (*after*)
4 Julie's newspaper never said much about green issues. She wrote her article. (*until*)
5 Julie's boss Karen read the article. She began thinking hard about Julie's ideas. (*when*)
6 Karen decided that the *Daily News* should go green. She saw all the letters from readers. (*once*)
7 Karen made this decision. She picked up the phone and called Julie to her office. (*as soon as*)
8 Julie left Karen's office 30 minutes later. She agreed to live a 'green year' and write about it. (*by the time*)
9 Paul accepted the idea. He and Julie discussed it carefully that evening. (*once*)
10 They decided to begin their new lifestyle. They immediately took the first step and turned down the heating. (*after*)

2 *IF*-SENTENCES TYPE 3

> Grammar summary S. 220

Put the verbs in the right forms to make *if*-sentences type 3. (The *if* part may be in first or second position.) Add a comma if necessary.

1 Julie (*not write*) her article on 'How to save the planet' / her boss (*not ask*) her to go green for a year
If Julie had not written her article on 'How to save the planet', her boss would not have asked her to go green for a year.

2 Paul (*not agree*) to go green for a year / Julie (*say*) no to her boss.
If Paul hadn't agreed ...

3 Julie and Paul (*not be able to*) pay for efficient roof insulation / they (*spend*) their money on wind or solar power instead
Julie and Paul would not have been able to ...

4 they (*keep*) their car / they (*not learn*) to get around the city in other ways
5 they (*not make*) some money from selling the car / they (*not be able to*) finish double glazing their house
6 they (*fly*) to India for their summer holiday / they (*add*) two tonnes of CO_2 emissions to the atmosphere
7 they (*not go*) to Wales instead / they (*not discover*) lots of beautiful places that were new to them

Modern ways to work

FOCUS

Holiday Club International operates ski and seaside resorts across Europe. Members buy points when they join, and these points allow them to use the resorts where and when they want.
Like other organizations, HCI needs a variety of staff and skills. Here are some of them.

F

D

A

B

C

E

1 accountant
2 bookings clerk
3 customer relations officer
4 IT technician
5 receptionist
6 publicity assistant
7 resort activities officer
8 salesperson
9 ski instructor
10 waiter

1 Match the people in the photos (A–F) to six of the jobs (1–10).

2 Say which of employees 1–10 you think said the following. Explain why.

My job is temporary because it's seasonal and it's not well paid. In high season, I have to work long, irregular hours. So it can be stressful. But I meet lots of people, and the job is fun. I love working outdoors, helping people to learn a new skill. I always have to be friendly and helpful, but that's me anyway. And I decide how to do things. I just love being independent.

My work is office-based and, with its regular routines, I suppose it's rather repetitive and not very challenging. But it's a responsible job and I have to be accurate. It's secure, permanent, full-time, and I like the regular hours. There's a reasonable salary with good fringe benefits. I work with numbers and don't have any customer contact, but I have to be a good team player in our small group.

3 Imagine you have a choice of jobs 1–10 at Holiday Club International. Say which you would or would not choose and why, using the highlighted vocabulary above.

I'd try the job of ... I think *I wouldn't try ... I don't think*	*it would be good* *I would enjoy it / be good at it* *I would like it / be good at it*	*because ...*

A Personal perspectives

BEFORE YOU READ

A student from another country asks you this question: 'After Class 10 in Germany, what routes can you take to get a good, permanent job by your early 20s?' How would you answer?

Routes to the modern workplace: complex but flexible

ANNA Haven't we met somewhere before? It's Ed, isn't it?

ED That's right. You were at Oxford CFE, weren't you?

ANNA Yes, I finished there a year ago, last July.

ED Me too. I was there for two years.

ANNA So was I. It's strange we didn't get to know each other.

ED Well, it's a big place, and we were on different courses. I did the one-year IT Diploma. And you did Business Studies, didn't you?

ANNA Not in the first year. When I came over from Germany, I joined the International Study Programme.

ED That sounds very grand!

ANNA Well, it included lots of English – and some IT and basic Business Studies. It was a bridge to my second year.

ED So what brought you over from Germany?

ANNA Well, after I left school, I did a one-year secretarial course in Dortmund. But then I found out I could get a business qualification over here for free, thanks to the EU. And I wanted to get some international work experience too.

ED Is that what you're doing now?

ANNA Yes, I scanned the internet for suitable job adverts, sent out loads of CVs and letters of application towards the end of my course, and I got some interviews – and a job offer from Mediscan. I've been there for a year now, and they're a good employer. The hours are a bit longer than at home, but the salary's reasonable and there are good benefits. I'm training in Export Sales now, and it's quite challenging. I'll probably stay for several years.

ED Great! Actually, your first year at CFE reminds me a bit of mine. I was on an 'access' programme.

ANNA What's that exactly?

ED It's for people who want to get back into education – and need some help getting there.

ANNA So what were you doing before that then?

ED It was stupid really. I left school and just drifted into a temporary job at a local factory that made car seats for Honda in Swindon. They put me in stock control as I'd done some ICT at school. It was a boring, dead-end job, but the pay was OK.

ANNA What happened then?

ED Well, after three years, the company decided to move production to Bulgaria and make us all redundant. Two months later, the factory was gone and so were 140 jobs! We were out of work!

ANNA Was that when you decided to go to CFE?

ED Yes, it was hard, but my redundancy pay helped, and I got a part-time job too. I upgraded my skills, and it worked. BSG, the solar heating company, were hiring as I was finishing. I applied for an IT job, and I got it. I'm finally in full-time, permanent work at last, the salary is good and I'm going to stay.

ANNA Let's hope BSG doesn't decide to move to Bulgaria too!

(462 words)

> INFO

CFE = college of further education: a local college that offers full-time and part-time vocational and school examination classes. Access courses are available for people who need to raise their basic educational level before joining other classes. Similarly, there may also be international study programmes, which are free to full-time students from other EU countries.
CV = curriculum vitae (AE: resume): a document giving personal details and details of qualifications and past employment. Often required by an employer as part of a job application. For more on CVs and resumes, see Unit 8.
ICT = information and communications technology: the school subject that used to be known as information technology.

1 LOOKING AT THE TEXT

A Compare and contrast Ed's and Anna's routes to their jobs today.

1 Contrast what they did after they left school.
2 Outline the college training that they each did in Oxford.
3 Compare their experiences since they finished their courses.

B Say what you think.

1 Who do you think was clearer and more organized at the beginning - Ed or Anna?
2 Do you think this mattered much?
3 Which person are you more like - Ed or Anna - and why?

2 BUILDING SKILLS: TAKING NOTES FROM READING

> TIP

When you take notes, organize them with sub-headings or dates (see below). Leave out unnecessary words such as pronouns and articles. Use abbreviations and symbols such as: *e.g., km, =, etc.*

A Copy and complete the notes about Ed and Anna from the past to now and to their future plans. (To work out dates in the past, work backwards from this year.)

1

Ed
Summer 20..: Left school, got job at ...
Summer 20..: Lost ...
... ...
... ...
Future plans: ...

2

Anna
Summer 20..: Left school., started a ...
Summer 20..: ...
... ...
... ...
Future plans: ...

B Use your notes to give an oral summary.

1 Work with a partner. Take turns to tell the stories of Ed and Anna.
2 Listen carefully to each other. Make sure that you have both noted the important information fully and accurately.

3 WORKING WITH WORDS

A Copy and complete the lists with 'employment' vocabulary from pages 85–86. Then add other words that you know.

Employment

Getting a job	*Things an employer wants*	*Pay and conditions*
job advertisement (advert/ad)	*experience*	*wages*
...	...	...
...	...	...

Describing work	*Types of employment*	*Being out of a job*
stressful	*permanent*	*redundancy pay*
...	...	...
...	...	...

B Rewrite the sentences using the words in brackets (all from pages 85–86) instead of the underlined words.

1 I had a lot of pressure in my old job. (*stressful*)
My old job was very stressful.
2 Susie is paid very well. (*salary*)
3 Tina works full-time now. (*job*)
4 Tony has responsibility for all export sales. (*responsible*)
5 Helping people is part of my job. (*helpful*)
6 Jo doesn't meet many customers in her work. (*customer contact*)
7 They closed the factory and put everybody out of work. (*redundant*)

4 BUILDING SKILLS: TAKING NOTES FROM LISTENING

> Das Hörverständnis üben S. 199

2 8 **A Listen for general understanding. Listen to Part 1 and answer these questions.**

1 Who is speaking?
2 Use your notes from exercise 2A to say when this phone conversation happened.
3 What do you think the speakers are going to talk about in Part 2?

> **TIP**
>
> This is harder than taking notes from reading because you can easily fall behind as you write. But don't panic! Speakers often make false starts and repeat themselves.

2 9 **B Listen for detail. Listen to Part 2 and do the following:**

1 Listen once. Try to remember as many details as you can, but do not write notes.
2 Briefly, report details that you remember to the class. Do you all remember the same?
3 Prepare headings, referring to exercise 3A for help. Start like this:
Job: Assistant IT ..., Marketing Support ...
Type of employment: full-time, ...
4 Listen again and take notes.
5 Work with a partner. Take turns to talk about the job from your notes. Make sure that you have both noted the important information fully and accurately. Add to or change your notes as necessary.

B The bigger picture

BEFORE YOU READ

A **What benefits beyond pay may temporary jobs in Germany offer?**

B **What further benefits do you expect when you get a permanent job?**

2 10

A contract too good to be true?

The aptitude tests and the interview were over: after several false starts, Steve finally had the 'right' job. The starting salary was not great, but his career prospects were good. Who could tell? After many years of commitment, Steve might even become a director.

In return, the company was also making big commitments. When Steve showed his family his new contract of employment, his long-retired grandad could hardly believe his eyes. The overall terms and conditions of service were generous and the fringe benefits excellent. 'We didn't have all this when I was your age,' he said.

He recognized cheap cafeteria prices, but subsidized travel, the rise from two weeks' paid holidays to five and the long-term sick pay were new to him. So were the free private healthcare, travel insurance and gym membership.

Then there was the flexitime system to help employees create a good work-life balance. There was also generous paid maternity and paternity leave, and subsidized creche facilities encouraged mothers to return to part-time or full-time work when they were ready.

Such employee benefits have developed over many years. Some have been due to union pressure, and some to government and EU laws. Others have come from business itself. A modern employer invests a lot of money in training its employees. In return, it wants to keep them - and to keep them working hard. It knows that a happy worker is a harder worker. Its workforce is its most valuable resource.

'But how can they afford all these benefits?' Grandad finally asked.

In today's competitive world of work, this is a very good question, and many European business leaders and politicians are asking it.

The big problem is this: business in rich, expensive Europe has to compete globally, most of all with low-cost East Asia. There, working hours are long, pay is low and benefits are few. In order to compete, European business has been taking tough action. First, it has sent manufacturing and now also many white-collar clerical and IT jobs to East Asia and other low-cost regions. It has also been taking away some of its generous benefits. For example, Europe's short, 35-hour week is dying. British business never accepted it. German firms have forced employees to accept longer hours. Now the French are starting to work longer hours too.

* * * * *

After an increasingly hard working life, Steve may one day have to answer his grandad's question like this: 'They really *couldn't* afford all those benefits - at least not for very long.'

(416 words)

1 LOOKING AT THE TEXT

A Read quickly to find information.

1 List the fringe benefits that the photos on page 89 illustrate.
2 List the benefits Steve's grandad had when he was young and those he did not.

B Copy and complete the notes on the text.

1 *Aspects of Steve's new job – good and bad:*

a starting salary: not great
b career: ...
c ...
d ...

2 *Examples of benefits:*

a ...
b ...
c ...

3 *Better benefits have come from:*

a ...
b ...
c ...

4 *Global pressure on European business means:*

a ...
b ...

5 *Conclusion:*

...

C Work with a partner and write a summary.

Use your notes to write a summary of the text in five short paragraphs. Choose one of the following to start each paragraph.

Better benefits for people like Steve have come from several sides. |
However, there is great pressure on European employers like Steve's. |
Steve's job offered many benefits, including the following. |
After a hard working life, it is probable that Steve will reach an unhappy conclusion. |
Most aspects of Steve's new job were very positive.

Start like this: *Most aspects of Steve's new job were very positive. Although ...*

2 WORKING WITH WORDS

A Use words from the text to complete Steve's answers to his family's questions.

1 *Does the company offer any help with children?* — *Yes, it gives ..., ... and ...*

2 *What about other paid time off work?* — *Well, we get ..., and we also get ...*

3 *And how about subsidized benefits? Is there anything like that?* — *Sure. They give us ..., and they offer ..., too.*

4 *And what about free benefits? Are there any completely free extras?* — *The answer's yes again. The company provides ..., ... and ...*

B Say what you think.

If you applied for Steve's job, which fringe benefits would interest you most/least? Why?

3 LISTENING

2 11 **A Listen for general understanding. Listen to conversations 1–4 from Anna's first day at Mediscan. Match them to pictures A–D.**

A

B

C

D

B Listen for detail. Listen to Anna's conversations again. Say which of these expressions you hear.

1 a Excuse me, but could you direct me to Marketing, please?
  b Excuse me, but can you tell me the way to Marketing, please?
2 a I'm sorry, but I need to see some form of ID, please.
  b I'm afraid I have to ask you for some kind of ID, please.
3 a I wonder if you could fill in some forms for me, please.
  b Perhaps you could fill in these forms for me, please.
4 a After that, would you like me to take you to your new office?
  b After that, shall I show you the way to your new office?
5 a If it's all right to ask, are you from Germany by any chance?
  b If you don't mind me asking, are you German perhaps?
6 a Shall I move it over to the window for you?
  b Would you like me to move it over to the window for you?
7 a Would it be all right if I came with you?
  b Would you mind if I came with you?
8 a Could you possibly wait for a moment while I save this document?
  b Do you think you could wait just a moment while I save this document?

4 CULTURE CHECK: POLITE EXPRESSIONS

Germans can often sound too direct, and even rude, to English speakers - especially the British. On the other hand, English speakers' politeness and indirectness can sound absurd to Germans. However, polite expressions are very important to English speakers, so use them!

please | thank you | certainly | of course | I'm afraid (that) ... | I'm sorry, but ... |

Polite expressions for asking, requesting and offering are also very important. Try not to answer requests or questions with only 'Yes' or 'No'. Fuller replies are more friendly and polite.

May/Can I ask ... | If you don't mind me asking ... | Perhaps you could tell me ... |
Could you/I (possibly) ... | Would you mind if ... | I wonder if you/I could ... |
Do you think you/I could ... | Would you like (me) to ... | Shall I ... for you?

A **Work with a partner. Practise offering and requesting in these situations.**

1 The room is very hot.
2 An elderly man is standing on the bus.
3 Your boss has given your colleague a lot of work.
4 You are carrying a heavy parcel.
5 You have forgotten to bring some money for lunch.

B **Work with a partner and act out the situations in exercise 3. You can vary the language from what you heard on the CD, but try to use expressions from exercises 3B and 4.**

5 DISCUSSION

> Diskussionen führen S. 210

Work in a group. Use the questions to guide your discussion.

1 What sort of work have you done up to now, and when did you do it?
2 What did you enjoy, and what did you not like so much?
3 Are you going to look for a job in the summer?
4 What sort of job would you like to have ten years from now?
5 What steps will you need to take to get there?

C Business options

Business Process Outsourcing (BPO) in Bangalore – India's outsourcing capital

Every evening when Yamini Rawat walks into the ultra-modern headquarters of XLN Back Office Services, she changes identities. By day she is Indian and speaks the local dialect to her family and friends. By night she is a Westerner and speaks 'neutralized English' to people 5,000 miles away. Bangalore is 5½ hours ahead of Britain. When someone in Liverpool phones their insurance company in London to ask about car insurance, they speak to Yamini in Bangalore. In the UK it's only 7 p.m. but for Yamini it's already past midnight and she still has more than four hours to work.

Before starting work Yamini is searched by security officers and hands in her camera phone. Next she puts on her headset and deals with call after call from the other side of the world. She gets free meals, free transport and medical support if she is ill at work. Yamini is 27 years old and has a university qualification in English literature. She learned to speak neutralized English in a special three-week voice-training programme. While she handles callers' insurance problems (100–200 calls per shift), she is constantly monitored by her team leader. 30% of her salary is called variable pay and is based on personal and corporate performance. It can be cut at any time. In a country where 800 million people live on less than 20 rupees ($0.50) per day, Yamini feels she is well paid for her work. (242 words)

Sally Field, 19
London, UK

Job description:
$ 14 per hour + commission
Working hours: Mon–Fri 9 a.m.–5.30 p.m. or 10 a.m.–6.30 p.m. (incl. alternate Saturdays)
Good spoken and written English needed
Experience of insurance business preferable

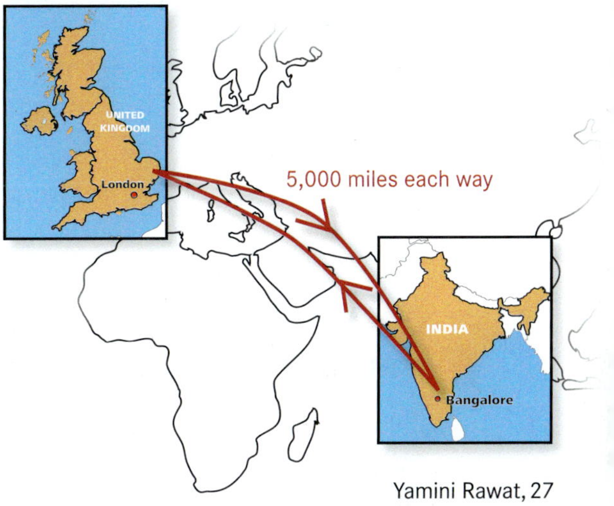

Yamini Rawat, 27
Bangalore, India

Job description:
$2.50 per hour + 30 % variable pay
Working hours: 10 – 12 hours per night
Only for graduates; English language and insurance training given

1 LOOKING AT THE TEXT

Are the following statements true, false or not mentioned in the text? Correct the false statements.

1 Yamini has a different name at work.
2 People in the UK know Yamini is in India.
3 Yamini studied English at university.
4 Yamini learned to speak English in three weeks.

2 LOOKING AT THE DIAGRAM

Contrast Sally's and Yamini's working conditions in about 80 – 100 words.

Begin with *Whereas Sally works in the daytime ...*

3 DISCUSSION

Discuss the following questions.

1 What other areas of business can you think of where outsourcing is common? Give reasons for your choices.
2 Is outsourcing a positive or negative development? Form two groups. One group is for outsourcing, the other is against it. Take turns to discuss the advantages and disadvantages.

D Grammar checkpoint

1 PRESENT PERFECT PROGRESSIVE

> Grammar summary S. 214

Write replies to the questions. Use the words in brackets and the present perfect progressive.

1 A Clara started her training course about two months ago, didn't she? (*do*)
B *Yes, she has been doing her training course for about two months now.*
2 A Alex joined Altman GmbH about a year ago, didn't he? (*work for*)
B *Yes,* ...
3 A Maria and Nick began studying German around ten weeks ago, didn't they? (*learn*)
B ...
4 A Eva and her sister moved into the apartment roughly a month ago, didn't they? (*share*)
...
5 A Tomas started looking for a new job nearly a month ago, didn't he? (*search*)
B ...
6 A Jenny asked for a college application form over a week ago, didn't she? (*wait for*)
B ...

2 PRESENT PERFECT PROGRESSIVE AND PRESENT PERFECT

Complete the dialogue. Sometimes more than one tense is possible.

> Grammar summary S. 214

TONY Hi, Emma! How are you?
EMMA Oh, hi, Tony! Fine, thanks. And how *have you been keeping*?[1] (*you/keep*)
TONY Really well. I ...[2] (*not see*) you for ages.
EMMA No, we ...[3] (*not meet*) since Lucy's party last summer. What ...[4] (*you/do*) since then?
TONY I ...[5] (*travel*) in South America. What about you?
EMMA Oh, I ...[6] (*not do*) anything as exciting as that. I ...[7] (*take*) a business studies course at college.
TONY ...[8] (*it/go*) well?
EMMA Yes, and I ...[9] (*just finish*) the first year. And guess what! I ...[10] (*pass*) with top grades! I found out this morning.
TONY That's really great! Let's go and celebrate!

3 GENERAL REVISION OF TENSES

> Grammar summary S. 212–216

It is 10th December, and Stefanie is in Ireland to study English. Use appropriate tenses to describe Stefanie's year.
Start like this: *In late May, after she had ...*

late May	*finish her final school exams, decide to study English in Ireland for a year*
June – Sept	*take a holiday job and save as much as possible*
	do this job, book a place at the Language Centre in Dublin
10th Sept	*fly to Ireland to start her course*
then – now	*go to classes five days a week*
every morning	*study at the Centre for three hours*
this morning	*different – meet some friends to do some Christmas shopping*
Christmas	*plan to visit her family in Dortmund and stay for 10 days*
Easter	*if have enough money, travel round Ireland*
June	*take her English exam and then travel home via London*
autumn	*want to go to college*

7 Going global

Main Course

FOCUS

Perhaps you have a laptop like this at home. If so, how did it get there? How was it made? This laptop and the products that run on it are the work of many people in many places.

1 Read the introduction above, and then make sentences like the one below.

The hardware was designed in Japan, and it was ...

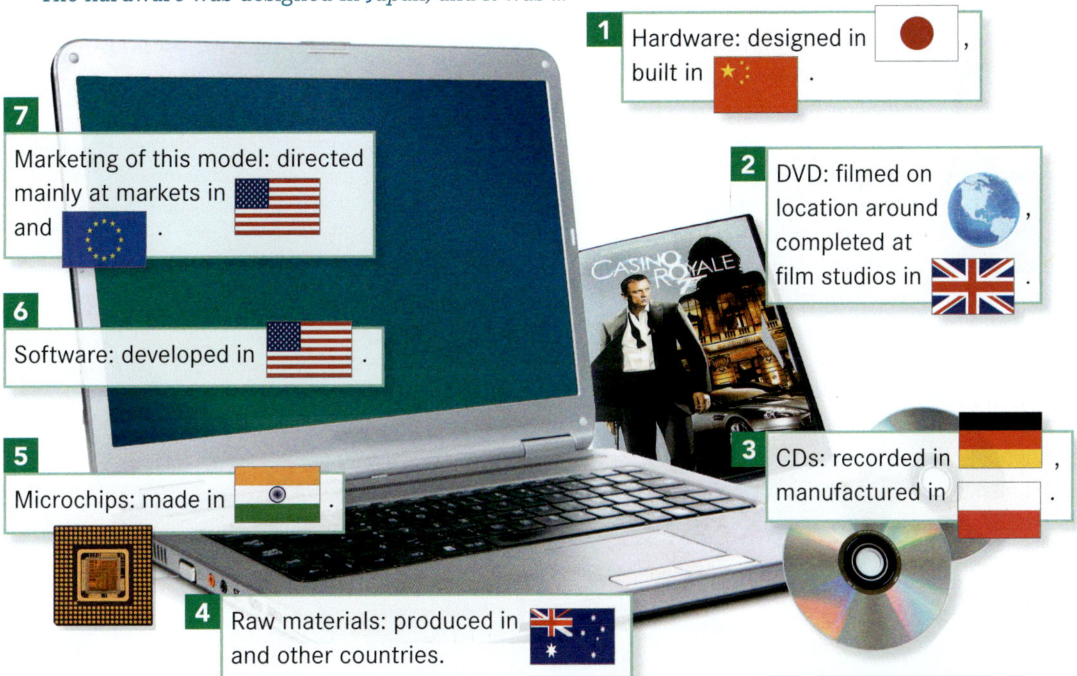

Key to flags > File 10, page 194

2 Discuss things that you have at home.

1 Use this checklist and note your 'Top 5' favourite things.

Accessories: e.g. bags, hats, shoes
Clothes: e.g. jeans, trainers,
Electronic goods: e.g. laptop, mobile phone, sound system, TV
Sports equipment: e.g. fitness machine, sports shoes
Transport: e.g. car, motorbike, scooter

2 Also note the brand name of each item, and where you think the following took place: development, design, production.

3 Work with a partner. Take turns to talk about things on your list like this:
(First) on my list is my ... It's a (brand name), and I think it was (produced) in ...

3 When you get home, check the labels on your favourite things. Were they made where you thought?

A Personal perspectives

BEFORE YOU READ

2 12 **You see lots of goods from around the world in the shops. What other effects of globalization can you also see?**

MONEY MATTERS

Globalization – good or bad?

WITH LISA HALL

They say globalization is good. But how good is it for ordinary people? Let's start by hearing from some ordinary people.

1 ARAND KRISHNAN

senior software programmer, InfoXL, India

Here in Bangalore, India's IT capital, we support the team in Houston, Texas. At the end of their working day, they send us problems, ready for our working day here. We process the material and send back solutions, ready for their next day.

Lots of western companies do this. It works well because we have good English and IT skills, and because data transmission is very cheap. But it's not all foreign companies here now. India is developing fast, and many local IT companies are being set up. In fact, I've been asked to help set one up now. It's a big risk, but a big opportunity too. (108 words)

2 NICK BELL ex-furniture factory worker, Galax, Virginia, USA

One day, we had our jobs, the next we were told production was going offshore to Indonesia. Two months later we were made redundant.

Our factory was the main employer in town, and since it closed every other business has been hit hard. So there are no other jobs for us, and people are leaving to find work somewhere else.

They say globalization puts cheap goods in the shops from places like China, but it's also taken my job away. If I could just get it back, I'd give up cheap goods tomorrow. What good are they if you don't have a paycheck? They're still too expensive!

(112 words)

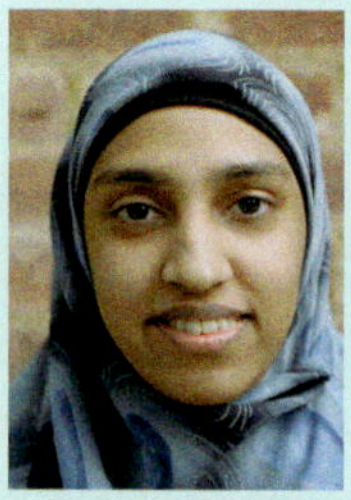

3 MALIKA AL-MAGRABI

textile worker, Tangier, Morocco

When I started here at 15, I was glad to find full-time work. But now it's terrible. Before, we were given 14 days to fill orders, but now we usually only get five. We're often required to work 16 hours a day, and we're sometimes forced to work through the night. People get ill, but that isn't allowed. I nearly lost my job when I was off sick for a day.

They're supposed to pay overtime for all the extra hours, but they never do. But what can we do? When my friend Fatima asked for her money, she was sacked immediately. We're just slaves. (105 words)

4 BORIS STEIN production engineer, BMW, Oxford, UK

I was one of many BMW staff sent to Britain to help rescue the Mini, a famous 1960s car that had never been brought up to date properly. It has been completely redeveloped by British and German engineers, and now the reborn Mini is as popular as ever. We're working flat out, and nearly 250,000 are being produced every year.

The Mini certainly isn't cheap, so price is not the main competitive advantage. Instead, it wins hearts and minds because it's fantastic to drive, it's beautifully made with cutting-edge technology, and it's one of the world's great brands. It shows that we can still win the globalization game right here in Europe. (121 words)

1 LOOKING AT THE TEXTS

A Complete the summaries with words from the first two texts.

Arand Krishnan is a senior software ...[1] with InfoXL in ...[2], India. His team provides overnight ...[3] for colleagues in America. InfoXL and other foreign ...[4] came to India because people speak English and have good ...[5] skills, and because the cost of sending ...[6] is very low. Now, many local IT businesses are appearing, and Arand may take the ...[7] and help ...[8] one up.

Nick Bell used to make ...[9] in Galax, Virginia in America, but then ...[10] moved to Indonesia and he became ...[11]. The factory was the biggest local ...[12], and its loss hit every other ...[13] in the town. People are now moving away to find work. Nick does not want the cheap ...[14] that globablization brings. He just wants the ...[15] back that ...[16] took away. Without it, he cannot buy these goods anyway.

B Use the third text to do a mediation task.

> Mediation S. 210

You are a Moroccan union official and a guide for a visiting group of German union officials. Write a short explanation of the situation at Malika's factory – past and present.

C Compare and contrast Boris Stein's experience with that of Nick Bell.

Find one similarity and several differences between them. Use this language:
Both of them have ... However, ... while ...
Concerning their recent experiences at work, ... but ...
Looking at the future, ... whereas ...

D Say what you think.

Our cutting edge technology means German jobs are safe.

Don't you believe it! Plenty of German jobs have gone abroad.

2 WORKING WITH WORDS

A Find opposites of these words in the text.

Text 1
1 problems (*lines 1–7*)
2 expensive (*lines 8–14*)
3 close down (*lines 8–14*)

Text 2
4 earlier (*lines 1–5*)
5 employee (*lines 6–9*)

Text 4
6 out of date (*lines 1–9*)
7 loses (*lines 10–16*)

B Use pairs of opposites from exercise A in the correct form to complete the following.

1 In countries such as Morocco, most ... do not allow their ... to join unions.
2 This IT equipment is ten years old, so it's completely .... If we want to stay in business, we'll have to buy equipment that's ...
3 All sorts of electronic equipment used to be much more ... than it is now. It is amazing to see how ... today's very powerful computers are.
4 Sadly, European manufacturers have ... a lot of business to Chinese producers. However, they can still ... new customers in world markets when they offer excellent quality.
5 Because of global competition, older, less efficient European industries have had to ... . At the same time though, new high-tech industries have continued to ... successfully.
6 Many developing countries still have big ... such as disease and poor infrastructure. But most are slowly finding ... to them – often with help from the west.

3 CULTURE CHECK: BODY LANGUAGE AND PERSONAL SPACE

Globalization is bringing together more and more people from different parts of the world. However, different cultures have different ideas about such basic things as body language and personal space. Something acceptable in one culture may be unacceptable in another.

You have probably already noticed some of the differences, for example through meeting people from other cultures, and you have certainly seen different cultural behaviours in films and on TV.

So try this quiz and see how culturally sensitive you are. Decide who you think is making each point.

EA = an East Asian, LA = a Latin American, NA = a North American, NE = a northern European, SE = a southern European

We don't like making too much eye contact when we talk. We feel that's quite rude and 'pushy'. If somebody does that while speaking, we feel that person is trying to dominate or control the listener.

A EA | LA

It's just natural to touch the other person's arm or shoulder when we're talking. It shows the warmth that we feel towards each other.

B EA | LA

When I meet somebody new, I like to shake hands firmly to show that I want to have a warm, friendly relationship with that person.

C NA | EA

I don't feel comfortable with somebody who doesn't look me in the eye when we talk. Rightly or wrongly, I feel there's something dishonest about that person – something that I can't quite trust.

D EA | NA

It's not polite in our culture to stand too close when we talk. We need to give each other as much personal space as possible. That's at least 80 centimetres.

E SE | EA

Answers > File 4, page 192

4 DISCUSSION

> Diskussionen führen S. 210

Discuss these questions in small groups.

1 Whatever the activists say, do you think any government can or should try to stop or slow down globalization?

2 How might globalization affect you in the future? Are you more likely to be a 'winner' or a 'loser' in the globalization process?

B The bigger picture

BEFORE YOU READ

A **What do you think Martin Luther King meant when he said, 'Before you've finished breakfast this morning, you'll have relied on half the world'?**

B **Have you seen products in the shops with a FAIRTRADE label on them? What do you think it means?**

2 13

Let's be fair about trade by Sally Pearson

The not-so-fair trading

We are told that free trade is a good thing. But is it? For many people it is not, and they are some of the poorest in the world.

'Always low prices' promises Walmart, America's – and the world's – largest retailer. Consumers like this, of course, and so sales rise. But the big retailers do not cut their own profits to reduce prices. They pass those 'low prices' along the supply chain to the producers, who are forced to compete with each other globally to be the cheapest. The producers are 'free' only to pass on the cost pressures to their workers.

It happens all over the world, in factories and on farms, and the results are the opposite of freedom.

Supply chain pressures create precarious employment

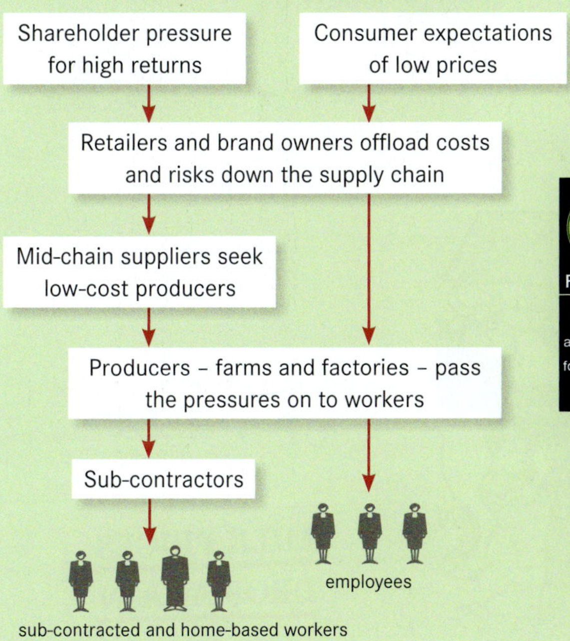

'We used to be well paid for meeting our targets,' Chandrika, a Sri Lankan textile worker reports. 'But now the targets they give us just cannot be met, so the bonus is never paid.'

'As a casual worker, I don't get a bonus, paid holidays or redundancy pay,' says Ragel, a fruit picker from South Africa.

Ana, a Bolivian factory worker, despairs: 'We have buried our dreams. Our only concern for the future is to make sure that the same thing doesn't happen to our children.'

The FAIRTRADE way

FAIRTRADE, with sales now expanding rapidly in Europe and North America, offers hope instead of despair. Coordinator Jack Carson explains:

'We visit potential suppliers to look at their products and their business strengths and weaknesses. If we are happy about these things, we develop an action plan. They may need design or technical support, for example, to get their products right for western markets. We also agree to buy directly and pay a fair, guaranteed price – and some of this immediately. This helps workers with things like paying for their children's education.

FAIRTRADE®
Guarantees **a better deal** for Third World Producers

We later offer training in marketing and other skills so that producers can gradually become independent.

As for the products, these range from food produce like coffee and bananas to crafts and fashion clothing. They are sold through our own shops and increasing numbers of other stores, including big supermarket chains. Sales are growing by nearly 50% per year. Consumers recognize the FAIRTRADE label and know that it promises quality products at competitive prices – and help for the producers. Instead of rising profits for middlemen, FAIRTRADE brings rising living standards to some of the world's poorest people.'

(401 words)

1 LOOKING AT THE TEXT

A Read the text carefully. Choose the best answer or answers.

1 Walmart sells more than ...
   a any other supermarket in the USA.
   b any other retailer in North America.
   c any other retail business in the world.
2 The three workers who speak about their problems ...
   a come from three different continents.
   b all work in factories.
   c all do badly under the free-trade system.
3 FAIRTRADE helps its suppliers by ...
   a helping them to improve their products.
   b helping them to help themselves as exporters.
   c building schools for their children's education.
4 More and more people are buying from FAIRTRADE because ...
   a its products are cheaper than normal supermarket products.
   b they want to pay a fair price for quality products.
   c they know this helps to improve life in poor parts of the world.

B Read the text again and do these activities.

1 Explain the 'word play' in the title of the text.
2 Find one similarity between each of the workers who speak in the text and Malika's situation - see page 96.
3 Identify the three sentences that relate to the diagram on page 99.
4 In your own words, explain the process that the diagram in the text illustrates.
5 Find the sentence that the photos represent.
6 Copy and complete the diagram on the right.
7 Cover the diagram and describe the process it illustrates.

C Say what you think.

FAIRTRADE SALES
UP AND UP

MILK PRICES
DROP AGAIN

2 WORKING WITH WORDS

A Match words from the box to 1–12 to form word pairs. Then look for the expressions in the text to check your answers.

1 free (*paragraph 1*)
2 supply (*paragraph 2*)
3 cost (*paragraph 2*)
4 paid (*paragraph 5*)
5 redundancy (*paragraph 5*)
6 fruit (*paragraph 5*)
7 factory (*paragraph 6*)
8 action (*paragraph 8*)
9 food (*paragraph 10*)
10 fashion (*paragraph 10*)
11 supermarket (*paragraph 10*)
12 living (*paragraph 10*)

chain | chains | clothing | holidays | pay | picker | plan | pressures | produce | standards | trade | worker

B Complete the following sentences with word pairs from exercise A. Use plural forms where necessary.

1 Every good employer should offer its employees good pay and conditions, including ... ... and, if jobs have to be cut, fair ... ...
2 The big ... ... like Walmart sell fresh ... ... as well as thousands of products in cans, packets and bottles.
3 The problems of poor working conditions apply to ... ... making trainers in Indonesia as well as to ... ... who gather oranges and lemons in countries around the Mediterranean.
4 Thanks to today's ... ... between different countries, there are huge ... ... that bring products to us from right around the world.

3 LISTENING

2 14 **A Listen for general understanding. Then answer these questions.**

Sally Pearson visited Guatemala with Jack Carson to write more about FAIRTRADE.

1 Who is Felipe Castro?
2 What is Manos Campesinas?
3 Has FAIRTRADE been a positive or a negative experience for Felipe and his colleagues as a group?
4 Has it been positive or negative for Felipe and his family?

B Listen for detail. Listen again and note points 1–12 missing from Sally's notes.

Felipe Castro: *age 48; wife & 3 children*
Farm: *1) ______ a hectare; 2) ______ coffee trees*
Co-operative – Manos Campesinas (= 'Workers' Hands'):
3) ______ members; 4) started in ______
What it does: *5) sells to ______*
6) gives ______
7) offers ______
Higher earnings allow farmers to build a new coffee mill:
What it will do: *8) add ______*
9) create ______
Higher earnings are also changing people's daily lives:
Farmers can now: *10) install ______*
11) keep ______
Felipe hopes to: *12) send ______*

4 BUILDING SKILLS: WRITING A COMMENT

> Eine Stellungnahme schreiben S. 203

A Prepare to write a comment:
Global competition is the only way.

1 Make a note of your own opinion. Consider first the views and experiences of everybody in this unit.
2 Copy and complete this mind map using words from the box.

> **TIP**
> When you write a comment, it is very important to collect and present the arguments for and against the topic. You can do this with notes and tables, but a mind map may be the most useful tool of all.

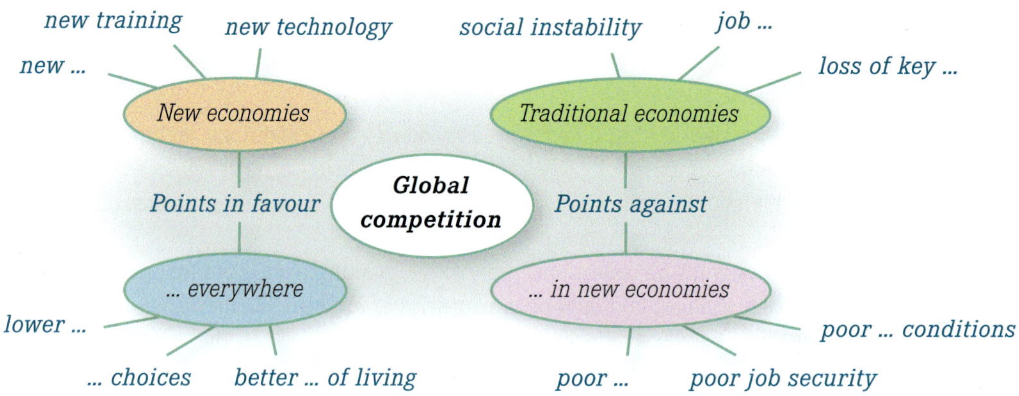

consumers | industries | jobs | losses | pay | prices | standard | wider | workers | working

B Write your comment.

1 Write a draft. Use this outline and keep to the point. Use the language shown to help you get started.

Introduction	Statement of the issue and your own opinion *We live in a world that is rapidly globalizing, and this is creating both benefits and great problems. It is therefore important to consider whether globalization is the only possible way forward. In my opinion, ...*
Development	Arguments for or against your own opinion, with evidence/examples *On the one hand, we should note the many good things that ... First of all, ... Secondly, ... For example,* *On the other hand, we must remember the huge difficulties that ... First, ... For instance, ...*
Conclusion	Restatement of opinion and brief summary of reasons *When I weigh up the good and the bad effects of globalization, I feel that on balance, it is ... My main reasons for this conclusion are that ...*

(For further useful connectors to help you in your writing, see **Language for writing** on the back cover flap.)

2 Check your draft for ideas. Make sure that it a) keeps to the point and b) is clear and logical.
3 Check your draft for correctness. Check a) language, including word order, b) vocabulary, c) spelling and d) punctuation.
4 When your draft is as good as possible, make a neat copy.

C Business options

Business as unusual

The Body Shop has branches all over the world and is famous for fair trade and human and animal rights. Here is an extract from its website.

The way we do business, the way we make products, the way we source ingredients, and the way we use our voice; we're different because of our values.

Our values

Right from the start, Anita Roddick founded The Body Shop with the belief that 'businesses have the power to do good'. We believe business can be both profitable and responsible.

Our campaigns

We've always seen ourselves as a lot more than just a beauty company. For years we've campaigned against injustices, stood up for the vulnerable and spoken out for those without a voice of their own.

Our charity

We believe in sharing our profits. Business should not just be about money, it should be about responsibility and the public good, not private greed. Our charity, The Body Shop Foundation, makes a difference. (133 words)

1 LOOKING AT THE TEXT

Complete the sentences using information from the text.

1 The Body Shop sources its products ...
2 It is possible to both make a profit and ...
3 The Body Shop tries to help people who ...
4 The intention of The Body Shop Foundation is to ...

2 DISCUSSION

Here are some of the campaigns organized by The Body Shop:

Stop Violence in the Home | Trafficking is Torture | Save the Whale

Put these campaigns in your own order of importance and explain your reasons to a partner. Then change partners and discuss the differences in your choices again.

3 WRITING

Write 80–100 words on one of the campaigns you looked at above or a campaign of your own choice.

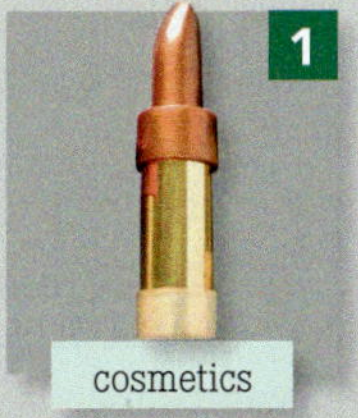

4 PRESENTATION

Work in pairs.

Choose one of the topics 1–4 and research how and where these products are manufactured. Pay particular attention to working conditions, the materials used and the impact they have on the environment. Then present your findings to the rest of the class.

D Grammar checkpoint

1 THE PASSIVE: MIXED TENSES

> Grammar summary S. 219

Jack Carson often interviews and writes reports about possible new FAIRTRADE suppliers. Write part of his report on 'Fruits of Africa' for him.

> Put the underlined sections into the passive.
> Use *by* + agent only where necessary.
> Think carefully about word order.

Start like this: *'Fruits of Africa' was started by Mr James Kasozi and some ...*

JACK Mr Kasozi, thanks for seeing me.
JAMES You're very welcome, but please call me James.
JACK Fine, well, when did you begin this project?
JAMES Some other fruit farmers and I started 'Fruits of Africa' five years ago.
JACK What made you do that?
JAMES Well, before that, we always lost our fresh fruit if we did not sell it quickly at the local market.
JACK And now?
JAMES Now we don't waste these valuable mangos, bananas and pineapples – we dry them instead in very cheap, simple dryers.
JACK Who supplies the dryers?
JAMES Our own organization is now making and selling these dryers as cheaply as possible.
JACK Do they run on electricity?
JAMES No, they don't use electricity. The natural heat of the sun does the drying.
JACK Are they popular?
JAMES Yes, farmers in the local area have already bought hundreds of the dryers. And we are now also receiving orders from all over the country.
JACK So what about the future?
JAMES If FAIRTRADE accepts our dried-fruit products, it will help a lot of poor farmers in this very poor part of Africa towards a much better life.

2 THE PASSIVE WITH MODAL VERBS

> Grammar summary S. 219

Jack and a colleague are summing up their ideas on another project. Use the underlined points and the passive to complete Jack's email to his boss.

JACK So let's sum up our ideas on the 'Baskets of Bengal' project.
LISA Right. First, they must improve their production quality control.
JACK And to help them do that, we should send our Technical Support Officer, Stephen Carter.
LISA Good idea. We could ask him to visit them early next month.
JACK Next, they have to supply a sample order so that we can test the market here.
LISA Right, and the next thing: we may need further basket designs at a later date.
JACK If so, we might supply a specialist product designer to work with them.
LISA And finally, about payment: we can make an immediate 30% payment with our first order, and we'll pay the rest 60 days after receipt of order.

Ema

Dear Margaret

Lisa and I have reached the following conclusions re. 'Baskets of Bengal':

1 Their production quality control must be improved.

8

Main Course

Finding a job in the EU

FOCUS

1 **Work with a partner or in a small group. Answer the questions and then check your score.**

A quiz about the EU

1. How many countries signed the original Treaty of Rome on 25 March 1957?
   A 4 **B** 6 **C** 9
2. Where is the headquarters of the European Commission?
   A Brussels **B** Luxemburg **C** Strasbourg
3. When was the euro introduced?
   A 2000 **B** 2001 **C** 2002
4. The voters of which two countries rejected the EU constitution in 2005?
   A Britain and Sweden **B** France and the Netherlands **C** France and Italy
5. Which country is not a member of the EU?
   A Belgium **B** Norway **C** Sweden
6. How many members does the EU have?
   A 25 **B** 27 **C** over 27
7. What is the Schengen Agreement about?
   A Cross-border policing **B** Open frontiers **C** The introduction of the euro
8. Who wrote the music to the 'European anthem'?
   A Edward Elgar **B** Guiseppe Verdi **C** Ludwig van Beethoven

Answers > File 3, page 192

2 **What is your own attitude to the EU? Choose the statement you agree with most and then do a class survey.**

I don't have an 'attitude'. The EU means nothing to me.

The EU has brought peace and prosperity to Europe, but I think that's enough. I don't want a United States of Europe with Brussels as its capital.

I'd like the EU to become like the USA. At the moment, national governments have more say than the people of Europe and that's a real problem.

A Personal perspectives

BEFORE YOU READ

What do you think applying for a six-month internship at a tourist information office involves?

An internship in the UK

Lisa Bach, 20, from Münster is studying tourism in Bremen. As part of her studies, she has to do six months' practical training as an intern in an English-speaking country. Lisa decides to look for an internship in the UK. She contacts a German online agency, SEC, that specializes in arranging internships abroad, and finds this offer:

Tourism internship

Location	Norwich, Norfolk, UK
Sector	tourism
Duties	dealing with enquiries, incl. accommodation; general office duties; occasional 'meeting & greeting' duties
Length	6 months, 1 April to 30 September 20..
Qualifications	18 or over; fluent English, one other major European language; MS Office; car driving licence; friendly, outgoing personality; ability to work well in a team
Remuneration	no salary; accommodation arranged; contribution towards travel/living expenses (by negotiation)
Application	email application, CV as attachment; host's name/email address and job reference number provided by SEC; phone interview will be arranged by email

Lisa fills in the SEC form, pays a fee and receives further details, including the name/email address and the job reference number.

Email

Betreff:	Application for tourism internship
Von:	Lisa Bach <lisa.bach@okipost.de>
Datum:	10 November 20.. 21:32
An:	Norwich City Council <human-resources@norwich.gov.uk>

Dear Sir or Madam

I refer to your offer of a tourism internship on SEC's website, reference ncc-tic-2064.
As you will see from my CV, I am studying Tourism Management at the University of Applied Sciences in Bremen, Germany. Students on this course are required to have a minimum of six months' practical work experience in an English-speaking country.
I am hoping to find an internship next year and would like to apply for the post you are offering. The dates 1 April to 30 September are fine, as are the duties you list in the job description. I worked for two months at the tourist office in Münster this summer, where I gained experience of similar work.
As requested, I attach my CV. If you have any further queries, please contact me by phone or email.
If you are interested in my application, I look forward to arranging a phone interview.

Yours faithfully

Lisa Bach

1 LOOKING AT THE TEXTS

A Do the following tasks.

1 What is Lisa's reason for applying for an internship?
2 Find information in the ad and email to show why Lisa chose this internship.
3 Say whether you think Lisa got a phone interview and explain your answer.

B Say what you think.

1 Could you imagine doing an internship abroad like Lisa? Say why/why not.
2 How would you feel about doing an unpaid internship?

2 WORKING WITH WORDS

A Find words or expressions in the ad (1–3) or email (4–6) to fit these definitions.

1 period of training – often unpaid
2 friendliness, enthusiasm for meeting new people
3 discussion to reach an agreement
4 department responsible for employees
5 opposite of 'theoretical'
6 summary of applicant's personal details, qualifications and work experience

B Write four sentences using some of the words and phrases from exercise A.

LISA BACH

	Personal details
Name:	Lisa Bach
Address:	Kreuzstraße 15, 48142 Münster, Germany
Date and place of birth:	28 May 1989, Münster
Nationality:	German
Daytime phone number:	+49-2571-547821
Email address:	lisa.bach@okipost.de
	Education
10/2007–present	Fachhochschule Bremen (University of Applied Sciences); 7-semester course, Touristik (Tourism Management)
08/2004–06/2007	Adolf-Kolping-Berufskolleg, Münster (vocational school); 3-year course, Hotelfachfrau (Hotel Administration); grade average: 1.9 on 6-point scale from 1 (very good) to 6 (very unsatisfactory)
08/1999–07/2004	Realschule im Kreuzviertel, Münster (secondary school); school-leaving certificate (equivalent of GCSE); grade average 2.1
	Work experience
2003	Altenzentrum St. Josef; assistant carer in home for the elderly
2002	Presto Supermarkt, Münster; sales assistant
	Paid employment
Summer 2009	vacation job, Verkehrsverein Münster; assistant in tourist information office
Summer 2008	vacation job, Hotel am Stadtgarten, Münster; assistant receptionist
	Interests and skills
Languages	English, advanced (some knowledge of business English)
IT skills	MS Office (Word, Excel, PowerPoint); HSTeam 2006 (hotel software); eComBot Travel (e-Tourism software)
Other	driving licence, EU class C
References	references can be supplied on request

3 LOOKING AT THE CV

Which part of a CV contains this information? Be careful: some information is not given in a CV at all.

1 ability to speak a foreign language
2 applicant's grade at end of Year 10
3 details of driving licence
4 details of unpaid jobs
5 how long an applicant went to primary school
6 information about paid holiday jobs
7 job applicant's email address
8 job applicant's name and address
9 names and addresses of referees
10 information regarding marital status and number of children

4 WORKING WITH WORDS

A Find the English equivalents of the following German words and expressions in the CV. They are not necessarily in the same order.

1 *Abschlusszeugnis*
2 *auf Wunsch*
3 *Berufserfahrung*
4 *bezahlte Beschäftigung*
5 *Empfangsassistentin*
6 *Ferienjob*
7 *fortgeschritten*
8 *Führerschein*
9 *Notendurchschnitt*
10 *Computerkenntnisse*

B Use some of the words and expressions from exercise A to explain the following in English.

Sie möchten jemandem sagen, dass ...
1 Sie etwas Berufserfahrung in der Touristikbranche haben.
2 Ihr Ferienjob als Empfangsassistentin Ihnen gut gefallen hat.
3 Sie nach einer bezahlten Beschäftigung suchen, bei der Sie Ihre Computerkenntnisse einsetzen können.
4 auf Wunsch Empfehlungsschreiben eingereicht werden können.
5 Sie fortgeschrittene Englischkenntnisse besitzen.
6 Sie seit zwei Jahren einen Führerschein haben.

5 MEDIATING

> Mediation S. 210

Explain Lisa Bach's CV in German.

You work in the human resources department of a big German tour operator. The company wants to hire an assistant to arrange hotel accommodation for its European tours. Use Lisa's CV to explain to your boss in German why you think she would be a good candidate for the job.

6 WRITING

Write an English letter of application and CV based on your personal profile.

Imagine you are applying for a three-month internship in any country or field of your choice. Write the letter of application and your CV in English. Include information about your school career, work experience, skills, etc.

7 LISTENING

3 2 **A Listen for general understanding. Read the email and then listen to the extract from the telephone interview. How did the interview go: *well*, *badly* or *all right*?**

Email

Subject:	Application for tourism internship
Date:	21 November 20.. 10:12
From:	Norwich City Council <human-resources@norwich.gov.uk>
To:	Lisa Bach <lisa.bach@okipost.de>

Dear Lisa Bach
Further to your application for an internship, I would like to arrange a date and time for a telephone interview. This should take place during our office hours, which are 9:00 a.m. to 6:00 p.m. (local time), Monday to Friday.

Could you please let me have a date and time this week when I can reach you on a landline phone?

Thank you and I look forward to hearing from you.

With regards

Ruth Morgan

B Listen for detail. Read the statements below. Then listen again and say if they are true or false. Correct the false statements.

1 Ruth suggested that they both use first names.
2 Lisa didn't react to Ruth's request for an interview date very promptly.
3 Ruth's first question was about Lisa's course in Bremen.
4 Lisa worked at the tourist information office in Münster last summer.
5 Lisa's main job at the tourst information office was dealing with callers' enquiries.
6 Almost all of these callers were only interested in accommodation.
7 Usually, Lisa just gave dog-owners the addresses of suitable accommodation.
8 Lisa's duties in Norwich will be very different from what she did in Münster.

C Summarize the phone interview in German.

8 ROLE-PLAY

Work with a partner. Read the suggestions below and add any ideas or information of your own to complete the interview. Then act out the interview together.

Ruth asks:
... about Lisa's knowledge of French.
... what Lisa hopes to get out of her internship.
... what Lisa thinks she can offer the tourist information centre in Norwich.
... how Lisa got on with co-workers/managers in Münster.
... how Lisa handled difficult customers/callers.

Lisa asks:
... about her accommodation in Norwich.
... what she will be expected to do on a typical day.
... if she will be allowed to deal with callers herself.

B The bigger picture

BEFORE YOU READ

3 3 **In this extract from *Now it's your turn*, a radio phone-in show, Helen Wood is asking callers about Britain and the EU. What opinions do you expect to hear?**

HELEN Is the EU good or bad for Britain? Or is it a mixture of both? That is the topic of our programme this evening. And my first caller is John Harris from Bristol. John, now it's your turn.

JOHN Hello. Uhm ... Yes, well, first I want to say that I'm certainly not anti-European, but I'm totally against the EU.

HELEN Oh yes. Why's that, John?

JOHN Well, I think the EU's a waste of time and money – just corruption, bureaucracy and interference in our affairs. What right has Brussels to tell us what to do? And it's so undemocratic. Just a bunch of unelected foreign bureaucrats. And who pays for it all? We do! I say we should leave tomorrow!

HELEN Phew! Well, we've certainly got off with a bang. Now our next caller is ... Oh, yes. Jane Garner from Hull, right?

JANE That's right, Helen. Good evening.

HELEN Hi. And what's your opinion, Jane?

JANE Well, my brother works for the EU in Brussels, and I think your last caller was very unfair – what he said was misleading, frankly.

HELEN Oh? And what makes you say that?

JANE Well, for example, the so-called 'Brussels bureaucracy'. Believe it or not, the EU is run by fewer people[1] than it takes to run a medium-sized city like Leeds[2].

HELEN Really? So why do so many people say that the EU is too bureaucratic, then?

JANE Well, it's all a question of perception. The trouble is that a lot of people blame Brussels for things that national governments do. The fact is that the European Commission has no legislative power at all. It can only inform, advise and recommend. The rest is up to the Council of Ministers.

HELEN In other words, national governments, right?

JANE Right – and unfortunately national politicians just defend their own national interests, that's the problem. The UK is particularly bad there, I'm sorry to say.

HELEN Well, thank you for that, Jane. And now my next caller is Dr Peter Brown from Manchester University. What's your take on this, Peter?

PETER Well, we've been doing research into corruption in Europe, and our findings show that the EU is much less corrupt than nearly all national governments. In actual fact, it's relatively clean.

HELEN Yes, but the media is full of stories about corruption, isn't it, Peter? They can't all be wrong, can they?

PETER Well, it's like the last caller said, I'm afraid. All too often, the EU gets the blame for the wrongdoing of national governments. It's like in sport. Where there's money, there's corruption. But the EU doesn't pay out any money directly, to farmers, for example. The member states are responsible for that, and there you really do find some corruption.

HELEN OK. Thanks, Peter. And now a caller from Europe is on the line. Beate König from Aachen in Germany. What would you like to say, Beate?

BEATE Good evening everybody. Well, I think the EU is much more than just trade and so on. It's open frontiers, a common currency, the freedom to live and work where we want.

And it's peace, stability and a European identity, too. I value those things a lot, that's all.

HELEN Fine. So you have no problem with Brussels interfering in German affairs?

BEATE Well, no, I don't. I think that in our globalized world, 'national sovereignty' doesn't mean much anyhow.

HELEN Oh yes? Why's that?

BEATE Well, what about global threats like climate change, scarcity of raw materials, terrorism, mass migration, cross-border crime and so on? No single country can fight those alone. We have no choice. We must integrate to survive. (608 words)

[1] The EU has just over 23,000 employees (2007) [2] Leeds City Council employs about 33,000 people (2008)

1 LOOKING AT THE TEXT

A Do the assignments.

1 List arguments the callers give for and against the EU.
2 Explain why many people have a negative view of the EU.

B Read the speech bubbles and say who is speaking.

1 *There are dishonest politicians in every country.*
2 *It's unfair that our taxes support these foreign politicians.*
3 *National governments alone can't solve international problems.*
4 *Individual countries decide how money from the EU is spent.*
5 *The EU doesn't control us, they make suggestions and recommendations.*
6 *People should stop and think about all the opportunities the EU offers.*
7 *The running of the EU is actually quite efficient if you look at the figures.*
8 *The British government should run our country – not the EU.*

C Say what you think.

1 Say which opinion is closest to your own, John Harris's or Beate König's, and why.
2 Which of the statements (a, b or c) do you agree with most? Give reasons for your choice.

I would like to see ...
a a further widening of the EU to include all European countries.
b no further widening but greater integration of the present members.
c the EU remain as it is at the moment – no further widening, no further integration.

2 WORKING WITH WORDS

A Complete the table with the missing forms from the phone-in.

	verb	*noun*	*adjective*
1	*mix*	...	*mixed*
2	*corrupt*	...	...
3	...	...	*interfering*
4	*perceive*	...	*perceptive*
5	...	*advice, adviser*	*advisory*
6	...	*recommendation*	*recommended*
7		*responsibility*	...
8	*threaten*	...	*threatening*

B Complete the sentences with some of the words that you found in exercise A.

1 You'll find that all opinion is based on a ...[1] of fact and ...[2]
2 Ask Jane Baker. She's ... for European affairs.
3 Unfortunately, where there's money, there's ...
4 I'm sorry. I can't help you. I strongly ... that you find a good lawyer.
5 Government ...[1] in our private lives is getting worse because of the ...[2] of terrorist attacks.

C Explain these sentences or phrases from the phone-in.

1 '... we've certainly got off with a bang.' (*line 17*)
2 '... what he said was misleading, frankly.' (*line 24*)
3 'The rest is up to the Council of Ministers.' (*line 37*)
4 'What's your take on this ...?' (*line 47*)
5 'In actual fact, it's relatively clean.' (*line 52*)

3 WRITING

> Eine Stellungnahme schreiben S. 203

Use these ideas to write a comment evaluating arguments for and against a fully united Europe.

For:
> balance power of USA/Russia/China
> threats now global, not national (climate change, terrorism, etc.)
> federal system more democratic
> more efficient/effective single market

Against:
> member states too diverse to unite
> differences in size/economies too great
> no official language
> too much power to bigger countries
> people prefer nation states

Use these expressions to emphasize or moderate what you say:

Emphasizing expressions
> it is clear that ...
> there can be no/little doubt that ...
> no matter how ...
> to begin/start with ...
> on top of that ...

Moderating expressions
> as far as I can see ...
> on the one hand ..., on the other (hand) ...
> perhaps/maybe ...
> it seems to me ...
> most would perhaps admit ...

C Business options

The euro – a powerful new currency

The euro was introduced as a physical currency in the form of notes and coins on 1 January 2002. The eurozone consists of all the countries whose sole currency is the euro. Not all the countries in the European Union (EU) have adopted the euro but it is intended to be the common currency for Europe, a trading bloc of approximately 500 million citizens. The UK, Denmark and Sweden are all outside the eurozone and have their own currencies. The euro is managed by the European Central Bank (ECB) in Frankfurt, which is a politically independent institution.

In 2008 the EU established the Single Euro Payments Area (SEPA) to make non-cash and cross-border payments much easier and cheaper in the eurozone. It should, for example, be easier to pay by mobile phone (e.g. in a supermarket) and by direct debit abroad. The goal is to make it possible for businesses and consumers to use a single bank account anywhere in the eurozone. (162 words)

1 *I'm glad we're outside the eurozone. The strong euro is good news for us. We export to Europe and our whisky is very attractive to foreign buyers. At the moment the pound is weak but I can't say what business will be like in five years' time.*

Duncan MacDonald (50), owner of a Scottish whisky distillery

2 *When the pound's strong, I transfer money to my German bank account and shop in Stuttgart. When it's weak, I shop in London. I have a bank account in both countries and this has its advantages and disadvantages.*

Carsten Fuchs (28), a German working in London

3 *While we were away, we paid for everything by credit card but they wouldn't accept it in one smaller restaurant, so we had to get cash from a cash machine. We got a real shock when we came back to the UK. The Italian bank had charged us a fee of £3, our own bank had charged us a foreign exchange fee and the exchange rate of the pound against the euro was really bad. Now I think the euro might be a good idea after all.*

Jenny Travis (37), just back from a holiday in Italy

1 LOOKING AT THE TEXT

A What are the benefits and drawbacks mentioned in the text of the UK using the pound and not the euro? Can you think of any others?

B Explain how the introduction of the euro in the UK would affect Duncan MacDonald, Carsten Fuchs and the Travis family.

Begin your answer with *If the UK introduced the euro, ... (would / wouldn't + infinitive)*

2 DISCUSSION

Find out more information about the SEPA. What advantages and disadvantages does it have for the eurozone?

D Grammar checkpoint

1 GERUND OR INFINITIVE?

> Grammar summary S. 221

Choose the correct form, a) or b).

1 We really enjoy a) travelling | b) to travel[1] within the Eurozone because we dislike a) having to | b) to have to[2] change money all the time. In fact, I think the UK should consider a) giving up | b) to give up[3] the pound and a) adopting | b) to adopt[4] the euro.

2 We chose a) joining | b) to join[1] the EU, didn't we? In my opinion, we should stop a) opting out | b) to opt out[2] of everything and start a) playing | b) to play[3] a full role in the union. If we don't, we risk a) becoming | b) to become[4] isolated on the edge of Europe. We really must avoid a) letting | b) to let[5] that happen.

3 My sister wants a) studying | b) to study[1] German so my dad suggested a) applying | b) to apply[2] to a university in a German-speaking country. Anyhow, she decided a) going | b) to go[3] to Dresden and she plans a) moving | b) to move[4] there in August.

4 Both Austria and France have promised a) holding | b) to hold[1] a referendum about Turkey joining the EU. If they do, I can't imagine Turkey a) winning | b) to win[2] the vote. Personally, I would like a) avoiding | b) to avoid[3] a referendum at any cost. I would prefer Turkey a) stopping | b) to stop[4] negotiations to join the union before that happened. Just think about it! It could mean a) closing | b) to close[5] the door to Europe in Turkey's face!

5 I will never forget a) visiting | b) to visit[1] the EU headquarters in Brussels for the first time. I had read so much about the 'gigantic EU bureaucracy' that I expected a) seeing | b) to see[2] huge office blocks and so on. I remember a) being | b) to be[3] very surprised at what I found. In fact, the EU building did not seem a) being | b) to be[4] any bigger than that of many big international firms. But when I tried a) telling | b) to tell[5] people back home, many of them simply refused a) believing | b) to believe[6] me. Some even told me to stop a) talking | b) to talk[7] such nonsense.

2 GERUND OR INFINITIVE?

> Grammar summary S. 221

Use the infinitive or *-ing* form to complete this dialogue.

A radio producer, Nick West, is talking to a reporter, Sue Green, about a request from a listener.

NICK Hi, Sue. Look, do you remember …[1] (*interview*) that guy about opening an office in Germany?

SUE Yes, of course. Greg Cox. Nice man but he just couldn't stop …[2] (*talk*). He's trying …[3] (*find*) an agent in the Ruhrgebiet, I think.

NICK Well, this email is from a guy called Lothar Moers in Bochum. He'd like …[4] (*get*) in touch with Greg Cox but he says he forgot …[5] (*note*) down his address. I meant …[6] (*deal*) with it yesterday, but I just didn't manage …[7] (*do*) it, I'm afraid. And I can't stop …[8] (*reply*) to it now. Do you think you could answer it for me?

SUE Sure. I'll stop …[9] (*work*) on this report and do it immediately.

NICK Thanks, a lot, Sue. I suppose it just means …[10] (*tell*) Greg Cox Mr Moer's email address and then he can take it from there. I don't want …[11] (*do*) it the other way round.

SUE Of course not. We always avoid …[12] (*give*) other people somebody's address. Anyhow, luckily, I decided …[13] (*keep*) Greg's contact details just in case anybody got in touch. I'll try his mobile number first and if I have no luck, I'll try …[14] (*get*) him on his office number.

9 Social challenges

Main Course

FOCUS

1 Do awareness activity 1: *Who are you?*

1 Work with a partner – someone you do not know well. Copy the chart below. Add extra writing space in columns 2–4.
2 Silently, fill in column 2 about yourself. Then guess your partner's answers and fill in column 3.
3 Next take turns to ask the questions and fill in column 4.
4 Discuss differences between your column 3 and 4 answers.

Who are you?	Myself	Partner (my guesses)	Partner (his/her answers)
1 What is your father's cultural heritage? (e.g. national/regional/ethnic/religious background)			
2 What is your mother's cultural heritage?			
3 Where were you born?			
4 What's your favourite school subject?			
5 What's your favourite sport?			
6 Who's your favourite musician/band?			
7 What's your favourite food?			
8 What's your biggest fear?			
9 What do you consider your best quality?			
10 How do you see yourself in ten years' time?			

2 Do awareness activity 2: *How does society help make me who I am?*

1 Use the diagram below to help you organize your thoughts. Think how different parts of society can benefit, control and influence you.

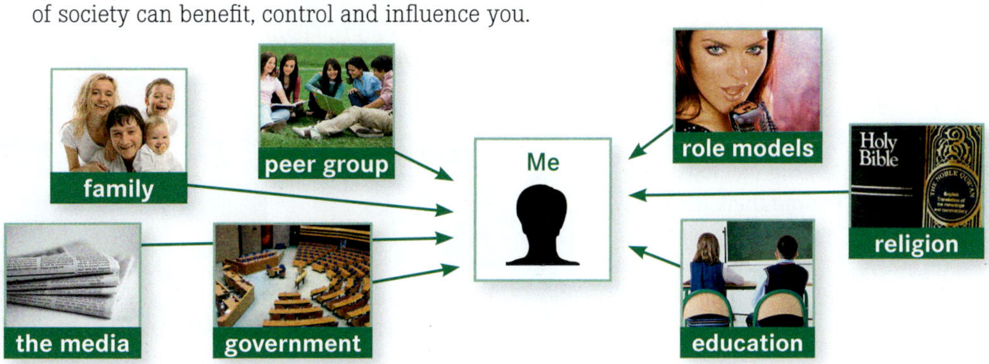

2 Work with a partner. Present your ideas to each other and discuss any differences.

A Personal perspectives

BEFORE YOU READ

3 4 **The first picture is from an old advert. What view of family life does it show? Is this your view?**

What's in a family?

Do you remember the 'perfect' family? You know, the one with the happy husband going off to his steady job in his clean, white shirt. And the happy wife looking after the perfect home while bringing up the perfect children.

Perhaps that family only ever existed in 1960s washing powder ads. Certainly, life today is much less tidy. The pressures on families are often huge. Few fathers have a steady job for life, and quite often there is no father. And the mother often works. Who then polishes the home and the children?

In fact, quite often there is no father *or* mother: in America about 4.5 million young people live with grandparents, and many more live with other relatives.

So can the family still do its traditional job for children? Can it still provide the steady structure, rules and role models that socialize the young, bringing them up to be responsible members of adult society? Every day the media seem to prove that street gangs have taken over – have become the only 'family' many teenagers have.

But there is better news too. When families break down, alternative arrangements with relatives can work well, as the stories of Brittany Hicks and Arianna Bianco show. Both have fathers they have never known. Brittany's mother could not look after her because of emotional problems. Arianna's mother had a drug addiction, making childcare impossible.

You might expect Brittany and Arianna to feel abandoned and angry. But both girls say they don't feel that way. 'I just deal with it,' says Arianna. 'I don't get mad at my mom. Being addicted to drugs was obviously a thing she couldn't stop.'

Brittany says she used to feel rejected by her mother, but, 'As I grew up, I came to realize that she loved me a lot. She told me, "I never abandoned you. I always knew where the best place was for you." And now I believe her.'

Brittany and Arianna both agree that they have to live by a tougher set of rules than kids in traditional families. 'My aunt is definitely stricter,' says Arianna. 'All my friends agree.' Brittany says her grand-parents check her activities more closely than she thinks they need to. 'I guess it's because they don't want me to run into the same problems my mom did.'

Talking about life outside the traditional family structure, Brittany speaks for both girls when she says, 'People think it's really different, but it's not. You're living with people who love you and want you to have a good life – just like any family.'

(426 words)

Brittany, who lives with her grandparents

Arianna, whose aunt and uncle care for her

1 LOOKING AT THE TEXT

A Read the text and do the following tasks.

1 Contrast the 'fantasy family' of the 1960s with the way that many real-world families are today.
2 Note things that Brittany and Arianna have in common in the way that they have been brought up.
3 Compare the way that Brittany and Arianna are being brought up with a more normal family upbringing.

B Say what you think.

"The only way I could get him to take any notice of me was to put myself on DVD."

"Couldn't you at least wait until half-time so we could discuss our communication problem?"

2 WORKING WITH WORDS

A Use the correct form of these phrasal verbs from the text to complete the story below.

break down | bring up | deal with | go off | grow up | look after | run into | take over

When Tony was three and his younger sister Lucy just two, their parents' marriage … …[1] big problems, and it … …[2] so badly that one day their father just disappeared. Years later, the family learned that he had … …[3] to start a new life in Australia.

For the next three years, their mother seemed to be able to … …[4] the situation. A child-minder … …[5] the children every day while she went to work. In the end, though, the problems of … …[6] two small children as a single mother were too much for her, and she had a nervous breakdown. Social Services then … …[7] from her, and the children were taken into care for several months. Then, after recovering, their mother was able to take them back again. She also met a new partner who soon became a real father to the children. So, in the end, Tony and Lucy … …[8] quite normally and happily.

B Find words or expressions in the text to express the underlined parts of the sentences below more efficiently.

The old ways and the new

1 It has gradually become clear to people that the old ways of family and working life have changed forever. (*paragraph 7*)
People *have come to realize* that the old ways of family and working life have changed forever.
2 For example, people often change jobs these days, and nobody expects to find a job that will continue until one retires at the age of 65. (*paragraph 2*)

Becoming a member of society

3 It is essential for every community to bring up its young people to become good members of that community. (*paragraph 4*)

4 Young people need to learn to do things according to the rules and customs of their community. (*paragraph 8*)

Helping a boy called Sam

5 It is clear that Sam's mother, Carrie, has severe psychiatric problems and that looking after her child has become impossible for her. (*paragraph 5*)

6 Carrie's illness is a big problem and Sam's father has lost contact with the family, and so we have been trying to make other plans for dealing with the situation. (*paragraph 5*)

7 Although his situtation is very bad, I can tell you something more positive. It seems that his aunt and uncle are happy to give him a home. (*paragraph 5*)

3 LISTENING

3 5 **A Listen for general understanding. Listen to someone else talking about his experiences and answer these questions.**

1 What is the family situation?

2 Does the speaker feel that he is dealing with it

a very well? b as well as can be expected? c very badly?

3 What is often the problem at the end of the working day?

B Listen for detail. Listen again and choose the correct answers.

1 Note which activities a–d the father believes his daughter and he are doing enough together.

a watching football
b playing with Barbie dolls
c playing board games
d talking

2 Say which of the following the father hopes that people outside the family can help to provide.

a understanding of make-up
b knowledge of hairstyling
c knowledge of the facts of life
d a female role model

3 Which problems a–d does the father say he has in finding a new partner?

a ability to trust someone new
b lack of time to find someone
c having a daughter
d inability to find a good role model

C Say what you think.

Imagine yourself as the girl above thinking back at the age of 18. What would you say to 'your' father about his efforts? Write your thoughts in the form of a letter to him. Use these ideas:

When I look back at those years after Mum left us, I (sometimes/often) feel ...
I (often/always) remember that (I/we/you) used to ...
I'm sure it was very (hard/depressing/tiring) for you to ...
I wish (you/we/I) (had/hadn't) ...
Finally, I'd just like to say ...

B The bigger picture

BEFORE YOU READ

Work with a partner. Try to decide which of these groups you trust most and least. Make a list from 1 (most trusted) to 7 (least trusted).

business managers | politicians | doctors and nurses | journalists | priests and ministers | teachers | solicitors and lawyers

3 6

Changing society

In a recent survey, Britons showed that the people they trust least are politicians (and journalists). Membership of political parties has dropped to record low levels, and numbers voting in elections have fallen. In a recent national election, only 55% of voters took part and just 42% of these voted for the winning party. The new government was chosen by roughly a quarter of the adult population!

Election numbers are falling across most of the western world. And, worryingly, the people who are least likely to vote are the young. Does this mean that young people have turned away from politics? For many the answer is yes but for others, no. The thing that these young people have turned away from is traditional party politics. Political parties work by bringing together many shades of opinion, and then uniting these into policies covering all areas of government. But these young people have a narrower focus – the environment, for example, or animal rights.

They live in the world of single-issue politics, and they see their particular issue as one requiring urgent action. They want to force the government to understand it and to act. This often means direct action to get public opinion on their side. They organize campaigns that may include demonstrations, marches and other ways of attracting attention. They may use non-violent acts of civil disobedience that lead to arrest by the police. Sometimes, they might even use violence – although this very often actually reduces rather than increases sympathy for their cause.

'There is nothing so powerful as an idea whose time has come,' Victor Hugo said, and this is true of some single-issue campaigns. Think of the suffragette movement that won women's right to vote in the early 20th century. Think of the Civil Rights movement in the 1950s and 1960s, finally bringing Black Americans their full freedom. Think of the students' movement of the late 1960s, which gave the voice of the young new power. These were campaigns that changed history.

Not every battle shakes the world though: smaller successes are possible too. Take the case of Julia Butterfly Hill, for example. Aged 23, she climbed a 180-foot, 1,000-year-old redwood tree in Stafford, California with the aim of preventing further logging in the area. She stayed there month after month, her friends supplying her with food by rope. After remaining in the tree for two years, she won. The loggers signed an agreement promising to save the tree and the surrounding forest forever.

Can traditional politicians attract people like Julia to join them? Sadly for mainstream politics they usually cannot.

(432 words)

1 LOOKING AT THE TEXT

A Read the text quickly and say what these numbers refer to.

55% ı the early 20th century ı the 1950s and 1960s ı 23 ı 180-foot

B Say whether these statements are true or false. Correct the ones that are false.

1 British people prefer to believe politicians rather than people in business.
2 Not so long ago, about 50% of the British population voted for the new government.
3 Young people are often more interested in single-issue politics than in traditional party politics.
4 The Civil Rights movement won the right to vote for American women.
5 Julia Butterfly Hill achieved nothing when she went to live up a tree.

C Say what you think.

1 Look again at the list of groups in Before you read.
   > Are politicians the only ones who can influence and change society?
   > Are they even the main influencers and changers?
   > Are there other groups in society that you would like to add to the list?

2

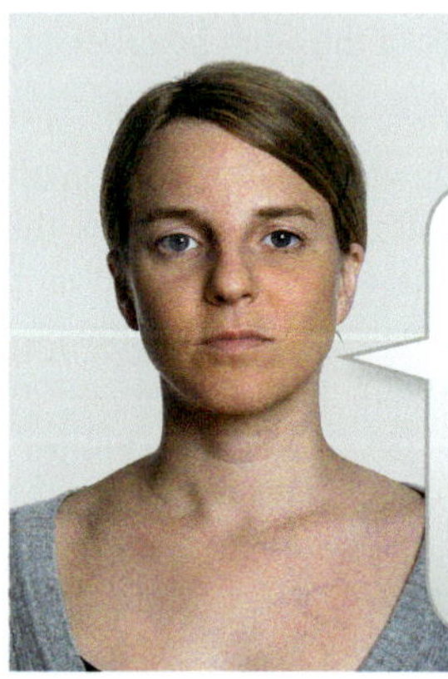

2 WORKING WITH WORDS

A Form adjectival compounds from the highlighted words.

1 Julia climbed a tree that was 180 feet tall.
Julia climbed a 180-foot tree.

2 She climbed a tree that was 1,000 years old.
3 She was a student who was 23 years old.
4 She began a protest that lasted for two years.
5 She was a good example of an activist who is concerned with a single issue.
6 In 1918, the suffragettes finally won the women's vote after a battle that had lasted 29 years.
7 The suffragettes and the Civil Rights movement were both important forces for change in the twentieth century.

> **TIP**
> - When plural nouns are used adjectivally, e.g. *a **180-foot** tree*, they usually become singular, e.g. *feet* > *foot*.
> - Adjectives disappear if the meaning is obvious, e.g. *tall* when talking about the height of a tree.

B **Find words or expressions in the text to express the underlined parts of the sentences below more efficiently.**

1 Membership of political parties has recently fallen to the smallest numbers that there have ever been. (*paragraph 1*)
Membership of political parties has recently fallen to record low levels.
2 Our festival is a great community event, and everybody in the village has a role to play in the various activities. (*paragraph 1*)
3 Our party is a very broad political group, and in it you can find lots of slightly different ideas. (*paragraph 2*)
4 Barbara is not interested in traditional political parties. She believes that fighting for just one political cause is the only way to change anything. (*paragraph 3*)
5 We believe that our new party is one that the world is now ready to listen to and follow. (*paragraph 4*)
6 The Civil Rights movement in America in the 1950s and 1960s was one that deeply affected everybody everywhere. (*paragraph 4*)

C **Make statements from the notes. Use language from the table to turn the percentages into appropriate expressions of proportion.**

Some statistics from the recent city elections:

1 Population registered to vote: 79%
Just under four-fifths of the population were registered to vote.
Or:
Approximately four out of five of the population were registered to vote.
2 Electorate who actually voted: 62%
3 Those over 50 who took part in the election: 76%
4 Voters aged 18-30 who voted: 25%
5 Those in the age range 30-40 who took part: 34%
6 Votes for the winning candidate, Sally Driscoll: 42%
7 Electors voting for the runner-up, David May: 39%
8 Votes going to the other five candidates: 19%

fewer than	*(one) out of (five)*
just under	*(three) out of (eight)*
a little under	*(seven) out of (ten)*
nearly	*half*
almost	*a third*
exactly	*a quarter*
about	*a tenth*
around	*(two) thirds*
roughly	*(three) quarters*
approximately	*(four) fifths*
just over	*(five) sixths*
a little over	*(six) sevenths*
more than	*(seven) eighths*
well over	*(nine) tenths*

3 LISTENING

3 7 **A** **Listen for general understanding. Two people are giving their opinions on an issue which is extremely important for them. Listen and answer these questions.**

1 What are they talking about?
2 What are they both against?
3 What are they both for?
4 Which presentation of their case is better?

B Listen for detail. Listen again to decide why one speaker is better than the other. Consider these points and give examples.

> clear delivery in simple English that the listeners can understand;
> organization of the presentation: introduction, presentation of ideas, summary;
> inclusion of relative ideas and information that is clearly connected (using *first of all, secondly, however, therefore,* etc.).

4 BUILDING SKILLS: GIVING A PRESENTATION

> Die Arbeitsergebnisse präsentieren S. 206

A Work with a partner. Look at the cartoon and do these activities.

1 Describe the cartoon.
2 Identify all the single-issue campaigns the man supports.
3 List more single-issue campaigns that you know about.
4 Discuss them and agree on one you would like to present.

B Prepare a 90-second presentation.

1 For the short introduction: collect essential information on the background to the campaign – why it was needed and how/when it was started.
2 For the main development: collect essential information on things that the campaign has done, with its successes and failures.
3 For the conclusion: agree on how you will re-state your opinion with a summary of supporting reasons.
4 Write notes for your presentation. Then practise and time it. Make necessary changes. Now you are ready to give your presentation, following the guidelines on page 206.

> **TIP**

- You may know all that you need to know for your presentation. However, you may want to collect information from books, magazines, campaign leaflets and from related websites.
- Sort and choose only the most important information to use. Remember: you have only a short time and every word must matter!

5 WRITING

> Eine Stellungnahme schreiben S. 203

Write a comment.

Choose an issue from the cartoon or any other that you do not support. Write a comment evaluating general arguments for and against it. Conclude with a short summary of your personal view.
Try to use some of the expressions that Julie used in her spoken presentation in exercise 3, for example:

First let's consider ...	*However, I believe that ...*	*Moreover, ...*
They also make the point that ...	*First of all, ...*	*So, to summarize, ...*
	Therefore, ...	

C Business options

The silver market

Emma Jones hosts a TV talk show. In this programme, she and her guests are talking about the life of elderly people.

EMMA Good evening. Our discussion topic tonight is: "Too old to enjoy life?" We'll be talking to a number of people on the show and we'd also like you to phone in or email your opinions. The lines are open now. Many people say that society has no use for us when we're old. What is your reaction to that, Vanessa?

VANESSA Well, I'm a journalist and I've just come back from Japan, which is known to have a high proportion of elderly citizens. Japan is years ahead of us in many ways, particularly with robotics. Old people there don't only have louder alarm clocks and books with large print, they have household robots to do the chores and humanoid robots as companions. It's a really big market. I think that helps them enjoy life more in their old age.

EMMA Very interesting indeed. Let's ask our IT expert, Dr Gerald Smart, what industry is doing about this over here.

DR SMART Basically, there are two aspects to this. Firstly there's the medical aspect – helping the old and disabled to improve mobility and independence with new hi-tech devices. Then there's the social aspect, which covers communication and home entertainment. My company is currently developing a robot which will respond to human speech and recognize people.

VANESSA If I can just come in on that, Emma. The Japanese have had this for years now. It's called the ifbot. It's a little human-like robot with a face-tracking system to keep eye contact. It shows emotions using the LEDs on its face and has a vocabulary of over 10,000 words, which makes it speak like a young child.

EMMA I see we have a lot to learn from Japan! Well, the first emails are coming in. Here's one from Sarah in Somerset. She's 65 and she writes: "I'm a widow but I keep in contact with my children over the internet. My daughter has installed a little camera on my computer so I can see my grandchildren and talk to them over my headset. It's not as nice as a visit but they live a long way away, so I only see them once a month." OK. We're all living longer nowadays, so what else must we do – or buy – to enjoy life in old age? Let's ask our marketing expert, Alastair Donald.

ALASTAIR I think we should give more thought to exactly which sections of the population are living longer. Currently, a third of the UK's population is over 50. Two thirds of them are women and their average life expectancy is 85. That's a big market – the so-called silver market – and we need to target them with special products. I mean special supermarkets, housing projects, holidays, furniture and so on ... (460 words)

1 LOOKING AT THE TEXT

Finish the following sentences with information from the text.

1 The Japanese help old people by ...
2 Jobs around the house are ...
3 The Japanese robot is able to ...
4 Sarah is able to ...
5 The average woman will ...

2 PROJECT

A **Choose three or four of the products and services mentioned in the text and explain how they would need to be adapted for an older person, e.g. *A mobile phone would need to have larger keys, a bigger display etc.***

B **In groups think of a product you think would be useful for an older person. Come up with some design ideas and present them to the rest of the class.**

D Grammar checkpoint

1 PARTICIPLE CLAUSES 1

> Grammar summary S. 224

Join the pairs of sentences. Use the word in brackets with the correct sentence and change the following verb into an *ing* participle.

1. Joey first got high on medical drugs at the age of 13. He grew up in a small town in Vermont. (*while*)
   Joey first got high on medical drugs at the age of 13 while growing up in a small town in Vermont.
2. He had used these drugs for two years. He finally allowed peer-group pressure to push him into trying heroin. (*after*)
3. He took this dangerous step. He had always been determined to avoid heroin because of all the frightening stories about it. (*before*)
4. He took the powerful new drug. He quickly found himself 'on the clouds'. (*on*)
5. He began selling heroin to pay for his $400-a-day habit. He moved from 'snorting' to using a needle. (*after*)
6. He studied at the University of Vermont. He knew he was reaching 'the bottom' and decided to visit the university's drug treatment centre. (*while*)
7. Soon after that, he realized that he really must break his addiction. He saw his best friend die of a drug overdose. (*on*)
8. He finally got clear of heroin ten months ago. He looks back on the whole experience now and says, 'I wouldn't wish it on my worst enemy.' (*after*)

2 PARTICIPLE CLAUSES 2

> Grammar summary S. 224

Change the relative clauses (starting with *who*, *which*, *that*) to *Ing* or *ed* participle clauses. See the example below.

Sheena Alston, social worker

Sheena Alston is an experienced social worker who works for Redbridge Social Services and who is employed in the Children's Services Department.

For many years her job was to find suitable homes for children who had been taken into care from broken homes and from families which had a history of violence. She had special responsibility for children who came from ethnic backgrounds, and it was her job to find 'foster' families which offered these children similar ethnic backgrounds.

More recently, she has taken over a newly created section that is called 'Friends and Family' and that is tasked with the job of placing children with relatives or with family friends. The children who are brought into the system often have serious psychological problems, and their successful placement is a job which requires hard work and great care both by Sheena and by the new families. However, a good result also brings great happiness to the child, to the family – and of course to Sheena herself.

*Sheena Alston is an experienced social worker **working** for Redbridge Social Services and **employed** in the Children's Services Department.*

10

Multiculturalism

FOCUS

1 **Look at the picture of a typical London market scene. Use the words in the box to talk about the ethnic minorities you can see.**

> Afro-Caribbean ׀ black ׀ British Asian ׀ Indian ׀ Pakistani ׀ white
> +
> bindi (red spot) ׀ hijab (headscarf) ׀ sari ׀ turban

2 **Which different cultures live in your region or neighbourhood? Which do you belong to?**

3 **Do you have social contact with people of other cultures? Where? When?**

A Personal perspectives

BEFORE YOU READ

A **Read the title and say what the story could be about.**

B **How would you expect a 'fanatic' to behave?**

My Son the Fanatic

Hanif Kureishi's short story is set in East London. Parvez, a 40-year-old Pakistani taxi driver, has been living in England for almost 20 years. He is worried about his son, Ali, who is behaving strangely. Now, Parvez has taken a night off to take Ali out for a meal. In this extract he is telling Bettina, his friend and confidant, about that evening ...

3 9

This time Parvez was trembling. Bettina put her arms around him.

"What's happened?"

"I've just had the worst experience of my life."

As Bettina rubbed his head Parvez told her that the previous evening he and Ali had gone to a restaurant. As they studied the menu, the waiter, whom Parvez knew, brought him his usual whisky and water. Parvez had been so nervous he had even prepared a question. He was going to ask Ali if he was worried about his imminent exams. But first, wanting to relax, he loosened his tie, crunched a popadom and took a long drink.

Before Parvez could speak, Ali made a face.

"Don't you know it's wrong to drink alcohol?" he said.

"He spoke to me very harshly," Parvez told Bettina. "I was about to castigate the boy for being insolent, but managed to control myself."

He had explained patiently to Ali that for years he had worked more than ten hours a day, that he had few enjoyments or hobbies and never went on holiday. Surely it wasn't a crime to have a drink when he wanted one?

"But it is forbidden," the boy said.

Parvez shrugged, "I know."

"And so is gambling, isn't it?"

"Yes. But surely we are only human?"

Each time Parvez took a drink, the boy winced, or made a fastidious face as an accompaniment. This made Parvez drink more quickly. The waiter, wanting to please his friend, brought another glass of whisky. Parvez knew he was getting drunk, but he couldn't stop himself. Ali had a horrible look on his face, full of disgust and censure. It was as if he hated his father.

Halfway through the meal Parvez suddenly lost his temper and threw a plate on the floor. He had felt like ripping the cloth from the table, but the waiters and other customers were staring at him. Yet he wouldn't stand for his own son telling him the difference between right and wrong. He knew he wasn't a bad man. He had a conscience. There were a few things of which he was ashamed, but on the whole he had lived a decent life. "When have I had time to be wicked?" he asked Ali.

In a low monotonous voice the boy explained that Parvez had not, in fact, lived a good life. He had broken countless rules of the Koran.

"For instance?" Parvez demanded.

7 imminent *bevorstehend*
8 crunch *kauen, im Mund zerbrechen*
popadom *Papadam (knuspriger dünner Fladen)*
11 castigate *züchtigen*
12 insolent *unverschämt*
17 shrug *mit den Schultern zucken*
20 wince *zusammenzucken*
fastidious *nörgelnd*
26 rip *reißen*
30 decent *anständig*
wicked *böse, gottlos*

Ali hadn't needed time to think. As if he had been waiting for this moment, he asked his father if he didn't relish pork pies.

"Well ..."

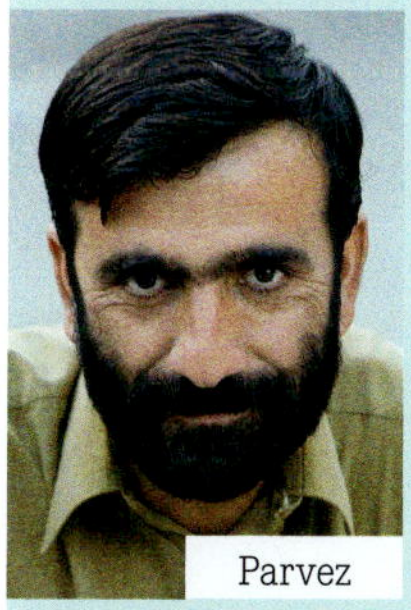

Parvez

Parvez couldn't deny that he loved crispy bacon smothered with mushrooms and mustard and sandwiched between slices of fried bread. In fact, he ate this for breakfast every morning.

Ali then reminded Parvez that he had ordered his own wife to cook pork sausages, saying to her, "You're not in the village now, this is England. We have to fit in!"

Parvez was so annoyed and perplexed by this attack that he called for more drink.

"The problem is this," the boy said. He leaned across the table. For the first time that night his eyes were alive. "You are too implicated in Western civilisation."

Parvez burped; he thought he was going to choke.

"Implicated!" he said. "But we live here!"

"The Western materialists hate us," Ali said. "Papa, how can you love something which hates you?"

"What is the answer then?" Parvez said miserably. "According to you."

Ali addressed his father fluently, as if Parvez were a rowdy crowd that had to be quelled and convinced. The Law of Islam would rule the world; the skin of the infidel would burn off again and again; the Jews and Christians would be routed. The West was a sink of hypocrites, adulterers, homosexuals, drug takers and prostitutes.

As Ali talked, Parvez looked out of the window as if to check that they were still in London.

"My people have taken enough. If the persecution doesn't stop there will be ***jihad***. I, and millions of others, will gladly give our lives for the cause."

Parvez' son Ali

"But why, why?" Parvez said.

"For us the reward will be in paradise."

"Paradise!"

Finally, as Parvez's eyes filled with tears, the boy urged him to mend his ways.

"How is that possible?" Parvez asked.

"Pray," Ali said. "Pray beside me."

Parvez called for the bill and ushered his boy out of the restaurant as soon as he was able. He couldn't take any more. Ali sounded as if he'd swallowed someone else's voice.

On the way home the boy sat in the back of the taxi, as if he were a customer. "What has made you like this?" Parvez asked him, afraid that somehow he was to blame for all this. "Is there a particular event which has influenced you?"

"Living in this country."

"But I love England," Parvez said, watching his boy in the mirror. "They let you do almost anything here."

"That is the problem," he replied.

(830 words)

35 relish *genießen*
37 smother *bedecken*
42 be implicated in *Teil von etw sein*
43 burp *aufstoßen*
choke *ersticken*
49 quell *bezwingen, beherrschen*
infidel *Ungläubige/r*
50 be routed *besiegen*
51 sink *hier: Sumpf*
hypocrite *Heuchler/in*
adulterer *Ehebrecher*
55 persecution *Hetzjagd*
62 urge *drängen*
mend one's ways *sich bessern*
65 usher out *hinausführen*

1 LOOKING AT THE TEXT

A Read the text and do the following activities.

1 Describe the setting of the incident and say from whose point of view it is told.
2 Copy and complete the table below. Outline Parvez's and Ali's conflicting opinions.

Parvez	*Ali*
drinks alcohol (whisky)	*rejects alcohol because it's against the Koran*

B Say what you think.

1 Explain the conflict between Parvez and Ali.
2 Describe Ali's idea of Muslim cultural identity in Britain and compare it to his father's.
3 Why do you think Ali has become a fanatic?

2 WORKING WITH WORDS

A Collect verbs and verb phrases that Hanif Kureishi uses to describe Ali's reaction to his father's behaviour.

Think about body language (facial expressions or gestures) that shows Ali's attitude, e.g. *(to) make a face*, as well as expressions such as *(to) speak harshly to sb, (to) be forbidden,* etc.

B How does Parvez defend himself against Ali's criticisms?

Find expressions Parvez uses to persuade his son that he is a hard-working and decent man who has integrated into English society, e.g. *(to) have few enjoyments/hobbies*, etc.

3 WRITING

Write a paragraph summarizing how you think the story could go on.

Work with a partner or in small groups. First, collect ideas on what happens when Parvez and Ali get home. Here are some ideas:

The argument continues and intensifies at home ...
Ali's mother tries to mediate ...
Finally, Ali leaves the house ...
His parents ...

Or

Ali goes up to his room ...
Parvez continues to drink ...
He feels misunderstood and unfairly treated ...
He works himself up into a rage and goes up to Ali's room ...

You could start like this:

For some time, they continued their journey in silence. "Can't we at least talk to each other?" Parvez asked miserably. "No," said Ali. "I have nothing more to say to you." When they got home, ...

B The bigger picture

BEFORE YOU READ

A **How would you describe the racial make-up of America?**

B **What do you think the 'new face of America' (see the title of the text) could be like?**

3 10

The New Face of America

Leo Jimenez

Vin Diesel

Jessica Alba

Leo Jimenez, 25, is a New York model. His high cheekbones and jet-colored black hair and eyes suggest Asian or American-Indian ancestry. In fact, Jimenez is Colombian by birth, a product of the mixed racial heritage of that Latin-American country. He says his melting-pot looks have definitely opened doors for him.

People like Jimenez are both defining and benefiting from a big shift in American attitudes to race, a shift that has led Louis Vuitton, YSL Beauty and H&M to employ racially-mixed models. The popularity of movie stars like Vin Diesel and Jessica Alba with young audiences is due in part to their diverse ethnic backgrounds - and the same applies to sports stars like Derek Jeter and Tiger Woods.

"Today what's ethnically neutral, diverse or simply unclear has tremendous appeal," says Ron Berger, the chief executive of a New York advertising and trend-research company.

The new attitudes are evident not only in fashion, the media and entertainment. Nearly 7 million Americans said they were members of more than one race in the 2000 census. In addition, more than 14 million Hispanics - about 42 percent of Hispanic respondents - ticked "some other race".

The increasingly multiracial American population, demographers say, is due to intermarriage - which has become much more common and socially acceptable since the ending of segregation in the 1960s - and to waves of mixed-race immigrants, particularly from Latin America.

The multiracial bonus

For decades, art directors, magazine editors and casting agents wanted tall, blond, blue-eyed models and actors. But now the demand for the "Nordic look" is on its way out. Vin Diesel, 36, the star of action movies like *The Fast and the Furious* (2001) once hid his racial heritage by saying that his mother is Irish and his father's race unknown. But now he admits that his racial mix has been a big career asset that has enabled him to play all types of roles and many ethnicities.

Even megastars like Jennifer Lopez and Christina Aguilera borrow from diverse cultures and ethnic backgrounds. Lopez, who is Puerto Rican, features as a mixed-race Latina-Asian princess in the latest Louis Vuitton ad, while Aguilera, half Ecuadorean, poses as an Indian film star on a recent cover of *Allure* magazine.

According to Linda Wells, the magazine's editor-in-chief, this reflects a current fascination with the racial hybrid. "Uniformity just isn't appealing anymore," she says.

A recent study by the Lewis Mumford Center at the State University of New York at Albany noted that while nearly half of Hispanics chose the "some other race" category in the 2000 census, a big majority of Hispanics had chosen the "white" category 20 years earlier. "There used to be a sense that to be white was to have arrived," says John R. Logan, the Mumford Center's director. "Today there's a trend towards rejecting whiteness as a badge of success."

(479 words)

1 LOOKING AT THE TEXT

A Read the article quickly to find and explain the following numbers. They are in the same order.

1 nearly 7 million
2 2000
3 more than 14 million
4 about 42 percent
5 the 1960s
6 for decades
7 36
8 nearly half of

B Find information in the article to support the following quotations.

1 Ron Berger: "Today what's ethnically neutral, diverse or simply unclear has tremendous appeal."
2 Linda Wells: "Uniformity just isn't appealing anymore."
3 John R. Logan: "Today there's a trend towards rejecting whiteness as a badge of success."

C Say what you think.

1 Do you agree with Ron Berger and Linda Wells? Say why (not).
2 Can you name any German racially-mixed celebrities? Think particularly of sport and pop music.

2 WORKING WITH WORDS

A The words in the table are all from the text. Give the missing verb or noun forms.

	Verb	*Noun*
1	*(to) suggest*	...
2	...	*product*
3	*(to) employ*	...
4	...	*entertainment*
5	...	*respondent*
6	...	*marriage*
7	...	*segregation*
8	...	*action*
9	...	*fascination*
10	*(to) choose*	...
11	*(to) arrive*	...
12	...	*director*

B Use some of the words from the table to write six sentences.

Leave gaps where the words should go. Then swap your sentences with a partner. Can you complete each other's sentences?

3 MEDIATION

> Mediation S. 210

Read the dialogue. Then pick out the main points and explain them in German.

KATE I think a lot of Europeans have a completely out-dated idea of what America's really like.
MIKE Oh? What makes you say that?
KATE Well, just to start with, a lot of people think that black Americans make up the biggest minority. But that's no longer true. I read that people of Spanish origin - you know, "Hispanics" - now outnumber African-Americans.
MIKE Really? I didn't know that.
KATE Today, about 15% of the total population say that they are Hispanic. The comparable figure for Blacks is just over 13%.
MIKE OK. And the hispanic population is growing much faster, isn't it?
KATE Right. The black - and by the way also the white - share of the population is actually shrinking. But what I really wanted to say is that people of mixed race are becoming just as important as the traditional minorities.

MIKE Oh, yes. Now you mention it, I remember reading something about that. That was one finding of the last US census, wasn't it?

KATE Yes, it was. For the first time, people were allowed to name more than one race in the 2000 census. And a lot of people did so.

MIKE What, before 2000 you could only give Black or White?

KATE Of course not, Mike. But you could only give one race. You know, African-American, Caucasian, Hispanic, Asian, Native American and so on. Take sports stars like Derek Jeter and Tiger Woods, for example. They're both a fairly complicated racial mix, but until 2000 they were just Black.

Derek Jeter

Tiger Woods

4 LISTENING

3 11 **A Listen for general understanding. Read the questions, then listen and answer them.**

1 What is the main topic of the radio discussion?
2 Who is taking part in the discussion?
3 Which speaker takes a hard, "anti-immigrant" line?
4 You are a big farmer in southern California. Which speaker seems to have most understanding of your situation?

B Listen for detail. First, make sure you understand the multiple-choice questions below. Then listen again and choose the correct answer, a), b) or c).

1 Frank claims that there are about **a)** 7 – **b)** 9 – **c)** 12 million illegal Mexican immigrants in the USA.
2 Julia thinks that a figure of about **a)** 5 – **b)** 7 – **c)** 9 million illegal immigrants is more accurate.
3 Julia says that the government has tolerated poor illegal immigrants for a long time for **a)** humanitarian – **b)** economic – **c)** religious reasons.
4 The majority of illegal immigrants work in **a)** farming, construction and manufacturing – **b)** their own business – **c)** domestic service and restaurants.
5 Julia feels that illegal immigrants should be allowed to stay in the USA provided that they **a)** have a home and a job – **b)** are willing to become US citizens – **c)** have nowhere to go in Mexico.
6 Frank argues that illegal immigrants should be deported because they **a)** have broken the US immigration laws – **b)** are taking jobs from Americans – **c)** are the Mexican government's responsibility.
7 Julia disagrees with Frank partly because immigrants **a)** work long hours for very low wages – **b)** do jobs that Americans aren't qualified to do – **c)** have become essential to the US economy.
8 Frank says that **a)** Americans wouldn't do immigrants' jobs even for a better wage – **b)** immigrants are taking jobs from Americans – **c)** immigrants are responsible for a rise in crime.

5 SPEAKING

Describe and interpret the cartoons.

> Interpretation von Bildern und Karikaturen S. 207

1

2

1 Work with a partner. Describe one cartoon each. Your partner should not look at the cartoon while you are doing so. Then look at the cartoons together and pick out any missing or incorrect details.

on the right/left ı in the middle ı in the foreground/background ı (to) close ı (to) dig a hole ı (to) cart sth away ı (to) represent/stand for ı to build ı border ı fence post ı barbed wire ı wire-netting (fence) ı spade

> **TIP**

Use the **present progessive** for what is happening now:
*Two Mexicans **are talking**.*
Use the **present perfect** for what has just or recently happened:
*The Americans **have built** a fence.*

2 Now interpret the cartoons. Present your results to the rest of the class.

> *... stands for/represents ...*
> *The cartoonist's message is ...*
> *... shows the contradictory positions of ... and ...*
> *On the one hand, the US government ..., on the other, employers ...*

6 WRITING

Read the press report and write the story from Lee's point of view.

Start like this: *I don't know how the accident happened. One minute we were on the road, the next we were crashing down the side of this canyon. Maybe Mom went to sleep for a moment, I don't know ...*

The life of 12-year-old Lee Wilson was saved by an illegal Mexican immigrant who found him wandering in the southern Arizona desert after his mother, 45-year-old Joan Wilson, had driven their car off the road and down the side of a canyon.

Lee crawled out of the wreck to get help. He was found frightened and confused about four hours later by Jesus Manuel Cordova, 26. After trying unsuccessfully to free the mother, Cordova cared for Lee while they waited for somebody to come by. Joan died a short time later.

As temperatures dropped, Cordova gave the boy his jacket, lit a fire and stayed with him until some hunters passed by and radioed for help. The boy was flown to a hospital in Tucson but was found to be unhurt.

C Business options

Some like it hot

Sally Price is a tourist guide in London. She is just finishing her tour for the day.

SALLY Okay, to end our tour of London's East End we're in Brick Lane. Can anyone tell me what Britain's most popular food is?
TOURIST Fish and chips?
SALLY That's what everyone thinks but I'm afraid you're wrong. It's actually chicken tikka masala – that's marinated chicken served in a curry sauce. It's absolutely delicious and I can thoroughly recommend it. If you look along Brick Lane, you'll see one curry house after another. There's food to suit all tastes but if you're not used to curry, go for a milder one, a korma for example. The hottest curries are generally the vindaloo ones, so be careful!
TOURIST That's interesting. Why is Indian food so popular here?
SALLY Well, traditionally, immigrants arriving in a new country can't speak the language very well but some occupations, in this case cooking, don't require language skills. That's why many Indians were first able to make a living by opening up restaurants. The first Indian curry house opened in London in 1809 and now there are well over 10,000. The Indian population of the UK stands at about 1.6 million at present but now just about everyone in the country eats Indian food. The whole industry is estimated to be worth around £3.5 billion!
TOURIST That's a lot of money! Could you recommend a restaurant for this evening?
SALLY I can recommend all the restaurants here really. Oh, and if you're lucky, you may well see a famous footballer or a TV celebrity.
TOURIST And what about the prices?
SALLY They're rising actually because of the shortage of rice on the world market and immigration restrictions on chefs from India.
TOURIST But can't the restaurant owners recruit chefs from the Indian community in the UK?
SALLY Well, the current generation of young Indians has set its sights on higher things and many are training to become engineers, doctors or lawyers. The restaurants are actually still quite reliant on new immigrants. Right, it's time to eat – I'm hungry! Enjoy your meal! (335 words)

1 LOOKING AT THE TEXT

True or false? Correct the false statements.

1 Fish and chips is less popular than chicken tikka masala.
2 Most Indians in the UK work in the restaurant business.
3 Not only Indians eat Indian food in the UK.
4 The Indian food industry is not very important to the UK economy.
5 Restaurant prices are rising because Indian food is so popular.

2 PROJECT

What different types of food are available in the area where you live? In groups choose one of these food types. Research its background and its impact on the economy and then present your findings to the class.

D Grammar checkpoint

1 REPORTED SPEECH – STATEMENTS

> Grammar summary S. 217

Read the statements and report the information.

1 There will soon be over ten million illegal immigrants in California alone.
Governor Schwarzenegger complained that ...
2 Fewer immigrants crossed the Rio Grande last year.
However, he added that ... the year before.
3 The US government has decided to build a fence along the border.
The Mayor of San Diego said that ...
4 Surveillance cameras have been installed at every crossing point.
An immigration official told reporters that ...
5 Maria Sanchez: "To be effective, the fence must be at least eight feet high."
Ms Sanchez pointed out that ...
6 Maria Sanchez: "They are also going to introduce much stricter border controls."
She went on to say that they ...

2 REPORTED SPEECH – QUESTIONS

> Grammar summary S. 219

A border guard has stopped a Mexican driver at a crossing point near San Diego. Report his questions.

1 "Can you understand English?"
The guard asked the truck driver ...
2 "Do you have a valid entry visa?"
He inquired ...
3 "May I see your vehicle papers, please?"
The guard asked politely ...
4 "What is the purpose of your visit to the USA?"
Then he wanted to know ...
5 "Where are you staying in California?"
After that, he asked ...
6 "How long do you plan to stay in California?"
He was interested to know ...

3 REPORTED SPEECH – INTRODUCTORY VERBS

> Grammar summary S. 217

Report the comments using as many different introductory verbs as you can.
These comments were made at a citizens' meeting in San Diego to discuss the problem of illegal immigration in southern California.

JEB DALE: In my opinion, the only answer is to build a high fence along the whole border. I'm a border guard and it's impossible to seal off a virtually open frontier.

SALLY-ANN MORRIS: Yes, but is that feasible? The fence would have to be at least eight feet high and the border's 1,400 miles long, for goodness' sake.

TOM BARNS: And it's not just the fence, either. There's the infrastructure, too – surveillance cameras and so on. And I know what I'm talking about, folks. I read something once about the iron curtain in Europe. You wouldn't believe it!

MADDY BARNS: It's good you mentioned the iron curtain. Is that what we really want? I mean do we want to build an iron curtain right across America?

ANNA GARCIA: I agree with that. No way! I think we need to do two things. First, a general amnesty for all illegal immigrants who already live and work here and, second, a fair quota system for poor Mexicans like for anybody else.

CARL HARMS: Well, I sure am glad that somebody has at last mentioned work, because that's what this is all about. I'm a fruit farmer and I'd go bust without the Mexicans, legal or illegal. The fact is, we need these people as much as they need us.

11

Main Course

Crime

FOCUS

1 Link the captions a–c to the cartoons 1–3.

a "... and our patience is exhausted. If you don't pay the ransom this year, we will ..."
b "You must admit, a strict diet, no alcohol and early to bed certainly keep you fit."
c "Open up, Benny. We know you're there. Fraud Squad."

1

2 Use the words and expressions below and the captions to describe the cartoons.

(to) be like a film set | (to) become an adult | breakout | (to) break out of/escape from prison | (to) deceive/trick sb into thinking sth | in captivity | kidnapper | (to) look over one's shoulder | victim (of a crime)

2

3 Which of these crimes do the cartoons focus on?

- graffiti-spraying
- kidnapping
- burglary
- escaping from prison
- drink driving
- shoplifting
- fraud
- armed robbery

3

4 Which of the eight crimes above do you think is the most/least serious? Why?

(to) be irresponsible | (to) be (relatively) trivial | minor/serious/trivial crime | (to) cause death/serious injury | (to) often involve children | (to) only involve property

A Personal perspectives

BEFORE YOU READ

A **Look at the headline and photos. What do you think the press report could be about?**

B **The US Constitution forbids 'cruel and unusual punishment' but the Supreme Court ruled that the death penalty is constitutional. What, then, do you think is meant by 'cruel and unusual punishment'?**

Karla Faye Tucker has an important place in American legal history. Her execution for murder broke the convention that women were not given the death penalty. Read on to find out more.

Execution by lethal injection

Death by lethal injection is painless. The victim is given a massive dose of a combination of fast-acting anaesthetics. Victims usually go into a coma almost immediately and die within about ten minutes.

3 12

A step too far?

1 ...

On the morning of Karla Faye Tucker's execution by lethal injection on 3 February 1998, the Governor's Office in Austin, Texas, received over 3,000 phone calls, faxes and emails, 80% of them asking the then governor, George W. Bush, to spare her life.

But nothing helped. Even if he had wanted to, Governor Bush felt he couldn't spare a convicted murderer's life 'just because she's a woman'. So the execution went ahead as planned, although even Texans – who routinely execute their killers without a thought – were troubled by it.

2 ...

By far the most important result of Ms Tucker's execution was to put an end to the legal convention that women may not be subjected to the death penalty. The last 'act of state' that discriminated between men and women simply because of their sex died with her. Since then, all attempts to save women from execution have similarly failed.

For feminists, Karla Faye's death was an awkward victory in the ongoing battle for equality with men. Whatever logic may say, many feel that equal wages and opportunity are one thing, capital and corporal punishment quite another. As civil rights activist Anna-Marie Barfield said, "Come on. We don't want to be that equal."

3 ...

The campaign for Karla Faye's life saw some surprising alliances. Civil rights campaigners, fundamentalist religious groups and male conservatives joined forces, although for widely differing reasons.

A large majority of civil righters are opposed to the death penalty on principle, seeing it as a 'cruel and unusual punishment' and hence unconstitutional. They also find the apparent racial bias repugnant. They would like to see the lives of all 369 offenders currently* on death row in Texas, of whom 40.9% are black and 27.9% Hispanic, spared.

Most fundamentalists are not opposed to capital punishment on principle – indeed, many are among its biggest fans – but nonetheless they thought that Ms Tucker's life should be spared. This was because during her 14 years on death row she had shown true remorse, had married a priest and had become a devout Christian. (The then Pope, John Paul II, agreed and sent a note to Governor Bush, himself a devout Christian, asking for clemency.)

Meanwhile, confused male conservatives just felt that women are, well, women and ought not to be executed. The more thoughtful among them pointed out that "as women don't kill by nature, those few that do must be insane".

4 ...

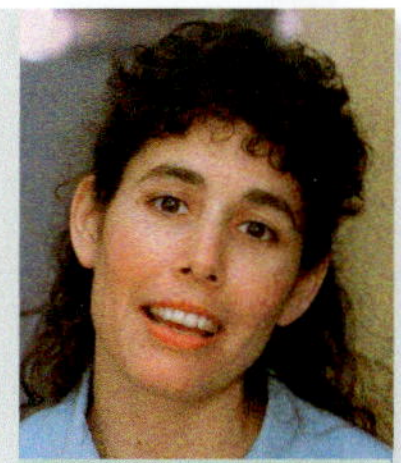

Karla Faye Tucker

Although many liberals also felt, at least in private, that executing women "somehow stinks", they were deeply worried by the passions aroused by the Tucker campaign. Would a reformed and repentant male have received such international attention? Would a black man who had killed an eldery white couple but then become a devout Muslim in prison have received such high-profile support? Almost certainly not. It was her sex and her prettiness and her uncanny natural ability to tear hearts on TV that made Karla Faye Tucker the campaigners' pin-up. (489 words)

* 15 February 2008

1 LOOKING AT THE TEXT

A Put four of these sub-headings into the text at the points shown.

Strange bedfellows | **Public opinion** | **Women's lib?** | **What about victims' rights?** | **The liberal dilemma** | **Pleas for clemency**

B Link the speech bubbles 1–8 to the people in the box. Say how you know.

an assistant in the Governor's Office, Austin, Texas | an aunt of Karla Faye's victim | a civil rights activist | a Christian fundamentalist | a feminist | Karla Faye's husband | a liberal | a male conservative

1 *Yes, gender equality can be really tough, but I believe inequality is even worse.*

2 *Being strapped to a bed and given a lethal injection is a cruel punishment. I believe humans deserve much better.*

3 *I'm not against capital punishment, but this is different. God has spoken to her. She's seen the Light.*

4 *I just feel that women – all women – should have our special protection and respect.*

5 *Look, Karla Faye Tucker's Christian, pretty and white, but what about the other 52 women on death row, not to mention the men?*

6 *This note has just arrived for the Governor. Guess who it's from?*

7 *What about victims' rights, I'd like to know? This woman killed our Jerry with an axe because she wanted to steal his motorcycle, for Pete's sake!*

8 *We didn't touch each other. We were only allowed to talk through a glass wall using microphones.*

2 WORKING WITH WORDS

A Show that you understand these expressions by using them in sentences of your own.

1 (to) spare sb's life (*line 8*)
2 act of state (*line 17*)
3 corporal punishment (*line 24*)
4 high-profile support (*line 66*)
5 (to) tear hearts (*line 68*)
6 campaigners' pin-up (*line 69*)

B Choose the most suitable connector, a) or b).

The US Supreme Court abolished the death penalty **a)** also | **b)** as[1] unconstitutional in 1972. **a)** However | **b)** Moreover[2], it was reintroduced in 1976 **a)** because of | **b)** because[3] a rise in violent crime **a)** what | **b)** which[4] many people saw **a)** as | **b)** like[5] being one result of abolition.

a) Furthermore | **b)** However[6], here we should be careful. The Supreme Court itself did not reintroduce capital punishment, **a)** and | **b)** but[7] only said that it was not unconstitutional - **a)** if | **b)** whether[8] to use it was for the states to decide.

Today, 36 states have reintroduced the death penalty, **a)** as a rule | **b)** in fact[9] by lethal injection **a)** because | **b)** while[10] this method is said to be more humane. **a)** But | **b)** Thus[11] this number can be a little misleading **a)** also | **b)** as[12] six of these states have not used the death penalty at all since reintroducing it, **a)** and | **b)** whereas[13] four more have only used it once. **a)** Moreover | **b)** Though[14] two-thirds of all executions since 1977 have been carried out in just five states, by far the most, 408, in Texas.

a) Although | **b)** Nonetheless[15], these states are not evenly spread throughout the country. **a)** For example, | **b)** Whereas[16] the northern and eastern states tend to be against capital punishment, those in the south and west make use of it.

3 WRITING

> Eine Stellungnahme schreiben S. 203

Comment on the suggestion that capital punishment should be used for particularly serious crimes such as murder and terrorism.

Think about the pros ...
- can never kill again
- cheaper than lifelong imprisonment
- retribution
- 'deterrent effect'
- enables victim's loved ones to 'draw a line'

and cons ...
- some innocent people will certainly be executed
- 'two wrongs do not make a right'
- suffering of guilty person's innocent family
- no rehabilitation possible
- most murders committed in the heat of the moment
- problem of mental instability at time of crime

According to FBI data, the murder rate in Non-Death Penalty States (green) has remained consistently lower than the rate in Death Penalty States (red).

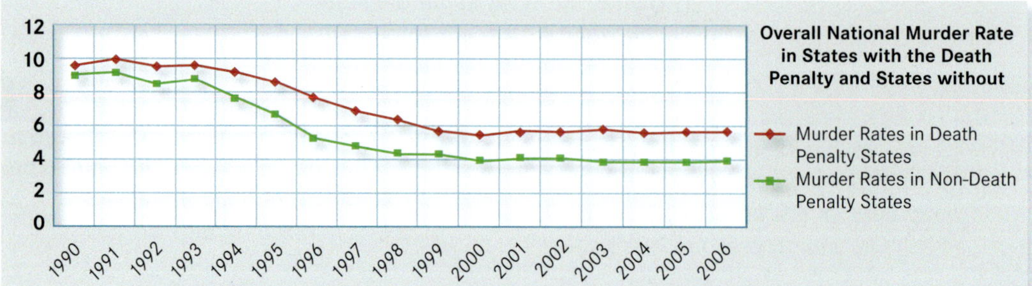

B The bigger picture

BEFORE YOU READ

A **What do you associate New York City with? Try to name at least three things.**

B **Have you ever come across the New York Police Department (NYPD)? Where?**

Although the New York Police Department (NYPD) features in many films and TV dramas, in fact until quite recently it was not much better than the criminals it was supposed to bring to justice. Read the article to find out more.

3 13

A stitch in time saves nine

In the early 1990s, New York City was sliding into lawlessness and chaos. South Bronx was just one of several 'no-go areas'; even the police only went there in heavily-armed groups. In 1991, the worst year for crime, the New York Police Department (NYPD) registered 2,245 murders, 2,818 rapes and 100,280 robberies. Few New Yorkers dared to use the subway or go into Central Park after dark. The city was fast becoming ungovernable.

Ten years later, New York had gone from being among America's most dangerous big cities to being one of its safest. In 2001, there were 633 murders, a drop of over 70%, 1,530 rapes and 27,229 robberies. And the subway? It had become one of the cleanest, safest and most efficient transport systems in the country.

What made this turnaround possible? First, there was a sea change in public opinion. Ordinary, decent, tolerant New Yorkers wanted their big apple back – and were willing to support a tough new mayor, Rudolph Giuliani, and a tough new police chief, William J. Bratton, to do it.

Bratton's first step was to clean up the NYPD itself. The force was rotten with drug abuse, bribery, racism and nepotism. That is one reason why Giuliani hired Bratton from Boston. He was a stranger to New York; he owed no favours. And Bratton was merciless. Corrupt officers were weeded out with 'zero tolerance'. That is where the term really comes from. They were not only sacked with the loss of all pension rights, but they were also prosecuted and given tough sentences. The 'bad apples' were replaced by 2,000 better-educated officers taken from all of New York's communities.

After cleaning up the police, Bratton then introduced a policy called 'Crimes and Quality of Life' (CQL). "In the past, we just cut down trees," said Bratton. "But that's not enough. You must kill the seeds, so that the trees never grow. That's what CQL is all about."

To stop the seeds from growing into trees, the new and reformed NYPD focused on seven main areas: drug dealing, domestic violence, bad and threatening behaviour in public places, car theft, guns on the street, school violence and graffiti spraying. "I told my officers never ever to look the other way," said Bratton. "It's like in school. The biggest deterrent isn't getting punished, but getting caught."

And it worked. As the seeds of crime were weeded out, the incidence of more serious crimes fell as well. "There's no such thing as a trivial crime," Bratton told his officers. "Never forget that most armed robbers started out as shoplifters." (431 words)

1 LOOKING AT THE TEXT

A Explain the title by referring to information in the article.

B Answer the questions.

1 Why is it possible to say that New York was 'becoming ungovernable' in the early 1990s?
2 What evidence is there to show that the situation in New York had improved radically by 2000?
3 How did Bratton go about reforming the NYPD?
4 Why was Bratton's policy of 'Crimes and Quality of Life' so successful?

2 WORKING WITH WORDS

A Link the words or expressions on the left with their meanings on the right.

1	no-go area (*line 3*)	a	completely different way of looking at a situation
2	turnaround (*line 19*)	b	catch criminals
3	sea change (*line 20*)	c	corrupt people
4	big apple (*line 21*)	d	diametrically opposed direction
5	zero tolerance (*line 30*)	e	nickname of New York City
6	bad apples (*line 34*)	f	part of city too dangerous to enter
7	cut down trees (*line 41*)	g	stop people becoming criminals
8	kill the seeds (*line 42*)	h	absolute refusal to show understanding in any circumstances

B Choose four more words or expressions from the text and write definitions – make sure they are in a different order. Swap with a partner. Can he/she match them?

3 SPEAKING

A Look at the photos and read the offenders' details. Which crimes do you think are most serious? Which are less serious or more understandable?

An eye for an eye?

1 

Chloe Martin, 35: caught stealing petrol from neighbour's car; single parent with two young children; first offence; says she can't afford to buy all the petrol she needs to drive to work

2 

Jake Wilson, 32: broke into warehouse to steal electronic equipment; injured security guard with flick knife; history of burglary/violence; resisted arrest

3 

Wim De Graf, 45: caused bad road accident (two people injured, one seriously) by dangerous driving; in UK on business and returning to Holland at end of week; first known offence; claims he was late for very important appointment

4 

Holly Chang, 19: stole £400 from employer to finance gambling habit; second offence in six months; refuses to accept help from Gamblers Anonymous

5 

Luke Hall, 15: sprayed graffiti on luxury villa; did it because "my dad says they should build more cheap homes"; says he won't do it again but he still agrees with his dad

B Study the possible punishments in the box and find one to fit each crime. Report your verdict to the class and give reasons for it.

Let the person off with a warning not to do it again |
Put him/her on probation with a suspended sentence (say how long) |
Make the offender do community service (say number of hours per week and for how long) |
Impose a fine of up to £3,000 |
Sentence person to prison for at last three years |
Make him/her repair or pay for any damage

4 GIVING A TALK

> Die Arbeitsergebnisse präsentieren S. 206

In small groups of three or four prepare a talk on crime trends in the USA.

Use the outline below (making any changes you wish) and the information in File 7, page 193. You may add any further information you have. Present your results to the rest of the class.

Outline: Crime trends in the USA

1 You could start your talk like this:
What impression do many Europeans have of crime in the US? Probably that the USA is a particularly violent and criminal place. But is this picture ...?

2 Go on:
We wonder whether this is supported by the latest statistics for the period ...
(= bridge to development sections)

3 Development I:
Refer to and explain nationwide general trends; point out biggest/smallest decrease(s)/increase(s) by region; speculate about possible causes, e.g. better policing, poverty, ...
Crime trends vary widely from region to region. For example, ...

4 Development II:
Refer to more detailed trends, including homicides; point out difference between crimes committed, crimes reported, crimes prosecuted, i.e. police involvement in fighting crime.
It is extremely important to recognize the difference between ...

5 Conclusion:
Conclude by referring back to your opening remarks and giving your group's opinion.
It is clear that Europeans' perception of crime in the USA is ...

5 LISTENING

3 14 **A Listen for general understanding. Listen to a story about an old lady who was stopped for speeding. Then put the drawings into the correct order.**

A

B

C

D

E

F

B Listen for detail. Listen again, then choose the correct statement, a), b) or c).

1 The deputy stopped the old lady because she ...
  a) was speeding.
  b) went through some red lights.
  c) was driving a stolen car.

2 The old lady said she had lost her licence because she had driven ...
  a) without vehicle registration papers.
  b) dangerously and caused an accident.
  c) while drunk.

3 The deputy sheriff ...
  a) called the sheriff.
  b) called for back-up.
  c) arrested the old lady for murder.

4 The punch line is ...
  a) 'I bet the liar told you I was speeding, too.'
  b) 'And I killed and hacked up the owner, too.'
  c) 'I'm sure everything's quite in order.'

C Business options

4 8 The cost of shoplifting

I was in the shopping centre near where I live. We were in a cosmetics store and everything there is expensive to buy, so we just stole some things. I got lipstick and nail varnish and my friend got eye liner and stuff. I had no money with me except to get the bus home. I just did it. I don't know why. Everyone does it. The store detective stopped us when we got outside though and I was really scared. I had to go to the police station with my mum and meet the store manager at a 'Final Warning Night'. We all sat in a circle and I had to say why I did it. It was very embarrassing for me, and my mum too, because she always goes to the shop where I was caught. She had no idea I was shoplifting. She was really ashamed and so was I. Now she'll never go there again and I'm banned. The manager said people like me made prices higher. **1**

Katie Jones (14), near Peterborough, UK

Police Constable Andrew Hunt

Shoplifters come from all social backgrounds. Their motives vary and can be anything from need, greed, excitement, peer-group pressure to mental illness or they can be professionals who sell the goods on, e.g. on the internet. Shoplifting costs retailers 1.7 billion pounds per year and they pass these losses on to the consumer, which means us, by putting up the prices. This money goes on replacing lost goods, employing plain clothes store detectives and uniformed guards, closed circuit television (CCTV), staff training and so on. **2**

3 *Girls – and to a lesser extent boys – start to go shopping without their parents at 13 or 14 and are attracted by the goods – typically clothes and cosmetics – but have no access to them. They have little cash, no store cards and no credit, so they steal them. They are normally low-value items and they want them for themselves. They don't sell them on to other people.*

Dr Fiona Byford, University of London

1 LOOKING AT THE TEXT

Match the following sentence halves.

1 Katie stole goods	A to catch the bus home.
2 She only had enough money on her	B to sell the goods on.
3 Katie had to explain	C to go to the cosmetics store.
4 She didn't intend	D from a cosmetics store.
5 Katie is no longer allowed	E why she had stolen the goods.

2 MEDIATION

One of your friends is doing a project on why teenagers shoplift. In German summarize the reasons that Police Constable Hunt and Dr Byford give.

3 OPINION

Dr Byford believes that teenagers shopping without their parents steal because they are attracted by the goods. What is your opinion? Why do you think teenagers shoplift? Write 80–100 words.

D Grammar checkpoint

1 ADVERB ORDER

> Grammar summary S. 223

Copy the table with eight writing lines into your exercise book and complete it with adverbs from the box. Sometimes more than one position is possible.

~~always~~ | ~~beautifully~~ | as a rule | at 6 o'clock | in the lesson | each spring | every day | fast | fortunately | in New York | in prison | last summer | loudly | naturally | nowadays | of course | often | once a month | on the whole | seldom | silently | since 2008

Front	*Mid*	*End-Position*		
		manner	*place*	*frequency/time*
	always	*beautifully*		

2 FORMING SENTENCES

> Grammar summary S. 223

Put the words or expressions in the correct order to make sensible sentences.

1 two hours' exercise | research | need | that | at least | a day | healthy prisoners | suggests
2 occupy | sometimes | a cell | two prisoners | unfortunately | designed for one
3 often | complain | critics | that | 'academies of crime' | are | prisons | in fact just
4 in street crime | has caused | mobile phones | it is said | that | a big increase | the theft of
5 clearly | a 'must have' status symbol | mobile phones | amongst | this is because | the young | have become
6 occur | or social group | most murders | within the family
7 no longer there | I returned | my car | to the car park | when | was
8 after dark | it's scandalous | many women | that | nervous | of walking | are | through our parks
9 in reality | crime | is falling | is increasing | it | many people | think | unfortunately, | when
10 FBI statistics | in states | less murders | perhaps surprisingly | show that | the death penalty | there are | without

3 TRANSLATING

Translate the sentences into English. Be careful about word order.

1 Vor dreißig Jahren war es noch möglich, ungefährdet auf der Straße zu spielen.
2 Viele New Yorker hatten Angst, nachts ihre Wohnungen zu verlassen.
3 Einige Wissenschaftler behaupten, dass Armut der Hauptgrund für Kriminalität ist.
4 Die Erfahrung zeigt, dass harte Bestrafung selten wirksam ist.
5 Leider ist eine große Mehrheit dafür, die Todesstrafe wieder einzuführen.
6 In der Tat wurde die Null-Toleranz hauptsächlich gegen korrupte Polizisten angewendet.
7 Selbverständlich wollte der Polizist wissen, wo wir uns zur Tatzeit aufgehalten haben.
8 Man sagt, dass der Dieb sich während der Flucht schwer verletzt hat.
9 Im Interesse der Gleichbehandlung werden heutzutage Frauen in den USA genauso hart bestraft wie Männer.
10 Laut einer Meinungsumfrage aus dem Jahre 2007 sind 74 % der Wahlberechtigten (*electorate*) in Texas für die Todesstrafe.

12

Main Course

Future life, future living

FOCUS

1 Link the photos 1–8 to the captions a–h.

1

2

3
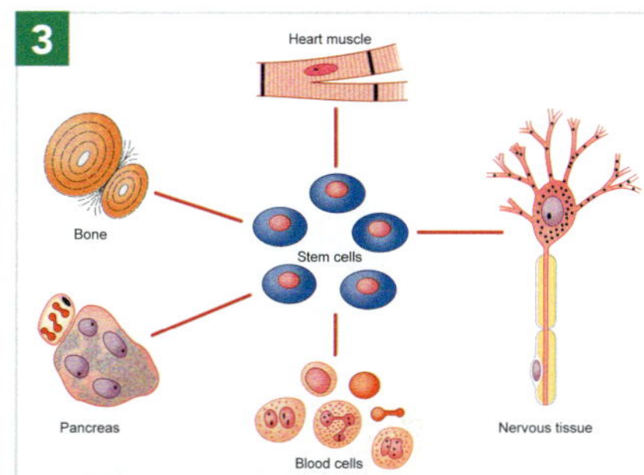

4

5
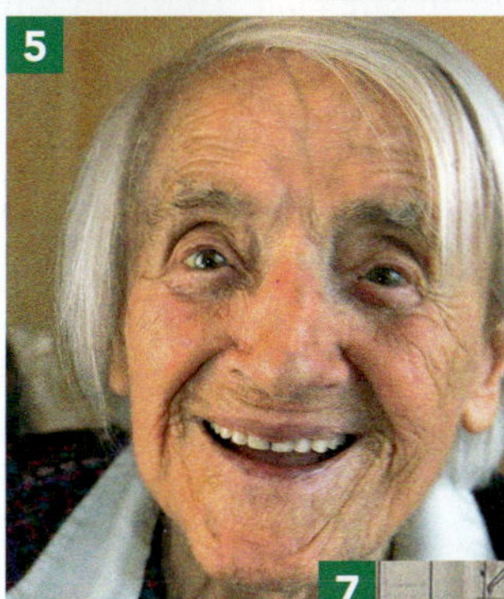

6

7

8
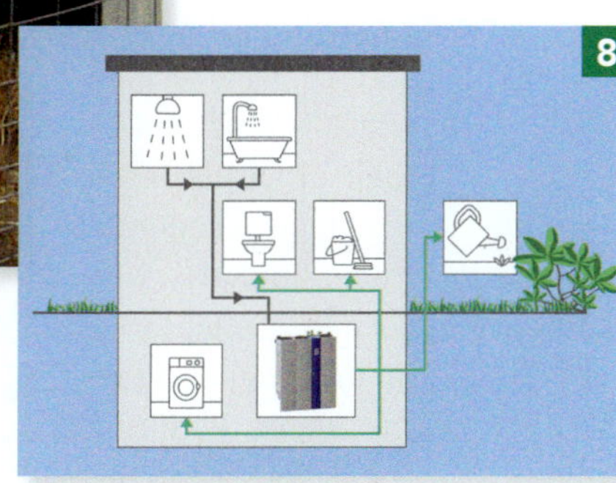

a your friend and helper
b more and better food
c 100+ and still going strong
d preventing hereditary diseases
e cloning
f conservation of resources
g the end of the service society
h cloned supercow's daughters give more milk

2 What is the overall theme of all the photos: a), b) or c)?
a) Future fears – b) Future developments – c) Future hopes

3 Which two developments do you find most interesting or useful? Say why. Then do a class survey.

4 How do you think life in Germany will have changed by, say, 2050?

A Personal perspectives

BEFORE YOU READ

A **What boycotts have you heard of, for example the USA's boycott of Iran?**

B **Do you think boycotts work or do they hurt the wrong people?**

C **Have you ever taken part in a boycott? If not, can you imagine doing so? Why (not)?**

According to this report from the Daily Mail*, the media and the big supermarkets are doing more to protect British consumers from the unknown risks of genetically-modified (GM) food than their government is.*

3 15

British supermarkets call for a boycott of 'cloned' meat and milk

Britain's biggest supermarkets last night announced a boycott of meat and milk from cloned farm animals and their offspring. The move follows Daily Mail revelations that a calf, the daugher of a US cloned cow, has been born on a British farm.

Separately, the government's Food Standards Agency (FSA) plans to hold emergency talks with EU officials tomorrow over the policing of food from cloned animals and their offspring.

Current food and health laws require the investigation and approval of any meat or milk from cloned farm animals. However, a loophole in the law means that there are no such controls on food which is produced by their offspring. As a result, meat and milk from animals who have a clone for a mother could be in the shops within a few years.

Last night, supermarkets, including Tesco, Sainsbury's, Asda, Morrisons and Marks & Spencer, reacted to this threat by announcing their own boycott. Tesco said: "We would not stock any products derived from cloned animals or their offspring." Marks & Spencer said: "We have long had a ban on all genetically modified ingredients in our food. That ban will now apply to any food from cloned animals and their offspring."

A Holstein calf called Dundee Paradise, the daughter of a US cloned cow, was born on a farm in Shropshire last month. This made clear that clone farming and the genetic modification of animals has now moved from science fiction to the reality of the supermarket.

In an astonishing failure, the government knew nothing at all about Dundee Paradise and the future birth of other calves from the same cloned cow.

Supporters of cloning claim that calves like Dundee Paradise will form the nucleus of the country's future dairy herds. And cloned and GM animals could, they say, provide cheap food for future generations. The idea is that 'supercows' will be capable of producing vast quantities of milk, as much as 70 pints (about 40 litres) a day.

However, the history of cloning and genetic modification is full of examples of animal suffering. The first cloned mammal, Dolly the sheep, died prematurely at the age of six in 2003 from a lung infection. She had also been diagnosed with the early onset of severe arthritis, and there are many more examples of miscarriages, ill health and abnormal organs.

Dundee Paradise and her sisters will start producing milk in around two years' time. As the law now stands, there is nothing to stop this going into stores without any form of labelling. (424 words)

from the *Daily Mail*, London, 10.01.07, abridged

1 LOOKING AT THE TEXT

A Do the assignments.

1 Explain why the *Daily Mail* can claim that British supermarkets and the media are doing more to protect consumers than the government is.
2 Point out the difference between Tesco's and Marks & Spencer's policy on GM food.
3 Say why the *Daily Mail* speaks of 'an astonishing failure' on the part of the British government.
4 Describe what role Dolly the sheep plays in the text.

B Use information from the text and any ideas of your own to list the pros and cons of cloning farm animals.

pros	cons
provide cheap food	*unpopular among consumers*

2 WORKING WITH WORDS

A Replace the highlighted words or phrases with a synonym from the text. They are not necessarily in the same order.

1 Supermarkets announced a refusal to sell[1] meat and milk from cloned animals or their young[2].
2 A serious omission in the regulations has allowed such meat to get into supermarkets.
3 This showed beyond a doubt[1] that the genetic alteration[2] of animals has now shifted[3] from science fiction to supermarket reality.
4 Dolly suffered an early death at the age of only six.
5 Exceptionally productive cows[1] will be able to deliver huge amounts[2] of milk.
6 As the law now stands, there is nothing to prevent[1] this milk finding its way[2] into stores without any type[3] of labelling.
7 The UK intends[1] to hold emergency discussions[2] with EU officials over the supervision[3] of food from cloned animals.
8 This calf and ones like her will make up the heart of Britain's future dairy herds.

B Work with a partner and complete the table.

The words in the table are all from the press report. If necessary, use a dictionary to find the missing forms. Please note: for some words, more than one noun is possible.

	Verb	*Noun(s)*	*Adjective*
1	*announce*	*...; ...*	
2	...	*revelation*	...
3		*law; ...*	...
4	*require*	...	
5	...	*investigation*	...
6	...	*approval*	...
7	*produce*	*...; ...*	...
8	...	*threat*	...
9	*apply*	*...; ...*	...
10	...	*modification*	...
11	...	...	*astonishing*
12	...	*infection*	...

C Replace the German words with words that you have found in exercise B.
Be careful with tenses, etc.

1 The ... (*Ankündigung*) shocked supporters of GM farming.
2 Cloned cows are said to be more ... (*leistungsfähig*) than their natural sisters.
3 It is a ... ... (*gesetzliche Auflage*) to get approval for food from cloned animals.
4 The *Daily Mail* ... (*untersuchen*) food from cloned animals in Britain and ... (*aufdecken*) a loophole in the law.
5 The EU ... (*drohen*) to introduce stricter labelling.
6 The findings ... (*erstaunen*) the journalists.
7 Farmers ... (*verändern*) plants by natural selection for thousands of years.
8 Is it true that cloned animals suffer from more ... (*ansteckende*) diseases than natural ones do?

3 WRITING

Write an email to the editor of the *Daily Mail* saying whether you would eat the meat of a cloned animal or its offspring.

Give reasons why or why not. You can use the outline on the right, adding any ideas of your own.

Email

Dear Sir or Madam

I am writing to express my personal opinion on ...

Supporters of GM food point out that ...
The opposite opinion is that ...

Personally, I have nothing against ... because ...

Yours faithfully

(your name)

B The bigger picture

BEFORE YOU READ

A Have you ever made use of FAQs yourself? If so, what did you want to find out?

B Work with a partner. Read this list of FAQs about gene technology. Then, skim the text and match as many questions as possible to the answers. Finally, read the text and match the remaining FAQs.

- a Can we trust the food we eat?
- b How do genetic engineers answer these arguments?
- c How does gene technology differ from selective breeding?
- d What are the ecological arguments against GM crops?
- e What are the medical applications of GM?
- f What is GM food?
- g Why do some people think GM food may be harmful?

3 16

1 ...

GM food is produced from plants or animals whose genes have been changed by scientists. All living organisms have genes written in their DNA. They are the chemical instructions for creating and maintaining life. By changing the genes, scientists can alter the characteristics of an organism. Maybe, for example, we want a plant to produce bigger yields or an animal to produce more meat. Gene technology can do this.

2 ...

A tendency to suffer from many illnesses is 'genetically programmed' by the genes in a person's DNA. By changing the right genes, it becomes possible to get rid of this tendency. At present, such techniques are very promising in the treatment of dementia and diabetes in old age. A further, more distant, medical application of gene technology could be the production of transplant organs.

3 ...

Farmers have used selective breeding to improve crops and animals for thousands of years. They have also created new plants and animals by cross-breeding closely-related species. This is how they produced wheat and mules, for example. However, this was a very time-consuming business. Gene technology delivers much faster and more predictable results because it enables scientists to select a single gene for a single characteristic.

4 ...

Critics argue that we do not know enough about how genes interact with each other and with the environment. This means that we can't say with certainty what the long-term result of any modification will be. They worry that manipulations could accidentally lead to substances being produced that are poisonous, or could trigger allergies. Critics also argue that antibiotic-resistant genes in plants and farm animals could be passed to the micro-organisms that make us ill. If this happens, we might not have effective antibiotic drugs to fight back.

5 ...

They point out that there is no evidence that GM food has any bad effects. They argue that a lot of non-GM food is processed to remove unwanted or toxic substances – and that the regulations that govern GM foods are far stricter than those for non-GM products. Genetic modification might cause new allergies but so, too, can traditional selective breeding. In fact, gene technology may make it possible to rid our food of such problems altogether. Furthermore, GM enables us to improve not only the flavour, texture and shelf life of food, but also its nutritional value.

▶

6 ...

All food is subject to regulation to ensure that it is safe for human consumption. Everybody involved in the production, processing and marketing of food, from farmers through to shopkeepers, must obey these strict rules. Food poisoning is usually caused by poor practice somewhere between the farm gate and the supermarket shelf. But consumers also have a responsibility. One of the main reasons why food poisoning has increased so dramatically in recent years is that we, the consumers, have not stored and prepared food properly in our own kitchens.

7 ...

The green lobby fears that certain genes from GM crops could be passed on to other species, with harmful results. For two reasons, they are particularly worried about genes that make GM plants resistant to herbicides. Firstly, these genes could produce 'superweeds' that are resistant to all but the most powerful herbicides and, secondly, they could destroy insects and birds as their food becomes contaminated. But is this really new? The fact is that 'factory farming' is already playing havoc with nature. On the contrary, bioengineers argue, GM technology offers a real chance of improving the situation in the countryside - GM crops require less of the fertilizers and pesticides that are later washed into the rivers. And because GM crops produce higher yields, they need less land. This could save the few surviving uncultivated habitats.

(607 words)

1 LOOKING AT THE TEXT

A Pick out arguments for and against the use of genetic technology.

What do you think of the arguments? Sort them into three categories: *most convincing* - *quite convincing* - *least convincing*. Then compare your results with others and see what the class thinks.

B Use the arguments and information you have picked out in exercise A to write a comment on the opinion on the right.

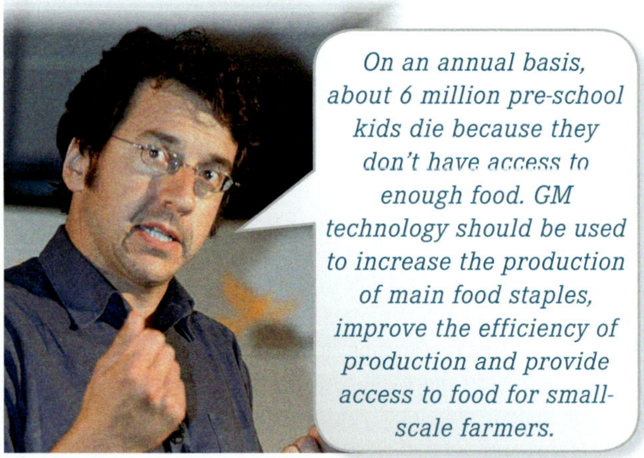

2 WORKING WITH WORDS

A Explain the following in your own words.

1 get rid of sth (*paragraph 2*)
2 more distant (*paragraph 2*)
3 time-consuming business (*paragraph 3*)
4 long-term result (*paragraph 4*)
5 trigger sth (*paragraph 4*)
6 toxic substance (*paragraph 5*)
7 shelf life (*paragraph 5*)
8 be subject to sth (*paragraph 6*)
9 poor practice (*paragraph 6*)
10 play havoc with sth (*paragraph 7*)

B Complete the sentences with the missing prepositions.

1 GM tomatoes, ...[1] example, are produced ...[2] plants that have been genetically modified ...[3] scientists.

2 DNA is often referred ...[1] as 'the blueprint ...[2] life', implying that it contains all the information needed to create life.

3 It is possible to get rid ...[1] a tendency to suffer ...[2] a particular illness by modifying the right genes ...[3] a person's DNA.

4 Critics are worried ...[1] the fact that not enough is known ...[2] how genes interact ...[3] each other ...[4] the long term.

5 The spread ...[1] seeds from GM crops could lead ...[2] the unintentional production ...[3] toxic substances ...[4] the natural environment.

6 Supporters ...[1] GM techniques point ...[2] that selective breeding can also result ...[3] the creation ...[4] new allergies.

7 The genetic modification ...[1] DNA is very promising ...[2] the treatment ...[3] conditions like dementia that occur ...[4] old age.

8 The control ...[1] so-called 'superweeds' depends ...[2] the use ...[3] very powerful herbicides because they are resistant ...[4] conventional methods ...[5] weed control.

3 TRANSLATION

> Übersetzung S. 211

Translate the text into German.

After climate change and the energy crisis, the world is now facing another catastrophe: the death of its bees. Almost 90% of bees have already died in some regions of the USA. In Germany, too, bee numbers have virtually halved in the last 15 years.

Maybe this would be sad rather than bad if bees just made honey. But honey is a by-product of a much more important job. Bees are essential for the pollination - and hence the growth - of over 90 different kinds of fruit and vegetable worldwide. The fact is that without bees, traditional farming is no longer possible.

But what are the causes of this catastrophe? The answer to this question is that nobody really knows. However, possible causes are new insecticides, that may kill bees as well as less friendly insects, air pollution, the destruction of natural habitats and, more recently, even radiation from mobile telephone masts. GM crops have also been named as a possible cause.

According to Manfred Hederer, a German expert, bee deaths could be caused by a highly toxic substance that still has to be identified.

(184 words)

4 LISTENING

3 17 **You are going to listen to an extract from the radio show *Be my guest*. Presenter Judy Patterson is talking to Ruth Morse and Luke Wilson about the use of gene technology (GT).**

A Listen for general understanding. Listen once and say what two main uses of GT are being discussed.

B Listen for detail. Read the ten statements below. Then listen to the extract again and say whether they are true or false. Correct the false statements.

1. Judy asks Ruth whether she thinks GT is a useful development.
2. Ruth is very sceptical about the medical value of GT.
3. Ruth says that GT will definitely enable scientists to produce transplant organs.
4. Luke sees human cloning as a big danger.
5. Ruth describes the excitement about human cloning as 'media hype'.
6. Ruth says that growing GM crops is the only answer to food shortages.
7. Luke agrees with Ruth that GM crops could help feed the world's growing population.
8. Judy thinks one benefit of GM crops is that they produce more food than natural ones.
9. Luke claims that GM crops are responsible for the destruction of the world's bees.
10. Ruth agees with Luke that the death of bees is a big disadvantage of GM farming.

5 SPEAKING

Hold a debate on the motion 'Gene technology is of great benefit to humankind'.

> INFO

- A **debate** is a **formal discussion** on a **clearly-defined motion** before an audience.
- In this kind of debate, there are normally four active **speakers**: the **proposer**, who argues for the motion, and the **opposer**, who argues against the motion, each with **seconds**, who support them with additional arguments or information.
- The debate is led by a neutral **chairperson**, who **a)** introduces the motion, **b)** calls on the participants to speak, **c)** makes sure that the speakers keep to the given time and **d)** calls on the audience to vote for or against the motion at the end of the debate. The chairperson may allow the audience to ask questions at the end.
- Debates make use of **formal spoken language**. In practice this means:
  > avoid very colloquial language
  > use full sentences
  > never 'get personal'
  > use emphasizing and moderating language, as necessary.

1. Choose the speakers and a chairperson.
2. The speakers prepare their 'speeches' for or against the motion by collecting arguments and ideas from the texts in this unit. (Don't forget the translation text!) Add any other information you may have.
3. Hold the debate. The proposer and opposer should speak for about three minutes each, their seconds for about two minutes.
4. Take a class vote for or against the motion at the end.

C Business options

The supermarket of the future

The British call it queuing and the Americans call it standing in line but we all hate it. One solution is to jump the queue or to hurry to the checkout with the fewest people, but soon this won't be necessary. The supermarket of the future will have customer power. The old supermarket trolley will be replaced by a smart cart and the customer will be able to scan in goods while walking around the shop and to pay at the checkout by mobile phone.

The trolley-based system is a computer, scanner and navigation system all in one. It will:

- lead you to what you're looking for using RFID (radio frequency identification device) technology.
- store your buying history and remind you what you bought last time.
- tell you what's on special offer.
- check items off against your personal shopping list, which you can upload to the shop.
- suggest recipes, which can be printed out in the shop or emailed to you.
- show advertisements on the screen.
- keep a running total of how much you've spent.

The total amount to be paid is registered by the self-checkout system, where you can choose to pay by credit, debit or store card, by mobile phone, by fingerprint or in cash. The mobile-phone based system will enable the customer to scan in goods using the phone's camera and then pay at the checkout by electronic means. The software for this is free of charge. (249 words)

1 LOOKING AT THE TEXT

Finish the following sentences with information from the text.

1 If smart carts and mobile-phone payment are introduced in supermarkets ...
2 With the help of RFID technology, customers ...
3 Before going to the shop customers will ...
4 If you have no cards or cash on you ...
5 The shop will give you free software to ...

2 A DEBATE

A **Would you like to shop in a hi-tech supermarket? What do you think are the advantages and disadvantages? Brainstorm in groups.**

B **Now form two groups. One group is for hi-tech supermarkets and one is against it. Using your ideas from above, take turns to discuss whether hi-tech supermarkets are a good development.**

D Grammar checkpoint

Here is a grammar quiz on what you have learned in this course. In each case, choose the correct alternative – a) or b).

1 MIXED TENSES

1 The firm **a)** makes | **b)** has been making bikes for over a hundred years.
2 Work on genes a) became | b) has become possible when they discovered DNA.
3 They **a)** publish | **b)** are publishing a new magazine next year.
4 **a)** Did you make | **b)** Have you made back-up copies of these files yesterday?
5 Luke **a)** talked | **b)** was talking to Maria when I arrived.
6 They met after they **a)** have both left | **b)** had both left university.
7 Sarah **a)** is often travelling | **b)** often travels to the US on business.
8 We **a)** aren't going to have | **b)** won't have a holiday this year.
9 I **a)** didn't see | **b)** haven't seen that movie yet.
10 According to the timetable, our train **a)** leaves | **b)** will leave at 10:32.
11 The minister expects the EU **a)** is going to allow | **b)** will allow GM crops soon.
12 We read the documents while we **a)** waited | **b)** were waiting for the meeting to begin.

2 MIXED STRUCTURES

1 Frank has avoided **a)** going | **b)** to go to a doctor for years.
2 Do you remember **a)** seeing | **b)** to see your girlfriend for the first time?
3 Humans can only survive a short time without **a)** drinking | **b)** they drink.
4 Jack **a)** told | **b)** told me that he'd be late for the meeting.
5 If you hadn't called the police, the thieves **a)** had got away | **b)** would have got away.
6 I'm sorry, but stamps **a)** can only bought | **b)** can only be bought at post offices.
7 We **a)** don't have to | **b)** mustn't finish the project this week – next week is fine.
8 The car's OK, but it would be better if it **a)** didn't use | **b)** wouldn't use so much fuel.
9 Somebody at the bus stop told **a)** me the way | **b)** the way to me.
10 I'm sure we **a)** have already seen | **b)** have seen already this film.
11 Frank stopped **a)** buying | **b)** to buy some petrol on his way home.
12 The mechanic **a)** explained | **b)** explained me how to switch on the lights.

3 FORMS OF WORDS

1 You can earn **a)** a lot of | **b)** much money designing websites.
2 The Greens don't seem to like **a)** each other | **b)** themselves very much.
3 Can you lend me **a)** any | **b)** some money, please? – Sure. How much?
4 This project has been **a)** good organized | **b)** well organized.
5 The customs officer spoke to us **a)** friendly | **b)** in a friendly way.
6 We enjoyed **a)** ourselves | **b)** us a lot at the party.
7 Do you think **a)** there is water | **b)** water is on Mars?
8 Do you have to wear **a)** a | **b)** an uniform at school?
9 Please try **a)** not to be | **b)** to not be late.
10 The news **a)** are | **b)** is not very good, I'm afraid.
11 You will find some more **a)** information | **b)** informations on the next page.
12 Joshua's dad doesn't want **a)** him to get married | **b)** that he gets married so young.

Business Topics

The New York Stock Exchange

4 10

Why do we need a stock market?

With the help of the stock market, very large sums of money can be raised in a short time. The general public are invited to buy stocks in a corporation. The corporation can then spend this money on things like expansion, research and development (R&D) and new ventures. If the corporation fails, the stockholders only lose the money they have invested. They are not liable (financially responsible) for any mistakes the company makes - the company is a separate legal entity. Legal action can be taken against the company but not against individual stockholders.

Out of a population of 300 million, 90 million Americans own stocks in American corporations. 80% of these stocks ($25 trillion in 2006) are traded on the New York Stock Exchange (NYSE) in Wall Street. The NYSE is the largest stock market in the world, followed by Tokyo ($5 trillion) and London ($2 trillion) and provides both face-to-face trading on the trading floor and electronic trading 24/7. As the market for stocks is so huge, however, the US stock market is not limited to the NYSE. There is also the NASDAQ (National Association of Securities Dealers Automated Quotation System), a fully electronic trading system which trades for smaller corporations and has a market share of approximately 15%.

What makes people want to buy stocks?

Stockholders are joint owners of the corporation they have invested in and are entitled to a share of its profits in the form of dividends. The general public can also buy and sell stock whenever they wish on the stock exchange. The prices are determined by supply and demand, so stockholders are able to make a profit through speculation. There is also an annual stockholders' meeting where important decisions are made and some stockholders have voting rights at this meeting. There are two types of stock - preferred stock and common stock. Preferred stockholders receive higher dividends but normally have no voting rights. Common stockholders are second in line for dividends but they have full voting rights.

(342 words)

1 LOOKING AT THE TEXT

A Match the two halves of the sentences.

1	The stock exchange enables people	A	for expansion and R&D.
2	Companies can	B	than preferred stockholders.
3	Companies need large amounts of cash	C	are stockholders.
4	Stockholders can only lose	D	for mistakes made by the company.
5	Stockholders are not responsible	E	through dividends and speculation.
6	A large number of Americans	F	is the second largest in the world.
7	The NYSE	G	to invest money in companies.
8	The Japanese Stock Exchange	H	the money they have invested.
9	Stockholders can make a profit	I	is not the only American stock exchange.
10	Common stockholders get less dividend	J	raise money on the stock exchange.

B Do the following tasks using your own words.

1 Identify who can buy stocks on the stock exchange.
2 Explain how the NYSE is different from the NASDAQ.
3 Describe how you can make a profit or a loss by buying stock in a company.
4 Summarize the differences between preferred and common stock.

2 WORKING WITH WORDS

A Find suitable prepositions in the text to fill in the gaps.

When you buy stocks ...1 a company, it gets more capital to spend ...2 expansion and R&D. At the same time stockholders can invest money ...3 a company without being liable ...4 any mistakes that are made. There is an enormous market ...5 stocks in the US but not all companies are entitled ...6 trade ...7 the NYSE and membership is limited ...8 reliable companies.

B Rewrite each sentence from the text so that it contains the words in capitals and has the same meaning.

1 If the corporation fails, the stockholders only lose the money they have invested.
NO MORE THAN
2 Out of a population of 300 million, 90 million Americans own stocks in American corporations.
ONE THIRD
3 As the market for stocks is so huge, the US stock market is not limited to the NYSE.
TOO BIG
4 The general public can buy and sell stock whenever they want on the stock exchange.
FREELY
5 The prices are determined by supply and demand.
DEPEND ON

3 PROJECT

Germany has eight different stock exchanges. In groups research one of these exchanges and compile a fact sheet. Focus on things like market share, turnover and which companies trade on it.

4 LISTENING

4 11 Chloe Dao is the guest speaker at a workshop for young entrepreneurs at a community college in the US. Chloe was seven when she arrived in Houston, Texas as a penniless refugee with her parents and seven sisters but she is now a successful business woman. Here she explains how she started her business.

A Listen to Chloe's presentation and complete the timeline showing the development of her business.

studied fashion in New York		took out loans to open her own store	
	work experience in different companies		...

B Chloe talks about her plans for the future. In groups discuss what you think she should do next.

5 GIVING A PRESENTATION

A Copy the table and put the phrases below under the right heading. Then listen to Chloe's presentation again and add further examples.

Opening	*Outlining the structure*	*Structuring within the presentation*	*Finishing*
It's a pleasure to be here.	*The first part of my presentation will look at ...*	*Now let's look at ...*	*Thank you for your attention.*

1 So to summarize, we've looked at ...
2 Feel free to ask any questions at the end of the presentation.
3 It's been a pleasure talking to you today.
4 Good morning. I work for ... and I'm here to talk to you about ...
5 After that, I will look at ...
6 Does anyone have any questions?
7 I'll start my presentation with ...
8 Let me now turn to ...

B Use the expressions you have collected to give a presentation on one of the following topics.

1 A holiday resort (e.g. who it is aimed at, what activities are available, how expensive it is, etc.)
2 A gym you go to (e.g. location, opening hours, equipment, fees, etc.)
3 Cosmetics (name, target group, price, how they are sold, etc.)
4 A house or housing project (location, use of energy, type of people, age, price, etc.)

How advertisers set the trend

The rise of jeans

Just about everybody in the western world has bought a pair of jeans at some time or other but, until the beginning of the 21st century, conservative America still viewed jeans as clothing for cowboys, manual workers and students. The traditional blue jeans were (and still are) cheap, mass-produced articles often made in low-wage countries and retailing at \$20-\$40 per pair. Office dress codes did not allow denims and there were even court cases in the 1990s against employees who wanted to wear jeans at work. In those days men wore a suit and tie and women wore a blouse and a jacket with matching trousers or a skirt. Denims were unthinkable for formal occasions.

The challenge for the advertisers was clear: How could they make denims universally acceptable and create a huge new lucrative market?

Their strategy was as simple as it was clever. They invented 'premium denim' and used it to make designer jeans. They improved the fit (which had been loose and shapeless) and retailed them at over \$150 per pair. Their best strategy, however, was to persuade celebrities to wear them. In 2000 media stars such as Jessica Simpson and Lindsay Lohan started wearing jeans made by Joe's Jeans and True Religion and since then more new brands (worn by even more stars) have emerged, such as 7 for All Mankind, Rock and Republic and Citizens of Humanity. Household names like Levi Strauß & Co. have lost a large amount of their market share to these new brands. Premium denim is better quality than the mass-produced material and is made in Japan or Italy. Designer jeans are sewn, washed and "distressed" (ripped and torn) in the US, so the manufacturers can respond quickly to changing fashion trends. Nowadays, while a pair of Levi's can still be bought for less than \$20 at Wal-Mart Stores for example, Dolce & Gabbana jeans sell at prices like \$2,995 - and the advertisers have succeeded again.

(326 words)

1 LOOKING AT THE TEXT

Answer the following questions.

1 What sort of people traditionally wore jeans in the US?
2 Explain why traditional blue jeans are so cheap.
3 Where and when could jeans not be worn in the 1990s?
4 Explain how designer jeans are different from the mass-produced article.
5 What strategies did the advertising industry use to create a market for designer jeans?
6 What is striking about the brand names of the designer jeans mentioned in the text?

2 DISCUSSION

A In your opinion, what makes someone pay $2,995 for a pair of jeans? Do you buy designer jeans or are you happy to wear traditional jeans? Explain your answers.

B What other trends have advertisers influenced in society?

Think about one or two examples of products you know (e.g. shoes/handbags/cosmetics) and consider factors such as product, price, place and promotion (i.e. the marketing mix).

3 AN ADVERTISING STRATEGY

A Look at the jeans and the price tags below. How much would you pay for the jeans? Give reasons for your answer.

A $85

B $4,000

C $10.50

B Now choose one of the price tags. In groups come up with a strategy for marketing the jeans which justifies this price.

Think about the advertising strategies from the text, the marketing mix and anything else you think is important.

4 WORKING WITH NUMBERS

A Label what you think the four percentages in the price breakdown of the regular jeans below are and give reasons for your answers.

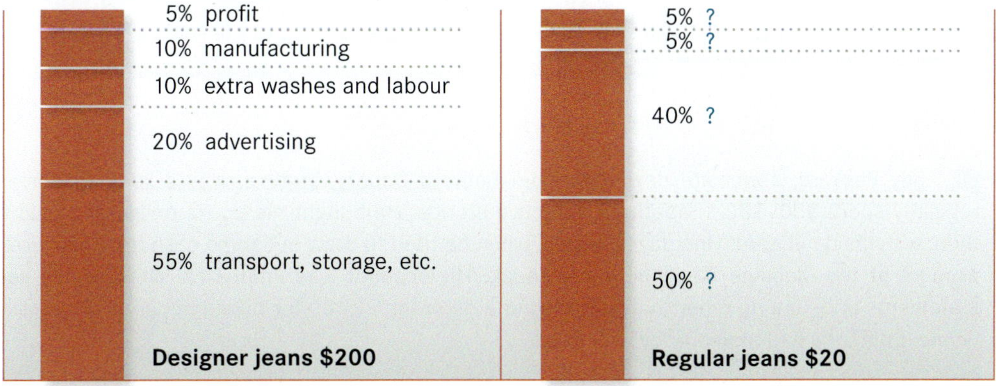

B Now look at the answers in the box at the bottom of the page and convert all the percentages into dollars. Explain which jeans are more profitable for the manufacturer.

5 LOOKING AT OFFERS

Compare the following two offers for jeans.

Ms Tanja Hartmann of Textilgroßhandel Weber in Hamburg would like to place a trial order for 100 pairs of low-priced jeans. Compare the two offers shown thinking about quantity required, unit price, terms of delivery and payment and any other factors you think should be considered. Then explain which offer you would accept and why.

Chinese offer tradetang.org Hangzhou

Email

Dear Friend
We thank you for your very important enquiry. Please see our excellent offer below. We can also arrange shipping (door-to-door). You can pay by PayPal (credit card). This offer is valid for one month from now. We will offer a bigger discount for a bigger order!

Best wishes
Jingyuan Wang

Article	*Quantity*	*Unit price*	*Delivery (days)*
'Champion' jeans	1-50	$7.00	5
	51-100 +	$4.75	8

Answer
50% manufacturing, 40% profit, 5% advertising, 5% transport, storage, etc.

Pakistani offer katif-fashions.com Karachi

Email

Dear Ms Hartmann
Many thanks for your enquiry. We are a major exporter of fashion wear with many customers in your country. This offer is valid for three months and we hope it is to your liking. Should you have any queries, please contact us.

Yours sincerely
Ahmed Iqbal

Article	'Roadrunner' denim jeans
Unit price	$6.50 – $7.50
Terms of payment	Bank transfer for up to 1,000 units; letter of credit (L/C) for more than 1,000 units
Minimum quantity	150 units
Maximum quantity	100,000 units per month
Shipping	Arranged to buyer's warehouse on request
Delivery period	30 days

3

Business Topics

The price of online shopping

4 13

1 Andy Packard, a website developer from Bedford County, Virginia, was a keen reader and regularly spent $50–$60 a month on detective stories. He bought his books online and paid for them with his debit card. One day, however, when he tried to draw out some cash from his current account at the Mainline Bank, he got a shock. His account was empty! He checked his bank statements and, among other things, he found a debit for $1,400 for books bought from Amazon online. Someone had stolen Andy's identity!

2 Andy called Amazon to find out more about the transaction but Amazon wouldn't give him any details over the phone. They would only talk to a customer's bank. However, Andy had a stroke of luck. By mistake the customer service representative at Amazon gave him the first part of the mysterious buyer's email address. Using his internet skills Andy traced the foreign-sounding name to Bangkok in Thailand.

3 Next, using ordinary search engines, Andy discovered the names, home addresses and phone numbers of a group of internet fraudsters. They were website development experts who were abusing their skills to break the law.

4 Andy and the police discovered that the fraudsters were also using 20 other stolen cards to buy goods and have them shipped to the same address in Bangkok. If the hackers had stolen Andy's credit card details, the maximum he could have lost would have been $50. However, they stole his debit card details, so they were able to clean out his current account. Andy's account was frozen for several weeks while the theft was investigated but then the bank and Amazon refunded him his money.

5 Andy had learned his lesson. Here are some guidelines Andy drew up and posted on his personal website:

> Never use a debit card on the internet.
> Always pay by credit card.
> Get the company's phone number.
> Check with directory information to make sure the number belongs to the company.
> Keep all your passwords private.
> Print out a record of your purchase order and confirmation number.

(347 words)

1 LOOKING AT THE TEXT

A Match these sentences to paragraphs 1–4.

A Andy wasn't the only person whose identity had been stolen.
B Amazon refused to tell Andy who had used his account.
C Somebody drew all the money out of Andy's bank account.
D The criminals were professional computer experts.

B Do the following tasks using your own words.

1 Explain what the thief did with Andy's identity.
2 Comment on why you think Amazon would only give details of transactions to the bank and not to Andy.
3 State how Andy was able to find out so much about the internet fraudsters.
4 Explain why it was better for the thieves to steal Andy's debit card details and not his credit card details.
5 Give reasons why it is important to get an online company's phone number and to check it with directory information.

2 WORKING WITH WORDS

Replace the underlined words with a word or expression from the box.

Banking and internet expressions

current | his bank statements | search engines | website development experts | hackers | debit card | clean out | frozen | refunded

1 Internet fraudsters stole money from Andy's personal bank account.
2 Somehow they were able to empty his account.
3 Andy got a shock when he looked at the printed list of his transactions.
4 Andy had a card with all the information needed to access his personal bank account.
5 Andy used online programs like Google to find the criminals.
6 They were professionals who made web pages on the internet.
7 Andy's current account was blocked for a long time.
8 Later the money Andy had lost was given back to him.

3 WRITING A FLOW CHART

Book shopping online is easy if you take it step by step. Put the following steps in the right order to create a flow chart.

1 Go online.
2 You receive an email acknowledgement immediately.
3 Choose your password.
4 Click on 'Proceed to checkout'.
5 Give your email address.
6 Place your order by clicking on the 'Order now' button.
7 Give your name and address.
8 The goods arrive by post.
9 Choose your book.
10 Give your credit card or bank account details.
11 You have 30 days to return the book if you're dissatisfied.
12 Access the online bookshop.

Go online. → [ ] → [ ] → ...

4 A DEBATE

A Look at the speech bubbles.

More and more people shop on the internet nowadays because it's quick and convenient. So what's the downside? Decide if the people below are for or against online shopping. What other advantages or disadvantages can you think of?

1 *There are a lot of empty shops in the city centre now. There just aren't enough customers.*

2 *I hate queuing so it's good that I don't have to worry about that any more. There's also no long search for a parking space now!*

3 *Online shopping is anonymous. You can buy anything – even children can buy goods which are bad for them.*

4 *I work shifts so it's great to be able to buy things 24 hours a day. And the goods are even delivered straight to my door!*

5 *For me, shopping is all about spending time with my friends. The internet is really impersonal.*

6 *I love bargain hunting and it's so easy to compare prices on the internet.*

B Form two groups.

One group is for online shopping and one is against it. Using the arguments above and your own ideas, take turns to discuss whether online shopping is a good idea.

5 PRESENTATION

Prepare a presentation on one of the following topics.

1 a shop that has closed down in your area (what it sells, why it has closed down, etc.)
2 your personal shopping habits (when and where you do most of your shopping, what you buy, etc.)
3 safety measures when shopping online (never use a debit card, make sure the website is protected, etc.)

Global freight forwarding

4 14

How freight forwarding has changed

It used to be so easy in the good old days when goods were produced from beginning to end in one factory. At the beginning of the 20th century at Henry Ford's famous car plant in Detroit for example, raw materials were shipped in and finished cars were shipped out. Up until the middle of the 20th century food, clothing and most consumer durables were still manufactured locally and only transported over short distances.

Nowadays, the massive expansion of cheap transportation using containerization has made it possible to outsource each stage of production to virtually anywhere on the planet. Consequently, manufacturing has moved from high-wage countries in the West to low-wage countries in the East. Shirts bought in New York will probably have been shipped to the US in containers from Malaysia or Hong Kong but will still be cheaper than any locally made product.

Today, the new challenge faced by international freight forwarders is global supply chain management. Companies rarely have their own transport divisions to supply their customers. Instead, they use one of the mega-carriers, such as DHL, UPS or Kühne & Nagel. These huge organizations have hundreds of thousands of employees in offices all over the globe and offer door-to-door, 'time definite' or 'day definite' deliveries of both small and large consignments. Their job is to get the goods to their destination cheaply and punctually. This requires sophisticated logistics and environmentally friendly means of transport to combat global warming. The services of such companies include:

- express delivery service
- air/sea/road/rail freight
- customs clearance
- online tracking and tracing
- groupage consignments (consolidated shipments)
- logistics (e.g. procurement, assembly/manufacturing, warehousing, distribution, installation, after-sales service, carbon footprint)

(280 words)

1 LOOKING AT THE TEXT

A Match the following definitions to five of the services mentioned at the end of the text.

1 transporting goods for different customers in one container
2 managing and coordinating the flow of goods from the point of origin to the consumer
3 getting the goods to the customer by an agreed deadline
4 permission for goods to enter a foreign country after paying taxes and completing other formalities
5 using the internet to find out where goods are or what has happened to them

B Choose the right answer to complete the sentences.

1. Until the middle of the 20th century most western consumers obtained their goods
   a from abroad. b locally. c from America.
2. By the beginning of the 21st century most goods in the West were manufactured in
   a the West. b Malaysia. c the East.
3. Nowadays, manufacturing companies usually
   a transport their goods in their own vehicles.
   b outsource transportation to small companies.
   c outsource transportation to large companies.
4. Modern freight forwarders
   a try to use environmentally friendly means of transport.
   b only use environmentally friendly means of transport.
   c must use environmentally friendly means of transport.

2 WORKING WITH WORDS

Replace the underlined words with expressions from the text.

1. Things were very different in the past.
2. Factories used wood, coal and iron ore to manufacture cars.
3. People bought their electrical equipment, household appliances and furniture locally.
4. Nowadays, goods are made by workers in low-wage countries.
5. Factories can be set up at almost any location in the world.
6. Manufacturers seldom use their own vehicles to deliver goods.
7. Companies now use very complex and technically advanced transport planning systems.
8. The planes, ships, trains and vehicles used should not be dangerous for the environment.

3 DESCRIBING DIAGRAMS

Use the diagram to describe global supply chain management. Begin with:

A manufacturing company in an industrialized country often outsources production to ...

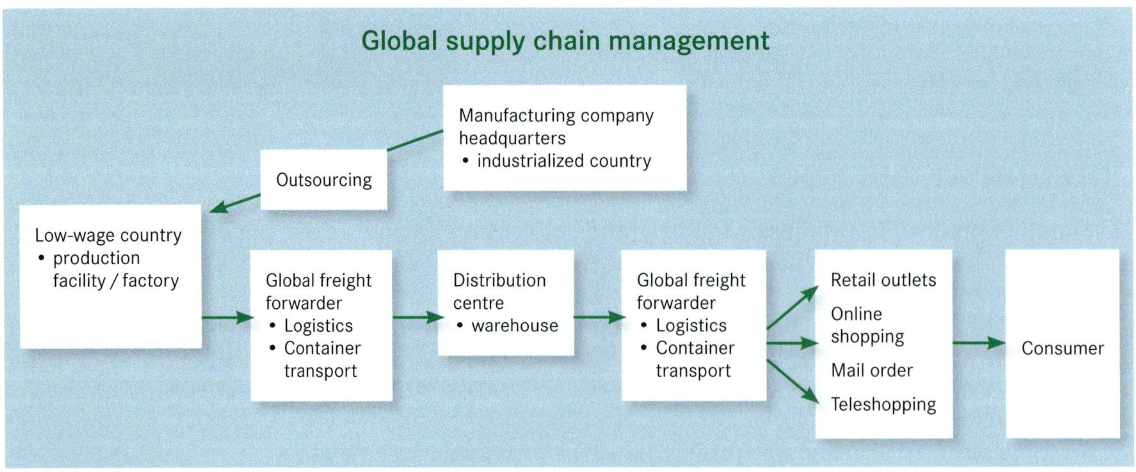

4 TELEPHONING

4 15 Frank Kaiser phones an American company to ask about a spare part for his Harley Davidson.

A Listen to the dialogue and decide whether the following sentences are true or false. Correct the false sentences.

1 Frank wishes to place a new order.
2 The order was dispatched five days ago.
3 Someone called Frank to tell him his order was on the way.
4 Frank needs to sign for the delivery when it arrives.
5 Frank was at home when the driver tried to make the delivery.
6 Frank can arrange delivery by calling 0049 201 8634-0.

B Listen again and complete the useful telephone language below. Then note down any other useful telephone phrases you hear.

1 Your call is being ...
2 Please ... the line.
3 This is Michelle ...
4 I'm calling ... my order for a gas tank.
5 ... me give you the number of the local package centre.
6 I'm sorry, I didn't quite ... that. It's a bad line.
7 Right, I think I've got that. Let me ... it back to you.
8 Is there ... I can do for you?

C Match these sentences to the ones above that can be used in the same way.

1 Good morning. This is James Clark.
2 Just a moment, please.
3 I'd like to speak to someone about a delivery, please.
4 I'm putting you through.
5 How can I help you?
6 I'm afraid I didn't hear that. The line's not very clear.
7 Here's the email address to write to.
8 Okay. Let me just check that. The number is ...

5 ROLE PLAY

Use the language from above to role play the following situations.

1 A from Office Shop Ltd in London phones B at Spedition Walter in Bonn to ask about a consignment of books (order no. GBC/2275 from 4 days ago). B tracks the consignment on the internet and tells A that the goods will arrive tomorrow. Invent further details as appropriate. Finish the call politely.

2 A at Weihnachtsschmuck Thomsen GmbH in Berlin phones B at Decor Incorporated in New York to talk about their order number CD-1225 from 30 days ago. A lets Decor Incorporated know that the Christmas decorations left their premises four days ago and will arrive in New York tomorrow. As the line is bad you have to repeat some of the details. Invent further details as appropriate. Finish the call politely.

Trends in the car industry

Current trend towards electricity

According to Shai Agassi, the CEO of Project Better Place (PBP), a California-based company specializing in personal transportation, electric vehicles are the way forward. His company has come up with a revolutionary new approach to personal mobility and has already found three countries, Denmark, Israel and Portugal, and a major car manufacturer, Renault-Nissan, who are willing to invest in his ideas.

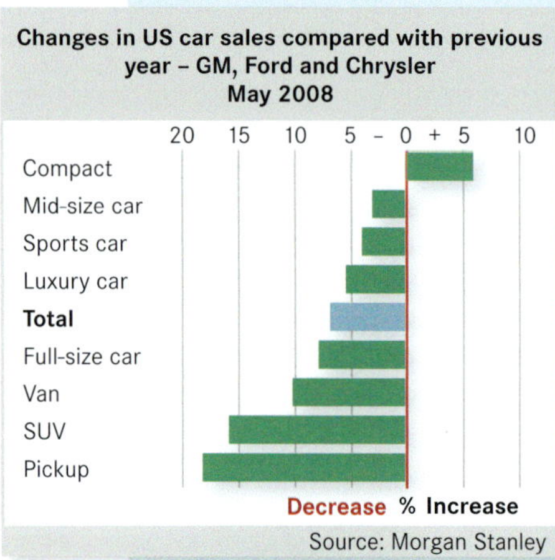

Agassi's vision is to install a network of recharging stations (Electric Recharge Grid) for zero-emission electric cars in these three countries by 2011. The rest of Europe, Asia and North America will be targeted as of 2012. Electric cars are still seen by many as too limited in range but drivers in smaller countries don't have this problem – in a country like Israel, 90% of Israelis drive less than 70 km a day. PBP plans to install up to 500,000 recharging stations there and use batteries that will give a car a range of approximately 160 km and a top speed of 150 kph. All three countries are also pioneering environmentally friendly forms of electricity generation with solar power in Portugal and Israel and wind power in Denmark.

Electric cars are still expensive to buy, so PBP has persuaded the governments of the three countries to offer tax incentives to electric vehicle users. In view of increasing fuel prices, many drivers are now considering either replacing the engines in their cars with electric motors or purchasing a new electric vehicle. In Israel, PBP plans to offer subscription-based ownership contracts for electric vehicles similar to those for mobile phones.

(261 words)

Electric cars – the vehicle of the future?

1 LOOKING AT THE TEXT

Use words from the text to complete the following summary.

PBP has decided to ...[1] in personal mobility and is now trying to persuade people to drive ...[2]. The company is being helped by three countries and a ...[3]. PBP is first going to ...[4] three smaller countries and then the larger markets. In Israel cars don't need to have a long ...[5] and electricity there is generated in an ...[6] way. Drivers of electric vehicles will pay less ...[7] and will pay for the cars in the way they now pay for their ...[8]

2 WORKING WITH WORDS

Rewrite these sentences using the words in capitals.

1 PBP is a California-based company. HEADQUARTERS
2 He has found three countries willing to invest in his ideas. SPONSOR
3 Agassi's vision is to install a network of recharging stations. INTEND
4 The rest of Europe, Asia and North America will be targeted as from 2012. MARKET
5 90% of Israelis drive less than 70 km a day. DISTANCE
6 The governments of the three countries will offer tax incentives to electric vehicle users. LESS

3 TALKING ABOUT GRAPHS

Use the graphs to describe the effect of oil prices on car sales in the US and predict how car manufacturers will react. Begin with:

At the beginning of 2007 oil only cost about $60 a barrel and Americans were still buying SUVs and pickups. By the end of the same year, however the price of oil ...

Useful expressions

to rocket/soar	to rise (rose, risen) very quickly	to survive	to stay alive
a compact	small car	fuel-efficient	with low petrol/diesel consumption
an SUV	sports utility vehicle		
to afford	to have enough money to buy	to adapt to	to change to

4 PROJECT

Form groups and pick a company which manufactures vehicles. Research what different types of technology they have on the market and give a presentation to the class. Consider their approach to costs, convenience and the carbon footprint.

What should your car engine run on?

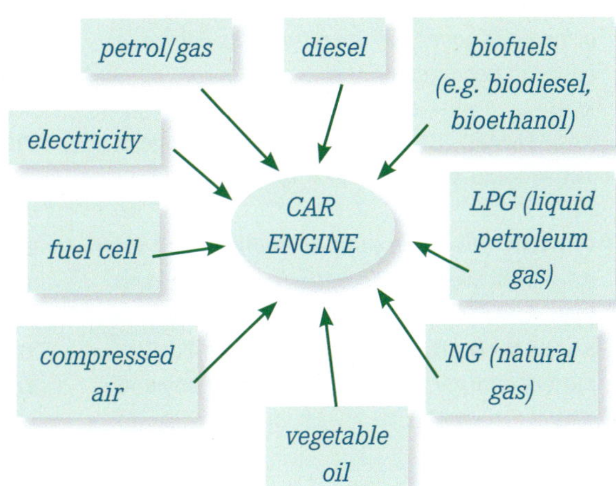

5 OPINION

Give your opinion in 80 – 100 words.

Germany is different to the three countries involved in Project Better Place. Do you think people in Germany would be prepared to drive a smaller, more fuel-efficient car with a shorter range to protect the environment?

6 LISTENING

4 17 Donald Macpherson is a businessman from Edinburgh. Today he's at the Frankfurt Motor Show.

A Listen to the dialogue and complete the following sentences.

1 Donald is interested in ...
2 The car uses the electric motor when ...
3 The car's computer ...
4 According to the salesman's statistics ...
5 The running costs would be less because ...
6 This car is environmentally friendly because ...

B Listen to the dialogue again and write a description of the vehicle. Use the keywords in the box.

spacious | hybrid | quiet | fuel-efficient | 100 mph | running costs | braking system | carbon emissions level

7 MEDIATION

Mediate between a German-speaking visitor to the Frankfurt Motor Show and a car salesman.

VISITOR *Bitte fragen Sie ihn, ob das ein Elektrofahrzeug ist.*
YOU ...
SALESMAN Yes, sir. It's a brand new electric vehicle, which we want to put on the market next year. Would you like to know more about it?
YOU ...
VISITOR *Ja, ich würde gerne mehr darüber erfahren. Können Sie ihn bitten, das Fahrzeug näher zu beschreiben?*
YOU ...
SALESMAN It's a two-seater with a range of 120 km and a top speed of 100 km/h.
YOU ...
VISITOR *Die Reichweite ist ziemlich kurz. Bitte fragen Sie, wo man die Batterie aufladen kann.*
YOU ...
SALESMAN The vehicle has its own 220V battery charger, so you can plug it in anywhere.
YOU ...
VISITOR *Bitte fragen Sie nach der Batterieladezeit.*
YOU ...
SALESMAN It takes 4–6 hours to recharge it 80% and 8 hours for 100%.
YOU ...
VISITOR *Danke. Ich würde gerne wissen, ob man die Batterie einfach austauschen kann.*
YOU ...
SALESMAN This will be possible in the future when there's a network of recharging stations.
YOU ...
VISITOR *Ich möchte gerne eine Probefahrt machen. Wäre das möglich?*
YOU ...
SALESMAN No problem at all! I'll call my colleague and he'll arrange an appointment for you.
YOU ...
VISITOR *Ich bedanke mich.*

The modern workplace

4 18

Amie's blog

What I want to get off my chest right now!!! My company is in the middle of a makeover and this morning my new line manager came in and asked me if I was flexible and interested in a challenge. I suddenly felt scared but told him I was ready for anything and would love to help in any way I possibly could. This is how the conversation went:

LM We really value your work, Amie but I'm sure you've heard from HR that there are going to be some major changes around here.
ME Thanks, I appreciate that. What sort of changes?
LM Well, the CEO has identified a number of departments, including Finance, where performance could be boosted and we think you could help us.
ME [*This is when I got really scared!*] I'm happy to help if I can. What is it you're thinking of?
LM Have you ever thought about teleworking?
ME Not really. What would I have to do?
LM Well, you would work on spreadsheets and access our database online in the comfort of your own home at the times that suit you best.
ME Sounds very interesting [*and I really meant that!*] but my computer's seen better days.
LM Oh, we'd take care of that, Amie. You'd get a new state-of-the-art computer with all the applications you need. We'd upgrade your internet access and you'd also have a dedicated phone line just for company work. We'd pay all the charges for you and equip your office with everything you need, including new furniture. We figure you'd put in about 20–30 hours a week including tele and video-conferencing, which would mean you'd get about the same paycheck as you do now. Think it over. Take your time and let me know how you feel about it.

I'm in shock! What does this mean? Can anybody out there tell me what's going to happen to me?

The writing's on the wall but you're lucky because you've effectively been offered a new job. Grab it with both hands! Soon the company will outsource your department and you'll be out on your ear!

Charleeze, Cleveland, OH

I'm a teleworker and although I'm glad I've got a job, it isn't all plain sailing. For example, all my breaks are unpaid and I have to take the kids to kindergarten before I can get started. At 3 and 4 they're too young to understand that I'm sometimes at work when I'm at home (which means I often work at night). My husband pulls his weight with the housework but I sometimes feel isolated and stressed out. I miss my co-workers and long to get out of the house and see other people!

Beth, Pascagoula, MS

At OGS telework makes sense. Our teleworkers don't have to worry about travelling long distances, bad weather or rising fuel prices. They choose their own working hours and workplace – some work in the garden, others by the pool or in a coffee shop. We log the number of hours they put in online and pay them accordingly. Meetings at OGS take the form of online video and telephone conferences and we put on interesting team-building seminars in Helsinki for co-workers from all over the world. Our employees are also trained to pick out different types of customers and colleagues and learn how to get on with them. Check out the link below with a demo of our teleconferencing tool and then take up this new challenge, Amie – you'll never regret it!

Reeta Ovaska, CEO of Ovaska Global Systems, Finland

(597 words)

1 LOOKING AT THE TEXT

Look at Amie's blog and the three comments and then copy and complete the table with the pros and cons of teleworking for both the employer and employee.

	Pros	*Cons*
Time	*[e.g. flexible]*	
Place		
Transport		
People		
Money		

2 WORKING WITH WORDS

Rewrite these sentences.

A phrasal verb has two parts - a verb (e.g. put) and a particle (e.g. on). Find the 6 phrasal verbs in Reeta Ovaska's comment and then use them to replace the underlined words in the following sentences.

1 Last weekend I worked two hours' overtime.
2 The company always has a party for the children at Christmas.
3 We went on a special course so we could recognize eight different personality types.
4 We learn to have a friendly relationship with customers.
5 Look at this website. It's really interesting!
6 I think you should accept your line manager's suggestion and become a teleworker.

3 OPINION

A What about you? Would you like to work from home? Discuss with a partner explaining your reasons.

B Now post your own comment on the blog.

Explain what you would do if you were Amie. Begin with *If I were you, I'd / I wouldn't ...*
Write 80 - 100 words.

4 LISTENING

4 19 Amie is taking part in a video conference.

A Copy the graph shown below. Now listen to the meeting and plot a graph of the company's sales figures over the last 12 months.

B Use your graph and other details from the meeting to write a summary in German.

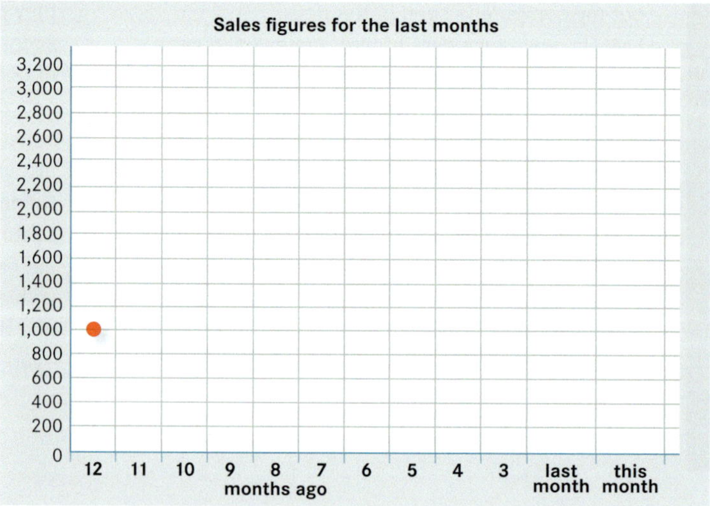

5 LOOKING AT LANGUAGE

Match the following expressions used at the meeting to the right headings from the box.

Introducing a speaker | Asking for clarification | Asking to speak | Summarizing | Returning to a topic | Giving permission to speak | Starting a new topic | Refusing/delaying permission to speak

1 As I was saying, ...
2 Can I come in on that?
3 Can you give us any information on ...?
4 Could I just make a point here?
5 Could we come back to that later, please?
6 Could we move on to ...?
7 Do you mean that ...?
8 For this I'll hand over to ...
9 Go ahead.
10 Let's get back to ...
11 The next topic on the agenda is ...
12 To sum up ...
13 We've just heard that ...
14 Yes, please do.

6 ONLINE CONFERENCING

Online conferencing is another alternative to video meetings. When the leader of the online conference gives a participant the microphone, it appears next to the participant's name and that participant can make a contribution. All participants can respond by clicking on other buttons.

Which buttons would you use in the following cases?

1 After a joke
2 To ask a question
3 At the end of a presentation
4 To leave the conference for a few minutes
5 To write a message to one of the participants

7 DISCUSSION

What do you think of video and internet conferencing? Is it better or worse than meeting face to face? Discuss in groups and then report back to the class.

1 *Video conferencing is difficult. If the person's not in the room, you are not as aware of their body language and it's not easy to sense how they really feel about something.*

2 *I love teleconferencing. It's really practical because it means that I never get stuck in traffic on the way to a meeting!*

Global giants

1 LOOKING AT GRAPHS

In 2004 Richard Parsons, the chairman of the board of the American Time Warner Corporation, said: *We've gone from a place where 200 years ago your market was where you could walk in a day, to a place where your market place is the whole globe ...*
However, the world market is dominated by a small number of countries and corporations.

A Use the lists to guess the names of the six biggest exporting countries and corporations shown.

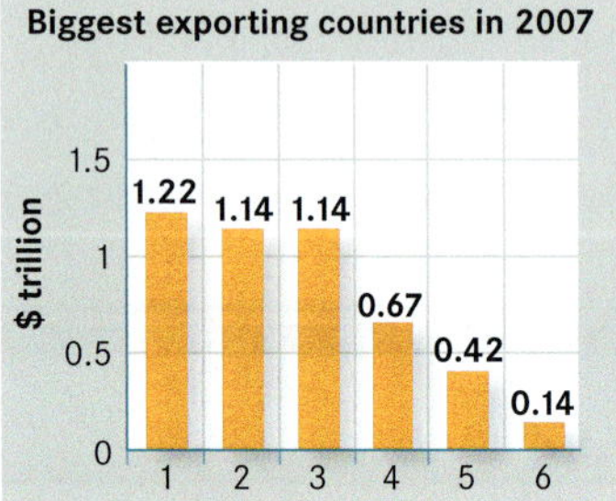

Biggest exporting countries in 2007

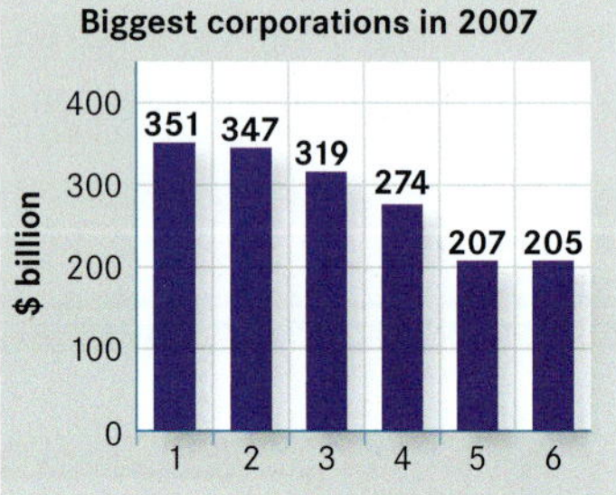

Biggest corporations in 2007

Countries
China | Germany | India | Japan | United Kingdom | USA

Corporations
BP (British)
Exxon Mobile (American)
General Motors (American)
Royal Dutch Shell (Dutch)
Toyota Motor (Japanese)
Wal-Mart Stores (American)

B Choose one of the countries or corporations and find out about the goods/services it exports or sells. Present your results to the class using charts, tables or photos.

2 GROUP WORK

Find out more about emerging markets.

Three of the world's six richest people in 2007 were from India, which is one of a group of rapidly industrializing countries known as the emerging markets. The three billionaires are:

> Lakshmi Mittal, ArcelorMittal, $45 billion, steel
> Mukesh Ambani, Reliance Industries Limited, $43 billion, petrochemicals
> Anil Ambani, Reliance Anil Dhirubhai Ambani Group, $42 billion, energy and communications

Use the internet to prepare a presentation on emerging markets with special reference to India and the billionaires mentioned or write 80-100 words on the same topic.

Think about:
> technological advances
> natural resources
> skills and cost of labour
> infrastructure
> anything else you think is important

> **INFO**
> In 2007 Warren Buffet ($62 billion, USA, investments), Carlos Slim Helu ($60 billion, Mexico, communications) and Bill Gates ($58 billion, USA, energy and communications) were the richest people in the world.

4 20

An emerging market

A Standing in an onion field in a village outside the city of Pune in India, Chandra Patil can check the weather report and find out how much onions cost at the local market, all on his mobile phone, for 175 rupees (€2.80) a quarter. The service is being offered by Reuters, better known for offering news and financial information.

B Pune is one of the world's most hi-tech cities. Wireless internet is available across the city and students from its top-ranked universities jam the streets on motorbikes and then compete for jobs at many of the West's biggest hi-tech companies once they have graduated.

C The city is a model of the tech-led renaissance of the subcontinent's economy and is also home to Tata Motors – the owner of Jaguar and Land Rover, two of Britain's most famous car companies.

Indian labour force by occupation	
agriculture	60%
industry	12%
services	28%

D Amit Mehra of Reuters says: "We have anecdotal evidence that farmers who cannot read ask their sons or daughters to read the text messages to them. And within a year we hope to move to a voice-based service. We have examples where people have made as much as £3,500 by getting the right information in time. There's a customer who gets a message that it will rain, so he deploys less labour. Another got a message that the supply of onions would go down so he held back his crop and made a $350 profit in one month."

(235 words)

Adapted from *The Sunday Times*, 2008

3 LOOKING AT THE TEXT

A Match four of the following headings (1–5) to the paragraphs of the text (A–D).

1 An exciting, modern environment
2 Industry is booming
3 The price of onions is rising
4 Mobile phones even help people who can't read and write
5 Mobile phone services are cheap by European standards

B Write a summary of the text using the keywords in the box.

mobile phone network | weather forecast | price of crops | latest technology | illiterate farmers

4 WORKING WITH WORDS

Rewrite each sentence from the text so that it contains the words in capitals and has the same meaning.

1 Chandra Patil can check the weather report on his mobile phone. USE
2 Students from its universities jam the streets on motorbikes. FULL OF
3 The city is also home to Tata Motors. LOCATED
4 Farmers who cannot read ask their sons or daughters to read the text messages to them. HELP
5 A customer got a message that the supply of onions would go down. SHORTAGE

5 OPINION

In today's global economy not all companies outsource. Germany's 'Mittelstand'*, made up of successful, medium-sized companies, provides the backbone of the German economy.

*translated as small and medium-sized companies

1 *German industry has skilled workers, an excellent research climate and reliable suppliers. Our employees have job security and profit-sharing. 70% of our sales are from exports.*

Anne Schmidt, head of a German 'Mittelstand' company

2 *This is a family-owned company with a long-term approach. We don't sack people or outsource production to maximize profits and shareholder value here! We also invest three times as much in research and development as they do abroad.*

Dieter Kampmann, a works council chairman

3 *The German motor industry is comprised of thousands of small companies making high-end products and developing advanced technologies. In Britain everything is outsourced. As a result, there is no core competence.*

Robert Schumann, Federation of German Industries (BDI)

4 *We have outsourced production and have global centers in India, Costa Rica and China for our customers all over the world. They want service 24/7 at the lowest possible price and this is what we deliver. There is no alternative in the 21st century.*

Maria Rodriguez, a sales executive at an American software company

A Look at the opinions above. Which are positive about outsourcing and which are negative?

B Group the following ideas from the speech bubbles into features of 'Mittelstand' services and production and features of outsourced services and production.

high-end products | job losses | job security | long-term approach | low prices | maximize profits | more investment in R&D | profit-sharing | 24/7 service | shareholder value

C Discuss in groups. Who do you agree with most and why?

6 PRESENTATION

Now choose a local 'Mittelstand' company and prepare a presentation about its services and attitude towards its workforce.

Who benefits from the EU?

4 21

The EU labour market

"I hate London", says Joanna (20), fighting back the tears. "I was attacked on the way home from work last night and my handbag was stolen. Luckily, I didn't have my papers in it. That would never have happened where I come from." Joanna is from a small town in Poland called Rodaki and has been living in London for two years. She works as a waitress in a restaurant in Hammersmith, a vibrant, multicultural part of West London. "It's all right here in the daytime," she says, "but at night it gets really bad. I'm only here because of the money." In London Joanna earns four times more than she would at home.

When Poland and nine other countries joined the EU in 2004, the British government expected about 13,000 Eastern Europeans to come to the UK in search of a job. In fact, half a million migrant workers streamed into the country and 64% of them were Polish. Whole sectors of the UK economy are now dependent on immigrant labour, including the hotel business, catering, agriculture and the building trade. "Don't believe for one minute that I would be doing this at home," she says. "I was going to work as a primary school teacher but the pay's not good. Here I can afford to buy some of the nice things in the shops." When she shows me her flat, I get a shock. It's tiny and she shares it with another Polish girl. "I'd like a bigger place but it's out of the question. The rents here are astronomical." Joanna spends most of her money on rent and the rest on food, the occasional trip back home and learning English. "We all go to English lessons," she says. "Everyone needs English these days and I've got to think of my future. One day I'll go back home and teach English at a university." But for the time being Joanna intends to stay in London, which now has a Polish newspaper (Polish Express) and a Polish radio station (Radio Orla). The local shops also stock Polish beer (Tyskie) and Polish bread and goulash.

Joanna is one of the many immigrant workers in the UK who earn the minimum wage of £5.50 per hour. In 2007 the average hourly wage for Polish workers was £7.40 as compared with £11.40 for their British counterparts. The arrival of cheap foreign labour has kept inflation down in the UK and Polish workers enjoy an excellent reputation for being well educated, hard working and reliable.

(423 words)

1 LOOKING AT THE TEXT

A Are the following statements true or false? Correct the false statements.

1 Joanna is not used to living in a big city.
2 Joanna has a well-paid job in London.
3 Joanna intends to return to her native country.
4 Most Polish workers only earn the minimum wage in the UK.
5 Polish workers are well respected in the UK.

B Make two lists: the disadvantages of living in London for Joanna and the advantages of using Polish labour for UK employers.

2 WORKING WITH WORDS

Find words in paragraph 2 of the text (When Poland ...) to replace the underlined words.

1 Ten new countries <u>became members of</u> the EU at the same time.
2 A lot of people went to the UK <u>because they were looking for</u> work.
3 Many employers use <u>workers from other countries</u>.
4 <u>The farming industry</u> is a major employer of overseas workers.
5 Joanna <u>has enough money</u> to buy more expensive things.
6 Joanna's flat is <u>very small</u>.
7 The <u>money she pays for her flat</u> is more than half of her income.
8 The local supermarket <u>sells</u> Polish food.

3 GROUP WORK

A Look at the graphs below. What do they tell us about migrant workers from the countries which joined the EU in 2004?

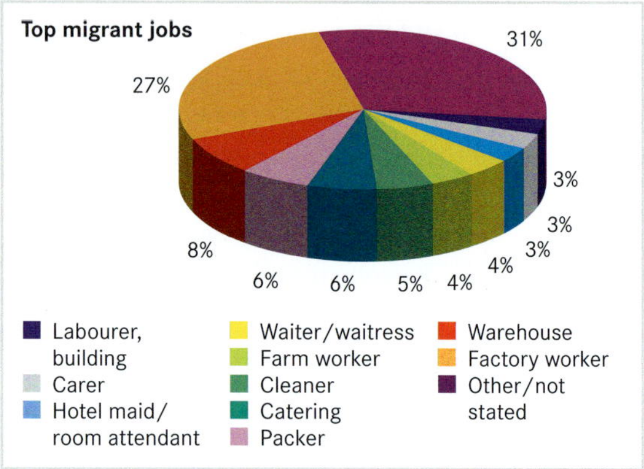

Source: Home Office/DWP

B Research in groups.

Statistics suggest that the number of workers moving from the new EU states to the UK is decreasing and some migrants have already left to go back home. What do you think could be the reasons for this? Think about the pound/euro exchange rate, the economic situation in the new member states, labour restrictions in the EU and anything else you can think of.

C Draw up a profile of an immigrant community in Germany or any other EU country.

4 MEDIATION

On 29 June 2008 Nokia opened a new €60 million mobile phone manufacturing facility in Jucu in Romania and officially closed its plant in Bochum the next day. 2,300 jobs were lost at the factory and 2,000 more at Nokia's German suppliers. The Romanian factory has a workforce of 500.

Mediate between a German works council representative visiting Jucu and the local mayor.

WCR *Bitte danken Sie ihm, dass er bereit ist, sich mit uns zu unterhalten.*

YOU ...

MAYOR I'm pleased to meet you and will tell you anything you would like to know.

YOU ...

WCR *Wusste er, dass durch die Eröffnung des Werks in Jucu 4.300 Menschen in Deutschland ihre Arbeitsplätze verloren haben?*

YOU ...

MAYOR I didn't know the exact figures but I'm sorry to hear that. We have 500 new jobs here and we hope that fewer Romanians will need to leave their families to look for work abroad now. Since 1989 2.5 million Romanian workers have left the country. That's one in ten of the workforce.

YOU ...

WCR *Das wusste ich nicht, aber kann er mir sagen, wie viel ein rumänischer Nokia-Arbeiter im Schnitt verdient?*

YOU ...

MAYOR About €450 per month gross. This is very good for Romania, where the minimum wage is € 114 per month. What did you earn at Nokia?

YOU ...

WCR *Brutto ca. 3.150€. Weiß er, dass es bei uns viele Härtefälle gibt? Einige meiner Kollegen mussten sogar ihre Häuser verkaufen, weil beide Ehepartner arbeitslos wurden.*

YOU ...

MAYOR That's tragic for those concerned but we Romanians are used to hardship. Here 25% of the population live below the poverty line. Did you know that before Nokia arrived Jucu used to be a village with no school and no doctor? Many houses still have outdoor toilets and no running water.

YOU ...

WCR *Das war mir nicht bekannt, aber geht er davon aus, dass Nokia in Jucu bleiben wird? Wir dachten auch, dass Nokia in Bochum bleibt, aber jetzt ist das Werk geschlossen worden.*

YOU ...

MAYOR We now have new roads, schools and hospitals. Even if Nokia shuts down after five years, the benefits to our community will remain.

YOU ...

5 DISCUSSION

A Do the following tasks in pairs.

1 Discuss how Nokia has helped the community in Jucu, Romania. Use ideas from the dialogue and any other benefits you can think of.

2 Consider how the closure of the factory affected Bochum. Do you know of any similar closures in Germany? To what extent did these affect the local community?

B Now form two groups.

Company closures are a fact of life. There is no alternative.

One group agrees with this statement, the other group disagrees. In class, conduct a debate on the topic considering different viewpoints. At the end, vote to decide which arguments were most convincing.

Women in business

4 22 Smashing the glass ceiling

1 In 2002 Ansgar Gabrielesen, Norway's trade and industry minister, 'shock bombed' his country's business world. He announced that 40% of the members of the boards of directors of Norwegian companies listed on the stock exchange would have to be women by 2005. At that point in time, 470 of the 611 companies listed did not have even one female board member and women only accounted for 6% of all board positions - affirmative action was needed. The day after his announcement the Norwegian press 'named and shamed' the worst companies, including Norway's largest company, Aker Solutions. Norway changed the law so that companies had to comply with Gabrielesen's decision or close down and it worked - there are more successful women now and businesses are making even larger profits. Marit Anderstet is one of Norway's new generation of high-flying female executives. In her blog she explains how she rose to a position of responsibility.

About me

2 I'm 35, married with two gorgeous kids (3 and 1) and I live in Oslo. My husband's in the oil business and I've been a member of the board of directors at a major Norwegian company for two years now. When I'm not at work or looking after my kids, I also give lectures at schools and universities on something that's very close to my heart - Female Future.

Female Future

3 This was set up by the Norwegian employers' association to get more women onto company boards. Big companies were told to 'pearl dive' for three rising junior female employees and they found me! The scheme was really great. I had a mentor at the company (I chose her myself) to help me understand how the hierarchy worked and what I needed to do to handle it. We had seminars once a month (Female Friday) and once every six months (Future Friday). At these seminars I learned to network, which was a skill I certainly didn't have before. In the past, Norwegian men would get top jobs by going on hunting and fishing trips together. It was enough to be a member of the 'old boys' club' and meet in places where women never went. We now have our own networks and we've also set up www. linkedin.com. This is a professional networking site, so if a company needs a woman for a top job, they can access LinkedIn and pick the person they need.

Life-work balance

4 This is a big thing in every woman's life and there's more to me than just my job! I don't want to spend 12 hours a day in the office just so people think I'm working. I tell people who do that to go home because they've got their life-work balance wrong. Norwegian law gives mothers a year's maternity leave and the right to go home for two hours a day to breast feed their babies. It gives men six weeks' leave too, so make sure you use it! (488 words)

1 LOOKING AT THE TEXT

A Choose the right answer to complete the sentences.

1 Ansgar Gabrielesen is a
   a businessman.
   b bomber pilot.
   c politician.

2 In 2002, 141 major Norwegian companies
   a had no women at all.
   b had women directors.
   c wanted 40% of their employees to be women.

3 As a result of the new law many Norwegian companies
   a closed down.
   b fired all their male directors.
   c appointed more women directors.

4 Marit Anderstet is
   a one of Norway's new female directors.
   b the director of a Norwegian school.
   c on the board of directors of an oil company.

5 Female Future helped Norwegian companies to
   a teach women to pearl dive.
   b find female talent.
   c teach women to be like men.

6 In the past Norwegian directors
   a met informally to decide on top jobs.
   b never met women in their free time.
   c only gave top jobs to women who could hunt and fish.

7 Nowadays, Norwegian women
   a can hunt and fish.
   b use networking sites to get top jobs.
   c can only get a top job by using a networking site.

8 Life-work balance means
   a it's illegal to spend 12 hours in the office.
   b home life is just as important as work.
   c men can take a year off work to look after a baby.

B Match four of the following seven headings to the paragraphs of the text.

End of 12-hour working day | Norway bans hunting and fishing | No place for workaholics | Men sacked to make way for women | Not just a housewife | End of male domination | New generation of company directors

2 WORKING WITH WORDS

A The following words and expressions in the text (1–5) are not meant literally. Match them to five of the explanations (A–H) given below.

1 a glass ceiling
2 to shock bomb
3 high-flying
4 to be close to someone's heart
5 to pearl dive

A to attack unexpectedly
B athletic
C dangerous
D to be very important
E extremely successful
F to steal
G an invisible barrier
H to look for talent

B Now use the expressions to replace some of the words in the following passage.

We stayed at a hotel full of very successful company executives. When I talked to one of them, he said the board of directors was all men – another company with a hidden barrier for women! However, he said that some of the directors were hoping to look for some capable women to join the board soon.

3 OPINION

Here are some of the emails Marit has received on her blog.

Email **1**

Hey Marit
Keep up the good work! Over here in the US we still have a male-dominated culture and I'm on what we call the 'mommy track'. I used to be in middle management at a local insurance company but when I got pregnant with my first child, the message was clear. I had no future in the company so I quit my job and now I'm at home. I love my kids but I'd sure like to find a company without a glass ceiling!
Abigail
Biloxi, Mississippi

2 Email

Dear Ms Anderstet
I am insulted at the idea that a woman should get a top job just because she is a woman. I have never heard such nonsense in my whole life! Jobs should be awarded on merit and not on the basis of the applicant's gender.
Margaret Fortescue, UK

Email **3**

Hi Marit
You've been fighting old men in Norway but let me give you a young man's view. Today's young man is different – at least he is in the UK. My partner and I (we aren't married) share all the responsibilities for our family and household. By this I mean work and the household chores. We both have part-time jobs and earn about the same. Things are changing and I don't think we need new laws to make things happen.
Ken (and Kath), London

A **Who do you agree or disagree with most? Explain your opinion in two or three sentences.**

B **Write an email to Marit in which you explain why you think it's a good or bad idea to introduce a 40% female quota for the boards of big companies. Write 80 – 100 words.**

4 DISCUSSION

A **Comment on the following statistics published by Fortune Magazine. What do they tell us about the gender gap?**

The highest paid men and women in America in 2007	
Bob Nardelli, $133.7 million *Former Chairman, President and CEO of Home Depot*	**Zoe Cruz, $30 million** *Co-President of Morgen Stanley*
Tom Freston, $78.3 million *Former President and CEO of Viacom*	**Susan L Decker, $25 million** *Executive Vice President, Finance and Administration of Yahoo*
Terry Semel, $71.7 million *Former Chairman, CEO of Yahoo*	**Irene B Rosenfeld, $19.2 million** *CEO of Kraft Foods*

B **In the past many jobs and professions were seen as typically male or female.**

1 Make two lists of typical men's and women's jobs and compare them in terms of pay, prospects and power.
2 To what extent do you think the situation has changed – are there still typical jobs for men and women? Do you know anyone who works in a field dominated by the other sex?
3 Having considered the questions above, to what extent do you think we need affirmative action to ensure that women get a fair chance of success?

10

Business Topics

A multicultural entrepreneur

4 23 My travel diary

After forking out a little over €100 for a return flight, I'm one of 156 passengers crammed into a modern jetliner. I'm on my way from Dortmund to Edinburgh courtesy of Sir Stelios Haji-Ioannou, better known as the founder of easyJet. (He advises people to call him Stelios because no one can pronounce the rest of his name.) I have a clear conscience about the environment because I paid €3.39 for carbon offsetting. According to Stelios, this money will go to a hydroelectric power plant in Ecuador. I also feel less worried about losing my suitcase (which cost me €18 to check in), because I paid €11.99 for travel insurance. All this cost the princely sum of €111.04. Well, actually it came to a bit more because right at the very end I had to pay another €7.50 for using my credit card. With all these extras my heart was in my mouth when I finally clicked on 'Book now' but luckily, that last click didn't cost me any more. The email I got one second later confirmed this. But who is the man behind the machine? Here's some of my research into the person who enabled me to go on a round trip of over 2,300 km for just €118.54. (211 words)

Stelios

Full name	Sir Stelios Haji-Ioannou
Born	February 14, 1967
Place of birth	Athens, Greece
Nationality	British
Residence	Monaco
Occupation	'serial entrepreneur'
Net worth	€1.6 billion
Marital status	single, no children
Education	Doukas High School in Athens, London School of Economics, City University, London

You were born into a wealthy shipping family and worked in the family business for a while. Why did you choose to get away from that?

I suppose I get bored easily. I am a workaholic; I can't sit still. I also fought very hard in the early years to get rid of the 'daddy's boy syndrome'.

How do you decide what to invest in?

I look for things that are price elastic, which means if you reduce the price, people are likely to consume more. Essentially, there are four areas:

- it has to be value for money
- it has to be innovative
- it has to be fun
- it has to have mass appeal

What charity plans do you have?

I'm very keen on scholarships. I think educating people can really change lives. It's the old proverb: if you give a man a fish, you feed him for a day. If you teach him to fish, you feed him for a lifetime.

Adapted from *The Prague Tribune*

1 LOOKING AT THE TEXTS

Match the following sentence halves.

1 The €3.39 the author pays will help to
2 He paid an extra €7.50 because
3 Stelios' business empire
4 He studied at
5 He feels happiest when
6 His company's products are for
7 He believes in
8 He believes in helping people

A the man on the street.
B to help themselves.
C he's working very hard.
D the value of a good education.
E protect the environment.
F two universities in London.
G he paid by credit card.
H has a total value of €1.6 billion.

2 WORKING WITH WORDS

Use words from the text to complete these sentences.

The last time I flew on a low-cost airline the fare came ...[1] £47. I think it was value ...[2] money because a scheduled flight would have cost me at least £100. Of course I wouldn't have been crammed ...[3] a narrow seat just 29 inches wide. Anyway, I think we'll soon have to fork ...[4] more for a flight because air fares are likely ...[5] rise in the near future. In fact, they might get rid ...[6] cheap flights altogether.

3 OPINION

Look at the interview and the list of easyGroup companies in the box below and explain why you think Stelios has chosen to sell these particular products and services. Write 80–100 words.

easyJet | easyInternetcafé | easyCar | easyValue | easyMoney | easyCinema | easyBus | easyHotel | easy4men | easyJobs | easyPizza | easyMusic | easyCruise | easyMobile | easyWatch | easyVan | easyOffice

4 COMPARING HOTELS

Accommodation is very expensive in London. Look at the two hotel adverts and then do the following tasks.

1 Draw up a list of the differences between the two hotel rooms offered. Use categories such as location, amenities, meal(s), price, etc.
2 Describe the sort of person you think would be prepared to stay in the easyHotel room without a window.
3 Explain which room you would choose for a short stay in London and why.

CITY HOTEL, Central London (near Regent's Park)
Price includes continental breakfast. All rooms are centrally heated with washbasins, one bathroom to every four bedrooms, radio, TV and telephone. There are tea and coffee making facilities in every room. Double or twin beds • £54 per room per night

easyHotel
London, South Kensington
Small room (no window), £25 per room per night; small room (with window), £55 per room per night
Close to Hyde Park and with fast access to Heathrow
All rooms: double bed (made up with towel, sheets, duvet and pillows), private shower room with WC, washbasin and shower, flat screen TV (remote control available from reception – £5 for 10 channels for 24 hours), air conditioning
The housekeeping service is an optional extra at a cost of £10. Should you want your room cleaned and the linen changed, please book with reception.

5 WORKING WITH WORDS

Match the following expressions from the hotel descriptions (1–6) to the definitions (A–F).

1 a washbasin
2 tea and coffee making facilities
3 access
4 a pillow
5 housekeeping
6 an optional extra

A room cleaning
B a sink
C transport links
D something which does not happen automatically
E you rest your head on this in bed
F a kettle, cups and saucers

6 BOOKING A HOTEL ROOM

Email

Good morning

Further to our phone conversation, I would like to confirm my reservation of a single room for Ms Julia Price for three nights from Wednesday 12 August to Saturday 15 August. The price of the room should include full breakfast and internet access. Ms Price will be arriving late on Wednesday, will the reception still be open?

I would also like to book a conference room for 8 people on Friday 14 August. Could you please let us know when the restaurant is open for lunch so we can plan the meeting?

Thanks and best wishes

Greg Scott

A The hotel receptionist took notes on the phone to Julia. Look at them and correct any mistakes.

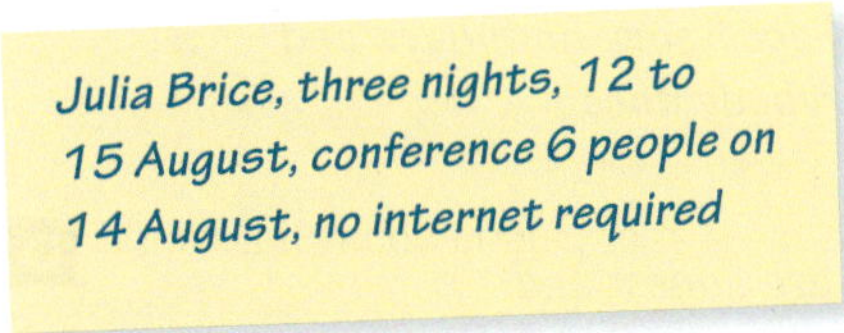

B Now write your own email.

You would like to book a room in one of the hotels from exercise 4. You need a double room for two nights and a meeting room for a day's conference. You need to know if there is parking space for your car. Invent any other details as necessary.

Fakes and imitations

1 WRITING

A Work in groups.

Make a list of counterfeit products sold on the black market (clothes, sunglasses, DVDs etc.) and then compare the prices of the fakes with the original prices. Present your findings to the class.

B Write a description of the graph. Begin like this:

In 2008 the most frequently pirated items were ...

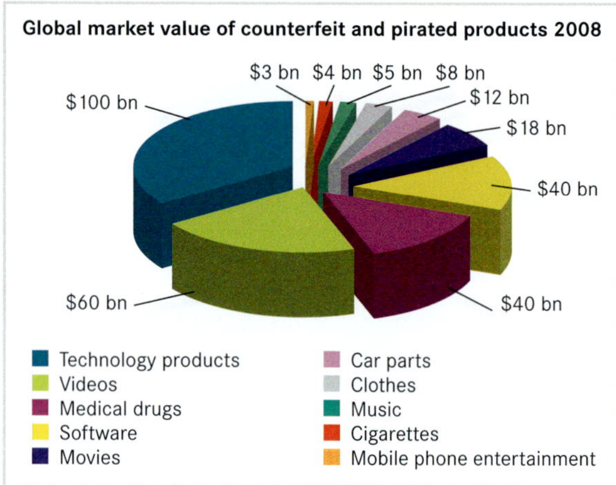

Source: www.havocscope.com

2 DISCUSSION

A Who says what? Look at the speech bubbles and match them to the statements below.

1 It's a crime to manufacture, sell and buy fakes.
2 I have to break the law to survive.
3 It's quite normal to have counterfeit goods.
4 The fashion companies don't need the money anyway.

A *In Hong Kong they come up to you in the street and say, "Missy – you want copy bag? Grade A copy bag?" OK, it's a fake but it's a must-have accessory nowadays and everybody does it.*

B *I love my fake Gucci glasses. $300 for the genuine article is just too expensive but I like to look good. And no one can tell me that Gucci and friends are short of cash so where's the problem?*

C *We are honest and admit that our bags are imitations. I moved here from Senegal and I support my family with the money from my Gucci bags. It's better than stealing or selling drugs.*

D *Anyone who intentionally purchases a counterfeit article is a thief and should be punished. Turnover of the genuine article suffers and jobs are lost. 10% of the world's products are fakes or imitations and this costs the global economy as much as $415 billion per year.*

B And what about you? Have you ever bought imitations or do you always buy the genuine article? Discuss in class and explain your reasons.

Free trade zones

When 74-year-old Lucía Cruz suddenly fell ill and died in agony shortly afterwards, she was victim no. 17. Victim no. 21 was Carlos Umanzor, aged 60. He was in hospital recovering from a heart attack and received some cough medicine for a cold. He was dead a few days later. In one respect, they were the lucky ones because most of the dead were children. Both the adults and the children had taken a poisonous cough syrup unwittingly provided by the Panamanian health care system. It contained diethylene glycol instead of glycerine. Both taste sweet but diethylene glycol is used in antifreeze and costs less than half the price of glycerine, which is used in drugs, food and toothpaste.

The Taixing Glycerine Factory is in the small town of Hengxiang, China. The locals call this area 'chemical country'. The factory's website shows a tall, futuristic-looking building but in reality it only has one storey and is made of brick. It is here that the fake glycerine began its long, complicated journey to Panama. On its way, it repeatedly received false certificates of analysis – in fact it was never analyzed – and passed from Hengxiang to Shanghai, to Barcelona, to the Colón Free Trade Zone near the Panama Canal and finally to Panama City, where government officials used it in 260,000 bottles of cough syrup. The final death toll is estimated at 365.

There are many cases like the one in Panama and in many of them, the counterfeit goods (including such items as spare aircraft parts and car brake linings) pass through free trade zones, such as Colón or the Jebel Ali Free Trade Zone in Dubai (UAE). Here there are minimal regulations, no tax is paid and the goods do not technically enter the host country at all. For this reason they can easily be transshipped to hide their origins and are particularly attractive to sellers of counterfeit goods.

(319 words)

3 LOOKING AT THE TEXT

Do the following tasks using your own words.

1 Explain what the cause of death was for Lucía Cruz and Carlos Umanzor.
2 Give your reaction to the statement "they were the lucky ones".
3 Find reasons in the text which suggest that the poisonous chemical was intentionally substituted for the safe substance.
4 Name the other products mentioned which are frequently counterfeited and explain the possible consequences.

4 WORKING WITH WORDS

Use words from the text to complete the sentences.

Many of the ...1 of fake drugs are too poor to buy ...2 or go to hospital. In this case the Panamanian authorities ...3 killed the poor people they wanted to help. No one knew the cough syrup was ...4 because it ...5 sweet. When the chemical passed through the Colón ...6, the importer didn't have to pay any ...7 on it because the chemical didn't enter the ...8. Places like Colón are very ...9 to criminals because they can ...10 where a drug has really come from.

5 OPINION

A Look at the material below.

How serious do you think the problem of counterfeit goods is? Should it be illegal to buy fakes as well as to sell them and how do you think this could be enforced?

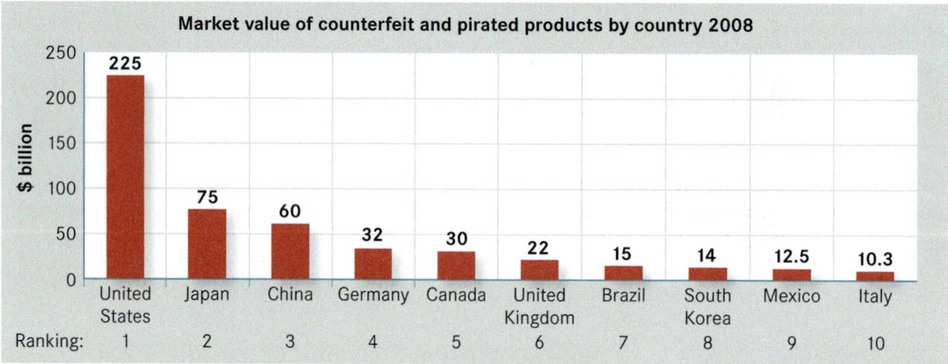

Source: www.havocscope.com

You're on holiday in Italy, home to fashion houses like Prada and Gucci, so of course it's tempting to get your hands on the latest bag or a cool pair of sunglasses. But beware! You will find many street vendors who are more than happy to sell you counterfeit goods for extremely low prices. Sounds great? Well, it is until the police catch up with you. Under Italian law, anyone caught buying fakes can face a fine of €3,333 to €10,000, and that goes for tourists too. So, start saving up now and buy the genuine item!

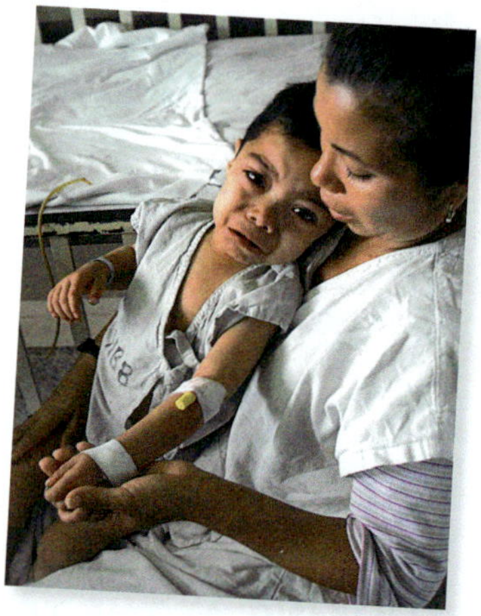

B Discuss your ideas with a partner. Then work with another pair and describe your partner's opinion.

C Now present the results of your discussions to the whole class.

Has your opinion changed as a result of your discussions? Write 80 - 100 words to say whether buying fakes should be made illegal or not.

12 Stem cell research

Singapore's $350 million biomedical science park

Why stem cells?

4 25

Stem cell therapy has been described as having awesome potential and as the body's biological self-repair kit. It is seen by many as the cure for cancer, Alzheimer's, Parkinson's disease and other major illnesses. Stem cells are 'master cells'. They are the body's building blocks and are used for growth, repair and regeneration. We all have stem cells but the most powerful ones are in embryos (fertilized eggs) because they can be used to regenerate virtually any part of the human body. Cloning technology is based on the use of embryonic stem cells, which so far has only been used to clone animals (e.g. Dolly the sheep), but could in theory be used to clone humans.

Stem cell research is highly controversial and rejected by many in the West on moral, ethical or religious grounds. They believe that fertilized human eggs are the beginning of human life and using them for research or therapy is the same as abortion. For this reason the US federal government, for example, has taken a negative view of stem cell research and it has been extremely hard to obtain government (US federal) funding and permission for treatment in the West. As it is also very expensive, there are now a number of government-backed initiatives outside the US and Europe, in particular in Thailand, Singapore, South Korea and China, which have attracted westerners seeking stem cell therapy.

It is against this backdrop that, in 2004, California launched a huge initiative to pump $3 billion of Californian tax-payers' money into human embryonic stem cell research over the next decade. Scientists are flocking to California, where universities and research centres expect to spend $831 million of taxpayers' and donated money on 800,000 square feet of new laboratory space to house 2,200 scientists. Stanford University, for example, is to receive $44 million to build a $200 million stem cell centre. It is hoped that this initiative will receive money from private enterprise and boost California's weak economy. American scientists are also optimistic that stem cell research will eventually receive federal funding. (343 words)

1 LOOKING AT THE TEXT

Choose the right answer to complete the sentences.

1 Major diseases
  a can be cured using stem cell therapy.
  b will be cured using stem cell therapy.
  c might be cured using stem cell therapy.

2 Stem cells can be used to
  a regenerate sheep.
  b regenerate human organs.
  c fertilize eggs.

3 In the US the federal government
  a is against stem cell therapy.
  b funds all stem cell therapy.
  c has banned stem cell therapy.

4 Stem cell therapy treatment outside the US is subsidized by
  a the US government.
  b foreign governments.
  c pharmaceutical companies.

5 Some of the money for stem cell research in California comes from
  a scientists.
  b the federal government.
  c the residents of California.

2 WORKING WITH WORDS

A Replace the underlined words with words from the box.

abortion | clone | controversial | disease | embryo | ethical | reject | stem cell

Nowadays, using <u>cells from which others can be grown</u>[1] is <u>something which makes many people very angry</u>[2] because people fear that they will be used to <u>make exact copies of</u>[3] humans. Others say that using <u>a fertilized egg</u>[4] to treat an illness is morally the same as <u>intentionally killing an unborn baby</u>[5]. They <u>are strictly against</u>[6] this type of biomedical research and say that their reasons are <u>based upon their moral principles</u>[7]. However, scientists still hope to treat <u>serious illnesses</u>[8] like cancer and Alzheimer's in this way.

B Rewrite each sentence from the text so that it contains the words in capitals and has the same meaning.

1 Stem cell therapy is seen by many as the cure for cancer. BELIEVE
2 Cloning technology could, in theory, be used to clone humans. POSSIBLE
3 It has been extremely hard to obtain government funding. GOVERNMENTS
4 Thailand, Singapore, South Korea and China have attracted westerners seeking stem cell therapy. WANT
5 It is hoped that this initiative will receive money from private enterprise. INVEST

3 LISTENING

4 26 Listen to a radio interview in which Tom Stokes explains how he overcame a serious illness.

A Make notes on the following key words while you listen.

symptoms | treatment | life today | hospital bill

B Listen again. Are the following statements true or false? Correct the false statements.

1 Tom became seriously ill after he retired.
2 Five million Americans have a heart transplant every year.
3 Tom's cousin worked at a hospital in Thailand.
4 Tom flew first to Israel then to Thailand.
5 Tom was treated with his own blood.
6 Tom was treated with embryonic stem cells.

C Explain in your own words why Tom chose to be treated in Thailand and not in the US.

D Would you be prepared to travel to a foreign country and pay to get medical treatment (e.g. stem cell therapy, dental treatment, laser eye surgery, cosmetic surgery)?

List the advantages and disadvantages in 80 - 100 words.

4 OPINION

Catholic priest: **1**
Human life is sacred. It is not for Man to interfere with God's will.

Director of stem cell treatment centre in Bangkok: **2**
Our patients pay a reasonable price for first-class treatment with an 80% success rate and no mortalities.

Son whose father has Alzheimer's: **3**
The government should do everything in its power to save lives by investing in embryonic stem cell therapy.

Anti-abortion activist: **4**
I want to protect life, not destroy it. The big pharmaceutical companies just want taxpayers' money so they don't have to risk their own!

German stem cell specialist working in Singapore: **5**
We love Germany but over here we have facilities the German government isn't prepared to pay for, so for the time being we intend to stay.

A Match five of the following eight captions to the speech bubbles.

1 Embryonic stem cell research will eventually cure all illnesses.
2 We would prefer to work back home.
3 Government funding would be used as insurance against big losses.
4 Taxpayers' money should be used to finance embryonic stem cell therapy.
5 Stem cell research is only acceptable in special circumstances.
6 We have found a profitable niche in the market for medical treatment.
7 Only 20% of our patients die after stem cell treatment.
8 We have no right to decide over life and death.

B What do you think? Is stem cell research ethical? Discuss in groups giving reasons for your opinions.

Files

FILE 1 Unit 3, exercise 3C, p. 58

Debbie

Personally, you would prefer the romantic comedy, and you particularly dislike science fiction, but you will watch it if that's what Dave wants. And anyway, you will accept the majority decision. You agree with Dave that a late movie would be a bad idea.
You would like to eat something before the film as you haven't had anything since breakfast.

role card

FILE 2 Unit 4, exercise 3, p. 71

Road commuter

You want much better public transport *before* congestion charging starts. You know that as things are, public transport can only carry up to 13% of commuters like you. You cannot afford to pay the daily congestion charge – (you know the figure for London is about £15 per day) – and you do not want to fight to find a place on public transport buses or trains every day.

role card

FILE 3 Unit 8, Focus, p. 105

1B | 2A | 3B | 4B | 5B | 6B (2008) | 7B | 8C

FILE 4 Unit 7, Culture Check, p. 98

a) EA | **b)** LA | **c)** NA | **d)** NA | **e)** EA

FILE 5 Unit 4, exercise 3, p. 71

City councillor

As the chairperson of the meeting, you must make sure everyone speaks and help the meeting come to an agreement. You think that congestion charging is necessary, but you worry that it will cause terrible problems. You need the government money to help develop public transport, but you can only provide the city's 50% of the money from congestion charges. The city has no other spare money.

role card

FILE 6 Unit 3, exercise 3C, p. 58

Dave

You are more interested in driving than anything else today, and you don't really mind which film you go to – although you would quite like to see *Journey to the Stars*.
However, you don't want to go to a late showing because you know your dad will be worried about the car. (You want to make sure he will lend you it many, many more times!)

role card

1 Nationwide general trends

U.S. crime statistics

According to the FBI's Preliminary Semiannual Uniform Crime Report, the nation experienced a 1.8 percent drop in violent crime and a 2.6 percent drop in property crime during the first six months of 2007 compared to the same period in 2006.

■ Crime by region

Percent change by geographic region

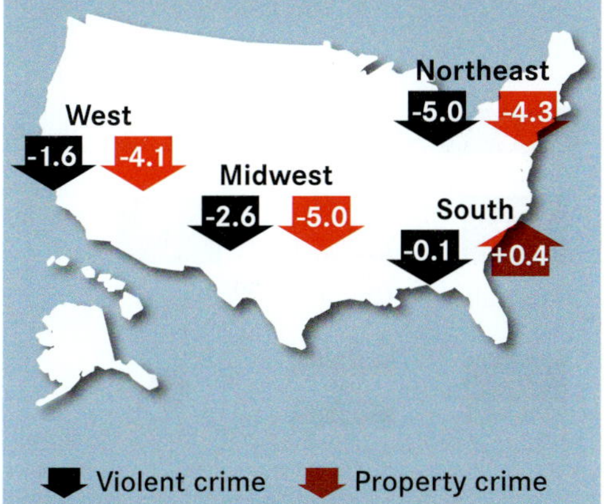

■ Violent Crime

Each of the violent crime offense categories decreased nationwide from January 2007 when compared to the corresponding months in 2006.

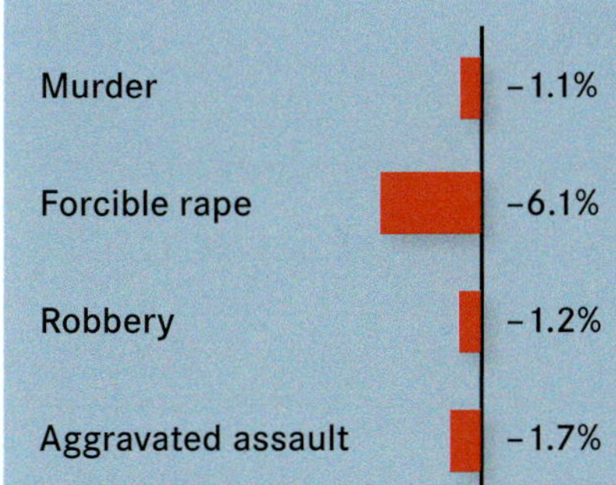

Source: U.S. Department of Justice, Bureau of Justice Statistics, http//www.ojp.usdoj.gov/bjs/

2 Violent crime

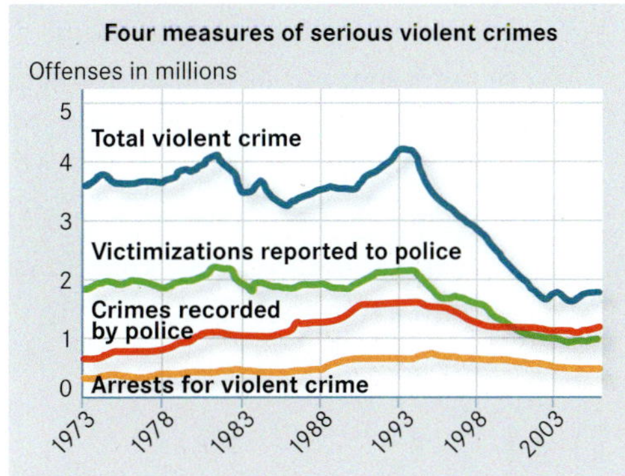

Serious violent crimes are 1) rape, 2) robbery, 3) armed assault and 4) homicide

Source: National Crime Victimization Survey

3 Homicide

4 Crime reported to the police

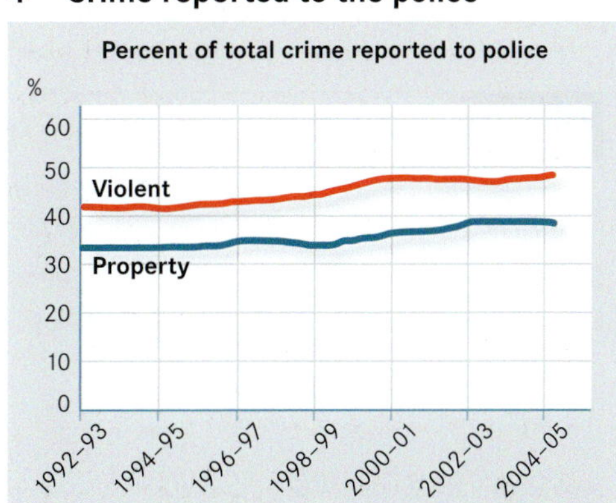

Source: http//www.fbi.gov/headlines/uscrimestatistics

FILE 8 Unit 3, exercise 3C, p. 58

Steve

You helped yourself to several things from the fridge before Claire arrived, so you're not hungry at all at the moment. Of all three films, you would much prefer to see *Pirates of the Caribbean*. (You have seen all the other 'Pirates' films at least twice each.) However, you know that Claire doesn't like *Pirates of the Caribbean*, and you don't want to have an argument with her. On the other hand, if you can quietly persuade Steve, then Debbie will probably agree with him – and then Claire will have to agree too.

role card

FILE 9 Unit 4, exercise 3, p. 71

Businessperson

You fear a large loss of trade, especially as car parking is already expensive in the city centre and the costs of running the business are high. You want the city councillor to understand clearly that if you have to close down, the city will lose your business rates (= local taxes). There may be thousands more like you.

role card

FILE 10 Unit 7, Focus, p. 95

Australia

China

the EU

Germany

India

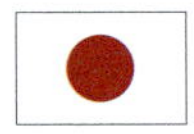
Japan

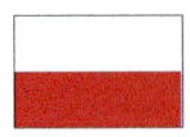
Poland

the UK

the USA

FILE 11 Unit 3, exercise 3C, p. 58

Claire

You would much prefer *One Night in New York*, and you think *Pirates of the Caribbean* is very silly – definitely something for 13-year-old boys. You are hungry and would quite like to eat before the film.

role card

FILE 12 Unit 4, exercise 3, p. 71

Government transport official

You accept that congestion charging will cause problems for some people but believe that it must be part of the answer to the congestion problem. You can provide government money to help develop public transport if the city council provides the other 50%.

role card

Appendix

REZEPTION

Lesen schwieriger Texte

Texte werden zu unterschiedlichen Zwecken gelesen. Manchmal braucht man nur zu wissen, worum es geht, dann reicht in der Regel ein aufmerksames Überfliegen des Textes. Oft müssen gezielt Informationen herausgesucht werden, dann kommt es darauf an, die richtigen Schlüsselwörter zu finden. Will man sich gründlich mit einem Text auseinandersetzen, um z. B. Fragen zu beantworten oder einen Aufsatz dazu zu schreiben, ist gründliches, möglicherweise zweimaliges Lesen erforderlich.

Grobverständnis: Sich einen schnellen Überblick über einen Text verschaffen

Manchmal werden Sie im Buch aufgefordert, einen Text schnell zu lesen, um das Thema grob zu erfassen.

1. Schritt: Suchen Sie nach Anhaltspunkten, die Ihnen Aufschluss über den Textinhalt geben: Titel und Zwischenüberschriften, fett gedruckte Wörter, Bilder und Bildunterschriften.

2. Schritt: Sind Sie noch unsicher, lesen Sie die ersten und letzten Sätze jedes Absatzes. Bleiben Sie nicht an Einzelwörtern, schwierigen Zitaten usw. hängen.

Suche nach Einzelinformationen im Text

Bei vielen Textverständnisfragen oder Aufgaben vom Typ *True or false* geht es darum, schnell bestimmte Informationen im Text zu finden und nicht jedesmal den ganzen Text neu zu lesen.

1. Schritt: Suchen Sie den Text nach Schlüsselbegriffen für die gesuchten Informationen ab. Geht es etwa um die Meinung des Autors zu einem bestimmten Thema, halten Sie nach Wörtern wie *think, believe, opinion* usw. Ausschau. Geht es um Informationen zu einem Thema, rufen Sie sich ein paar Schlüsselbegriffe in Erinnerung, nach denen Sie Ausschau halten. Manchmal hilft es, sich den gesuchten Begriff als gedrucktes Wort vor dem geistigen Auge vorzustellen.

2. Schritt: Gehen Sie falls nötig mit dem Finger die Zeilen entlang, während Sie suchen. Wenn Sie sich wie oben beschrieben vorbereitet haben, springen Ihnen die gesuchten Begriffe sofort ins Auge.

Detailverständnis: Gründliches Lesen

Lesen Sie nicht einfach drauflos. Ein paar einfache Schritte helfen Ihnen, den Text besser zu verstehen, ohne sich in Details zu verlieren.

1. Schritt: Der erste Schritt sollte darin bestehen, sich ein grobes Verständnis vom Textinhalt zu verschaffen (siehe oben). So werden Sie unklare Stellen besser in den Gesamtzusammenhang einordnen können. Es ist hilfreich, sich die wichtigsten Stichwörter kurz zu notieren. Zu dem Text *A step too far* auf S. 136 etwa könnten Sie nach kurzem Überfliegen aufschreiben: *The text is about the death penalty in the United States, in particular about the first woman who was executed.*

2. Schritt: Machen Sie sich die Struktur des Textes bewusst. Wo ist die Einleitung? Welcher Teil enthält die Hauptinformationen, und wie sind sie aufgebaut (Zwischenüberschriften, Absätze usw.)? Achten Sie auf Strukturwörter wie *only, but while, that's why, while, however* usw., mit denen der Verfasser seine Argumentation gliedert.

3. Schritt: Lesen Sie den Text nun aufmerksam. Notieren Sie sich Schlüsselstellen, z.B: *Karla Faye Tucker - first woman to be executed in the US; executed in Texas on 3 February 1998; case attracted a lot of interest - some felt because she was white, attractive and showed remorse (married a priest and became a Christian); many pleas for clemency to Governor Bush from different groups and even from the Pope.* Schlagen Sie Wörter beim ersten Lesen nur nach, wenn die Bedeutung des ganzen Satzes an ihnen hängt. Oft lässt sich die wesentliche Bedeutung durch den Kontext erschließen.

4. Schritt: Notieren Sie sich den Textinhalt in strukturierter Form, etwa einer Mind Map oder einer Liste (Themen, pro/kontra). Fügen Sie auch Formulierungen hinzu, die Ihnen später helfen, sich in eigenen Worten über den Textinhalt zu äußern. Schlagen Sie jetzt das notwendige Vokabular nach. > Note Making S. 201, Mind Mapping S. 202

Umgang mit unbekannten Vokabeln

Fragen Sie sich bei neuen Vokabeln immer, ob sie für das Verständnis des Zusammenhangs unbedingt notwendig sind. Nachschlagen kostet Zeit und hilft oft nicht beim Verständnis des wirklich Wichtigen.

Erschließen der Bedeutung aus dem Kontext

> Ein Wort, das unbekannt scheint, kann z. B. mit einem anderen, Ihnen bekannten Wort verwandt sein (Ableitungen wie *aggressor* von *aggressive*). Oder das Wort hat einen bekannten Wortstamm und einen angehängten Wortteil, mit dessen Hilfe Sie die Bedeutung erkennen können (*formal - **in**formal, clockwise - **anti**clockwise, change - change**able**, stupid - stupid**ity***). Manche Wörter haben Ähnlichkeiten mit einem deutschen Wort (vgl. etwa *initial* und „Initialen“, *potential* und „potenziell“).

> Sind Sie sich immer noch nicht sicher, kann der Satzzusammenhang Aufschluss geben. Machen Sie sich zunächst die Wortart bewusst: Suchen Sie nach einem Substantiv? Wofür steht das gesuchte Substantiv wahrscheinlich - für ein Gebäude? Eine Person? Handelt es sich um ein Adjektiv, das die Situation näher beschreibt oder jemanden charakterisiert?
Schauen Sie sich den folgenden Absatz an und versuchen Sie die Bedeutung der fett gedruckten Wörter aus dem Zusammenhang zu erschließen:
*Business is bad at the moment and we don't expect it to **rally** for at least a year. All the signals are very **inauspicious**, I'm afraid.*
Auch wenn man *rally* und *inauspicious* nicht kennt, kann man aus dem Kontext erschliessen, dass *rally* ein Verb ist, das eine positive Entwickling beschreibt und *inauspicious* ein Adjektiv mit negativer Bedeutung ist

Umgang mit dem einsprachigen Wörterbuch

Machen Sie sich mit Ihrem Wörterbuch vertraut, so dass Sie die Symbole, Abkürzungen und die Lautschrift verstehen und die Hilfen, die vorne und hinten im Wörterbuch oder auf Zusatzseiten angeboten werden, nutzen können. Auf der folgenden Seite sehen Sie ein Beispiel eines typischen Wörtbucheintrags.

Wörterbucheintrag

uncountable = unzählbares Nomen

North American English = Aussprachevariante

Wortart

Erste Bedeutung

Verweis auf einen anderen Eintrag

alarm /ə'lɑːm; *NamE* ə'lɑːrm/ *noun, verb*
■ *noun* **1** [U] fear and anxiety that sb feels when sth dangerous or unpleasant might happen: *'What have you done? Ellie cried in alarm.* ◇ *I felt a growing sense of alarm when he did not return that night.* ◇ *The doctor said there was no cause for alarm.* ⇨ note at FEAR **2** [C, usually sing.] a loud noise or a signal that warns people of danger or of a problem: *She decided to* ***sound the alarm*** (= warn people that the situation was dangerous). ◇ *I hammered on all the doors to* ***raise the alarm.*** – see also FALSE ALARM **3** [C] a device that warns people of a particular danger: *a* ***burglar/fire/smoke alarm.*** ◇ *The cat* ***set off the alarm*** (= made it start ringing). ◇ *A car* ***alarm went off*** *in the middle of the night* (= started ringing). **4** = ALARM CLOCK: *The* ***alarm went off*** *at 7 o'clock.* **IDM** **a'larm bells ring/start ringing** if you say that **alarm bells are ringing**, you mean that people are starting to feel worried and suspicious
■ *verb* **1** to make sb anxious or afraid **SYN** WORRY: [VN] *The captain knew there was an engine fault but didn't want to alarm the passengers.* [also VN **to** inf] ⇨ note at FRIGHTEN **2** [VN] to fit sth such as a door with a device that warns people when sb is trying to enter illegally

Zweite Bedeutung

countable = zählbares Nomen

idiom = Redewendung

Synonym

verb/noun + *'to' infinitive* = zusammengesetzter Ausdruck, in dem das Verb von *to* + Infinitiv gefolgt wird

verb/noun = zusammengesetzter Ausdruck aus Verb und Nomen

> Notieren Sie sich alle Wörter, deren Bedeutung Sie suchen, und schlagen Sie dann alle hintereinander nach.
> Lesen Sie nicht den gesamten Eintrag, sondern beschränken Sie sich auf die Verwendung Ihres Stichworts in der gesuchten Wortart (z. B. Sie suchen *alarm* als Verb, also ignorieren Sie den ersten Teil des oben stehenden Eintrags). Den entsprechenden Abschnitt mit allen zusammengesetzten Ausdrücken und den Beispielsätzen, die Ihnen helfen zu unterscheiden, in welchen Zusammenhängen welche Bedeutung zutrifft, müssen Sie dann allerdings gründlich lesen.
> Schauen Sie sich auch die Einträge in der unmittelbaren Umgebung Ihres Stichworts an, um eine Vorstellung von dem Wortfeld zu bekommen.
> Notieren Sie sich die passende Bedeutung, damit Sie sie nicht wieder vergessen.

Lernen neuer Vokabeln

Es gibt verschiedene Möglichkeiten, Vokabeln zu lernen – suchen Sie sich die, die Ihnen am besten liegt. Eines gilt jedoch für alle Methoden: Wörter prägen sich am besten ein, wenn man nicht nur das Stichwort aufschreibt, sondern auch noch dazugehörige Ausdrücke, Synonyme, Gegenteile, verwandte Wörter und Verwendungsbeispiele, evtl. auch Aussprachehinweise. Besonders wichtig sind zusammengesetzte Ausdrücke. Dazu gehören auch *phrasal verbs* (*set about, put off* usw.). Der Eintrag für das Stichwort *pay* könnte z. B. so aussehen:

pay (noun)	–	*Bezahlung, Gehalt, Lohn*
payslip	–	*Gehaltsabrechnung*
pay day	–	*Zahltag*
pay-off	–	*Abfindung*
pay (verb)	–	*zahlen*
pay for sth	–	*etw bezahlen*
pay off	–	*auszahlen*
pay as you go (phone)	–	*Prepaid(-Handy)*

Natürlich brauchen Sie nicht gleich komplette Wörterbucheinträge aufzuschreiben. Überlegen Sie sich jedoch, welche Ableitungen Ihnen zu dem neuen Wort schon bekannt sein könnten oder in welchem zusammengesetzten Ausdruck es Ihnen begegnet ist. Lassen Sie Platz für spätere Hinzufügungen, so dass die Einträge nach und nach „wachsen".

Karteikarten: Sie benötigen Karteikarten und einen Karteikasten mit mehreren Abteilungen. Schreiben Sie das englische Wort mit den dazugehörigen Ergänzungen auf eine Seite einer Karteikarte und die deutschen Bedeutungen auf die Rückseite. Sobald Sie ein Wort wissen, wandert es von der ersten in die zweite Abteilung des Karteikastens. Die Wörter in der zweiten Abteilung schauen Sie sich in größeren Abständen nochmal an, um diejenigen, die Sie wissen, dann in die dritte Abteilung fürs Langzeitgedächtnis abzulegen. Was Sie nicht wissen, kommt zurück in die erste Abteilung, die Sie sich möglichst oft anschauen sollten.

Vokabelheft: Wenn Sie im Unterricht neue Vokabeln mitschreiben wollen, bietet sich ein Vokabelheft an. Benutzen Sie ein zweispaltiges Heft, damit Sie eine Spalte leicht bedecken können. Gestalten Sie das Lernen weniger schematisch, indem Sie die Seiten, die Sie lernen wollen, zufällig auswählen und ab und zu mal Deutsch-Englisch statt Englisch-Deutsch lernen.

Wortfamilien: Fertigen Sie Listen mit Wortfamilien an, um sich zusammen mit einem neuen Wort auch noch seine Ableitungen einzuprägen (*approve - approval - approving - disapprove - disapproval*).

Wortfelder: Die beste Methode, Wortfelder, also zusammenhängende Wortgruppen zu einem Thema zu lernen, sind Mind Maps, also grafisch angelegte Wortnetze. Diese Methode ist gut geeignet, um den Themenwortschatz für eine Klassenarbeit zu lernen. Um den Schlüsselbegriff herum werden einzelne Oberbegriffe für die wichtigsten Aspekte des Themas angeordnet. Um jeden Oberbegriff werden nun die dazugehörigen Vokabeln herumgeschrieben.

> Mind Mapping S. 202

Vokabeltrainer: Wer gerne am Computer lernt, findet problemlos einen geeigneten Vokabeltrainer im Handel. Solche Software enthält meistens vielerlei Übungen, die das Vokabellernen unterhaltsam und spielerisch gestalten. Achten Sie darauf, dass es sich um eine Software handelt, die auf Ihre Schulart abgestimmt ist. Es gibt auch zahlreiche kostenlose Online-Vokabeltrainer im Internet.

Das Hörverständnis üben

Um gesprochenes Englisch zu verstehen, z. B. in Unterhaltungen, Telefongesprächen, Vorstellungsgesprächen, im Fernsehen u. a., sollten Sie sich gut auf die jeweilige Situation vorbereiten. Oft beeinträchtigen der Akzent, Hintergrundgeräusche und andere Störungen das Verständnis so, dass man sich auf das Wichtigste konzentrieren muss. Eignen Sie sich die unten beschriebene Methode an, wenn Sie die Hörverständnisaufgaben in *Focus on Success* bearbeiten. Damit lassen sich Barrieren bei schwierigen Hörtexten leicht abbauen.

Vor dem Hören

- Lesen Sie die gesamte Aufgabenstellung sorgfältig durch. Nutzen Sie alle Hilfen, die Ihnen zur Verfügung stehen - Abbildungen, Überschriften usw.
- Schreiben Sie wenn möglich **Schlüsselbegriffe** auf und rufen Sie sich, wenn genug Zeit ist, kurz wichtige Wortfelder zum Thema in Erinnerung.

Während des Hörens

- Hören Sie sich den gesamten Hörtext zunächst in Ruhe an, um zu verstehen, worum es geht. Machen Sie in dieser Phase keine Notizen.
- Achten Sie bei einem zweiten Hören nur auf die für die Aufgabe wichtigen Informationen. Konzentrieren Sie sich nicht auf einzelne Wörter und Ausdrücke, die Sie nicht verstehen.

- Achten Sie auf Ausdrücke, die den logischen Gedankengang verdeutlichen, z. B. *however, in my view, in conclusion* usw. Sie helfen Ihnen, den roten Faden nicht zu verlieren.
- Notieren Sie Informationen nur **stichpunktartig**, nie in ganzen Sätzen. Dabei kann ein Raster sehr hilfreich sein. In diesem Beispiel handelt es sich um den Wandel der Geschlechterrollen in unserer Gesellschaft:

	changed role	*reasons*	*consequences*
men			
women			

- Verwenden Sie Zeichen, Abkürzungen und Wortverkürzungen, um beim Notieren Zeit zu sparen:

Zeichen	
=	*the same as*
≠	*not the same as*
+	*and*

Abkürzungen	
e.g.	*for example*
km	*kilometres*
w., w/o	*with, without*

Wortverkürzungen	
govt	*government*
impt	*important*
kids	*children*

Nach dem Hören

- Formulieren Sie Ihre Stichpunkte so schnell wie möglich aus - vielleicht können Sie später Ihre Aufzeichnungen nicht mehr lesen oder Ihre Wortverkürzungen nicht mehr verstehen.
- Versuchen Sie, alle Fragen zu beantworten. Wenn Sie einige Informationen nicht verstanden haben, stellen Sie eine begründete Vermutung an.

Suche nach Informationen im Internet

Das Internet bietet riesige Ressourcen für die Recherche, z. B. für Aufsätze oder Präsentationen, aber es ist wichtig zu wissen, wo und wie man am besten sucht.

1. Schritt: Notieren Sie, wonach Sie genau suchen, und halten Sie passende Suchbegriffe fest. Ohne eine solche Vorgabe, die so spezifisch wie möglich sein sollte, gerät man vom Suchen leicht ins Surfen.

2. Schritt: Überlegen Sie sich, wo Sie mit der Suche beginnen sollten. Es ist sinnvoll, sich mit der Zeit einen Grundstock an englischsprachigen Ressourcen zusammenzustellen, z. B. *online encyclopedias* (etwa www.encyclopedia.com), *online dictionaries* (z. B. www.leo.org), *facts and figures about different countries* (etwa https://www.cia.gov/cia/publications/factbook/), *news sites* (z. B. www.bbc.co.uk), *science and technology sites* (etwa www.howstuffworks.com).

3. Schritt: Suchen Sie sich die beste Suchmaschine und geben Sie möglichst spezifische Suchbegriffe ein. Machen Sie sich mit allen Suchfunktionen vertraut. Schränken Sie die Sprache der angezeigten Ergebnisseiten auf Englisch ein.

4. Schritt: Achten Sie darauf, nur verlässliche Quellen zu benutzen. Im Durchschnitt ist das Internet nicht sehr zuverlässig, da jeder Nutzer beliebige Informationen einstellen kann. Prüfen Sie immer, wer für die jeweiligen Inhalte verantwortlich ist, und verlassen Sie sich nicht auf die nächstbeste Information.

5. Schritt: Bevor Sie einzelne Artikel Satz für Satz lesen, überfliegen Sie sie. Sind nur einzelne Abschnitte für Ihr Thema relevant, suchen Sie sich diese heraus und ignorieren Sie die übrigen Teile. > Grobverständnis S. 196

6. Schritt: Anstatt ganze Textabschnitte in Ihr Dokument herüberzukopieren, machen Sie sich gezielt Notizen. Speichern Sie die Seite unter Ihren Favoriten, wenn Sie später noch einmal darauf zurückkommen oder Materialien bzw. Zitate von der Seite verwenden möchten. > Note Making S. 201

PRODUKTION

Note Making

Es ist sinnvoll, sich beim Lesen und Hören eines Textes Notizen zu machen. So können Sie später leichter auf die Informationen zurückgreifen.

Beim Lesen

Auf den ersten Blick scheint es ziemlich leicht, sich beim Lesen eines Textes Notizen zu machen. Trotzdem fällt es vielen schwer, wirklich kurze, sinnvolle Stichpunkte zu notieren. Oft führt die Sorge, etwas Wichtiges auszulassen, dazu, dass ganze Sätze des Originaltextes abgeschrieben werden. Damit verliert man nicht nur Zeit, sondern es wird später auch schwierig, seinen Text in eigenen Worten zu formulieren.

Hier einige Tipps, damit Sie diese Falle umgehen:

> Geben Sie Ihren Notizen eine Überschrift, die Ihr Thema klar umreißt, z. B. *Effects of genetic engineering on the environment*.
> Gehen Sie den Text durch und filtern Sie die wesentlichen Unterthemen heraus, die Sie als Überschriften verwenden können. Denken Sie daran, unter den Überschriften genug Platz für Ihre Stichpunkte zu lassen. > Detailverständnis S. 196
> Halten Sie Ausschau nach Signalen wie Hervorhebungen, Wiederholungen und bedeutungstragenden Adjektiven wie *huge, incredible, devastating* usw. Diese zeigen, was der Verfasser für wichtig hält.
> Notieren Sie nur Stichwörter, nicht ganze Sätze.
> Verdeutlichen Sie den logischen Aufbau der Informationen, z. B. indem Sie bestimmte Punkte in einer Liste untereinanderschreiben, Themen durch Leerzeilen voneinander abheben oder die wichtigsten Begriffe unterstreichen.
> Kontrollieren Sie, ob Sie alle notwendigen Informationen zusammengetragen haben. Vergessen Sie nicht, dass sie oft über den gesamten Text verstreut sind.

Beim Hören

In diesem Fall ist es schwieriger Notizen zu machen, da man oft sehr schnell schreiben muss. Man muss sich auf das Wesentliche konzentrieren und sollte Abkürzungen verwenden, damit man den Faden nicht verliert. > Das Hörverständnis üben S. 199

Mind Mapping

Eine Mind Map ist eine sinnvolle Methode, Begriffe und Angaben übersichtlich in einem Netz um einen Oberbegriff herum anzuordnen. Sie eignet sich z. B. zum Vokabellernen, zum Brainstorming, zum Ideensammeln und zur Vorbereitung eines Aufsatzes oder einer Präsentation.

> Umgang mit unbekannten Vokabeln S. 197

Materialien: Ein großes Blatt (z. B. DIN A3), farbige Stifte.

1. Schritt: Schreiben Sie den Oberbegriff (wenn es um Wortfelder geht) bzw. das Thema (wenn es um eine Ideensammlung geht) deutlich und groß in die Mitte.

2. Schritt: Schreiben Sie die wichtigsten Begriffe zum Thema um den Oberbegriff herum; sie sollten durch starke „Äste" mit dem Oberbegriff verbunden sein.

3. Schritt: Fügen Sie nach demselben Prinzip weitere Wörter und Ideen zu den einzelnen Unterthemen hinzu. Je spezieller, desto kleiner die Verzweigungen, d.h. der Weg vom Thema nach außen führt vom Allgemeinen zum Speziellen. Sie können jederzeit und überall neue Ideen hinzufügen.

4. Schritt: Heben Sie wichtige Begriffe durch farbige Markierungen und Symbole hervor.

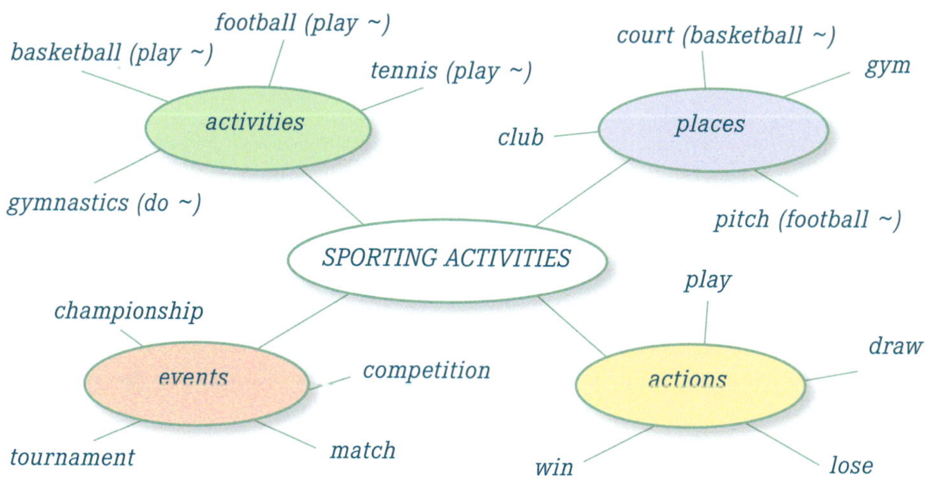

Fragen zum Text beantworten

> Lesen schwieriger Texte S. 196

Bevor Sie mit dem Schreiben beginnen, vergewissern Sie sich, dass Sie den gesamten Text verstanden haben. (Nicht jedes Wort ist wichtig - überlegen Sie sich, ob Sie die Bedeutung des Satzes auch verstehen, ohne jedes Wort zu kennen.) Lesen Sie die Aufgabenstellung immer genau, um zu verstehen, worauf es bei der Beantwortung genau ankommt - ein häufiger Fehler ist das „Vorbeischreiben" an der Frage. Achten Sie auch darauf, keine Informationen zu „verpulvern", die Sie möglicherweise für die Beantwortung einer anderen Frage benötigen.

- Wenn Sie im Buch nichts anstreichen dürfen, machen Sie sich Notizen in Form von Stichpunkten und Listen, anstatt ganze Sätze aus dem Text herauszuschreiben. In der Klassenarbeit bzw. Prüfung sollten Sie die wichtigsten Passagen im Text markieren. Am besten markieren Sie alles, was für eine Textverständnisfrage wichtig ist, mit einer bestimmten Farbe, und nehmen dann eine andere Frage für die nächste Textverständnisfrage.
- Verwenden Sie in der Antwort die Zeitform der Fragestellung.

- Verwenden Sie so viele Synonyme und Umschreibungen der Begriffe und Formulierungen aus dem Text wie möglich, z. B. *recently - in recent years; violent crime - crime involving violence; think - believe; to a great extent - greatly; when she was a child - in her childhood* usw.
- Suchen Sie Signale im Text wie Hervorhebungen, Wiederholungen und bedeutungstragende Adjektive und Adverbien wie *absolutely, unbelievably, amazing*. Dies sind Signale dafür, was der Verfasser für wichtig hält.
- Versuchen Sie nicht, Ihre eigene Meinung einzubringen, wenn dies nicht in der Fragestellung gefordert ist.

Formulierungen für das Schreiben über den Text

- *According to the author, ...*
- *The article goes on to say that ...*
- *The text says that ...*
- *The author makes the point that ...*

Aus dem Text zitieren

Wenn Sie wirklich einmal eine wichtige Aussage aus dem Text zitieren möchten, um einen Punkt zu unterstreichen, so tun Sie dies nicht, indem Sie einfach die Formulierung des Textes übernehmen, sondern zeigen Sie, dass Sie bewusst zitieren und dies auch sprachlich deutlich machen können. Zitieren Sie in Ihrer Antwort höchstens einmal aus dem Text.

Zitate in die Antwort einbauen

- *To quote the author, ...*
- *According to the article, many stars are 'both defining and benefiting from a big shift in American attitudes to race'.*
- *Ron Berger highlights the positive aspects of this shift by saying 'what's ethnically neutral, diverse or simply unclear has tremendous appeal'.*

Eine Stellungnahme (*comment*) schreiben

Bei einer Stellungnahme geht es darum, Ihre Meinung zu einem bestimmten Thema darzulegen. Wichtig ist, dass Ihre Meinung begründet und mit Beispielen belegt ist.

1. Schritt: Machen Sie sich genau bewusst, worüber Sie schreiben sollen. Lesen Sie die Aufgabenstellung mehrmals durch.

2. Schritt: Machen Sie sich Notizen. Ordnen Sie Ihre Stichwörter übersichtlich an, z. B. in einer Mind Map, einer Liste oder einer Übersicht.

> Note Making S. 201, Mind Mapping S. 202

3. Schritt: Schreiben Sie einen Einleitungssatz, der sich auf die Aufgabenstellung beziehen sollte.

4. Schritt: Behandeln Sie jedes Argument in einem Absatz. Handelt es sich um ein Pro-/Kontra-Thema, können Sie erst die Pro- und dann die Kontra-Argumente anführen. Verdeutlichen Sie Ihre Argumentation durch die Verwendung von Strukturwörtern; hierzu siehe die Liste auf der hinteren Umschlagklappe dieses Buches (*Language for writing*).

> Einen Text sinnvoll gliedern S. 205

5. Schritt: Bringen Sie Ihre Argumentation in einem prägnanten Schlusssatz auf den Punkt.

Eine Stellungnahme einleiten
- > *In the following I shall deal with the problem/subject/issue of ...*
- > *I would like to discuss ...*
- > *I intend to present arguments in favour of ... and against ...*

Eine Stellungnahme abschließen
- > *All in all, I think it can be said that ...*
- > *In conclusion, I would like to say that ...*
- > *I would like to conclude by saying that ...*

Einen Text zusammenfassen

Die Fähigkeit, einen gelesenen Text zusammenzufassen, ist nicht nur wichtig, um den Text richtig zu verstehen, sondern sie hilft auch bei anderen Situationen, in denen Sie Informationen aus einem Text auf das Wesentliche reduzieren müssen. Zu solchen Situationen gehören z. B. die Beantwortung von Textverständnisfragen oder eine Mediation.

> Fragen zum Text beantworten S. 202, Mediation S. 210

1. Schritt: Lesen Sie den Text so oft wie möglich, bis Sie sicher sind, alles verstanden zu haben.

> Detailverständnis S. 196, Umgang mit unbekannten Vokabeln S. 197

2. Schritt: Fassen Sie in ein oder zwei einleitenden Sätzen zusammen, worum es in dem Text geht, z. B.: *The text is an extract from a radio phone-in show which is looking at people's attitudes to the EU.*

3. Schritt: Machen Sie sich bewusst, welche Informationen für den Leser wichtig sind, indem Sie *Wh*-Fragen beantworten: *Who? What? When? Where? Why?*, z. B.:
- > *Who: Dr Peter Brown from Manchester University*
- > *What: has been doing research into corruption in the EU*

4. Schritt: Machen Sie sich Notizen in Form von Stichwörtern. > Note Making S. 201

5. Schritt: Schreiben Sie Ihren Text. Beachten Sie dabei folgende Punkte:
- > Lassen Sie Unwesentliches weg. Dazu gehören etwa Beispiele, Aufzählungen, Namen, Zitate usw.
- > Verwenden Sie so weit wie möglich Ihre eigenen Worte.
- > Vermeiden Sie es, zu dem Text Stellung zu nehmen. Dies gehört in der Regel nicht zur Aufgabenstellung.
- > Denken Sie daran, Zitate in indirekte Rede umzuwandeln. > Reported speech S. 217

6. Schritt: Kontrollieren Sie Ihren Text auf Fehler und vergewissern Sie sich, dass Sie alle wichtigen Aspekte des Textes berücksichtigt haben.

Einen Aufsatz schreiben

Im Laufe der Oberstufe, in der Abschlussprüfung und auch später, z. B. im Studium, werden Sie immer wieder Aufsätze zu unterschiedlichsten Themen schreiben müssen. Es ist sinnvoll, sich von Anfang an einige Regeln zu eigen zu machen, um das Vorgehen möglichst zu automatisieren und sich gleich auf den Inhalt konzentrieren zu können. Dies ist besonders wichtig, wenn es - wie in der Abschlussprüfung - auf die Zeit ankommt.

1. Schritt: Verschaffen Sie sich Klarheit über Ihr Thema. Welche Aspekte gehören dazu, welche nicht?

2. Schritt: Machen Sie ein Brainstorming, indem Sie alle Ideen aufschreiben, die Ihnen zum Thema in den Kopf kommen. Wichtig: Die Ideen sollten Sie gleich in eine Struktur bringen, um nicht in einem Wust von ungeordnetem Gekritzel zu enden. Zur Strukturierung eignen sich z. B. Listen oder Mind Maps.

> Note Making S. 201, Mind Mapping S. 202

3. Schritt: Überlegen Sie sich einen Aufbau für Ihren Text. Dies kann z. B. in Form einer Mind Map geschehen. Eine andere Möglichkeit ist eine Übersicht (*outline*) wie die folgende:

Should old towns be closed to private vehicles?

Einleitung: Umreißen des Themas
Hauptteil: Ausführung zum Thema, z. B.:

1. *Disadvantages for business*
- **1.1** *Job losses*
  - **1.1.1** *retail trade*
  - **1.1.2** *fewer tourists*
    - **1.1.2.1** *less money for tourist attractions*
    - **1.1.2.2** *job losses in cafés, etc.*
- **1.2** *What about town centre residents, delivery vehicles, etc.?*

2. *Advantages, positive effects on town and people*

...

Schluss: Zusammenfassung, Fazit

4. Schritt: Schreiben Sie Ihren Text. Lassen Sie Platz für Korrekturen, Änderungen oder Ergänzungen. Wichtig: Verdeutlichen Sie Ihre Argumentation durch die Verwendung von Strukturwörtern; hierzu siehe die Liste auf der hinteren Umschlagklappe dieses Buches (*Language for writing*) und den Abschnitt unten „Einen Text sinnvoll gliedern“.

5. Schritt: Überprüfen Sie Ihren Entwurf auf:

- **Rechtschreibfehler** (z. B. gleichlautende Wörter wie *there/their*, *meet/meat* usw.)
- **Grammatikfehler** (z. B. Gebrauch der Zeitformen; *-ly*-Endung für Adverbien)
- **Wortwahl** (z. B. Wiederholungen; *False friends* wie „aktuell“ ≠ *actual*, „eventuell“ ≠ *eventual*, „spenden“ ≠ *spend*)
- **Satzbau** (z. B. unvollständige Antworten, die mit *Because* beginnen)
- **Gedankenführung** (z. B. Klarheit des Ausdrucks; Verwendung von Strukturwörtern wie *However, On the other hand, In addition, As a result* usw.)

Einen Text sinnvoll gliedern

Wann immer es darum geht, einen zusammenhängenden Text zu schreiben, sei es eine Antwort auf eine Frage zum Text, einen Aufsatz, eine Zusammenfassung o. Ä., ist es ganz wichtig, die Gedanken in einen logischen Zusammenhang zu bringen, damit der Leser den Faden nicht verliert. Dies alles gilt ebenso für mündliche Präsentationen, nur werden Sie dabei Ihre Materialien nicht Wort für Wort ablesen, sondern frei sprechen. Daher ist es wichtig, Formulierungen für die Gliederung auch mündlich parat zu haben.

Die wichtigsten Strukturwörter finden Sie auf der hinteren Umschlagklappe dieses Buches (*Language for writing*). Im Folgenden sehen Sie einige Beispiele, wie man diese Formulierungen in einen Text einbauen kann.

Argumente gliedern

> *In his text 'The world's changing energy supplies' Knapp discusses many aspects of energy and the environment. Firstly, he states that ... Secondly / Then he goes on to say that ... Another point he makes is that ... Finally, ...*

Eine Begründung anführen

> *Due to / Because of / As a result of all the discussions about renewable sources of energy ...*
> *Renewable energy has been talked about a lot. Therefore, the public ...*
> *Renewable energy has been talked about a lot, so the public ...*

Aspekte ergänzen

> *Brian Knapp states that many renewable sources of energy include high development costs. In addition, / Moreover, he points out that they these energy forms still only offer a small amount of the world's rising energy requirements.*
> *In addition to / Besides / As well as mentioning the high development costs of many renewable forms of energy, Knapp points out that these energy forms still only offer a small amount of the world's rising energy requirements.*

Einen Gegensatz ausdrücken

> *Although the demand for cheap energy is continuing to rise, our current main sources of energy – fossil fuels – are running out.*
> *In spite of the rising demand for cheap energy, our current main sources of energy are running out.*
> *While/Whereas the demand for cheap energy is continuing to rise, our current main sources of energy are running out.*
> *Our current main sources of energy are running out. However, / But nevertheless, the demand for cheap energy is continuing to rise.*
> *On the one hand, our current main sources of energy are running out; on the other hand, the demand for cheap energy is continuing to rise.*

Beispiele anführen

> *The writer is of the opinion that nuclear fusion is a safe energy source compared with other energy sources, for example / for instance / such as / e.g. ...*

Ein Fazit ziehen

> *As a consequence, / All in all, / Consequently, Brian Knapp thinks that ...*
> *To sum up / To conclude, I would like to say that ...*

Diese Strukturwörter (*connectors*) sollten Sie sich so zu eigen machen, dass Sie sie möglichst in jedem Text verwenden. Dadurch gewöhnen Sie sich eine genaue und logische Ausdrucksweise an. Achten Sie auch beim Lesen von Texten auf Strukturwörter; so können Sie der Gedankenführung leichter folgen.

Die Arbeitsergebnisse präsentieren

Die Fähigkeit, wirkungsvoll vor einem Publikum zu referieren, ist wichtig im Berufsleben und zunehmend auch in der Schule. Dabei kommt es nicht nur auf den Inhalt an, sondern auch darauf, wie anschaulich Sie den Inhalt „verpacken", d.h. dass Sie Ihren Vortrag leicht nachvollziehbar gliedern, abwechslungsreich gestalten und lebendig illustrieren.

Vor der Präsentation

1. Schritt: Bereiten Sie Ihr Thema gründlich vor und machen Sie sich dabei schon Notizen auf Englisch.

2. Schritt: Prüfen Sie Ihre Stichpunkte sprachlich und vergewissern Sie sich, dass Sie alles richtig aussprechen (anhand der Lautschrift in einem Wörterbuch oder der Aussprachebeispiele in gängigen Online-Wörterbüchern oder auf Wörterbuch-CD-ROMs).

3. Schritt: Überlegen Sie sich, wie Sie Ihren Vortrag interessanter und lebendiger machen können (Anschauungsmaterial, Audiobeispiele, Anekdoten usw.).

4. Schritt: Organisieren Sie alle Hilfsmittel, die Sie benötigen (OHP, Flipchart usw.).

5. Schritt: Üben Sie die Präsentation, am besten vor Zuhörern.

Während der Präsentation

1. Schritt: Steigen Sie nicht gleich mitten ins Thema ein, sondern geben Sie einen Überblick über Ihre Präsentation.

2. Schritt: Machen Sie es den Zuhörern leicht, indem Sie sich klar ausdrücken, kurze Sätze benutzen und langsam sprechen.

3. Schritt: Die Zuhörer bleiben am ehesten interessiert, wenn Sie Ihre Präsentation so abwechslungsreich wie möglich gestalten: Ziehen Sie zwischendurch Anschauungsmaterial (OHP, Beamer usw.) heran und teilen Sie Handouts aus. Wenn Sie Folien benutzen, halten Sie sie klar und übersichtlich, anstatt sie mit Grafiken zu überladen.

4. Schritt: Achten Sie auf Ihre Körpersprache: Wenden Sie sich dem Publikum zu, halten Sie Blickkontakt mit den Zuhörern, sprechen Sie langsam und deutlich und benutzen Sie Gesten, um den Inhalt zu verdeutlichen.

5. Schritt: Fassen Sie zum Schluss das Wichtigste zusammen. Bedanken Sie sich bei den Zuhörern für ihre Aufmerksamkeit und ermuntern Sie sie, Fragen zu stellen.

Interpretation von Bildern und Karikaturen

Am besten eignen Sie sich einen Grundstock an Formulierungen zur Beschreibung und Interpretation von Bildern und Karikaturen an. Achten Sie darauf, sich auf die wesentlichen Bildaussagen zu konzentrieren, anstatt sich in Details zu verlieren.
Halten Sie die folgenden Schritte ein, um Ihre Antwort sinnvoll zu gliedern:

1. Schritt: **Beschreibung des Bildes.** Betrachten Sie alle Einzelheiten der Bildvorlage, aber beschränken Sie sich bei der Beschreibung auf die Elemente, die für die Aussage wichtig sind.
Verwenden Sie bei der Beschreibung der Bildinhalte das *Present progressive* (außer bei Verben, die gewöhnlich nicht in dieser Zeitform vorkommen). Zu dem Cartoon auf S. 62 könnten Sie z. B. schreiben: *The cartoon shows two dogs in an office. The bigger dog is sitting at a computer. he is explaining to the smaller dog how safe the internet is because ...* Aber Vorsicht: Das *Present progressive* gilt nur für die Handlungen und Situationen, die im Bild dargestellt sind, nicht für die Verben, mit denen Sie den Cartoon beschreiben und interpretieren (*The cartoon* ***shows/describes*** *... / It* ***seems*** *as if the dog on the left ...*).

> Present progressive S. 212

2. Schritt: **Interpretation des Bildes.** Wenn Ihnen das Bild nicht viel sagt, können Sie dies in Ihre Interpretation miteinbeziehen, indem Sie es als *ambiguous* oder *unclear* bezeichnen.

3. Schritt: **Stellungnahme zur Bildaussage.** Bringen Sie die Hauptaussage der Bildvorlage auf den Punkt und/oder beziehen Sie Stellung, indem Sie z. B. die Wirkung des Bildes auf den Betrachter beurteilen.

1. Beschreibung des Bildes

> *In the foreground/background/centre there is ...*
> *The speech bubble* (Sprechblase) / *thought bubble* (Denkblase) / *caption* (Bildunterschrift) / *label* (Aufschrift) *says that ...*
> *The cartoon shows / appears to show ...*
> *The scene depicts/shows ...*
> *In the foreground/background, there is/are ...*
> *On the left/right you can see ...*
> *The ... looks as if ...*
> *The person on the left appears to ... / It seems as if the person ...*
> *He/She is wearing/holding ...*

2. Interpretation der Bildaussage

> *The picture/cartoon deals with the recent discussion of ...*
> *I think the cartoonist's/artist's/photographer's use of irony/exaggeration is intended to create ... / is aimed at making ... / conveys ...*
> *The person in the centre represents/symbolizes/shows ...*
> *This indicates/shows/reveals that ...*
> *The ... represents / is in fact / stands for ...*
> *The cartoonist/artist/photographer criticizes / wants to say / express the idea that ...*
> *Because the foreground / background is ..., the impression is given that ...*
> *From the way the people are depicted, it is obvious that ...*
> *The point of the cartoon seems to be that ...*

3. Stellungnahme, Beschreibung der Wirkung auf den Betrachter

> *I think the cartoon is quite right / makes a fair point.*
> *I agree with the cartoonist / artist, but ...*
> *In my opinion, the cartoonist is partly right / exaggerates a little / a lot / is quite wrong.*
> *For example, / For instance, ...*
> *Because of ..., the picture touches me / leaves me cold.*
> *I think the ... is a symbol of ...*
> *The ... helps to create a ... atmosphere, which forces you to / has the effect of ...*

Interpretation von Grafiken, Diagrammen und Tabellen

Wie im Falle von Cartoons ist es auch bei Grafiken, Diagrammen und Tabellen sinnvoll, einen Grundstock an Formulierungen zur Beschreibung und Interpretation parat zu haben. Halten Sie die folgenden Schritte ein, um Ihre Antwort sinnvoll zu gliedern:

1. Schritt: **Beschreibung der Vorlage.** Hier geht es nicht darum, alle Details aufzuzählen, sondern zu beschreiben, worum es in der Vorlage geht und welche Daten dargestellt werden.

2. Schritt: **Zusammenfassung der dargestellten Tendenzen, Entwicklungen bzw. Größen.** Welche Schlussfolgerungen ergeben sich aus den Daten? Kann man zusammenfassend ein Ergebnis oder Fazit formulieren?

Typen von Diagrammen

Tabelle (*table*)

	USA	UK
1995	495	105
2005	718	85

Kurvendiagramm (*graph, line graph*)

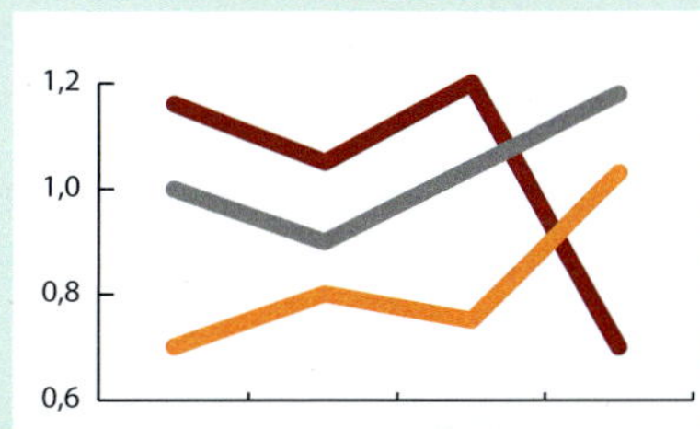

Balkendiagramm (*bar chart*)

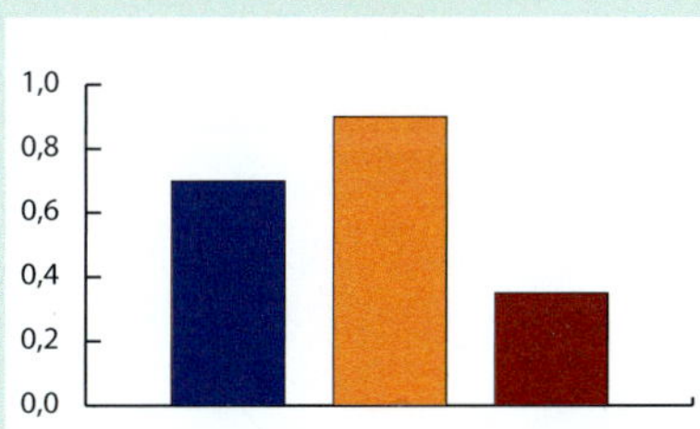

Kreis-/Tortendiagramm (*pie chart*)

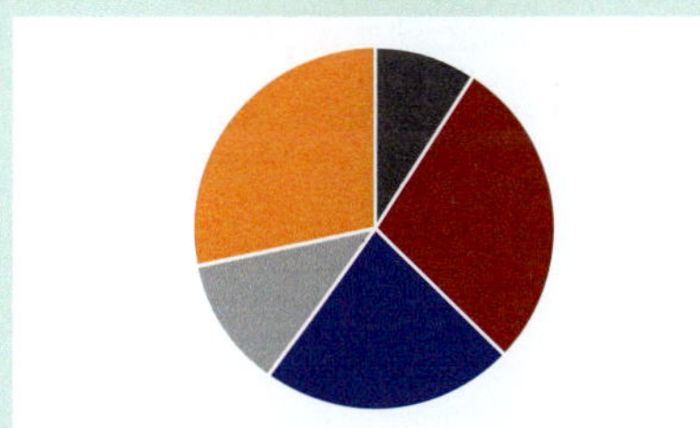

Sprechen über Zahlen und Mengenangaben (*values, amounts*)

- *more / less than ...*
- *no less than ...*
- *eighty-five per cent (said that ...)*
- *On the other hand, almost ...*

Sprechen über Proportionen (*proportions, shares, percentages*)

- *(over) half of*
- *more / less than one third / quarter of ...*
- *the (vast) majority of*
- *a mere third of ...*

Sprechen über Entwicklungen (*developments*) und Tendenzen (*tendencies*)

- *a huge / sharp increase / decrease*
- *a small / slight raise / dip*
- *levels out, remains constant*
- *drastically, gradually, sharply, steadily*
- *rises / increases / hits a maximum*
- *drops / decreases / falls / plunges*
- *over a period of ...*
- *between 2000 and 2008*

INTERAKTION

Gruppengespräche und Diskussionen führen

Ob es um Gruppengespräche, Diskussionen oder Rollenspiele geht: Machen Sie das meiste daraus, indem Sie die folgenden Punkte beherzigen.

> Lernen Sie die Formulierungen auf der hinteren Umschlagklappe dieses Buches (*Language for discussion*). Klappen Sie diese während des Unterrichts aus. Die Formulierungen helfen Ihnen, sich klar und logisch auszudrücken.
> Bereiten Sie sich inhaltlich vor, indem Sie sich einzelne Aspekte des Themas nochmal in Stichworten ins Gedächtnis rufen und Schlüsselbegriffe auf Englisch notieren.
> Legen Sie sich, wenn genügend Zeit ist, ein paar Fragen/Antworten zum Thema zurecht.
> Bleiben Sie immer ruhig und denken Sie nach, bevor Sie sprechen.
> Bleiben Sie beim Thema und schweifen Sie nicht ab.
> Gehen Sie auf Ihre Gesprächspartner ein und halten Sie Blickkontakt.
> Beteiligen Sie sich und hören Sie nicht bloß still zu: Gruppenarbeit ist eine hervorragende Gelegenheit zum freien Sprechen.

Melden Sie sich auch immer mal wieder spontan zu Wort und lassen Sie Ausdrücke einfließen, die Interesse, Überraschung, Skepsis usw. äußern - so etwas macht das Gespräch gleich viel lebendiger:

Sich zu Wort melden	
> *Can I just say that ...*	> *Well, if you ask me ...*
Jemand anderen ins Gespräch einbringen	
> *What do you think, Sven / Svenja?*	
Verständnis, Erstaunen usw. ausdrücken	
Ach so. / Ah ja.	*I see. / Right. / Oh, right.*
Oh je!	*Oh dear!*
Echt?	*Really?*
Gut. / Okay.	*Fine.*
Alles klar.	*OK then.*
Das ist doch wohl nicht dein Ernst!	*You're kidding!*

MEDIATION

Mediation

Schriftliche Mediation bedeutet das sinngemäße Übertragen von Texten in eine andere Sprache für jemanden, der das Original nicht versteht. Wichtig bei einer Mediation ist immer die Konzentration auf das Wesentliche, im Unterschied zur Übersetzung. Einzelheiten sind bei einer Mediation ebenso zweitrangig wie stilistische Feinheiten.

1. Schritt: Lesen Sie genau, **für welche Situation** Sie den Text zusammenfassen müssen und **für wen**. Meist bestimmt die jeweilige Situation, worauf es ankommt.

2. Schritt: Lesen Sie den gesamten Text durch, ohne sich dabei auf Einzelwörter zu konzentrieren. Ignorieren Sie unbekannte Vokabeln wenn möglich, oft sind sie für das Verständnis des Hauptinhalts nicht wesentlich.

3. Schritt: Lesen Sie nochmals, worauf es in der Aufgabenstellung ankommt und in welcher Form die Lösung abgefasst sein soll. Wenn es einzelne Fragen gibt, markieren Sie die für die jeweiligen Fragen wichtigen Textpassagen in unterschiedlichen Farben.

4. Schritt: Fassen Sie die Hauptpunkte des Textes zusammen. Drücken Sie sich klar und verständlich aus; vereinfachen Sie die Sprache des Originals, indem Sie sich darauf konzentrieren, **was** gesagt wird, nicht **wie** es gesagt wird.

5. Schritt: Lesen Sie Ihren Text nochmals durch und vergewissern Sie sich, dass der Inhalt des Originals angemessen und verständlich ausgedrückt ist.

Übersetzung

Im Gegensatz zur Mediation ist bei der Übersetzung jedes Wort des Originaltextes wichtig. Oft muss im Deutschen jedoch eine andere Satzkonstruktion gewählt werden. Besonders knifflig sind z. B. die folgenden Konstruktionen; übersetzen Sie die Beispielsätze ins Deutsche:

> **Partizipialkonstruktionen**
z. B. *The jobs done by women are often badly paid. / Some people say that feminism has been a great success pointing to the progress in the last 30 years.*

> **Konstruktionen mit Gerundium**
z. B. *I avoided looking at her. / She achieved her aims by working very hard.*

> **Passivkonstruktionen**
z. B. *He was offered a good job. / He is said to be rich.*

Außerdem muss häufig die Wortart geändert werden, z. B. *There is a need to ...* (Es ist notwendig, zu ...) oder *She used to work in France.* (Früher arbeitete sie in Frankreich.).

Eine weitere Schwierigkeit sind kleinere Partikel und Ausdrücke, die sich vom Deutschen oft unterscheiden, z. B. *after all, as, as to, as for, at all, at least, however, neither ... nor, not ... either, not ... until, unless.*

1. Schritt: Lesen Sie den gesamten Text einmal zügig durch.

2. Schritt: Lesen Sie den Text nun Wort für Wort und schlagen Sie schwierige Wörter nach. Vergewissern Sie sich, dass Sie den Satzbau jedes Satzes richtig erfasst haben (siehe die Liste schwieriger Konstruktionen oben).

3. Schritt: Fertigen Sie eine Rohfassung an, die Sie am besten doppelzeilig schreiben, um Korrekturen einfügen zu können.

4. Schritt: Bevor Sie die Reinschrift anfertigen, prüfen Sie Ihren Text auf:
Rechtschreib- und Grammatikfehler (z. B. Partizipien, Gerundien, Zeitenfolge)
Ausdruck (z. B. Sätze, an denen man noch das englische Original erkennt)
Verständlichkeit (z. B. zu lange oder verschachtelte Sätze)
Vollständigkeit (ausgelassene Wörter oder Satzteile).

Grammar Summary

THE SIMPLE PRESENT

1 I **go** to the disco once a week.
2 We **live** in Bavaria.
3 Mr Brown **teaches** us English every day.
4 **I don't like** chocolate.
5 **Does** he **like** chocolate?

> Man gebraucht das **simple present** für regelmäßige, sich wiederholende Ereignisse oder Handlungen (1, 3) und für Dauerzustände (2, 4, 5).
> Mit Ausnahme der 3. Person Singular (*he, she, it*) hat das **simple present** dieselbe Form wie der Infinitiv (1, 2).
⚠ Die **3. Person Singular** endet auf *-(e)s* (3).
> Ist **kein Hilfsverb** im Satz vorhanden, werden **Verneinung** und **Fragen** mit der entsprechenden Form von *to do* gebildet (4, 5).

Das **simple present** wird häufig mit den folgenden **Zeitangaben** benutzt:

> *always, never, often, rarely, seldom, sometimes*
> *generally, mostly, normally, regularly, usually*
> *every day/week/month/..., every morning/afternoon/...*
> *on Mondays/Tuesdays/..., on weekdays*
> *in (the) summer/winter/...*
> *at Christmas/Easter, at weekends*

THE PRESENT PROGRESSIVE

1 **I'm calling** to say that Ben's ill.
2 He**'s staying** in bed today.
3 The computer **isn't working**.
4 **Are** you **sleeping**?

> Man benutzt das **present progressive** (auch **present continuous** genannt) für Vorgänge oder Handlungen, die im Moment des Sprechens oder Schreibens passieren und noch nicht abgeschlossen sind (1, 3, 4).
> Es wird auch für vorübergehende Situationen gebraucht (2).
> Das **present progressive** wird mit dem Präsens von *to be* und der *-ing*-Form des Vollverbs gebildet.
> Da beim **present progressive** immer ein Hilfsverb vorhanden ist, wird die **Verneinung** mit *not/n't* gebildet (3).
> Fragen werden durch Umstellung gebildet (4).

Das **present progressive** wird oft mit den folgenden **Zeitangaben** benutzt:

at the moment, at present, now, this week/month

⚠ Diese Verben bilden normalerweise **keine progressive-Form**:

be, believe, doubt, feel (meinen), *hate, hear, imagine, know, like/dislike, love, mean, notice, prefer, realize, recognize, remember, see* (begreifen), *seem, suppose, think* (meinen), *understand, want, wish*

THE SIMPLE PAST

1 We **wanted** to go to the USA last year.
2 She **went** on a school trip to London.
3 Jasmin **did not enjoy** her holiday in Rimini last summer.
4 Where **did** you **go** last year?

> Man benutzt das **simple past**, um über Vergangenes zu berichten.
> Das **simple past** wird auch gebraucht, wenn man sagen will, **wann** etwas geschehen ist (1, 3, 4).
> Bei **regelmäßigen** Verben wird das **simple past** durch das Anhängen von *-ed* an den Infinitiv gebildet (1).
⚠ Die unregelmäßigen Verben haben eine Sonderform (2), die man sich merken - auswendig lernen! - muss.
> Irregular Verbs (S. 300)
> Ist **kein Hilfsverb** im Satz vorhanden, bildet man die **Verneinung** und **Fragen** mit *did/didn't* (3, 4).

Das **simple past** wird häufig mit den folgenden **Zeitangaben** benutzt:

> *yesterday, the day before yesterday, the week/month/... before last*
> *last night/week/month/summer/December/Easter/...*
> *two/three/... hours/days/years/... ago*
> *in 2005/in the 20th century ...*
> *at that time, in those days*

THE PAST PROGRESSIVE

1 The teacher **was talking** to Heather **during the break**.
2 The tourists **were taking** photos when a lion (suddenly) **sprang** towards them.
3 I **wasn't doing** anything particular when he **arrived**.
4 **Were** you **having** breakfast when I **phoned**?

> Wenn man ausdrücken möchte, dass eine Handlung zu einem bestimmten Zeitpunkt oder während eines bestimmten Zeitraumes in der Vergangenheit **im Gange** war, benutzt man das **past progressive** (auch **past continuous** genannt)(1).
> Das **past progressive** wird auch benutzt, um zu verdeutlichen, dass eine Handlung im Gange war, als ein neues Ereignis (plötzlich) eintrat (2-4).
> Man bildet das **past progressive** mit *was/were* und der *-ing*-Form des Vollverbs (1).
> Die **Verneinung** wird mit *was not/wasn't* bzw. *were not/weren't* gebildet (3).
> **Fragen** bildet man durch Umstellung (4).
⚠ Einige Verben haben **keine progressive-Form** (siehe die Liste unter **present progressive**).

THE PRESENT PERFECT

1 I've **bought** a new car.
2 I **haven't seen** the new film yet.
3 How long **have** you **had** a laptop?
4 We'**ve had** snow **for** two weeks.
5 She'**s had** a cold **since** December.

> Wenn man ausdrücken will, dass etwas geschehen ist, ohne dass der genaue Zeitpunkt des Ereignisses wichtig ist, wird das **present perfect** benutzt (1, 2).
> Man gebraucht das **present perfect** auch, um zu sagen, seit wann oder wie lange ein Zustand oder eine Handlung schon andauert (3-5). Dafür wird sehr oft *for* bzw. *since* verwendet. (Im Deutschen steht dafür „seit" plus Gegenwart.)
> Das **present perfect** wird mit *have/has* und der 3. Form des Vollverbs gebildet (1, 4, 5).
⚠ Die unregelmäßigen Verben haben eine Sonderform (1, 2), die man auswendig lernen muss.

> Irregular verbs (S. 300)

> Die **Verneinung** wird durch das Einfügen von *not/n't* nach *have/has* gebildet (2).
> **Fragen** bildet man durch Umstellung (3).

Das **present perfect** wird oft mit den folgenden Zeitangaben benutzt:

> *already, still (not), (not) yet*
> *(not) ever, just, lately, never, recently*
> *so far this week/month/..., till/until now*

THE PRESENT PERFECT PROGRESSIVE

1 I'**ve been learning** English since I was 10.
2 They'**ve not been speaking** to each other lately.
3 **Has** he **been singing** in the choir for long?

> Das **present perfect progressive** (auch **present perfect continuous** genannt) benutzt man für Handlungen und Vorgänge, die in der Vergangenheit begonnen haben und zum Zeitpunkt des Sprechens bzw. Schreibens noch nicht beendet sind.
> Das **present perfect progressive** wird mit *have/has been* und der *-ing*-Form des Vollverbs gebildet (1).
> Die **Verneinung** bildet man durch das Einfügen von *not/n't* unmittelbar nach *have/has* (2).
> **Fragen** werden durch Umstellung gebildet (3).
⚠ Einige Verben haben normalerweise **keine progressive-Form** (siehe die Liste unter **present progressive**, S. 212).

THE PAST PERFECT

1 Laura couldn't pay. She **had forgotten** her purse.
2 Nina **had** already **left** the coffee bar by the time I arrived.
3 When I visited John in hospital, he **had been** there for ten days.

> Mit Hilfe des **past perfect** drückt man aus, dass zwei Handlungen oder Vorgänge in der Vergangenheit aufeinander folgten (1, 2). Die Handlung, die zeitlich voranging, steht im **past perfect**.
> Das **past perfect** wird auch verwendet, um auszudrücken, dass ein Zustand vor einem Zeitpunkt der Vergangenheit begann und zu diesem Zeitpunkt noch andauerte (3).

⚠ Wenn zwei oder mehrere kurze Handlungen in der Vergangenheit direkt aufeinander folgen, wird für alle Handlungen das **simple past** verwendet:
*The cat **ran** out when Joanne **opened** the door.*

THE PAST PERFECT PROGRESSIVE

1 Rod **had been travelling** for three months when he ran out of money.
2 When I found Mary, I could see that she **had been crying**.

> Das **past perfect progressive** (auch **past perfect continous** genannt) wird verwendet, wenn man ausdrücken will, dass eine Handlung oder ein Vorgang vor einem Zeitpunkt in der Vergangenheit begonnen hatte und bis (oder fast bis) zu diesem Zeitpunkt andauerte.

THE FUTURE

A will

1 In the future people **will use** public transport more often.
2 We can only hope that everyone **will accept** this shift in attitudes.
3 You've forgotten your purse? Don't worry. I**'ll lend** you some money.
4 Ms Smith **will not be** at the meeting this afternoon.
5 I **won't come** either.
6 **Will** he **get** the job?

> Das **will future** benutzt man, um Vorhersagen zu machen (1) oder Vermutungen über die Zukunft zu äußern (2).
> Man benutzt es auch, wenn man sich spontan zu etwas entschließt, Angebote oder Versprechen macht (3).
> Das **will future** wird mit *will* + Infinitiv des Vollverbs gebildet. Es hat für alle Personen die gleiche Form (1-3).
> Die **Verneinung** bildet man durch das Einfügen von *not* unmittelbar nach *will* (4). Im gesprochenen Englisch sagt man häufig *won't* (5).
> **Fragen** werden durch Umstellung gebildet (6).

Das **will future** kommt häufig mit den folgenden einleitenden Verben und Ausdrücken vor:

> *believe, expect, forecast, hope, imagine, suppose, think*
> *It's clear/obvious that ..., There's no doubt that ...*

B going to

1 Look at these clouds. It**'s going to rain** soon.
2 This time I**'m going to get** good marks in the class test.
3 Tom **isn't going to work** at the club any more.
4 When **are** you **going to take** your driving test?

> Das **going to future** benutzt man für Ereignisse und Situationen, die nach Meinung des Sprechers bald eintreten werden (weil es bereits Anzeichen dafür gibt) (1).
> Es wird auch für Pläne und Absichten gebraucht (2).
> Das **going to future** wird mit *am/is/are* + *going to* + Infinitiv gebildet (1, 2).
> Die **Verneinung** bildet man durch das Einfügen von *not/n't* unmittelbar nach *am/is/are* (3).
> **Fragen** werden durch Umstellung gebildet (4).

⚠ Der **Gebrauch des Futurs** hängt in gewissem Maße von der Absicht oder Sichtweise des Sprechers ab. Dies gilt insbesondere für das **going to future** und für zukünftige Ereignisse. Daher ist es im Zweifelsfall ratsam, das neutralere **will future** zu benutzen.

C The present progressive / The simple present

1 We'**re leaving** the house at 10.30.
2 The bus **goes** at 11 o'clock.

> Man kann das **present progressive** auch **mit einer Zeitbestimmung der Zukunft** (*at 10.30, this afternoon, on Sunday*) für bereits feststehende Pläne und Verabredungen verwenden (1).

> Genau wie im Deutschen wird auch im Englischen das **simple present mit einer Zeitangabe** benutzt, um fest terminierte Vorgänge (Fahrpläne, Stundenpläne, Programme usw.) anzugeben (2).

MODAL AUXILIARY VERBS

1 He **can speak** several languages.
2 You **must accept** your new situation.
3 We **needn't go** to work today.
4 **May** I **interrupt** you?

> Um zu sagen, was geschehen kann, muss, darf, soll usw., benutzt man ein modales Hilfsverb in Verbindung mit einem Vollverb (1-4).

⚠ Im Englischen steht ein Hilfsverb - anders als im Deutschen - nie ohne Vollverb:
- Lena kann Spanisch. ⟶ *Lena can speak Spanish.* NICHT: ~~Lena can Spanish.~~

> Modale Hilfsverben - nicht jedoch die Ersatzverben (siehe unten) - haben bei allen Personen immer die gleiche Form, einschließlich der 3. Person Singular (keine *-s*-Endung) (1, 2).

> Die **Verneinung** wird durch das Einfügen von *not/n't* unmittelbar nach dem Hilfsverb gebildet (3).

> **Fragen** bildet man durch Umstellung (4).

> Abgesehen von *could* (wenn es für eine Fähigkeit gebraucht wird) kann man modale Hilfsverben nur im Präsens und - mit einer geeigneten Zeitangabe - mit zukünftiger Bedeutung benutzen, zum Beispiel:
- *You **can go** home now.* (Präsens)
  *You **can go** home an hour early tomorrow.* (Futur)
- *I **must write** these letters now.* (Präsens)
  *I **must write** a long report next week.* (Futur)

⚠ Um andere Zeitformen bei modalen Hilfsverben zu bilden, z. B. die Vergangenheit, muss ein geeignetes Ersatzverb gebraucht werden:

must *The provider **had to block** access to the internet last December.*
can *I **couldn't start** the car yesterday.* (Fähigkeit)
*We **weren't allowed to go** home early last Friday.* (Erlaubnis)

Übersicht der modalen Hilfsverben nach Funktion

Funktion	Modale(s) Hilfsverb(en)	
Fähigkeit	*He **can** speak several languages.* *The first satellites **could** only transmit sound.*	
Möglichkeit	*With your qualifications you **could** work abroad.* *The boss **may** come in at any moment.* *He **might** ask you what you are doing.*	
Bitte	***Can** I have a word with Ms Sims, please?* ***Could** I speak to Ms Sims, please?* ***May** I interrupt you?* ***Might** I ask you a personal question?*	(neutral) (höflich) (betont höflich) (äußerst höflich)
Erlaubnis	*You **can** go in now.* *The boss is free. You **may** go in now.*	(neutral) (gefällig)
Verbot	*We **mustn't** be late for work tomorrow.*	
Pflicht	*You **must** wear a hard hat in the factory.*	
Wahl	*Most shop workers **needn't** work on Sundays.*	
Empfehlung	*You **should** get better qualifications.* *You **ought to** get better qualifications.* *You **must** get better qualifications.*	(neutral) (betont) (streng)

REPORTED SPEECH

A Aussagesätze

1 Some people **claim** that 'servant' robots **are putting** people out of work.
2 The speaker **reminded** his audience that there **were** some jobs robots **couldn't do**.

> Wenn man einem Dritten berichten möchte, was während eines Gespräches gesagt wurde, benutzt man die **indirekte Rede**.

> Bei Verwendung der indirekten Rede benutzt man ein einleitendes Verb wie *claim, say, remind, answer, think, mention* usw., um zu verdeutlichen, dass eine Äußerung wiedergegeben wird.
Steht das einleitende Verb in der Vergangenheit - also *said, answered, mentioned* usw. -, dann verschieben sich die Zeiten wie folgt:

direkte Rede		indirekte Rede
simple present *she works hard*	→	**simple past** *she worked hard*
present progressive *she is working hard*	→	**past progressive** *she was working hard*
simple past *she worked hard*	→	**past perfect** *she had worked hard*
past progressive *she was working hard*	→	**past perfect progressive** *she had been working hard*
present perfect *she has worked hard*	→	**past perfect** *she had worked hard*

present perfect progressive *she has been working hard*	⟶	**past perfect progressive** *she had been working hard*
past perfect *she had worked hard*		(keine Verschiebung) –
past perfect progressive *she had been working hard*		(keine Verschiebung) –
will *she will work hard*	⟶	**would** *she would work hard*
am/is/are going to *she is going to work hard*	⟶	**was/were going to** *she was going to work hard*
would/might etc. *she would work hard*		(keine Verschiebung) –
would have/might have etc. *she had been working hard*		(keine Verschiebung) –

⚠ Die modalen Hilfsverben werden folgendermaßen verschoben:

Modalverb	Bedeutung	indirekte Rede
can	Fähigkeit	*could, was/were able to*
can	Erlaubnis	*was/were allowed to*
may	Möglichkeit	*might*
may	Erlaubnis	*was/were allowed to*
must	Pflicht	*had to*
mustn't	Verbot	*was/were not allowed to*
needn't	freie Wahl	*did not/didn't have to*

> Außer wenn man über ein Gespräch berichtet, das am selben Tag stattgefunden hat, müssen fast alle **Zeit**- und einige **Ortsangaben** entsprechend der folgenden Tabelle geändert werden. (Angaben, die nicht aufgeführt sind, bleiben unverändert.)

direkte Rede		indirekte Rede
today	⟶	*on that day*
tomorrow	⟶	*the next day*
yesterday	⟶	*the day before*
the day after tomorrow	⟶	*two days later*
the day before yesterday	⟶	*two days before*
next day/Friday/week/Christmas/...	⟶	*the following day/Friday/week/Christmas/...*
last Friday/week/summer/...	⟶	*the Friday/week/summer/... before*
two years/months/weeks/... ago	⟶	*two years/months/weeks/... before*
now, at present	⟶	*then*
at the moment	⟶	*at that moment*
at this time	⟶	*at that time*
here	⟶	*there*
in this place	⟶	*at that place*
this	⟶	*that*
these	⟶	*those*

B Fragesätze

1 A member of the audience **asked what had led** to the widespread use of robots in factories.
2 She **wanted to know if/whether** her job **was endangered**.

> Bei indirekten **Fragen** unterscheidet man zwischen Fragen mit Fragewort (1) und Fragen ohne Fragewort (2).
> Bei Fragen **mit Fragewort** wird das Fragewort übernommen (1).
> Bei Fragen **ohne Fragewort** benutzt man *if* bzw. *whether* (= ob), um zu verdeutlichen, dass es sich um eine Frage handelt (2).
> Alle anderen Änderungen erfolgen wie bei den Aussagesätzen (siehe **Aussagesätze** S. 217).

C Bitten, Aufforderungen und Befehle

1 Lucy **asked the engineer to show her** the robot.
2 He **told her not to go** too close to it.

> **Bitten** werden meist durch *asked* (= bitten) (1), **Aufforderungen** und **Befehle** durch *told* (= sagen) (2) eingeleitet.
> Bei **positiven Sätzen** erscheint das Verb als *to* + Infinitiv (1).
> Bei **negativen Sätzen** setzen wir *not* unmittelbar vor *to* (2).

⚠ Die beiden Verben *to tell* und *to ask* stehen immer mit einem Objekt, das die angesprochene Person erwähnt (1, 2). Ist dies vom Kontext her nicht erkennbar, wird einfach ein passender Begriff eingesetzt:

- *Ben said, 'Don't enter the studio when the red light is on.'*
  Ben ***told everybody*** *not to enter the studio when the red light was on.*

THE PASSIVE

1 Measures **are being introduced** to reduce traffic pollution.
2 Pollution **is caused by** some thoughtless people.

> Ist der Verursacher einer Handlung unbekannt oder zweitrangig, benutzt man das Passiv. Im Vordergrund steht also das Ergebnis des Vorgangs (1).
> Möchte man den Verursacher doch angeben, benutzt man einen *by agent* (2).
⚠ Der Verursacher wird mit *by* - auf keinen mit Fall *from* - eingeleitet.
> Das Passiv wird mit einer Zeitform von *to be* und der 3. Form des Vollverbs gebildet:

Zeit	Zeitform von *to be*	3. Form
simple present	*am/is/are*	*caused*
present progressive	*am/is/are being*	*introduced*
simple past	*was/were*	*buried*
past progressive	*was/were being*	*built*
present perfect	*has/have been*	*installed*
will-Futur	*will be*	*blocked*
going to-Futur	*am/is/are going to be*	*sacked*

> Beim Gebrauch von modalen Hilfsverben wird nach folgendem Muster verfahren:

bei Aussagen	Hilfsverb + *to be* + 3. Form	*must be displayed*
bei Fragen	Hilfsverb + Subjekt + *to be* + 3. Form	*Can ... be persuaded?*

⚠ Das Verb *to be* bleibt im Infinitiv immer unverändert.

THE IMPERSONAL PASSIVE

1 **It is said that** petrol will soon cost more.
2 He **is thought** to have gone to hospital.

> Das **impersonal passive** wird vor allem dann benutzt, wenn man sich objektiv bzw. unbeteiligt ausdrücken möchte. Daher kommt diese Struktur oft in Polizeiberichten, seriösen Zeitungsartikeln usw. vor.

> Bei Verben des Berichtens, Denkens usw. benutzt man häufig das Satzmuster:
It is/was/... + 3. Form des einleitenden Verbs + *that*-Satz (1).
Hier sind weitere Beispiele dieses Musters:

Aktiv	*Some **say** that companies which cause pollution should be heavily fined.*
Passiv	***It is said that** companies which cause pollution should be heavily fined.*
Aktiv	*Experts **recommended** that more be spent on public transport.*
Passiv	***It was recommended** that more be spent on public transport.*

> Um das Subjekt des *that*-Satzes zu betonen, kann man folgendes Muster benutzen:
Subjekt + *is/was/...* + 3. Form + *to be* + andere Satzteile (2):

Aktiv	*Many **believe** that the minister is thinking of raising fuel taxes.*
Passiv	*The minister **is believed to be** thinking of raising fuel taxes.*

⚠ Der *by agent* wird in solchen Passivsätzen folgendermaßen verwendet:

Aktiv	*The speaker felt that the idea was too radical.*
Passiv	*The idea was felt to be too radical **by** the speaker.*

CONDITIONALS

1 If we **invest** in new technology, a lot of people **will lose** their jobs.
2 A lot of people **will lose** their jobs if we **invest** in new technology.
3 If more people **took part** in re-training schemes, they **wouldn't have to worry** about finding new employment.
4 We **won't have** political censorship if we **don't start** to censor the internet.
5 **Will** we soon **have** political censorship if we **start** to censor the internet?

> Ein **Konditionalsatz** besteht aus zwei Teilen: dem ***if*-Teil** und dem **Hauptteil**.
Der ***if*-Teil** drückt eine **Bedingung** aus, der Hauptteil eine **Folge**.

> Bei **Konditionalsätzen** kommen folgende **Zeitmuster** am häufigsten vor:

Typ I	*If + simple present*	+	*will*-Futur
Typ II	*If + simple past*	+	*would* + Infinitiv
Typ III	*If + past perfect*	+	*would have* + 3. Form des Verbs

Der *if*-Teil kann hinter dem Hauptteil stehen. In diesem Fall steht kein Komma dazwischen (2).

> Je nach Sinn kann der *if*-Teil, der Hauptteil oder beide Teile des Satzes **verneint** werden (3, 4).

> Bei **Fragen** kann nur der **Hauptteil** zu einer Frage geformt werden. Dann steht dieser Teil **an erster Stelle** (5).

> *if*-Sätze werden gemäß der **Wahrscheinlichkeit** der zu erwartenden Folge eingesetzt:
Typ I: Folge (fast) sicher.
*If we **invest in** new technology, a lot of people **will lose** their jobs.*
D.h. viele Leute werden (vermutlich) ihre Stellen verlieren, da wir (sehr wahrscheinlich) in die neue Technologie investieren werden.
Typ II: Folge theoretisch möglich, aber kaum wahrscheinlich.
*If we **invested in** new technology, a lot of people **would lose** their jobs.*
D.h. es ist kaum zu erwarten, dass viele Leute ihre Stellen verlieren werden, da wir (wahrscheinlich) nicht in die neue Technologie investieren werden.
Typ III: Folge unmöglich, da die Bedingung nicht erfüllt wurde und bereits in der Vergangenheit liegt.
*If we **had invested in** new technology, a lot of people **would have lost** their jobs.*
D.h. der Sprecher weiß schon, dass keiner den Job verloren hat, da wir in die neue Technologie nicht investiert haben.

GERUND/INFINITIVE

1 Max **enjoys playing** football.
2 Can you **afford to buy** that DVD collection?
3 Cem and Julie **continued to meet** even though they had spilt up.
4 Cem and Julie **continued meeting** even though they had split up.
5 Alison **normally likes going** to parties, but **today** she would **prefer to stay** at home.

> Nach einigen Verben folgt immer die *-ing*-Form **(gerund)** (1).
Am wichtigsten sind:

admit, avoid, consider, deny, enjoy, finish, give up, imagine, mention, (not) mind (etwas/nichts dagegen haben), *miss, practise, recommend, risk, stop, suggest*

> **Nach einigen Verben** folgt immer der Infinitiv **(infinitive)** (2).
Die **wichtigsten** Verben dieser Gruppe sind:

afford, choose, decide, expect, hope, manage, mean, plan, promise, refuse, want

⚠ Nach den Verben *begin, continue, intend* und *start* kann der **Infinitiv** oder die ***-ing*-Form beliebig benutzt werden** (3, 4).

> Einige Verben werden **je nach Bedeutung** entweder mit dem **Infinitiv** oder mit der ***-ing*-Form** benutzt. Die **wichtigsten** Verben dieser Gruppe sind:

like, dislike, love, hate, prefer

> Wenn von einer **allgemeingültigen Situation** die Rede ist, folgt auf diese Verben die ***-ing*-Form**. Handelt es sich aber um eine **Ausnahmesituation**, dann verwendet man den **Infinitiv** (5).

advise, allow, encourage, forbid, permit, recommend
Handelt es sich um einen **konkreten Einzelfall**, wird mit diesen Verben ein **Objekt + Infinitiv** verwendet.
*I strongly **advise you to** be more polite to people.*
Wenn es sich aber um eine **allgemeine Situation** handelt, dann steht das nachfolgende Verb in der ***-ing*-Form**.
*Most firms don't **allow smoking** in their offices.*

forget/remember

Die Struktur ***forget/remember*** **+ *-ing*-Form** bezieht sich auf die Vergangenheit. Sie drückt etwa die Idee „Ich werde nie vergessen ..." aus.

⚠ „Vergangenheit" bezieht sich hier nicht auf *forget/remember*, sondern auf das nachfolgende Verb.

*I still **remember getting** my first bicycle.*

*I'll never **forget going** to the Rock against Hunger concert last year.*

Die Struktur ***forget/remember*** **+ Infinitiv** dagegen bezieht sich auf die Zukunft. Sie drückt etwa die Idee aus „Ich darf nicht vergessen, etwas zu tun" bzw. „ich habe noch etwas zu tun, weil ich es bis jetzt vergessen habe".

*Dad, please **remember / don't forget to pick me up** from the station.*

*Oh dear. I **forgot / didn't remember to pick Sally up** from the station.*

regret

Die Struktur ***regret*** **+ *-ing*-Form** drückt Bedauern über eine vergangene Situation bzw. einen vergangenen Vorfall aus. Häufig geht es dabei um verpasste Chancen.

*I really **regret leaving** school without any qualifications.*

*I know they will **regret buying** such a big, expensive car.*

Die Struktur ***regret*** **+ Infinitiv** – fast immer mit einem Verb des Mitteilens wie *inform, say, tell* kombiniert – drückt eine schlechte Nachricht aus.

*I **regret to say** that I can't attend the meeting tomorrow.*

*We **regret to inform** you that the vacancy has now been filled.*

stop

Bedeutet ***stop*** „aufhören, etwas zu tun", steht das nachfolgende Verb in der ***-ing*-Form**.
Bedeutet aber ***stop*** „kurz anhalten, um etwas anderes zu tun", folgt ein Verb im **Infinitiv**.

*For heaven's sake **stop shouting** at me.*

*I'm a little late because I **stopped to give** somebody a lift.*

try

Bedeutet ***try*** „etwas ausprobieren", steht das nachfolgende Verb in der ***-ing*-Form**. Bedeutet aber ***try*** „sich anstrengen, etwas zu tun", folgt ein Verb im **Infinitiv**.

*I **tried phoning** Ellie, but she wasn't at home.*

*We'll **try to repair** your computer by the weekend.*

ADJECTIVES AND ADVERBS

1 John has a **new** DVD player.
2 He always buys **expensive** equipment.
3 My computer has become **very slow**.
4 That CD sounds **terrible**.
5 We can make printouts **quickly** and **cheaply**.

> Um **Personen** oder **Sachen** näher zu beschreiben, benutzt man **Adjektive** (1–4).
> Adjektive stehen **unmittelbar** vor Substantiven oder **unmittelbar nach** einer Form von *be* (bzw. *become* oder *seem*, die *be* ersetzen können) (3).
> **Adjektive** können mit Verben wie *feel, look* (aussehen), *sound, smell* und *taste* eine **sinnliche Wahrnehmung** ausdrücken (4).
> Um einen **Tätigkeitsverb** näher zu beschreiben, setzt man ein Adverb **unmittelbar hinter das Verb** bzw. Verb + Objekt (5).

⚠ Im Englischen können ein Verb und sein Objekt - anders als im Deutschen - nicht durch ein Adverb getrennt werden. Also NICHT: ~~We can make quickly printouts~~. (siehe Word order unten)

> Adverbien werden auch benutzt, um **Adjektive, andere Adverbien** und **ganze Sätze** näher zu bestimmen:
MP3 players have become ***surprisingly cheap.*** (Adverb + Adjektiv)
My fax machine prints out ***terribly slowly.*** (Adverb + Adverb)
Luckily *Gerd left a message on my mailbox.* (Satzadverb)

> Die meisten Adverbien werden durch Anhängen von *-ly* an das Adjektiv gebildet (5). Eine kleine Anzahl von Adverbien hat dieselbe Form wie Adjektive; die häufigsten sind *fast, hard, early late, long, daily*.

COMPARISON OF ADJECTIVES AND ADVERBS

1 A hundred years ago life was **slower** and people may have been **happier**.
2 Which technological innovation is the **most/least important**?
3 Today you can copy data **more easily than** ever before.

> **Einsilbige** und **zweisilbige Adjektive**, die auf *-y* enden - zum Beispiel *easy, happy* und *lucky* -, werden mit *-(i)er/-(i)est* gesteigert (1).

> **Mehrsilbige Adjektive** und **Adverbien**, die auf *-ly* enden, werden mit *more/most* gesteigert (2, 3).
⚠ Die Adverbien, die dieselbe Form wie das entsprechende Adjektiv haben (*fast, hard, early* usw.), werden mit *-er/-est* gesteigert.

> Um Personen oder Sachen im Satz miteinander zu vergleichen, gibt es folgende Möglichkeiten:

Kein Unterschied	*as good as*	genau so gut wie
Unterschied	*not as good as*	nicht so gut wie
Unterschied	*better than*	besser als

WORD ORDER

positions of adverbs of time, place and frequency

1 She goes shopping **every week**.
2 They play in a club **in Doherty Street**.
3 **Last year** we went to India for our holidays.
4 Paul and Emily went to **the USA last year**.
5 She **always finishes** school early on Fridays.
6 He **is never** at home when I call.
7 I like to stay at home **now and then**.
8 Gina acted **strangely at the party last night**.

> Zeitangaben (Wann?) und Ortsangaben (Wo?, Wohin?) stehen in der Regel am Satzende (1, 2).

> Um die Zeit eines bestimmten Ereignisses hervorheben, kann man die Zeitangabe an die erste Stelle setzen (3).

> Stehen eine Zeitangabe und eine Ortsangabe zusammen am Satzende, dann gilt die Reihenfolge Ort vor Zeit (alphabetisch merken: O vor Z!) (4).

> Besteht eine Häufigkeitsangabe aus einem Wort, z.B. *always, often, sometimes*, steht sie unmittelbar vor dem Vollverb (5).

> Lautet das Vollverb *to be*, steht das Adverb direkt dahinter (6).

- > Besteht die Häufigkeitsangabe aus mehreren Wörtern, z.B. *every day, now and then*, steht sie wie eine Zeitangabe am Satzende (7).
- > Adverbien der Art und Weise stehen in der Regel am Satzende. Kommen noch Zeit- oder Ortsadverbien hinzu, lautet die Reihenfolge: Art und Weise - Ort - Zeit (AOZ) (8).

RELATIVE CLAUSES AND CONTACT CLAUSES

1 Car manufacturers are designing cars **which/that** can use hydrogen fuel cells.
2 Wildernesses are being spoiled by tourists **who/that** want to go to 'unspoiled' places.
3 Tony filled in a Dateline questionnaire **(which/that)** he found on the internet.
4 Fred Foley is a paparazzo **whose** photos sell for huge sums of money.
5 Call centre employees, most **of whom** come from India, work long hours.
6 Some non-GM crops are attacked by pests **against which** they have no resistance.

- > Relativsätze werden benutzt, um den Hauptsatz durch zusätzliche Informationen genauer zu bestimmen.
- > Für **Sachen** benutzt man das Relativpronomen *which* bzw. *that* (1) und für Personen *who* bzw. *that* (2).
- > Steht das Relativpronomen für das **Objekt des Hauptsatzes**, dann kann man es weglassen (3). Solche Relativsätze heißen **contact clauses**.
- > Um **Besitz** bzw. **Zugehörigkeit** anzuzeigen, gebraucht man *whose* unmittelbar vor dem **Substantiv** bei Personen und Sachen (4).
- > Steht eine **Präposition** vor dem **Relativpronomen**, wird *whom* für Personen und *which* für Sachen benutzt (5, 6). In solchen Fällen ist der Gebrauch von *that* nicht möglich.

DEFINING AND NON-DEFINING RELATIVE CLAUSES

1 The first Europeans **who** settled in Australia came from Britain.
2 Sydney, **which** is famous for its unusually designed opera house, is situated on the south-eastern coast of Australia.

- > Im **ersten Beispielsatz** ist der Sinn des Hauptsatzes *The first Europeans came from Britain* ohne den Relativsatz *who settled in Australia* offensichtlich falsch bzw. unvollständig. Relativsätze dieser Art - die wesentlich für das Verständnis des gesamten Satzes sind - nennt man **defining relative clauses** (notwendige oder bestimmende Relativsätze).
- > Im **zweiten Beispielsatz** ist die Aussage des Hauptsatzes *Sydney is situated on the south-eastern coast of Australia* ohne den Relativsatz völlig verständlich, weil der Relativsatz *which is famous for its unusually designed opera house* eine zusätzliche, also nebensächliche, Information enhält. Daher werden solche Relativsätze ***non-defining relative clauses*** (nicht notwendige oder nicht bestimmende Relativsätze) genannt.
  ⚠ Notwendige Relativsätze werden immer **ohne** trennende **Kommas** benutzt. Dies signalisiert, dass sie fester Bestandteil der Hauptaussage sind.

PARTICIPLE CONSTRUCTIONS

1 Malaria, preventable with a treated bed net **costing** less than one pound, is endemic.
2 Many men believe that any work **involved** with cooking is a woman's chore.
3 **Losing** more and more people to AIDS, Africa now needs effective help more urgently than ever before.

4 **Burdened** with declining life-expectancy, large parts of Africa are caught in a poverty trap.
5 **Having fetched** water from a river for many years, some women in developing countries are now happy to be able to use the Hippo Roller.
6 **Despite facing** extreme destitution, many rural residents haven't given up hope.
7 Donors should invest in projects that help local inhabitants become self-supporting, **thereby making** sure that the money isn't wasted.
8 Poor infrastructure is a key barrier to economic growth in Nepal, **thus causing** huge additional costs to the transport of commercial goods.
9 Life is becoming hard in the developing countries, **with** many small farmers **going** out of business.
10 AIDS represents a major challenge to sub-Saharan Africa, currently **killing** more than two million people every year.

Die englische Sprache ist geprägt durch häufige Verwendung von Partizipialkonstruktionen. Diese ermöglichen einen eleganteren Sprachfluss.

> Partizipialkonstruktionen verkürzen Relativsätze; dabei kann entweder das **present participle** (1) oder das **past participle** (2) verwendet werden.
> Sie werden auch verwendet, um adverbiale Nebensätze zu vekürzen. In diesen Fällen unterscheidet man zwischen Partizipialkonstruktionen ohne Konjunktion (3-5) und solchen mit Konjunktion (6-9). In Sätzen ohne Konjunktion ist der Inhalt des Satzes auch ohne eine solche klar. Dagegen sind Konjunktionen nötig, um zu verhindern, dass der logische Zusammenhang des Satzes verloren geht. Zum Beispiel wird der Inhalt von Satz 6 unklar, wenn die Konjunktion *despite* ausgelassen wird.
> Wie bei der Verkürzung von Relativsätzen kommen auch bei der Verkürzung von adverbialen Nebensätzen das **present participle** (3, 6-9) und das **past participle** (4) zur Anwendung. Darüber hinaus wird hier auch noch das **perfect participle** verwendet (5), und zwar um die Vorzeitigkeit der Handlung im Nebensatz auszudrücken. *(Nachdem sie jahrelang Wasser aus dem Fluss geholt hatten, ...)*
> Schließlich verknüpft man mit einer Partizipialkonstruktion zwei Hauptsätze zu einem einzigen Satz, und zwar ausnahmslos mittels **present participle** (10).

COUNTABLE AND UNCOUNTABLE NOUNS

1	Visit our website for more **information** on our firm.	NICHT ~~informations~~
2	Have you read the paper today? The political **news** is interesting.	NICHT ~~news are~~
3	Where can I get some **advice**?	NICHT ~~an advice~~

> Einige wichtige **Substantive** sind **zählbar im Deutschen, nicht jedoch im Englischen**. Diese Substantive können also nicht ohne weiteres mit dem unbestimmten Artikel *a/an* oder mit einem Zahlwort benutzt werden.
Hier ist eine Liste solcher Wörter, die Sie auswendig lernen sollten:

advice, baggage, damage, data, equipment, evidence, furniture, information, knowledge, luck, luggage, machinery, news, progress, research, rubbish, work (housework, homework)

> Um diese Substantive im Plural zu verwenden, muss *some, a bit of* bzw. *a piece of* hinzugefügt werden (3).

THE DEFINITE ARTICLE

1 **Sociologists** say that **violence** is increasing among young people.
2 Is **the current trend** partly caused by **the violent films** they watch?
3 **Most sentences** are not tough enough.
4 Nearly **half the prisoners** in **British prisons** are under 25.
5 **Spring** is my favourite season but **the spring** we're having this year is more like **winter**.
6 We had **breakfast** late this morning so we came to school **by car** instead of **by bus**.
7 They are thinking of legalizing soft drugs in **the Netherlands**.

> Hat ein Substantiv eine allgemeine, uneingeschränkte Bedeutung - also „alle ohne Ausnahme" - dann steht es ohne Artikel (1, 5).

> Ist die Bedeutung eines Substantives auf bestimmte Fälle eingeschränkt, benutzt man den Artikel (2, 5).

> Ferner wird der Artikel in den folgenden Fällen und Wendungen im Englischen - z. T. anders als im Deutschen - nicht gebraucht:
- bei *most* in der Bedeutung „die meisten" (3),
- bei öffentlichen Gebäuden im allgemeinen Sinn (4),
- bei Mahlzeiten (6),
- bei Verkehrsmitteln (6),
- bei Straßennamen,
- bei Tageszeiten, Wochentagen, Monaten und Jahreszeiten im allgemeinen Sinn (5).

> Der Artikel wird verwendet nach *all* und *half* (4) und mit den Pluralnamen von Staaten (7).
⚠ Der bestimmte Artikel steht im Englischen (viel) seltener als im Deutschen. Daher: *When in doubt, leave it out!*

Basic word list

Diese Liste enthält ca. 1000 Wörter und Ausdrücke, die in Focus on Success – The new edition: Ausgabe Wirtschaft als bekannt vorausgesetzt werden. Nicht aufgeführt, jedoch vorausgesetzt, sind einige elementare Wörter wie einfache Strukturwörter, Präpositionen, Zahlen, Wochentage usw. sowie internationale Wörter wie *email*, *hotel*, *cowboy* usw.

> **TIP**
>
> Die folgende Grundwortschatzliste ist nach Themenbereichen angelegt. Auch innerhalb der Themenbereiche sind die Vokabeln nach sinnvollen Wortfeldern angeordnet. Dadurch eignet sich die Liste nicht nur zum Nachschlagen, sondern auch zum Lernen. Hierzu gibt es eine einfache, aber effektive Übung. Nehmen Sie sich einen Themenbereich vor und verdecken Sie ein paar Wörter in der linken Spalte. Schauen Sie nun auf die Übersetzungen in der rechten Spalte und bilden Sie englische Sätze, die so viele Übersetzungen der verdeckten deutschen Wörter wie möglich enthalten. Anschließend kontrollieren Sie Ihre Übersetzungen, indem Sie die linke Spalte aufdecken.

PEOPLE
(Menschen)

people *Personen*
population *Bevölkerung, Einwohner*
nationality *Staatsangehörigkeit*
race *Rasse*
racist *rassistisch; Rassist/in*
society *Gesellschaft*
social *sozial*
human *menschlich*
adult *Erwachsene/r*
child *Kind*
teenager *Teenager/in*
sex *Geschlecht*
lady *Dame*
man *Mann, Mensch*
men *Männer, Menschen*
woman *Frau*
women *Frauen*
male *männlich*
female *weiblich, Frauen-*
boy *Junge*
girl *Mädchen*
couple *Paar*
married *verheiratet*
to get married *heiraten*
Mr *Herr*
Mrs, Ms *Frau*
name *Name*
age *Alter*
born *geboren*
life *Leben*
death *Tod*
anybody *jemand, jede/r/s*
anyone *jemand, jede/r/s*
nobody *niemand*
some *einige, etwas*
somebody *jemand*
someone *jemand*
everybody *jede/r/s*
everyone *jede/r/s, alle*
friend *Freund/in*
guest *Gast*
host *Gastgeber/in*
leader *Leiter/in*
loser *Verlierer/in*
member *Mitglied*
group *Gruppe*
crowd *(Menschen-)Menge*
together *zusammen*

FAMILY
(Familie)

family *Familie*
parents *Eltern*
father *Vater*
mother *Mutter*
dad *Papa*
mum, mom *(AE)* *Mama*
stepfather *Stiefvater*
stepmother *Stiefmutter*
husband *(Ehe-)Mann*
wife *(Ehe-)Frau*
children *Kinder*
son *Sohn*
daughter *Tochter*
brother *Bruder*
sister *Schwester*
brothers and sisters *Geschwister*
cousin *Cousin/e*
grandparents *Großeltern*
grandfather *Großvater*
grandmother *Großmutter*
grandchildren *Enkel(kinder)*

EMOTIONS
(Gefühle)

to feel *(sich) fühlen*
feeling, emotion *Gefühl*
happy *glücklich, froh, zufrieden*
joy *Freude*
pleased *zufrieden*
(to) surprise *Überraschung; überraschen*
mad *verrückt, toll*
unhappy *unglücklich*
sad *traurig*
to cry *schreien, weinen*
angry *wütend, zornig*
crazy *verrückt*
afraid of *ängstlich*
to be frightened of *sich fürchten vor*
tired *müde*
care *Sorge*

BODY AND CLOTHING
(Körper und Kleidung)

body *Körper*
physical *physisch, körperlich*
leg *Bein*
arm *Arm*
hand *Hand*
shoulder *Schulter*
hair *Haar(e)*
to touch *anfassen, berühren*
head *Kopf*
face *Gesicht*
eye *Auge*
to look *(aus)sehen, blicken*
nose *Nase*

to smell *riechen*
mouth *Mund*
voice *Stimme*
to smile *lächeln*
to speak *sprechen, reden*
ear *Ohr*
to listen *zuhören*
to hear *hören*
to sound *klingen*
tooth *Zahn*
heart *Herz*
skin *Haut*
health *Gesundheit*
healthy *gesund*
well *gesund, gut*
able *fähig, in der Lage*
flexible *flexibel*
illness *Krankheit*
ill/sick *krank*
painful *schmerzhaft*
fat *dick*
thin *dünn*
short *kurz, klein*
small *klein*
tall/big *groß*
weak *schwach*
strong *stark, kräftig*
old *alt*
young *jung*
clothing *Bekleidung*
clothes *Kleidung, Kleider*
fashion *Mode*
design *Design*
(to) dress *Kleid; (be)kleiden*
to wear *tragen, anhaben*
to cover *(be)decken*
to wash *waschen*
to spray *(be)sprühen*
comfortable *bequem*
uncomfortable *unbequem*
elegant *elegant*
coat *Mantel*
shirt *Hemd*
shoes *Schuhe*
trainers *Turnschuhe*
boot *Stiefel*
bag *Tasche*
uniform *Uniform*

JOBS AND WORK
(Jobs und Arbeit)

to work *arbeiten, funktionieren*
worker *Arbeiter/in*
job *Arbeit, Stelle*
factory *Fabrik*
business *Geschäft, Firma*
company *Firma, Unternehmen*
firm *Firma*
office *Büro, Amt*
assistant *Assistent/in, Verkäufer/in*
director *Direktor/in, Geschäftsführer/in*
boss *Chef/in*
customer *Kunde, Kundin*
meeting *Konferenz, Besprechung*
model *Modell, Model*
project *Projekt*
programme *Programm*
expert *Fachmann/frau*
doctor *Arzt, Ärztin*
police *Polizei*
politician *Politiker/in*
farmer *Bauer, Bäuerin*

SCHOOL
(Schule)

education *Erziehung, (Ausbildung)*
school *Schule*
to learn *lernen, erfahren*
college *Fachhochschule*
to train *trainieren, ausbilden*
university *Universität*
to study *lernen, studieren*
course *Kurs, Lehrgang,*
class *Klasse*
desk *(Schreib-)Tisch*
seat *Sitz(platz)*
teacher *Lehrer/in*
to teach *unterrichten, lehren*
pupil *Schüler/in*
student *Student/in, Lernende/r*
subject *(Schul-)Fach, Thema*
English *englisch*
German *deutsch*
history *Geschichte*
topic *Thema*
question *Frage*
exercise *Übung*
homework *Hausaufgaben*
rule *Vorschrift, Regel*
to match *zuordnen, (zusammen) passen*
correct *richtig*
true *richtig, wahr*
false *falsch*

HOUSES AND HOMES
(Haus und Einrichtung)

house *Haus*
home *Zuhause, Heim; nach Hause*
flat *Wohnung*
to live *wohnen, leben*
address *Adresse*
door *Tür*
key *Schlüssel*
roof *Dach*
window *Fenster*
stairs *Treppe*
room *Zimmer, Raum*
(to) clean *sauber; reinigen, säubern*
furniture *Möbel*
bed *Bett*
table *Tisch*
bath *Bad*
shower *Dusche*
kitchen *Küche*
floor *Etage, (Fuß-)Boden*
alarm *Alarm(anlage)*

HOBBIES AND SPORT
(Hobbys und Sport)

to like *mögen, gern tun*
to interest *interessieren*
to enjoy *genießen, gefallen*
to love *lieben, sehr gern mögen*
favourite *Lieblings-*
fun *Spaß*
sport *Sport*
active *aktiv, tätig, aktiviert*
to play *spielen*
match *Spiel, Wettkampf*
game *Spiel*
ball *Ball, Kugel*
to kick *treten*
score *Ergebnis, Punkt(estand)*
to win *gewinnen, siegen*
winner *Gewinner/in, Sieger/in*
to swim *schwimmen*
to fish *angeln*
cycling *Radfahren*
bike *Rad*
to ride *reiten, (Rad) fahren*
(to) dance *Tanz; tanzen*
dancer *Tänzer/in*
television *Fernsehen, Fernseher*
viewer *Zuschauer/in*
TV programme *Fernsehprogramm*
to smoke *rauchen*

SOCIETY AND SOCIAL PROBLEMS
(Gesellschaft und soziale Probleme)

religion *Religion*
politics *Politik*
political *politisch*
rights *Rechte*
vote *Stimme, Abstimmung*
to allow *erlauben, (zu)lassen*
to control *kontrollieren, regeln*
control *Kontrolle*
poor *arm, schlecht, mangelhaft*
rich *reich, wohlhabend*
protest *Protest*
crime *Verbrechen*
conflict *Konflikt*
problem *Problem*
crisis *Krise*

danger *Gefahr*
dangerous *gefährlich*
serious *schwer, ernst*
wrong *falsch*
to hurt *verletzen*
to hit *schlagen, treffen*
to break *brechen*
to burn *(ver)brennen*
to fight *(be)kämpfen*
to die *sterben*
dead *tot*
to kill *töten*
gun *Schusswaffe, Pistole*
to protect *(be)schützen*
to hide *verstecken, verbergen*
drug *Droge*
risk *Risiko*
mistake *Fehler, Irrtum*
to forbid *verbieten*
to forget *vergessen*
to ignore *ignorieren*
to steal *stehlen*
personal *persönlich*
chance *Chance, Gelegenheit*
responsible *verantwortlich*
law *Gesetz, Recht*
case *Fall*

INTERACTING WITH PEOPLE
(Umgehen mit Menschen)

to communicate *sich mit jdm verständigen*
to talk *sprechen, reden*
to say *sagen*
to tell *sagen, erzählen*
truth *Wahrheit*
to ask *fragen, bitten*
to answer *(be)antworten*
to reply *antworten*
to realize *bemerken, realisieren*
to understand *verstehen, begreifen*
to translate *übersetzen, -tragen*
to explain *erklären*
to repeat *wiederholen*
to agree *zustimmen, vereinbaren*
to express *ausdrücken*
to be sorry *leidtun*
to discuss *diskutieren (über), besprechen*
to argue *argumentieren, streiten*
argument *Argument; Streit*
to shout *schreien*
to order *befehlen, bestellen, ordnen*
to direct *leiten*
to shock *erschüttern, schockieren*
reaction *Reaktion*
to warn *warnen*
to disappoint *enttäuschen*
to promise *versprechen*
to help *helfen*
to share *(sich) teilen, gemeinsam (be)nutzen*
to show *zeigen*
to connect *verbinden*
to call *(an)rufen*
to phone *anrufen*
to ring *läuten, anrufen*
to chat *sich unterhalten, chatten (mit)*
dialogue *Dialog*
conversation *Unterhaltung*
to introduce *(sich) vorstellen*
to meet *(zusammen)treffen, begegnen*
to greet *(be)grüßen*
(to) kiss *Kuss; küssen*
to laugh *lachen*
(to) joke *Witz; scherzen*
(to) offer *Angebot; (an)bieten*
to invite *einladen*
party *Party, Partei*
to arrange *arrangieren, vereinbaren*
to inform *informieren*
to report *berichten*
to notice *bemerken*
to guess *raten, schätzen*

READING AND WRITING
(Lesen und Schreiben)

to read *lesen*
reader *Leser/in*
story *Erzählung, Geschichte*
mail *Post*
letter *Brief, Buchstabe*
to send *senden, schicken*
document *Dokument, Papier*
briefcase *Aktentasche*
key *Taste*
table *Tabelle*
diagram *Diagramm, Grafik*
content *Inhalt*
to write *schreiben*
paper *Papier, Zeitung*
pencil *Bleistift*
point *Punkt; Sinn*
word *Wort*
sentence *Satz*
message *Mitteilung, Nachricht*
slogan *Werbespruch*
form *Form, Formular*
summary *Zusammenfassung*
page *Seite*
title *Titel*
information *Auskunft, Information(en)*
dictionary *Wörterbuch*
to mean *bedeuten, meinen, heißen*
meaning *Bedeutung*
emphasis *Hervorhebung*
to copy *kopieren*
to list *auflisten, notieren*
to note *beachten, notieren*
to complete *vervollständigen*
to comment *kommentieren*
to describe *beschreiben*
description *Beschreibung, Schilderung*
detail *Detail*
stereotype *Klischee*
example *Beispiel*
language *Sprache*
grammar *Grammatik*
vocabulary *Wortschatz*
style *Stil*
clear *klar, deutlich*
formal *formell, förmlich*
dear *liebe/r*

BELIEFS AND ATTITUDES
(Glaube und Einstellungen)

to believe *glauben*
to consider *nachdenken über, halten für*
to think *denken, meinen, finden, glauben*
view *Ansicht, Aussicht*
opinion *Meinung, Einschätzung*
positive *positiv, bejahend*
opposite *Gegenteil; gegensätzlich*
to dislike *nicht mögen*
to hate *hassen, nicht mögen*
option *Option, Wahl, Alternative*
idea *Idee, Gedanke*
to hope *hoffen*
(to) dream *Traum; träumen*
to want *wollen*
to wish *wünschen*
to remember *sich erinnern, daran denken*
to suppose *vermuten*
to imagine *sich vorstellen*
to seem *(er)scheinen*
to prove *beweisen*
real *echt, wirklich*
to worry *sich Sorgen machen*
to know *kennen, wissen*
reason *Vernunft, Grund*
to need *brauchen, benötigen*
necessary *nötig, erforderlich*

MOVEMENT
(Bewegung)

to move *(sich) bewegen, umziehen*
fast *schnell*
slow *langsam*
to go *gehen, fahren*
to walk *(zu Fuß) gehen*
step *Schritt*
to run *laufen*
to jump *springen*

to climb *klettern, steigen*
to fall *fallen*
to sit *sitzen, sich hinsetzen*
to stand *stehen, aushalten*
to rise *steigen*
to turn *(sich) drehen*
to arrive *ankommen*
to come *kommen*
to enter *eintreten, eingeben*
to leave *(ver)lassen*
to bring *bringen, holen*
to carry *tragen*
to put *setzen, stellen, legen*
to press *drücken*
to push *drücken, schieben*
to pull *ziehen*
to lead *führen*
to follow *(be)folgen*
to pass *vorbeigehen, vergehen; bestehen*
to hurry *sich beeilen*
to rush *sich beeilen*
to reach *greifen, erreichen*
to catch *fangen*
to disappear *verschwinden*

TOWNS AND BUILDINGS
(Städte und Gebäude)

city *(Groß-)Stadt*
town *Stadt*
village *Dorf*
neighbourhood *Nachbarschaft*
street *Straße*
path *(Fuß-)Weg, Pfad*
road *(Land-)Straße*
sign *Zeichen, Schild*
corner *Ecke*
map *Karte*
local *örtlich, lokal*
building *Gebäude*
bank *Bank*
church *Kirche*
tower *Turm*
hospital *Krankenhaus*
supermarket *Supermarkt*
market *Markt*
entrance *Eingang, Einfahrt*
bridge *Brücke*
farm *Bauernhof*

TRAFFIC, TRAVEL AND HOLIDAYS
(Verkehr, Reisen und Urlaub)

holiday *Ferien, Urlaub, Feiertag*
abroad *im/ins Ausland*
foreign *fremd*
international *international*
national *national, staatlich*
country *Land, Staat*
European *europäisch*
American *amerikanisch*
tour *Tour, Rundgang*
trip *Ausflug, Reise, Besuch*
tourist *Tourist/in*
visitor *Besucher/in, Gast*
to travel *reisen, fahren*
to visit *besuchen, besichtigen*
to plan *planen*
boat *Boot, Schiff*
ship *Schiff*
bus *(Linien-)Bus*
truck *Laster, Lkw*
car *Auto*
vehicle *Fahrzeug, Wagen*
to drive *(Auto) fahren*
driver *Fahrer/in*
plane *Flugzeug*
helicopter *Hubschrauber*
flight *Flug*
to fly *fliegen*
airport *Flughafen*
train *Zug*
underground *unterirdisch; U-Bahn*
station *Bahnhof*
ticket *Fahrkarte, Eintrittskarte*
to miss *verpassen, vermissen*
to return *zurückkehren, -gehen*
hotel *Hotel*
beach *Strand*
to relax *sich erholen*
photo *Foto*

MONEY AND SHOPPING
(Geld und Einkaufen)

money *Geld*
to earn *verdienen*
to afford *es sich leisten können*
to spend *ausgeben, verbringen*
to buy *kaufen*
to pay *(be)zahlen*
to sell *(sich) verkaufen*
to charge *berechnen, verlangen, (auf)laden*
to cost *kosten*
price *(Kauf-)Preis*
worth *wert*
bill *Rechnung*
present *Geschenk*
prize *Preis*
free *kostenlos, frei*
cheap *billig, günstig*
expensive *teuer*
luxury *Luxus*
card *Karte*
cash *Bargeld*
to change *(aus)wechseln, (sich) ändern*
to borrow *borgen, leihen*
to belong *gehören zu*
to own *besitzen*
to prefer *vorziehen, bevorzugen*
to choose *(aus)wählen*
available *verfügbar*
product *Produkt, Erzeugnis*
to produce *produzieren, herstellen*
shop *Laden, Geschäft*
shopping *Einkaufen*
sale *Verkauf*
success *Erfolg*
to open *öffnen*
to close *schließen*
open *offen*
closed *geschlossen*

EATING AND DRINKING
(Essen und Trinken)

to eat *essen*
food *Essen, Nahrung*
to cook *kochen*
to prepare *(sich) vorbereiten*
meal *Essen, Mahlzeit*
breakfast *Frühstück*
lunch *Mittagessen*
dinner *(Abend-)Essen*
to taste *schmecken*
hunger *Hunger*
hungry *hungrig*
thirst *Durst*
thirsty *durstig*
meat *Fleisch*
potato *Kartoffel*
vegetable *Gemüse*
fruit *Obst, Frucht*
fresh *frisch*
salt *Salz*
burger *Hamburger*
chicken *Huhn, Hähnchen*
egg *Ei*
cheese *Käse*
chocolate *Schokolade, Praline*
cake *Kuchen, Torte*
sweet *süß; Süßigkeit*
to drink *trinken*
mineral water *Mineralwasser*
tea *Tee*
juice *Saft*
alcohol *Alkohol*
wine *Wein*
beer *Bier*
bar *Bar*
cup *Tasse*
glass *Glas*
bottle *Flasche*
knife *Messer*
fork *Gabel*
spoon *Löffel*
plate *Platte, Teller*
bowl *Schüssel*
box *Kiste, Kästchen, Schachtel*
packet *Schachtel, Packung*

NATURE AND WEATHER
(Natur und Wetter)

nature *Natur*
natural *natürlich*
planet *Planet*
world *Welt*
continent *Erdteil, Kontinent*
environment *Umwelt, Umfeld*
earth *Erde*
air *Luft*
water *Wasser*
ice *Eis*
fire *Feuer*
sky *Himmel*
mountain *(größerer) Berg*
river *Fluss*
wind *Wind*
rain *Regen*
sun *Sonne*
storm *Sturm*
heat *Hitze*
hot *heiß, warm*
warm *warm*
cold *kalt*
to dry *trocknen*
wet *nass*
light *Licht, hell, leicht*
to shine *scheinen*
dark *dunkel*
animal *Tier*
dog *Hund*
cat *Katze*
bird *Vogel*
fish *Fisch*
flower *Blume*
plant *Pflanze*
tree *Baum*
to recycle *wieder verwerten*
to waste *verschwenden*

SCIENCE AND TECHNOLOGY
(Wissenschaft und Technik)

science *Wissenschaft*
scientist *Wissenschaftler/in*
chemical *chemisch; Chemikalie*
technical *technisch*
to build *(auf)bauen*
tool *Werkzeug*
device *Gerät, Apparat*
machine *Maschine*
computer *Computer*
data *Daten*
image *Bild*
to switch on *an-, einschalten*
to click *klicken*
to print *drucken*
electric *elektrisch, Strom-*
electricity *Elektrizität, Strom*
power *Kraft, Strom*
instruction *Anleitung*
method *Methode, Verfahren*
system *System*
to repair *reparieren*
modern *modern*
new *neu*
safe *sicher*
automatic *automatisch*

ART AND CULTURE
(Kunst und Kultur)

art *Kunst*
picture *Bild*
symbol *Symbol, Zeichen*
to draw *zeichnen*
scene *Szene*
to represent *darstellen*
culture *Kultur*
to act *handeln*
movie *Film*
book *Buch*
author *Autor/in*
article *Artikel*
newspaper *Zeitung*
magazine *Zeitschrift*
news *Neuigkeit(en), Nachricht(en)*
media *Medien*
song *Lied*
singer *Sänger/in*
music *Musik*
band *Kapelle*

QUALITIES AND CHARACTERISTICS
(Eigenschaften und Besonderheiten)

character *Charakter*
kind *Art, Sorte*
similar *ähnlich*
different *anders, verschieden*
difference *Unterschied*
advantage *Vorteil*
disadvantage *Nachteil*
to be *sein*
to become *werden*

DESCRIBING PEOPLE AND SITUATIONS
(Menschen und Situationen beschreiben)

friendly *freund(schaft)lich*
kind *nett*
interesting *interessant*
individual *individuell*
boring *langweilig*
funny *komisch, merkwürdig*
busy *beschäftigt, besetzt*
lazy *faul*
helpful *hilfreich, nützlich*
careful *vorsichtig, sorgfältig*
creative *gestalterisch, kreativ*
romantic *romantisch*
smart *schick, clever*
stupid *dumm*
silly *albern*
nice *schön, nett*
tough *zäh*
strict *streng, strikt*
polite *höflich*
rude *unhöflich, rüde*
pretty *hübsch*
beautiful *schön*
ugly *hässlich*
positive *positiv*
negative *negativ, verneinend*
strange *fremd, seltsam*
normal *normal*
perfect *vollkommen, perfekt*
special *besondere*
well-known *sehr bekannt, berühmt*
famous *berühmt*
popular *beliebt, populär*
unknown *unbekannt*
good *gut*
better *besser*
best *beste/r/s, am besten*
great *groß(artig)*
amazing *erstaunlich*
excellent *ausgezeichnet*
wonderful *wunderbar, -voll*
fantastic *fantastisch, wunderbar*
bad *schlecht, schlimm*
worse *schlechter, schlimmer*
worst *schlechteste/r/s, schlimmste/r/s*
horrible, awful, terrible *furchtbar, schrecklich*
easy *leicht, einfach*
basic *elementar*
simple *einfach*
hard *schwer, schwierig, hart*
difficult *schwer, schwierig*
important *wichtig*
successful *erfolgreich*
exciting *aufregend, spannend*
useful *nützlich*
unfair *unfair*
poor *arm*
wealthy *reich*
loud *laut*
quiet, silent *ruhig, still*
wet *nass*
dry *trocken*
slow *langsam*
quick *schnell, rasch*

DESCRIBING OBJECTS
(Gegenstände beschreiben)

type *Typ, Art*
object *Gegenstand*
thing *Sache, Ding, Gegenstand*
piece *Stück, Teil*
unit *Unit, Einheit*
colour *Farbe*
this *dies, diese/r/s*
that *das*
these *diese*
those *jene*
their *ihr/e/r/s*

Size – shape – weight
(Größe – Form – Gewicht)
line *Linie*
circle *Kreis*
hole *Loch*
size *Größe*
little *klein, wenig*
to grow *wachsen*
big *groß*
large *groß, umfangreich*
weight *Gewicht*
heavy *stark, schwer*
light *leicht*
to fill *füllen*
full *voll, vollständig*
empty *leer*
wide *breit, weit*
narrow *eng*
metre *Meter*
long *lang*
short *kurz*
hard *fest*
soft *weich*

ACTIONS AND PROCESSES
(Handlungen und Prozesse)

action *Aktion, Handlung*
activity *Tätigkeit*
to do *tun, machen*
to happen *passieren, geschehen*
to start *anfangen, starten, beginnen*
to continue *fortsetzen*
to finish *beenden, erledigen*
to stop *(an) halten, aufhören (mit)*
to result from *folgen aus*
to let *erlauben, (zu)lassen*

Necessity, probability, possibility
(Notwendigkeit, Wahrscheinlichkeit, Möglichkeit)
condition *Bedingung*
may *dürfen, können, mögen*
maybe *vielleicht*
possible *möglich, denkbar*
impossible *unmöglich*
probably *wahrscheinlich*
can *können, dürfen*
could *konnte/n, könnte/n*
would *würde/n*
will *werde(n), wollen*
should *soll/en, sollte/n*
must *müssen*
to have to *müssen*

Everyday actions
(Alltagshandlungen)
to take *nehmen, bringen, dauern*
to decide *(sich) entscheiden, beschließen*
decision *Entscheidung*
to make *machen*
to fix *festlegen, reparieren*
to check *(über)prüfen*
to organize *organisieren*
to get *holen, bekommen, werden*
to give *geben*
to hold *abhalten, veranstalten*
to keep *(be)halten*
to spare *übrig haben*
to set *setzen*
to mix *mischen*
to remove *entfernen*
to avoid *vermeiden*
to wait *warten*
to watch *beobachten*
to see *sehen*
to search *(durch)suchen*
to find *finden, suchen*
to use *benutzen, verwenden*
to try *versuchen, probieren*
to experience *erfahren, erleben*
to open *öffnen, beginnen*
to develop *entwickeln*
to save *retten, sichern*
to recover *sich erholen*
to sleep *schlafen*
to wake up *aufwachen, aufwecken*

TIME *(Zeit)*

period *Periode, Zeitraum*
date *Datum, Termin*
beginning *Anfang*
to begin *anfangen, beginnen*
(to) end *Ende, Schluss; (be)enden*
final *letzte/r/s*
first *erste/r/s, zuerst*
last *letzte/r/s, zuletzt*
time *Zeit, Mal*

Days, months, ...
(Tage, Monate, ...)
second *Sekunde*
minute *Minute*
hour *Stunde*
o'clock *... Uhr*
day *Tag*
morning *Morgen*
afternoon *Nachmittag*
evening *Abend*
night *Nacht*
tonight *heute Abend/Nacht*
today *heute*
yesterday *gestern*
tomorrow *morgen*
week *Woche*
weekend *Wochenende*
month *Monat*
year *Jahr*
season *Saison, Jahreszeit*
spring *Frühling*
summer *Sommer*
autumn *Herbst*
winter *Winter*
Christmas *Weihnachten*
Easter *Ostern*
birthday *Geburtstag*
age *Zeitalter*

Frequency
(Häufigkeit)
sometimes *manchmal*
often *oft, häufig*
usual *gewöhnlich, normal*
usually *normalerweise, gewöhnlich, meistens*
common *üblich, gemeinsam*
regular *regelmäßig, regulär*
daily *täglich*
always *immer*
never *nie(mals)*

Other words for talking about time *(andere Zeitangaben)*
early *früh*
late *spät*
later *später*
until *bis*
now *nun, jetzt*
then *dann*
ago *vor*
as *wie, als, da*
yet *noch*
before *vor(her)*
after *nach*
past *vorbei, nach; Vergangenheit*
future *Zukunft; (zu)künftig*
soon *bald*
suddenly *plötzlich*
only *nur, einzig*
once *einmal, einst*
again *wieder*
next *nächste/r/s; danach*
already *schon, bereits*
recent *letzt, jüngst*
while *während*
at the moment *momentan, augenblicklich*
nowadays *heutzutage*
forever *für immer*
ever *je(mals)*

ready *fertig, bereit*

PLACE AND DIRECTION
(Orts- und Richtungsangaben)

space *(Zwischen-)Raum, Abstand, Platz, Weltall*
place *Stelle, Platz*
situation *Situation, Lage*
outside *außer(halb)*
outdoors *draußen, im Freien*
inside *innerhalb, drinnen*
far *weit (entfernt)*
near *bei, nahe*
around *herum*
away *weg, entfernt*
back *zurück*
forward *vorwärts*

Prepositions *(Präpositionen)*

from *von*
across *(quer) über*
along *entlang*
over *(vor)über*
under *unter*
between *zwischen*
through *durch*
behind *hinter, hinten*

Other words for describing places *(andere Ortsangaben)*

direct *direkt*
state *Zustand, Staat*
to stay *bleiben*
here *hier*
there *da, dort(hin)*
anywhere *irgendwo(hin)*
somewhere *irgendwo(hin)*
nowhere *nirgends*
front *Vorderseite*
side *Seite, Rand*
top *Spitze, Gipfel; Spitzen-*
bottom *Boden, Unterseite*
high *hoch*
low *tief, niedrig*
distance *Entfernung, Abstand*
kilometre *Kilometer*
north *Norden, Nord-*
east *Osten*
south *Süden, Süd-*
west *Westen*
middle *Mitte*
left *linke/r/s, links*
right *rechts*

QUANTITY *(Menge)*

number *Nummer, Zahl*
count *zählen*
to add *zusammenzählen, hinzufügen*
plus *plus*
kilo *Kilo(gramm)*
litre *Liter*
limit *Grenze*
all *alle(s)*
whole *ganz*
almost *fast, beinahe*
nearly *beinahe, fast*
very *sehr*
really *wirklich, eigentlich, tatsächlich*
a lot *viel, sehr*
lots of *viel, viele*
many *viele*
most *meist*
much *viel*
more *mehr*
extra *zusätzlich*
double *doppelt*
both *beide*
pair *Paar*
enough *ausreichend, genug*
half *Hälfte; halb*
part *Teil*
quite *ziemlich, ganz*
less *weniger, abzüglich*
few *ein paar, wenig/e/r/s*
a little *ein wenig, etwas*
alone *allein(e)*
minimum *Minimum; minimal*
none *kein/e/r/s*
nothing *nichts*
neither *auch nicht, keine/r/s*
any *irgendetwas, welche/r/s, jede/r/s*
anything *etwas, alles*
another *noch eine*
other *andere/r/s*
each *jede/r/s*
every *jede/r/s*
everything *alles*
exactly *exakt, genau*
specific *spezifisch*
just *einfach, nur, genau*
about *über, etwa*
to include *einschließen*

CONNECTORS *(Strukturwörter)*

because *weil*
so *also, damit, deshalb, so (dass)*
simply *einfach*
certainly *sicherlich, bestimmt*
for example *zum Beispiel*
such as *wie zum Beispiel*
(in this) way *Weg, Methode, auf diese Art (und Weise)*
but *aber, sondern*
however *doch, jedoch*
except *außer*
else *andere/r/s*
than *als*
whether *ob*
if *wenn, falls, ob*
or *oder*
same *gleiche/r/s, der-, die-, dasselbe*
also *auch, außerdem*
too *zu, auch*
with *mit, bei*
without *ohne*
in case *falls*
perhaps *vielleicht, eventuell*
even *sogar (noch)*
anyway *jedenfalls, sowieso*

USEFUL WORDS AND PHRASES
(Nützliche Wörter und Ausdrücke)

to welcome *willkommen*
excuse me *Entschuldigung*
please *bitte*
of course *natürlich, selbstverständlich*
sure *freilich, sicher(lich)*
thanks *Dank; danke*
unfortunately *leider*
total *(End-)Summe; völlig, (ins) gesamt*
main *hauptsächlich, wichtigste/r/s*
something *etwas*
fact *Tatsache, Fakt*
tip *Vorschlag, Hinweis, Tipp*
pro *für*
con *wider*
against *gegen*

QUESTION WORDS
(Fragewörter)

what? *was?, welche/r/s?*
where? *wo(hin)?*
when? *wenn?, wann?*
who? *wer?, welche(r/s)?*
which? *welche/r/s?*
why? *warum?*
how? *wie?*

Unit word list

Dieses Wörterverzeichnis enthält alle Wörter in **Focus on Success – The new edition: Ausgabe Wirtschaft** in der Reihenfolge ihres Erscheinens. Nicht aufgeführt sind die Wörter aus der *Basic word list* sowie internationale Wörter wie *hotel, email* usw.
Die Wörter der *Business Options*-Seiten werden in den darauf folgenden Units nicht vorausgesetzt. Wörter, die in den Hörverständnistexten vorkommen, sind mit einem CD-Symbol gekennzeichnet.

AE = American English
BE = British English
abbrev = abbreviation (*Abkürzung*)
n = noun (*Substantiv*)
v = verb
adj = adjective
adv = adverb

inf = informal (*informell, Umgangssprache*)
phr = phrase (*feststehende Wendung*)
<> = opposite (*Gegensatz*)
fem = feminine
pl = plural
esp = especially

REFRESHER COURSE

UNIT A

page 6

to chill out	[ˌtʃɪl 'aʊt]	*(inf)* to relax	*sich entspannen*
to hang around	[ˌhæŋ ə'raʊnd]	*(inf)* to spend a lot of time in a place	*rumhängen*
speech bubble	['spi:tʃ bʌbl]	circle with words to show what someone says	*Sprechblase*
text message	['tekst mesɪdʒ]	written message sent by phone	*SMS*
chatroom	['tʃætru:m]	internet site where you can communicate with other people online	*Chatroom, Diskussionsforum*
to discover	[dɪ'skʌvə]	*n* discovery	*entdecken*
movies	['mu:viz]	*(AE) BE:* cinema	*Kino*
to go clubbing	[gəʊ 'klʌbɪŋ]	to go out to clubs	*in Discos gehen*
net	[net]	*(abbrev)* internet	*Internet*
to carry out	[ˌkæri 'aʊt]	to do (a task)	*ausführen*
survey	['sɜ:veɪ]	set of questions used to find out people's opinions	*Umfrage*

page 7

according to	[ə'kɔ:dɪŋ tə]	as reported by	*nach, gemäß*
Red Cross	[ˌred 'krɒs]	a community service that helps people in need	*Rotes Kreuz*
worthwhile	[ˌwɜ:θ'waɪl]	important, worth doing	*der Mühe wert*
the box	[ðə 'bɒks]	*(inf)* television	*die Kiste*
the homeless	[ðə 'həʊmləs]	people who have no home	*die Obdachlosen*
to get a lot out of sth	[ˌget ə lɒt 'aʊt əv]	to benefit from sth	*viel davon haben*
Are you joking?	[ɑ: ju 'dʒəʊkɪŋ]	used to show surprise	*Ist das dein Ernst?*
schoolwork	['sku:lwɜ:k]	homework	*Hausaufgaben*
to suffer	['sʌfə]	to become worse	*leiden*
to look round	[ˌlʊk 'raʊnd]	to visit a place and see what is there	*sich umsehen*
I'm afraid	[aɪm ə'freɪd]	unfortunately, sorry	*leider*
coach	[kəʊtʃ]	trainer	*Trainer/in*
to expect	[ɪk'spekt]	*phr* to expect sb to do sth	*erwarten*
violent	['vaɪələnt]	*n* violence	*gewalttätig*
stuff	[stʌf]	things	*Zeug*
to test	[test]	to examine	*prüfen*
skill	[skɪl]	thing you are good at	*Fähigkeit, Geschick*
to network	['netwɜ:k]	to link up with	*vernetzen*

all over the place	[ɔ:l ˌəʊvə ðə 'pleɪs]	everywhere	*überall*
voluntary	['vɒləntri]	*v* to volunteer	*freiwillig*
competitive	[kəm'petətɪv]	*phr* competitive sports	*Wettkampf-*
part-time job	[ˌpɑ:t 'taɪm dʒɒb]	*v* to work part-time	*Teilzeitjob*
expression	[ɪk'spreʃn]	word or phrase	*Ausdruck*
definition	[ˌdefɪ'nɪʃn]	explanation of a word	*Definition*
valuable	['væljuəbl]	useful, important	*wertvoll*
permanent	['pɜ:mənənt]	<> temporary	*ständig, dauerhaft*
certain	['sɜ:tn]	definite	*gewiss, sicher*
ability	[ə'bɪləti]	skill	*Fähigkeit*

page 8

not necessarily	[nɒt ˌnesə'serəli]	*adj* necessary	*nicht unbedingt*
order	['ɔ:də]	sequence	*Reihenfolge*
employer	[ɪm'plɔɪə]	*v* to employ	*Unternehmer, Arbeitgeber*
qualification	[ˌkwɒlɪfɪ'keɪʃn]	*phr* job qualifications	*Qualifikation, Ausbildung*
cinema	['sɪnəmə]	*(BE) AE:* movie theater	*Kino*
instead of	[ɪn'sted əv]	rather than	*statt, anstatt (von)*
petrol	['petrəl]	*(BE) AE:* gas	*Benzin*
to refer to	[rɪ'fɜ: tə]	to talk about sth specific	*sich beziehen auf*
to replace	[rɪ'pleɪs]	to put sth in the place of sth else	*ersetzen*
underlined	[ˌʌndə'laɪnd]	with a line underneath the word	*unterstrichen*
suitable	['su:təbl]	appropriate	*passend, geeignet*
to score a goal	[skɔ:r ə 'gəʊl]	e.g. Ronaldo scored three goals.	*ein Tor erzielen*
to be lucky	[bi 'lʌki]	not: ~~to have luck~~	*Glück haben*
times	[taɪmz]	*phr* many times	*mal*

page 9

rare	['reə]	not very often, unusual	*selten*
seldom	['seldəm]	not very often, rarely	*selten*
general	['dʒenrəl]	most of the time, basic	*allgemein*
weekday	['wi:kdeɪ]	*phr* on weekdays	*Wochentag*
drum	[drʌm]	*phr* to play the drums	*Trommel*
to surf	[sɜ:f]	*phr* to surf the net	*surfen*
mark	[mɑ:k]	result at school	*Note*
better	['betə]	<> worse	*besser*

page 10

below	[bɪ'ləʊ]	<> above	*unten*
pub	[pʌb]	*(BE) AE:* bar	*Kneipe*
mate	[meɪt]	*(inf)* friend	*Kumpel*
at present	[ət 'preznt]	at the moment	*gegenwärtig*
currently	['kʌrəntli]	at the moment	*zurzeit*

page 11

to serve	[sɜ:v]	to give (a meal) to sb	*servieren*
ordinary	['ɔ:dnri]	normal	*gewöhnlich, normal*
exercise bike	['eksəsaɪz baɪk]	bike which is used for keeping fit	*Heimtrainer*
to practise	['præktɪs]	*n* practice	*üben*
penalty	['penlti]	*phr* to take a penalty	*Strafstoß*
cash machine	['kæʃ məʃi:n]	machine which lets people take money from their bank accounts	*Geldautomat*
to manage	['mænɪdʒ]	to control sth, to deal with sth	*zurechtkommen, fertig werden (mit), (es) schaffen*
to try on	[ˌtraɪ 'ɒn]	to put on a piece of clothing to see whether you like it	*anprobieren*

UNIT B

page 12

to ban	[bæn]	to say that sth is not allowed	*verbieten*
discrimination	[dɪˌskrɪmɪ'neɪʃn]	*v* to discriminate against	*Diskriminierung*
public school	[ˌpʌblɪk 'sku:l]	*(AE) BE:* state school	*staatliche Schule*
requirement	[rɪ'kwaɪəmənt]	thing that is necessary	*Erfordernis*
to make up	[ˌmeɪk 'ʌp]	to form	*bilden*
awesome	['ɔ:səm]	very difficult or impressive	*überwältigend*
challenge	[tʃælɪndʒ]	a difficult task	*Herausforderung*

to wrestle	['resl]	to fight sb as a sport	*ringen*
mat	[mæt]	piece of material that people wrestle on	*Matte*
rival	['raɪvl]	person or team who plays against sb	*Gegner/in, Rivale, -lin*
unblinking	[ʌn'blɪŋkɪŋ]	to blink = blinzeln	*unbewegt*
shiver	['ʃɪvə]	*phr* a shiver of fear	*Zittern*
fear	[fɪə]	*v* to fear	*Furcht*
hulk	[hʌlk]	big strong man	*Kerl wie ein Baum*
stretcher	['stretʃə]	piece of equipment used to carry sb who has been hurt	*Trage*
hold	[həʊld]	*v* to hold	*Griff*
to twist	[twɪst]	to turn	*(ver)drehen*
muscle	['mʌsl]	⚠ Aussprache	*Muskel*
to injure	['ɪndʒə]	to hurt	*verletzen*
stereotype	['steriətaɪp]	e.g. racial stereotype	*Klischee*
to compete	[kəm'pi:t]	to play against other people or teams	*konkurrieren*
teammate	['ti:mmeɪt]	person who is on the same team as you	*Mannschaftskamerad/in*
session	['seʃn]	time spent doing a particular activity	*Treffen, Termin*
nasty	['nɑ:sti]	not nice	*gemein*
sweetie	['swi:ti]	*(inf)* darling	*Liebling, Schatz*
next door	[ˌnekst 'dɔ:]	in the next room or building	*nebenan*
to set to work	[set tə 'wɜ:k]	to begin a task or project	*ans Werk gehen*
to impress	[ɪm'pres]	*adj* impressive	*imponieren*
to beat	[bi:t]	to win against sb	*schlagen*
to back off	[ˌbæk 'ɒf]	to stop making things difficult for sb	*zurücktreten*
warrior	['wɒriə]	someone who fights in a war	*Krieger*
princess	[ˌprɪn'ses]	daughter of king or queen	*Prinzessin*
guy	[gaɪ]	*(inf)* boy, man	*Kerl, Typ*
equal	['i:kwəl]	person who is treated the same as others	*Gleichberechtigte/r, Ebenbürtige/r*
page 13			
statement	['steɪtmənt]	*v* to state	*Aussage*
proud	[praʊd]	pleased with oneself	*stolz*
ice-hockey	['aɪs hɒki]	hockey played on ice	*Eishockey*
first aider	[ˌfɜ:st 'eɪdə]	*phr* first aid	*Sanitäter*
opponent	[ə'pəʊnənt]	person or team who plays against sb	*Gegner/in*
feminine	['femənɪn]	connected with women	*weiblich*
to teach sb a lesson	[ti:tʃ ə 'lesn]	to show sb they were wrong by making sth bad happen to them	*jdm eine Lektion erteilen*
glad	[glæd]	pleased	*froh*
to accept	[ək'sept]	*adj* acceptable	*akzeptieren*
private	['praɪvət]	<> public	*privat, persönlich*
precise	[prɪ'saɪs]	exactly	*genau*
frightening	['fraɪtnɪŋ]	scary	*beängstigend, erschreckend*
increasing	[ɪn'kri:sɪŋ]	getting bigger	*zunehmend*
pleasant	['pleznt]	nice	*angenehm*
to discriminate	[dɪ'skrɪmɪneɪt]	to contrast, but: to discriminate against sb	*unterscheiden, diskriminieren*
to require	[rɪ'kwaɪə]	*n* requirement	*erfordern*
injury	['ɪndʒəri]	*v* to injure	*Verletzung*
competition	[ˌkɒmpə'tɪʃn]	*v* to compete	*Wettkampf*
impression	[ɪm'preʃn]	a feeling or an idea about sth	*Eindruck*
to challenge	['tʃælɪndʒ]	to test sb's skills with a difficult task	*herausfordern*
to rival	['raɪvl]	to compete with	*konkurrieren*
wrestler	['reslə]	*v* to wrestle	*Ringer/in*
missing	['mɪsɪŋ]	absent	*fehlend*
page 14			
EU	[ˌi: 'ju:]	*(abbrev)* European Union	*EU*
football	['fʊtbɔ:l]	*AE:* American football	*American Football (BE: Fußball)*
phenomenal	[fə'nɒmɪnl]	*n* phenomenon	*phänomenal*
talent	['tælənt]	special natural ability	*Talent*
although	[ɔ:l'ðəʊ]	even though	*obwohl*
grade	[greɪd]	result in school	*Note*

page 15

planner	['plænə]	book in which people write their plans	*(Termin-)Kalender*
further	['fɜːðə]	additional	*weiter*
lunchtime	['lʌntʃtaɪm]	time when people eat their mid-day meal	*Mittagspause*
ironing	['aɪənɪŋ]	*v* to iron	*Bügeln*
hairdresser	['heədresə]	person who cuts and styles hair	*Friseur/in*
to record	[rɪ'kɔːd]	to store a film or TV programme on video/DVD	*aufzeichnen*
BBC	[ˌbiː biː 'siː]	*(abbrev)* British Broadcasting Corporation	*BBC*
to swap	[swɒp]	to switch	*tauschen*
role	[rəʊl]	role-play	*Rolle*
at least	[ət 'liːst]	at the minimum	*mindestens*
to go camping	[gəʊ 'kæmpɪŋ]	to go on holiday in a tent or caravan	*campen*
leisure centre	['leʒə sentə]	place where people go to keep fit	*Freizeitzentrum*
to go on a date	[gəʊ ɒn ə 'deɪt]	to meet a (possible) boyfriend or girlfriend	*eine Verabredung haben*

UNIT C

page 16

case study	['keɪs stʌdi]	detailed description of a particular person/situation	*Fallstudie*
double life	['dʌbl laɪf]	*phr* to lead a double life	*Doppelleben*
genuine	['dʒenjuɪn]	real	*echt*
eating disorder	[ˌiːtɪŋ dɪs'ɔːdə]	e.g. anorexia, bulimia	*Essstörung*
anorexia	[ˌænə'reksiə]	illness where people don't eat because they want to be very thin	*Magersucht*
bulimia	[bjuː'lɪmiə]	illness where people eat and make themselves sick to stay thin	*Bulimie, Ess-Brech-Sucht*
charming	['tʃɑːmɪŋ]	*n* charm	*charmant*
attractive	[ə'træktɪv]	*v* to attract	*attraktiv*
community	[kə'mjuːnəti]	people who live together in an area/ a society	*Gemeinde*
secret	['siːkrɪt]	*phr* to keep sth secret	*geheim*
double-decker	[ˌdʌbl 'dekə]	*phr* double-decker bus	*Doppeldecker*
packet	['pækɪt]	small paper or plastic container	*Schachtel, Packung, Tüte*
tub	[tʌb]	small round plastic container	*Becher*
to scream	[skriːm]	here: to attract attention with big writing and bright colours	*schreien*
familiar	[fə'mɪliə]	*n* familiarity	*bekannt*
tingling	['tɪŋglɪŋ]	*v* to tingle	*kribbelnd, prickelnd*
to lose control over	[luːz kən'trəʊl əʊvə]	to no longer be able to control sth	*die Beherrschung verlieren*
to stuff	[stʌf]	to push sth into a space	*stopfen*
greedy	['griːdi]	*n* greed	*gierig*
in no time	[ɪn 'nəʊ taɪm]	very quickly	*im Handumdrehen*
counter	['kaʊntə]	*phr* over the counter	*Tresen, Ladentisch*
dessert	[dɪ'zɜːt]	sweet food eaten at the end of a meal	*Nachspeise, -tisch*
caramel	['kærəmel]	sweet sauce made by melting sugar	*Karamel*
donut	['dəʊnʌt]	*(AE) BE:* doughnut	*Pfannkuchen, Krapfen*
cheeky	['tʃiːki]	a bit rude but in a funny way	*frech, kess*
to grin	[grɪn]	smile	*lächeln, grinsen*
to sink	[sɪŋk]	to go down	*sinken*
dirty	['dɜːti]	<> clean	*schmutzig*
guilty	['gɪlti]	<> innocent	*schuldig*
cubicle	['kjuːbɪkl]	e.g. shower/toilet cubicle	*Kabine*
to bend	[bend]	*phr* to bend over	*(sich) beugen*
toilet pan	['tɔɪlət pæn]	*(AE) BE:* toilet bowl	*Kloschüssel*
to throw up	[ˌθrəʊ 'ʌp]	to be sick	*(sich) erbrechen*
to not be able to help	[nɒt bi ˌeɪbl tə 'help]	to not be able to avoid sth	*nicht umhin können*
association	[əˌsəʊsi'eɪʃn]	group of people with a common goal or interest	*Verband, Verein*
to go down a road	[gəʊ ˌdaʊn ə 'rəʊd]	to experience sth	*etwas erleben*

to refuse	[rɪ'fjuːz]	to reject, turn down	*ablehnen, sich weigern, widerstehen*
to put on weight	[ˌpʊt ɒn 'weɪt]	<> to lose weight	*zunehmen*
addiction	[ə'dɪkʃn]	*v* to be addicted	*Sucht, Abhängigkeit*
to vomit	['vɒmɪt]	to throw up	*erbrechen*

page 17

task	[tɑːsk]	work, assignment	*Aufgabe*
to compare	[kəm'peə]	*n* comparison	*vergleichen*
evidence	['evɪdəns]	proof	*Beweis, Beleg*
embarrassed	[ɪm'bærəst]	*n* embarrassment	*verlegen*
ashamed	[ə'ʃeɪmd]	*n* shame	*beschämt*
attitude	['ætɪtjuːd]	*phr* attitude towards sth	*Haltung, Einstellung*
to disagree (with)	[ˌdɪsə'griː wɪð]	<> agree	*widersprechen, nicht zustimmen*
choice	[tʃɔɪs]	*v* to choose	*Wahl*
to starve yourself	[stɑːv]	to not allow yourself to eat	*hungern*
otherwise	['ʌðəwaɪz]	if not	*sonst, ansonsten*
to get real	[get 'riːəl]	to accept the truth	*die Realität anerkennen*
to pull oneself together	[ˌpʊl wʌnself tə'geðə]	to take control of your feelings	*sich zusammenreißen*
mental	['mentl]	*n* mentality	*mental*
treatment	['triːtmənt]	*v* to treat	*Behandlung*
sufferer	['sʌfərə]	sb who suffers from an illness	*Leidende/r*
sympathetic	[ˌsɪmpə'θetɪk]	*n* sympathy	*mitfühlend, verständnisvoll*
medical	['medɪkl]	connected with illnesses and treatments	*medizinisch*
criticism	['krɪtɪsɪzəm]	negative feedback	*Kritik*
phrase	[freiʒ]	expression	*Wendung, Ausdruck*
waiter	['weɪtə]	*fem* waitress	*Kellner, Ober*

page 18

to attract	[ə'trækt]	to draw attention to	*anziehen, anlocken*
special offer	[ˌspeʃl 'ɒfə]	*phr* on special offer	*Sonderangebot*
to get drunk	[get 'drʌŋk]	to drink so much alcohol that you can no longer think clearly	*sich betrinken*
good-looking	[ˌgʊd 'lʊkɪŋ]	attractive	*gut aussehend*
ad	[æd]	*(inf)* advertisement	*Anzeige*
disgusting	[dɪs'gʌstɪŋ]	*n* disgust	*ekelhaft*
to overcome	[ˌəʊvə'kʌm]	to beat or deal with (a problem or illness)	*überwinden*
capital	['kæpɪtl]	main city in a country	*Hauptstadt*
equivalent (of)	[ɪ'kwɪvələnt əv]	sth that is equal in size/importance, etc. to sth else	*Entsprechung*
curable	['kjʊərəbl]	*v* to cure	*heilbar*
fatty	['fæti]	containing a large amount of fat	*fetthaltig, fettig*
What's the matter with ...?	[ˌwɒts ðə 'mætə wɪð]	What's wrong with ...?	*Was ist los mit ...?*

page 19

countable	['kaʊntəbl]	which can be counted	*zählbar*
uncountable	[ˌʌn'kaʊntəbl]	which cannot be counted	*nicht zählbar*
ham	[hæm]	type of meat from a pig	*Schinken*
research	[rɪ'sɜːtʃ]	study to find out more about a subject	*Forschung*
advice	[əd'vaɪs]	suggestion	*Rat(schlag)*
luggage	['lʌgɪdʒ]	suitcases	*Gepäck*
hardware	['hɑːdweə]	parts of a computer	*Hardware, Geräte*
software	['sɒftweə]	computer programs	*Software, Programme*
knowledge	['nɒlɪdʒ]	what sb knows	*Wissen*
police officer	[pə'liːs ɒfɪsə]	policeman/-woman	*Polizeibeamter/-beamtin*
column	['kɒləm]	vertical sections which separate a page	*Spalte*
mustard	['mʌstəd]	yellow-brown sauce usually served with meat	*Senf*
paint	[peɪnt]	*v* to paint	*Farbe*
can	[kæn]	e.g. a can of beans	*Dose*
queue	[kjuː]	*v* to queue up for sth	*(Warte-)Schlange*
loaf	[ləʊf]	e.g. a loaf of bread	*(Laib) Brot*
tube	[tjuːb]	e.g. a tube of toothpaste	*Tube*
jar	[dʒɑː]	e.g. a jam jar	*(Einmach)Glas*

page 20

unspecified	[ˌʌn'spesɪfaɪd]	unclear	*unbestimmt*
quantity	['kwɒntəti]	amount	*Menge, Quantität*
cookbook	['kʊkbʊk]	book that shows how to cook different meals	*Kochbuch*
to have room	[həv 'ru:m]	to have enough space for	*Platz haben*
barbecue	['bɑ:bɪkju:]	outdoor party where food is cooked on a metal frame over a fire	*Grillparty*
plenty of	['plenti əv]	many of	*viel(e)*
freezer	['fri:zə]	cupboard where food can be stored at a very low temperature	*Gefrierschrank*

page 21

to panic	['pænɪk]	<> to stay calm	*in Panik geraten*
Why on earth?	[ˌwaɪ ɒn 'ɜ:θ]	phrase used to emphasize the question 'why?'	*Warum um Himmels willen?*
not ... either	[nɒt 'aɪðə]	e.g. Pete can't go and I can't either.	*auch nicht*
carrot	['kærət]	long orange vegetable	*Karotte*
fridge	[frɪdʒ]	cupboard where food can be stored at a low temperature	*Kühlschrank*
understandable	[ˌʌndə'stændəbl]	which can be understood	*verständlich*
time off	[ˌtaɪm 'ɒf]	*phr* to take time off	*Freizeit*

UNIT D

page 22

time out	[ˌtaɪm 'aʊt]	*phr* to take time out	*Freizeit*
financial	[faɪ'nænʃə]	connected with money	*finanziell*
exotic	[ɪg'zɒtɪk]	exciting because it is strange or unusual	*exotisch*
destination	[ˌdestɪ'neɪʃn]	place to which people travel, the end of a journey	*(Fahrt-)Ziel*
proper	['prɒpə]	real, full, correct	*richtig, geeignet, korrekt, ordentlich*
bright	[braɪt]	clever	*hell; glänzend, schlau*
to pick fruit	[pik 'fru:t]	to take fruit from trees or plants	*Obst pflücken*
absolutely	['æbsəlu:tli]	definitely	*absolut*
especially	[ɪ'speʃəli]	particularly	*besonders, insbesondere*
uncool	[ˌʌn'ku:l]	⚠ Betonung	*uncool*
come on	[ˌkʌm 'ɒn]	used to show that you think sb is wrong	*komm (schon)*
living expenses	[ˌlɪvɪŋ ɪk'spensɪz]	money spent on everyday things	*Lebenshaltungskosten*

page 23

to break into	['breɪk ɪntə]	to enter by force	*einbrechen*

page 24

to give a lift	[gɪv ə 'lɪft]	to give sb a ride	*mit dem Auto mitnehmen*
weatherman	['weðəmæn]	man on TV who predicts the weather	*Meteorologe*
to watch out	[ˌwɒtʃ 'aʊt]	to be careful	*aufpassen*
visa	['vi:zə]	mark in a passport which allows you to enter a country	*Visum*
to take off	[ˌteɪk 'ɒf]	(of an aeroplane) to leave the ground	*starten*

page 25

several	['sevrəl]	a few more than one	*mehrere, einige*
school-leaver	[ˌsku:l 'li:və]	person who has just left school	*Schulabgänger/in*
farewell	[ˌfeə'wel]	saying goodbye to sb	*Abschied*
definitely	['defɪnətli]	certainly	*bestimmt, definitiv*

UNIT E

page 26

pushy	['pʊʃi]	trying to persuade sb to do sth	*aufdringlich*
sales	[seɪlz]	selling goods	*Verkaufs-*
staff	[stɑ:f]	a group of workers or employees	*Personal, Angestellte, Mitarbeiter/innen*
virtual	['vɜ:tʃuəl]	existing only on a computer screen	*virtuell*
mail-order catalogue	[meɪl 'ɔ:də kætəlɒg]	book with a list of goods that will be sent to customers by post	*Versandhauskatalog*

bargain	['bɑ:gɪn]	special offer	*Sonderangebot*
department store	[dɪ'pɑ:tmənt stɔ:]	large shop selling clothes, food, etc.	*Kauf-, Warenhaus*
purchase	['pɜ:tʃəs]	*v* to purchase	*(Ein-) Kauf*
fabulous	['fæbjələs]	great, wonderful	*fabelhaft*
blouse	[blaʊz]	piece of clothing like a shirt for women	*Bluse*
quality	['kwɒləti]	<> quantity	*Qualität*
fashion-conscious	['fæʃn kɒnʃəs]	very interested in fashionable clothes	*modebewusst*
exclusive	[ɪk'sklu:sɪv]	good quality and expensive and only bought by a small number of people	*exklusiv*
label	['leɪbl]	*phr* brand label	*Label, Marke*
wardrobe	['wɔ:drəʊb]	large cupboard for clothes	*Kleiderschrank, Garderobe*
thrill	[θrɪl]	*adj* thrilling	*Spannung*
lovely	['lʌvli]	nice, pleasant	*hübsch*
pure	[pjʊə]	*n* purity	*rein*
silk	[sɪlk]	a soft shiny material	*Seide*
site	[saɪt]	*(inf)* website	*Website*
shopping trolley	['ʃɒpɪn trɒli]	*AE:* shopping cart	*Einkaufswagen*
in the meantime	[ɪn ðə 'mi:ntaɪm]	in the time between two events	*inzwischen*
to run up debts	[ˌrʌn 'ʌp dets]	to spend more money than you have	*sich verschulden, Schulden anhäufen*

page 27

second-hand	[ˌsekənd 'hænd]	which used to belong to somebody else	*gebraucht*
auction	['ɔ:kʃn]	*phr* to put sth up for auction	*Auktion*
to link	[lɪŋk]	to connect, to join	*verbinden*

page 28

sceptical	['skeptɪkl]	having doubts	*skeptisch*
to keep in touch with	[ˌki:p ɪn 'tʌtʃ wɪð]	to stay in contact with	*in Verbindung bleiben*
creditor	['kredɪtə]	person who gives money to people who must pay it back later	*Gläubiger/in*
to repay	[rɪ'peɪ]	*n* repayment	*zurückzahlen*
convenient	[kən'vi:niənt]	*n* convenience	*bequem*
honest	['ɒnɪst]	*n* honesty	*ehrlich*
display	[dɪ'spleɪ]	⚠ Betonung	*Ausstellung*
row	[rəʊ]	line	*Reihe*
occasional	[ə'keɪʒənl]	now and then, sometimes	*gelegentlich*
fixed	[fɪkst]	set in place	*befestigt*
anti-theft pad	['æntɪ θeft pæd]	piece of material designed to stop people stealing goods	*Diebstahlsicherung*
to glow	[gləʊ]	to produce light	*leuchten*
reliable	[rɪ'laɪəbl]	which can be trusted	*zuverlässig*
value	['vælju:]	how much sth is worth	*Wert*
feature	['fi:tʃə]	aspect of a product	*Eigenschaft*
to switch off	[ˌswɪtʃ 'ɒf]	to turn off	*abschalten*

page 29

position	[pə'zɪʃn]	arrangement	*Stellung*
fortunately	['fɔ:tʃənətli]	luckily	*glücklicherweise*
actually	['æktʃuəli]	in fact	*tatsächlich, eigentlich*
unluckily	[ʌn'lʌkɪli]	unfortunately	*unglücklicherweise*
obviously	['ɒbviəsli]	clearly	*offensichtlich*
irresponsible	[ˌɪrɪ'spɒnsəbl]	<> responsible	*unverantwortlich*
from time to time	[frəm ˌtaɪm tə 'taɪm]	sometimes	*von Zeit zu Zeit*
now and then	[naʊ ənd 'ðen]	sometimes	*ab und zu*
frequency	['fri:kwənsi]	*adj* frequent	*Häufigkeit*
retailer	['ri:teɪlə]	person or company that sells products	*Einzelhändler/in*
shoplifting	['ʃɒplɪftɪŋ]	stealing from a shop	*Ladendiebstahl*
punishment	['pʌnɪʃmənt]	*v* to punish	*Strafe, Bestrafung*
shoplifter	['ʃɒplɪftə]	person who steals things from a shop	*Ladendieb/in*
sale	[seɪl]	event where goods are sold at a cheaper price	*Schlussverkauf*
to buy sth on credit	[baɪ ɒn 'kredɪt]	to buy sth using borrowed money	*etw auf Kredit kaufen*

congratulations	[kənˌgrætʃu'leɪʃnz]	*v* to congratulate	*Glückwunsch*

UNIT F

page 30

questionnaire	[ˌkwestʃə'neə]	list of questions	*Fragebogen*
to fit	[fɪt]	to be suitable	*passen*
to stay up	[ˌsteɪ 'ʌp]	to not go to bed	*aufbleiben*
to text	[tekst]	to write a text message	*SMS schicken, simsen*
loads	[ləʊdz]	*(inf)* a lot	*eine Menge*
to depend	[dɪ'pend]	to be dependent upon	*abhängen von*
social life	[ˌsəʊʃl 'laɪf]	time spent meeting friends	*Sozialkontakte*
to hand in	[ˌhænd 'ɪn]	to give in (e.g. your homework)	*abgeben*
to sit back	[ˌsɪt 'bæk]	to relax and not play an active role in sth	*sich zurückhalten, sich zurücklehnen*

page 31

sensible	['sensəbl]	<> silly	*vernünftig*
careers adviser	[kə'rɪəz ədvaɪzə]	person whose job is to give people advice about different jobs	*Berufsberater/in*
to interview	['ɪntəvju:]	to have a conversation with questions and answers	*interviewen*
theme	[θi:m]	a topic or subject	*Thema*
don't mention it	['menʃn]	you're welcome	*gern geschehen*
to concentrate	['kɒnsntreɪt]	to focus on sth	*sich konzentrieren*
to get by	[ˌget 'baɪ]	to have just enough money to live	*durchkommen*
to increase	[ɪn'kri:s]	to grow	*ansteigen, zunehmen*
since	[sɪns]	before the present time	*seit*
generation	[ˌdʒenə'reɪʃn]	people born around the same time	*Generation*
at a disadvantage	[ət ə ˌdɪsəd'vɑ:ntɪdʒ]	having more problems than other people	*benachteiligt*
job-related	['dʒɒb rɪleɪtɪd]	having to do with the job	*beruflich*
shelf	[ʃelf]	flat surface on a wall or in a cupboard where things can be placed	*Regal*

page 32

objection to	[əb'dʒekʃn tə]	*v* to object to	*Ablehnung gegenüber*
misunderstanding	[ˌmɪsʌndə'stændɪŋ]	*v* to misunderstand	*Missverständnis*
cartoon	[kɑ:'tu:n]	a humorous drawing	*Karikatur*
brochure	['brəʊʃə]	e.g. advertising brochure	*Broschüre, Prospekt*
careless	['keələs]	<> careful	*sorglos, nachlässig*
travel agency	['trævl eɪdʒənsi]	company that helps to organize holidays	*Reisebüro*
rack	[ræk]	object used to hold things or hang things from	*Ständer*
to sort	[sɔ:t]	to organize	*sortieren*
to deal with	['di:l wɪð]	to work with	*sich beschäftigen mit, mit jdm zu tun haben*
to complain	[kəm'pleɪn]	*n* complaint	*reklamieren, sich beklagen, beschweren*

page 33

to take it in turns	[ˌteɪk ɪt ɪn 'tɜ:nz]	to alternate	*sich abwechseln*
bartender	['bɑ:tendə]	*(AE) BE:* barman, barmaid	*Barmann, -frau*
cashier	[kæ'ʃɪə]	person who takes money from and gives money to customers in a shop or bank	*Kassierer/in*
shelf-stacker	['ʃelf stækə]	person who works in a supermarket putting products on shelves	*Regalauffüller/in*
tuition	[tju'ɪʃn]	*v* to tutor	*Unterricht*
old people's home	[ˌəʊld 'pi:plz həʊm]	place where old people live together and are cared for	*Seniorenheim*
filling station	['fɪlɪŋ steɪʃn]	petrol station	*Tankstelle*
recently	['ri:sntli]	lately, not long ago	*kürzlich, neulich*

page 34

day off	[ˌdeɪ 'ɒf]	*phr* to take a day off	*freier Tag*
part-timer	[ˌpɑ:t 'taɪmə]	person who works part-time	*Teilzeitarbeiter/in*
arrival	[ə'raɪvl]	*v* to arrive	*Ankunft*

MAIN COURSE

UNIT 1

page 35

focus	['fəʊkəs]	theme	*Blickpunkt*
quotation	[kwəʊ'teɪʃn]	*v* to quote	*Zitat*
to set foot in	[set 'fʊt ɪn]	to enter	*betreten*
to feature	['fi:tʃə]	to appear	*eine Rolle spielen*
sequence	['si:kwəns]	part of a film	*Episode, Sequenz*

page 36

perspective	[pə'spektɪv]	view point	*Perspektive, Ansicht*
to contrast	[kən'trɑ:st]	to compare differences	*gegenüberstellen*
to scan	[skæn]	read sth quickly to find a piece of information	*überfliegen, absuchen*
roughly	['rʌfli]	<> exactly	*ungefähr*
event	[ɪ'vent]	sth that is happening	*Ereignis, Veranstaltung*
particularly	[pə'tɪkjələli]	specific, especially	*bestimmt, speziell, besonders*
urban	['ɜ:bən]	<> rural	*städtisch*
rural	['rʊərəl]	<> urban	*ländlich*
calm	[kɑ:m]	quiet	*ruhig*
enjoyable	[ɪn'dʒɔɪəbl]	*v* to enjoy	*angenehm*
gentle	['dʒentl]	kind	*freundlich*
intense	[ɪn'tens]	*n* intensity	*intensiv*

page 37

to check out	[ˌtʃek 'aʊt]	to find out about	*herausfinden*
pretty soon	[ˌprɪti 'su:n]	very soon	*sehr bald*
to get used to	[get 'ju:st tə]	to become familiar with sth	*sich gewöhnen an*
to yell	[jel]	to shout	*schreien*
really something	['ri:əli sʌmθɪŋ]	something impressive	*toll, beeindruckend*
downtown	['daʊntaʊn]	*(esp AE)* in the city centre	*im Stadtzentrum*
skyline	['skaɪlaɪn]	buildings, etc. that can be seen against the background of the sky	*Silhouette*
to blow sb away	[ˌbləʊ ə'weɪ]	to really impress sb	*jdn überwältigen*
scary	['skeəri]	frightening	*unheimlich, beängstigend*
elevator	['elɪveɪtə]	*(AE) BE:* lift	*Lift*
senior	['si:niə]	student in the last year of high school in the US	*Schüler/in im letzten Schuljahr*
skyscraper	['skaɪskreɪpə]	very tall building	*Wolkenkratzer*
huge	[hju:dʒ]	very big	*gewaltig*
forest	['fɒrɪst]	woods	*Wald*
waterfall	['wɔ:təfɔ:l]		*Wasserfall*
to be stuck	[bi 'stʌk]	to be unable to get away	*feststecken*
nightmare	['naɪtmeə]	*adj* nightmarish	*Albtraum*

page 38

context	['kɒntekst]	circumstances	*Kontext, Zusammenhang*
shopping mall	['ʃɒpɪŋ mɔ:l]	a large building with many shops inside	*Einkaufszentrum*
exhibition	[ˌeksɪ'bɪʃn]	*v* to exhibit	*Ausstellung*
tourist guide	['tʊərɪst gaɪd]	person whose job is to show tourists around	*Reiseführer/in*
presenter	[prɪ'zentə]	*v* to present	*Moderator/in*
to cross out	[ˌkrɒs 'aʊt]	to draw a line through	*durchstreichen*
suggestion	[sə'dʒestʃən]	recommendation	*Vorschlag*
ferry	['feri]	a large boat used to transport people	*Fähre*
geography	[dʒi'ɒgrəfi]	layout	*Lage, Geographie*
gateway	['geɪtweɪ]	entrance	*Tor, Pforte*
to rent	[rent]	to hire	*mieten*
lake	[leɪk]	area of water surrounded by land	*(Binnen-)See*
ride	[raɪd]	*phr* to go for a ride	*Tour, Fahrt, Flug*
tight	[taɪt]	*phr* a tight fit	*knapp, eng*
budget	['bʌdʒɪt]	amount of money you plan to spend	*Budget, Etat*

security check	[sɪ'kjʊərəti tʃek]	a measure to stop dangerous items/ people entering a building/country, etc.	*Sicherheitskontrolle*
greeting	['gri:tɪŋ]	*v* to greet	*Begrüßung*
to receive	[rɪ'si:v]	to get	*empfangen*
relationship	[rɪ'leɪʃnʃɪp]	a connection between two or more people	*Verhältnis*

page 39

immigrant	['ɪmɪgrənt]	*v* to immigrate	*Einwanderer/Einwanderin*
bite	[baɪt]	*phr* to take a bite of sth	*Bissen, Happen*
sub-heading	[ˌsʌb 'hedɪŋ]	title that comes under the main title	*Untertitel*
encyclopedia	[ɪnˌsaɪklə'pi:diə]	book that gives information about many different subjects	*Lexikon, Enzyklopädie*
entry	['entri]	piece of written information in a book	*Eintrag*
novel	['nɒvl]	book containing a story	*Roman*
guidebook	['gaɪdbʊk]	book which gives information on a particular place	*Reiseführer*

page 40

distant	['dɪstənt]	*n* distance	*fern*
to shine	[ʃaɪn]	*adj* shiny	*glänzen*
magical	['mædʒɪkl]	wonderful	*magisch*
to take sb's breath away	[teɪk 'breθ əweɪ]	to surprise sb by being very impressive	*jdm den Atem rauben*
to explore	[ɪk'splɔ:]	to travel around and see different areas	*erkunden*
borough	['bʌrə]	area, quarter in a city	*(Stadt-)Bezirk*
shore	[ʃɔ:]	place where land meets water	*Ufer*
island	['aɪlənd]	land which is surrounded by water	*Insel*
within	[wɪ'ðɪn]	inside	*innerhalb*
characteristic	[ˌkærəktə'rɪstɪk]	quality	*Eigenschaft, Merkmal*
sense	[sens]	a feeling	*Sinn, Gefühl*
melting pot	['meltɪŋ pɒt]	place where people from different cultures live together	*Schmelztiegel*
variety	[və'raɪəti]	*adj* various	*Vielfalt*
cultural	['kʌltʃərəl]	connected with culture	*kulturell*
ethnic	['eθnɪk]	connected with origin or race	*ethnisch*
tradition	[trə'dɪʃn]	*adj* traditional	*Tradition*
wave	[weɪv]	large number of people moving somewhere	*Welle*
effect	[ɪ'fekt]	result	*Auswirkung*
dish	[dɪʃ]	plate or shallow bowl	*Gericht*
crowded	['kraʊdɪd]	filled with people	*überfüllt*
energy	['enədʒi]	force	*Energie*
newly	['nju:li]	recently	*kürzlich*
to invent	[ɪn'vent]	*n* invention	*erfinden*
steel-frame	['sti:l freɪm]	with a frame of steel (strong metal)	*Stahlträger*
construction	[kən'strʌkʃn]	building	*Bau, Bauweise*
area	['eəriə]	a space	*Gebiet, Bereich*
including	[ɪn'klu:dɪŋ]	*abbrev:* incl.	*einschließlich, inbegriffen, darunter*
finance	['faɪnæns]	*adj* financial	*Finanzen*
advertising	['ædvətaɪzɪŋ]	industry connected with producing adverts	*Werbung*
to take over	[ˌteɪk 'əʊvə]	to start to have control over people or things	*übernehmen*
taxpayer	['tækspeɪə]	person who pays taxes	*Steuerzahler/in*
bankrupt	['bæŋkrʌpt]	*n* bankruptcy	*bankrott, pleite*
terrorist	['terərɪst]	person who takes part in political attacks	*Terrorist/in*
attack	[ə'tæk]	assault	*Angriff*
failure	['feɪljə]	<> success	*Versagen*
unemployment	[ˌʌnɪm'plɔɪmənt]	*adj* unemployed	*Arbeitslosigkeit*
former	['fɔ:mə]	from an earlier time	*früher*
recovery	[rɪ'kʌvəri]	*v* to recover	*Erholung*

page 41

structure	['strʌktʃə]	something that has been built, a foundation and organized system	*Gebäude, Struktur, Aufbau*

man-made	['mæn meɪd]	<> natural	*von Menschenhand*
industry	['ɪndəstri]		*Industrie*
birth	[bɜːθ]	*v* to be born	*Geburt*
aspect	['æspekt]	area, part	*Aspekt, Seite*
to collect	[kə'lekt]	to bring together	*sammeln*
to differ	['dɪfə]	to be different	*sich unterscheiden*
to immigrate	['ɪmɪgreɪt]	to come to live in a new country	*einwandern*
attraction	[ə'trækʃn]	feeling of being attracted to sth/sb	*Anziehung*
sleepy	['sliːpi]	tired	*müde*
informative	[ɪn'fɔːmətɪv]	*v* to inform	*informativ*
to strengthen	['streŋθn]	to make stronger	*stärken*
page 42			
comprehension	[ˌkɒmprɪ'henʃn]	*v* to comprehend	*Verständnis*
large-scale	['lɑːdʒ skeɪl]	in large numbers	*in großer Zahl*
timetable	['taɪmteɪbl]	e.g. train timetable	*Zeitplan, Fahrplan*
rather	['rɑːðə]	*phr* rather you than me	*lieber, eher*
page 43			
mass tourism	[ˌmæs 'tʊərɪzəm]	large-scale tourism	*Massentourismus*
profitable	['prɒfɪtəbl]	lucrative, likely to make money	*gewinnbringend, rentabel*
location	[ləʊ'keɪʃn]	area, site, setting	*(Stand-)Ort, Lage*
accessible	[ək'sesəbl]	easy to reach	*zugänglich*
up-market	[ˌʌp 'mɑːkɪt]	of good quality	*im oberen Marktsegment*
accommodation	[əˌkɒmə'deɪʃn]	a place to stay/live	*Unterkunft, Wohnraum*
wide range	[waɪd 'reɪndʒ]	big choice or selection	*breite Palette*
affordable	[ə'fɔːdəbl]	<> high-priced, expensive	*erschwinglich*
to realize one's potential	[ˌrɪəlaɪz wʌnz pə'tenʃl]	to do as well as one can	*seine Möglichkeiten verwirklichen*
infamous	['ɪnfəməs]	having a bad reputation	*berüchtigt*
crime rate	['kraɪm reɪt]	the number of crimes in an area	*Kriminalitätsrate*
to plague	[pleɪg]	to harass, to trouble	*plagen*
beggar	['begə]	a person who asks people for money to live off or survive	*Bettler/in*
vandal	['vændl]	a person who damages public property	*Vandale*
mayor	[meə]	elected leader of a town or city council	*Bürgermeister/in*
organized crime	['ɔːgənaɪzd kraɪm]	large amount of crime organized by a single group of criminals	*organisierte Kriminalität*
chief	[tʃiːf]	boss, commander	*Chef*
to clean up the streets	[ˌkliːn 'ʌp ðə striːts]	to stop crime in an area	*die Straßen säubern*
policy	['pɒləsi]	a plan of action, a principle	*(praktische) Politik*
tough	[tʌf]	hard, strict	*hart, streng*
controversial	[ˌkɒntrə'vɜːʃl]	causing argument or discussion	*kontrovers, umstritten*
to elect	[ɪ'lekt]	to choose by vote	*wählen*
term	[tɜːm]	a period of time of a specific length	*Amtszeit*
despite	[dɪ'spaɪt]	in spite of, regardless of	*trotz*
to flock	[flɒk]	to go in large numbers	*strömen*
increasing	[ɪn'kriːsɪŋ]	getting bigger	*steigend, zunehmend*
to contribute	[kən'trɪbjuːt]	to support, to add to	*beitragen*
airfare	['eəfeə]	cost of a flight	*Flugkosten, -preis*
temporary	['temprəri]	<> permanent	*vorübergehend, zeitweilig*
impact	['ɪmpækt]	effect, influence	*(Aus-)Wirkung, Einfluss*
to rise	[raɪz]	to go up, to increase	*(an)steigen*
to fall	[fɔːl]	to go down, to decrease	*fallen*
to climb	[klaɪm]	to go up, to increase	*klettern, steigen*
to bottom out	[ˌbɒtəm 'aʊt]	to reach the lowest point possible	*die Talsohle erreichen*
to peak	[piːk]	to reach the highest point possible	*den Höhepunkt erreichen, gipfeln*
page 44			
comparison	[kəm'pærɪsn]	comparing things	*Vergleich, Steigerung*
approx.	[ə'prɒksɪmətli]	*(abbrev)* approximately	*ungefähr, etwa, zirka*
clue	[kluː]	something which helps solve a puzzle	*Schlüssel*
farther	['fɑːðə]	= further	*weiter*
to guess	[ges]	to try to answer	*raten*

junior	['dʒu:niə]	low-ranking	*untergeordnet*
comment	['kɒment]	*v* to comment	*Kommentar*
length	[leŋθ]	measurement of time, distance, etc.	*Länge, Dauer*
departure	[dɪ'pɑ:tʃə]	*v* to depart	*Abfahrt*
frequent	['fri:kwənt]	*n* frequency	*häufig*
service	['sɜ:vɪs]	assistance	*(Bus-/Zug-)Verbindung*

UNIT 2

page 45

advertisement	[əd'vɜ:tɪsmənt]	*abbrev:* ad, advert	*Anzeige, Werbespot*
classified	['klæsɪfaɪd]	arranged by subject	*nach Rubriken geordnet*
panel	['pænl]	section of a page	*hier: Spalte, Fläche*
leaflet	['li:flət]	flyer	*Broschüre, Flugblatt*
pop-up ad	['pɒp ʌp æd]	advert that appears on the screen when you are online	*Internet-Anzeige*
banner ad	['bænər æd]	advert that covers the top/bottom/side of an internet page	*Bannerwerbung*
product placement	['prɒdʌkt pleɪsmənt]	advertising products by showing them in films or on TV shows	*Schleichwerbung*
commercial	[kə'mɜ:ʃl]	advertisement	*Anzeige, Werbespot*
sponsorship	['spɒnsəʃɪp]	giving financial support to a group/event, etc.	*finanzielle Unterstützung*
annoying	[ə'nɔɪɪŋ]	irritating	*lästig, ärgerlich*
glamorous	['glæmərəs]	*n* glamour	*glamourös*
aim	[eɪm]	goal	*Ziel*
to vary	['veəri]	*n* variety	*variieren*
to promote	[prə'məʊt]	to advertise	*fördern*
brand	[brænd]	*phr* brand name	*Marke*

page 46

agency	['eɪdʒənsi]	e.g. advertising agency	*Agentur*
to design	[dɪ'zaɪn]	to create	*entwerfen*
sponsor	['spɒnsə]	*v* to sponsor	*Sponsor/in*
freelance	['fri:lɑ:ns]	e.g. freelance journalist	*freiberuflich*
developer	[dɪ'veləpə]	person whose job is to create new products	*Entwickler/in*
to expand	[ɪk'spænd]	to get bigger	*expandieren, (sich) ausdehnen*
potential	[pə'tenʃl]	possible	*potentiell*
client	['klaɪənt]	customer	*Kunde/Kundin*
campaign	[kæm'peɪn]	*phr* advertising campaign	*(Werbe-)Feldzug, Kampagne*
to pitch	[pɪtʃ]	to present an idea or a product to persuade people to use or buy it	*anbieten, anpreisen*
contract	['kɒntrækt]	a formal document or agreement	*(Arbeits-)Vertrag*
account manager	[ə'kaʊnt mænɪdʒə]	person who looks after regular customers	*Kundenbetreuer/in*
to get the green light	[get ðə ˌgri:n 'laɪt]	to be allowed to begin	*grünes Licht erhalten*
to launch	[lɔ:ntʃ]	to start	*einführen, starten*
journey	['dʒɜ:ni]	trip	*Reise, Fahrt*

page 47

innovative	['ɪnəveɪtɪv]	*n* innovation	*innovativ*
to decline	[dɪ'klaɪn]	to decrease	*abnehmen, sinken, zurückgehen*
fairly	['feəli]	quite	*ziemlich*
slight	['slaɪt]	a little, small	*leicht*
stable	['steɪbl]	*n* stability	*fest*
flow chart	['fləʊ tʃɑ:t]	diagram showing the order in which a process happens	*Flussdiagramm*
to set up	[ˌset 'ʌp]	to found	*begründen*
booker	['bʊkə]	person whose job is to book appointments	*Besteller/in*
slot	[slɒt]	appointment	*Termin*
PA	[ˌpi: 'eɪ]	*(abbrev)* personal assistant	*persönliche/r Assistent/in*
to be due to	[bi 'dju: tə]	due to = because of	*darauf zurückzuführen sein*
stressful	['stresfl]	*n* stress	*stressig, anstrengend*
process	['prəʊses]	systematic action	*Prozess, Vorgang*

page 48

to sponsor	['spɒnsə]	*n* sponsor, sponsorship	*finanziell unterstützen*
to supply	[sə'plaɪ]	to provide	*liefern*
supply	[sə'plaɪ]	giving people what they want or need	*Lieferung; Stoff, Material*
urgent	['ɜːdʒənt]	*n* urgency	*dringend, eilig*
application	[ˌæplɪ'keɪʃn] (fɔːm)]	*v* to apply to/for	*Bewerbung*
Human Resources	[ˌhjuːmən rɪ'sɔːsɪz]	*abbrev:* HR	*Personal(abteilung)*
candidate	['kændɪdət]	person who has applied for a job	*Kandidat/in, Bewerber/in*
shortlisted	['ʃɔːtlɪstɪd]	chosen to go on a list of possible candidates	*in der engeren Wahl*
to confirm	[kən'fɜːm]	*n* confirmation	*bestätigen*
to attend	[ə'tend]	to be present at	*teilnehmen (an)*
correspondence	[ˌkɒrɪ'spɒndəns]	letters sent and received by people	*Korrespondenz*
to suggest	[sə'dʒest]	*n* suggestion	*vorschlagen, andeuten*
closeness	['kləʊsnəs]	*adj* close	*Vertrautheit*

page 49

heading	['hedɪŋ]	title	*Überschrift*
forum	['fɔːrəm]	discussion	*Forum*
discussion	[dɪ'skʌʃn]	*v* to discuss sth	*Diskussion*
to drown in	['draʊn ɪn]	to be surrounded by	*ertränken in*
terrible	['terəbl]	awful	*schrecklich, furchtbar*
commercial break	[kəˌmɜːʃl 'breɪk]	pause between TV programmes when adverts are shown	*Werbepause*
to cut	[kʌt]	to get rid of sth	*ausblenden*
lively	['laɪvli]	fun	*lebhaft*
to lighten up	[ˌlaɪtn 'ʌp]	to feel less worried	*aufheitern*
to escape	[ɪ'skeɪp]	to get away from	*flüchten*
advertiser	['ædvətaɪzə]	person or company that advertises	*Werbefirma*
branded	['brændɪd]	showing the name of a company	*Marken-*
entertainment	[ˌentə'teɪnmənt]	amusement	*Unterhaltung*
placement	['pleɪsmənt]	*v* to place	*(Produkt-)Werbung*
extended	[ɪk'stendɪd]	*n* extension	*verlängert*
competing	[kəm'piːtɪŋ]	*v* to compete	*konkurrierend*
viral	['vaɪrəl]	like a virus	*viral, Virus-*
to pass	[pɑːs]	to move, go by	*weitergegeben werden*
to spread	[spred]	*n* spread	*(sich) verbreiten*
word of mouth	[ˌwɜːd əv 'maʊθ]	*phr* to spread by word of mouth	*Mundpropaganda*
to recognize	['rekəgnaɪz]	to see sth or sb familiar	*erkennen*
channel	['tʃænl]	*phr* to change channels	*Kanal*
to admit	[əd'mɪt]	to confess	*zugeben, gestehen*
wasteful	['weɪstfə]	*v* to waste	*verschwenderisch*
to drop	[drɒp]	to fall	*fallen*
to collapse	[kə'læps]	to fail suddenly	*zusammenbrechen*
to fail	[feɪl]	to not succeed	*versagen, scheitern*
Middle Ages	[ˌmɪdl 'eɪdʒɪz]	period from about 600 AD to 1450 AD	*Mittelalter*

page 50

to mention	['menʃn]	to be mentioned = to appear in a text	*erwähnen*
hard sell	[ˌhɑːd 'sel]	selling technique that puts a lot of pressure on the customer	*aggressive Verkaufstechnik*
soft sell	[ˌsɒft 'sel]	selling technique that persuades customers without putting pressure on them	*zurückhaltende Verkaufstechnik*
to influence	['ɪnfluəns]	*n* influence	*beinflussen*
raw material	[ˌrɔː mə'tɪəriəl]	material that is used to make a product	*Rohstoff*
disagreement	[ˌdɪsə'griːmənt]	*v* to disagree	*Widerspruch, Uneinigkeit*
to exaggerate	[ɪg'zædʒəreɪt]	*n* exaggeration	*übertreiben*
one-sided	[ˌwʌn 'saɪdɪd]	showing only one aspect of a situation	*einseitig*

page 51

leading	['liːdɪŋ]	*v* to lead	*führend*
technique	[tek'niːk]	method	*Methode, (Arbeits-)Technik*

college of further education	[ˌkɒlɪdʒ əv ˌfɜːðər ˌedʒuˈkeɪʃn]	vocational school	*Fachoberschule, Weiterbildungskolleg*
to stand for sth	[ˈstænd fə]	to mean	*für etw stehen*
formula	[ˈfɔːmjələ]	method	*Formel*
immediate	[ɪˈmiːdiət]	happening without delay, straight away	*umgehend, sofort*
acronym	[ˈækrənɪm]	an abbreviation pronounced as a word	*Akronym, Initialwort*
attention	[əˈtenʃn]	*phr* to pay attention to	*Aufmerksamkeit*
to raise	[reɪz]	to build up	*wecken*
to create	[kriˈeɪt]	*adj* creative	*hervorrufen, erzeugen, wecken*
desire	[dɪˈzaɪə]	*adj* desirable	*Begehren, Verlangen*
to encourage	[ɪnˈkʌrɪdʒ]	to promote	*anregen*
to analyze	[ˈænəlaɪz]	to study in detail	*analysieren*
aimed at	[ˈeɪmd ət]	*v* to aim sth at	*abgezielt auf, gerichtet an*
play on words	[pleɪ ɒn ˈwɜːdz]	pun	*Wortspiel*
to work out	[ˌwɜːk ˈaʊt]	to train	*trainieren*
membership	[ˈmembəʃɪp]	*phr* gym membership	*Mitgliedschaft*
to join	[dʒɔɪn]	to sign up	*beitreten, sich anmelden*
statistical	[stəˈtɪstɪkl]	*n* statistic	*statistisch*
presentation	[ˌpreznˈteɪʃn]	a business talk	*Vorstellung, Präsentation*
to decrease	[dɪˈkriːs]	to go down	*fallen, sinken*
rapid	[ˈræpɪd]	happening in a short period	*rapide, schnell*
sharp	[ˈʃɑːp]	sudden(ly) and by a large amount	*rasch, schnell, stark*
steady	[ˈstedi, -li]	even(ly), stable	*stetig, fest, regelmäßig*
gradual	[ˈgrædʒuə]	happening slowly over a period of time	*allmählich, nach und nach*
decline	[dɪˈklaɪn]	decrease	*Rückgang*
to remain	[rɪˈmeɪn]	to stay the same	*bleiben*

page 52

trend	[trend]	general way in which things are changing, fashion	*Trend*
timeline	[ˈtaɪmlaɪn]	diagram showing the order in which events happened	*Zeitachse, -leiste*
abbreviation	[əˌbriːviˈeɪʃn]	short form of a word or phrase	*Abkürzung*
crash	[kræʃ]	*phr* a market crash	*Zusammenbruch*
to go bankrupt	[gəʊ ˈbæŋkrʌpt]	to no longer have enough money to pay off your debts	*in Konkurs gehen, Pleite gehen*
to hire sb/sth	[ˈhaɪə]	*(esp AE)* to give sb a job, to pay to borrow sth	*ein-/anstellen, mieten, anheuern*
award	[əˈwɔːd]	prize	*Auszeichnung*
expansion	[ɪkˈspænʃn]	act of making sth bigger	*Erweiterung*

page 53

to start up	[ˌstɑːt ˈʌp]	to begin, to found	*starten, gründen*
search engine	[ˈsɜːtʃ endʒɪn]	a program which searches the internet for information	*Suchmaschine*
founder	[ˈfaʊndə]	a person who establishes or begins something	*Gründer/in*
flashing banner	[ˌflæʃɪŋ ˈbænə]	an advert at the top of a web page which flashes	*blinkende Bannerwerbung*
source	[sɔːs]	provider	*Quelle*
revenue	[ˈrevənjuː]	amount of money a company makes	*Einkünfte, Einnahmen, Gewinn*
targeted	[ˈtɑːgɪtɪd]	aimed at	*gezielt*
to soar	[sɔː]	to increase greatly	*steil ansteigen*
experiment	[ɪkˈsperɪmənt]	test	*Versuch, Experiment*
screen	[skriːn]	display, monitor	*Bildschirm*
context-sensitive	[ˌkɒntekst ˈsensətɪv]	considering the surrounding information	*kontextbezogen*
to scan	[skæn]	to analyse quickly	*überfliegen, absuchen*
input	[ˈɪnpʊt]	information entered into a computer	*Eingabe*
to consider	[kənˈsɪdə]	to pay attention to	*berücksichtigen*
internet connection	[ˌɪntənet kəˈnekʃn]	computer link to the internet	*Internetanschluss, -verbindung*
profile	[ˈprəʊfaɪl]	description	*Profil*
database	[ˈdeɪtəbeɪs]	set of information	*Datenbank*
to place	[pleɪs]	e.g. to place an advert	*aufgeben*

to charge	[tʃɑːdʒ]	to sell for a certain amount of money	*berechnen*
click-through	['klɪk θruː]	when sb clicks on an internet advertisement	*Anklicken*
auction	['ɔːkʃn]	a way of selling sth for the highest amount of money possible	*Auktion, Versteigerung*
bid	[bɪd]	an offer of money, usually in an auction	*(An-)Gebot*
budget	['bʌdʒɪt]	amount of money that can be used for a particular purpose	*Etat, Budget*
to generate	['dʒenəreɪt]	to make	*aufbringen, erzielen*

page 54

sales figures	['seilz fɪgəz]	the amount of things that have been sold	*Verkaufszahlen*
account executive	[əˌkaʊnt ɪg'zekjətɪv]	manager for regular customers or clients	*Kundenberater/in, -betreuer/in*
microwave	['maɪkrəweɪv]	oven which heats food quickly using electromagnetic waves	*Mikrowelle*
to not break the bank	[nɒt ˌbreɪk ðə 'bæŋk]	to not cost too much	*nicht die Welt kosten*

UNIT 3

page 55

madness	['mædnəs]	*adj* mad	*Wahnsinn*
contact	['kɒntækt]	*phr* to stay in contact	*Kontakt, Verbindung*
celebrity	[sə'lebrəti]	sb famous	*Promi(nente/r)*
interactive	[ˌɪntər'æktɪv]	*v* to interact with sb	*interaktiv*
newsletter	['njuːzletə]	printed report of news	*Rundschreiben, (Info-)Blatt*
blog	[blɒg]	an online journal	*Blog*
to react	[ri'ækt]	*n* reaction	*reagieren*
hurricane	['hʌrɪkən]	severe storm	*Orkan, Wirbelsturm*
latest	['leɪtɪst]	newest	*neueste, letzte*
public	['pʌblɪk]	in front of other people	*öffentlich*
to raise	[reɪz]	*phr* to raise money for sth	*sammeln*
charity	['tʃærəti]	*phr* an act of charity	*wohltätiger Verein*
in need	[ɪn 'niːd]	needing help	*bedürftig*
communication	[kəˌmjuːnɪ'keɪʃn]	*v* to communicate	*Kommunikation, Mitteilung, Benachrichtigung*
refugee	[ˌrefju'dʒiː]	sb fleeing their country	*Flüchtling*
background	['bækgraʊnd]	origin	*Hintergrund, Herkunft*
library	['laɪbrəri]	place where books can be borrowed	*Bücherei, Bibliothek*

page 56

reality TV	[riˌæləti tiː 'viː]	shows using real people, not actors	*Reality TV*
bother	['bɒðə]	difficulty, trouble	*Ärger*
long-running	['lɒŋrʌnɪŋ]	having been on TV for a long time	*mit langer Laufzeit*
to screen	['skriːnɪŋ]	to show a programme on TV	*ausstrahlen*
series	['sɪəriːz]	programme in episodes	*Serie*
producer	[prə'djuːsə]	film-maker, manufacturer	*Produzent/in, Erzeuger*
action	['ækʃn]	*phr* to take action	*Aktion, Handlung*
entertaining	[ˌentə'teɪnɪŋ]	*n* entertainment	*unterhaltsam*
audience	['ɔːdiəns]	viewers	*Zuschauer*
to vote	[vəʊt]	*phr* to vote in favour of/against	*abstimmen, wählen*
to throw out	[ˌθrəʊ 'aʊt]	to force sb to leave	*hinauswerfen*
trouble	['trʌbl]	problem	*Schwierigkeiten, Ärger*
actress	['æktrəs]	female actor	*Schauspielerin*
popular press	[ˌpɒpjələ 'pres]	media that aims to reach a wide audience	*Boulevardpresse*
to exploit	[ɪk'splɔɪt]	*n* exploitation	*be-, ausnutzen*
abuse	[ə'bjuːs]	*v* to abuse sb	*Anpöbelung, Beschimpfung(en)*
to blame sb	[bleɪm]	to think that sb is responsible for sth	*die Schuld geben, verantwortlich machen*
psychological	[ˌsaɪkə'lɒdʒɪkl]	mental	*psychologisch*
profile	['prəʊfaɪl]	description	*Profil, Ansicht, Herkunft, Berufsbild, Porträt*
personality	[ˌpɜːsə'næləti]	a person's character	*Persönlichkeit*
clash	[klæʃ]	conflict	*Konflikt, Zusammenstoß*
profit	['prɒfɪt]	*adj* profitable	*Profit, Gewinn*

to survive	[sə'vaɪv]	*n* survival	*überleben*
addicted	[ə'dɪktɪd tə]	*n* addiction	*süchtig nach*
to appear	[ə'pɪə]	*n* appearance	*erscheinen*
embarrassing	[ɪm'bærəsɪŋ]	*v* to embarrass	*peinlich*
fame	[feɪm]	*adj* famous	*Ruhm*
to wonder	['wʌndə]	to think about	*sich fragen, sich wundern*
psychology	[saɪ'kɒlədʒi]	*adj* psychological	*Psychologie*
to behave	[bɪ'heɪv]	to act in a certain way	*sich benehmen, sich verhalten*
contestant	[kən'testənt]	sb taking part in a contest	*Kandidat/in*
grotesque	[grəʊ'tesk]	terrible	*grotesk*
Roman	['rəʊmən]	inhabitant of the ancient Roman empire	*Römer/in*
page 57			
to force	[fɔ:s]	to make sb do sth that they don't want to do	*zwingen*
housemate	['haʊsmeɪt]	person that you share a house with	*Mitbewohner/in*
remark	[rɪ'mɑ:k]	*phr* to make a remark about sth	*Bemerkung*
abusive	[ə'bju:sɪv]	*n* abuse	*beleidigend, ausfallend*
accurate	['ækjərət]	correct, precise	*genau*
legal	['li:gl]	*v* to legalize	*legal*
legible	['ledʒəbl]	clear enough to read	*leserlich*
logical	['lɒdʒɪkl]	sensible or reasonable	*logisch*
moral	['mɒrəl]	*n* morality	*moralisch*
perfect	['pɜ:fɪkt]	*n* perfection	*vollkommen*
relevant	['reləvənt]	*phr* to be relevant to sth/sb	*relevant, wichtig*
behaviour	[bɪ'heɪvjə]	*phr* good/bad behaviour	*Verhalten, Benehmen*
page 58			
brave	[breɪv]	*n* bravery	*tapfer*
to be up for	[bi 'ʌp fə]	to be keen to do	*bereit sein für, Lust haben auf*
to pick up	[,pɪk 'ʌp]	to collect	*abholen*
either	['aɪðə]	*phr* either one or the other	*hier: beides*
genre	['ʒɑ:nrə]	type or style	*Genre*
comedy	['kɒmədi]	funny film	*Komödie, Comedy*
documentary	[,dɒkju'mentri]	programme about sth real	*Dokumentarbericht, -film*
satire	['sætaɪə]	*adj* satirical	*Satire*
sci-fi	['saɪ faɪ]	*(abbrev)* science fiction	*Science-Fiction, wissenschaftlich-utopisch*
spy	[spaɪ]	person who tries to find out secret information	*Spion/in, Spionage-*
pirate	['paɪrət]	*phr* pirate DVDs	*Pirat*
all-star	['ɔ:l stɑ:]	full of celebrities	*Star-, mit vielen Stars*
to put forward	[,pʊt 'fɔ:wəd]	to suggest or present	*vorbringen, zur Diskussion stellen*
point of view	[,pɔɪnt əv 'vju:]	opinion	*Standpunkt, Ansicht*
ought to	['ɔ:t tə]	should	*sollte/n*
it's a pity	[ɪts ə 'pɪti]	it's a shame	*es ist schade*
whatever	[wɒt'evə]	no matter what	*was (auch) immer*
page 59			
medium	['mi:diəm]	way of communicating	*Medium*
butterfly	['bʌtəflaɪ]	type of winged insect	*Schmetterling*
altogether	[,ɔ:ltə'geðə]	in total	*alles in allem*
stranger	['streɪndʒə]	person you don't know	*Fremde/r*
unusual	[ʌn'ju:ʒuəl]	strange	*ungewöhnlich*
applicant	['æplɪkənt]	person who applies for a job, etc.	*Bewerber/in*
offline	['ɒflaɪn]	<> online	*offline, nicht im Internet*
to make no sense	[meɪk nəʊ 'sens]	to be hard to understand	*nicht sinnvoll sein*
freely	['fri:li]	willingly and honestly	*freimütig*
provider	[prə'vaɪdə]	*v* to provide	*Anbieter*
user	['ju:zə]	person who uses sth	*Anwender/in, Benutzer/in*
at risk	[ət 'rɪsk]	in danger of	*gefährdet*
to be worried	[bi 'wʌrid]	to be afraid	*befürchten*
identity	[aɪ'dentəti]	who sb is	*Identität*
thief	[θi:f]	*pl:* thieves	*Dieb/in*

researcher	[rɪ'sɜːtʃə]	*v* to research sth	*Forscher/in*
reunion	[riː'juːniən]	*v* to reunite	*Treffen, Wiedersehen*
to abridge	[ə'brɪdʒ]	to make (a text) shorter	*(ab)kürzen*
to adapt	[ə'dæpt]	to change	*adaptieren*

page 60

to lie	[laɪ]	<> to tell the truth	*lügen*
circle	['sɜːkl]	*phr* circle of friends	*Kreis*
to pay attention to	[peɪ ə'tenʃn tə]	to be careful with	*beachten, achten auf*

page 61

to reduce	[rɪ'djuːs]	*n* reduction	*reduzieren, verringern*
component	[kəm'pəʊnənt]	part	*Bestandteil*
to shorten	['ʃɔːtn]	to make sth shorter	*(ver)kürzen*
keyboard	['kiːbɔːd]	set of keys for controlling a computer	*Tastatur*
over the top	[ˌəʊvə ðə 'tɒp]	too much	*übertrieben*
to bet	[bet]	to be sure that	*wetten*
experience	[ɪk'spɪəriəns]	*phr* to have experience of sth	*Erfahrung*

page 62

netiquette	['netɪket]	*(inf)* rules for behaving correctly online	*Netiquette, Umgangsformen (im Internet)*
range	[reɪndʒ]	*phr* a wide range of	*Reihe, Spektrum*
polite	[pə'laɪt]	*n* politeness	*höflich*
capital (letter)	['kæpɪtl]	e.g. A, B, C	*Groß(buchstabe)*
to be considered	[bɪ kən'sɪdəd]	to be thought of as	*berücksichtigt werden*
to emphasize	['emfəsaɪz]	*n* emphasis	*betonen, hervorheben*
bold	[bəʊld]	in a thick dark print	*fett*
to underline	[ˌʌndə'laɪn]	to draw a line under a word	*unterstreichen*
spelling	['spelɪŋ]	*phr* a spelling mistake	*Rechtschreibung*
to avoid	[ə'vɔɪd]	to try not to do sth	*(ver)meiden*
punctuation	[ˌpʌŋktʃu'eɪʃn]	marks used to separate phrases/ sentences	*Zeichensetzung, Interpunktion*
unnecessary	[ʌn'nesəsəri]	<> necessary	*unnötig*
to shut up	[ˌʃʌt 'ʌp]	*(inf)* to be quiet	*den Mund halten*
kid	[kɪd]	*(inf)* child	*Kind*

page 63

mobile	['məʊbaɪl]	*abbrev* mobile phone	*Handy, Mobiltelefon*
to be seen as	[bi 'siːn əz]	to think of sth as	*gesehen werden als*
to feel lost	[fiːl 'lɒst]	to feel unable to cope	*sich verloren fühlen*
continuously	[kən'tɪnjuəsli]	frequently, again and again	*ständig*
to refuse	[rɪ'fjuːz]	to not accept, to say no to	*ablehnen*
ring tone	['rɪŋ təʊn]	sound a phone makes when sb calls it	*Klingelton*
text message	['tekst mesɪdʒ]	a written message sent from a mobile	*SMS(-Nachricht)*
to locate	[ləʊ'keɪt]	*n* location	*orten*
to trace	[treɪs]	to follow	*(zurück)verfolgen*
to find the way	[faɪnd ðə 'weɪ]	to discover the route to somewhere	*den Weg finden*
appointment	[ə'pɔɪntmənt]	an arranged meeting	*Termin, Verabredung*
must-have item	[ˌmʌst 'hæv aɪtəm]	sth that is essential or very desirable	*was man unbedingt haben muss*
organizer	['ɔːgənaɪzə]	diary, calendar	*elektronischer Kalender*
reminder function	[rɪ'maɪndə fʌŋkʃn]	a function on a mobile that helps you remember something	*Erinnerungsfunktion*
posting	['pəʊstɪŋ]	message on a website or chat room	*Posting, Leserbrief im Internet*
gran	[græn]	*abbrev* grandmother	*Oma*
mailbox	['meɪlbɒks]	answer phone	*Anrufbeantworter*
pix	[pɪks]	*inf* pictures	*Bilder*
debt	[det]	money that sb owes	*Schuld(en)*
pay-as-you-go	[ˌpeɪ əz ju 'gəʊ]	paid for before being used	*mit Karte, vorausbezahlt*
contract	['kɒntrækt]	a formal document or agreement	*Vertrag*
in instalments	[ɪn ɪn'stɔːlmənts]	bit by bit	*ratenweise*
MMS	[ˌem em 'es]	*abbrev* Multimedia Messaging Services	*multimediale Nachricht per Mobiltelefon*

page 64

fundraising	['fʌndreɪzɪŋ]	raising money for a charity/organization	*Wohltätigkeitsveranstaltung, Spendensammeln*
bouncy castle	['baʊnsi kɑːsl]	plastic castle filled with air for children to play on	*Hüpfburg*
soft drink	[ˌsɒft 'drɪŋk]	cold drink containing no alcohol	*alkoholfreies Getränk*
exchange	[ɪks'tʃeɪndʒ]	conversation	*(Kurz-)Dialog*
exam results	[ɪgˌzæm rɪ'zʌlts]	grades or marks	*Examensnoten*
secure	[sɪ'kjuə]	*n* security, safe	*sicher*

UNIT 4

page 65

on the move	[ɒn ðə 'muːv]	travelling	*unterwegs*
various	['veəriəs]	a range of	*verschieden*
transport	['trænspɔːt]	*phr* means of transport	*Verkehr(smittel)*
salesman	['seɪlzmən]	man whose job is to sell goods	*Verkäufer*
ideal	[aɪ'diːəl]	perfect	*ideal*
budget	['bʌdʒɪt]	cheap	*hier: Billig-*
extent	[ɪk'stent]	*phr* to a certain extent	*(Aus-)Maß, Umfang, Grad*
reality	[ri'æləti]	*adj* real	*Wirklichkeit*
amazed	[ə'meɪzd]	*n* amazement	*erstaunt*
annoyed	[ə'nɔɪd]	*v* to annoy sb	*verärgert*
anxious	['æŋkʃəs]	*n* anxiety	*besorgt, beunruhigt*
delighted	[dɪ'laɪtɪd]	happy	*(sehr) erfreut, entzückt*
depressed	[dɪ'prest]	*n* depression	*deprimiert, niedergeschlagen*
disappointed	[ˌdɪsə'pɔɪntɪd]	*n* disappointment	*enttäuscht*
excited	[ɪk'saɪtɪd]	*n* excitement	*aufgeregt, erregt*
exhausted	[ɪg'zɔːstɪd]	*n* exhaustion	*erschöpft*
frustrated	[frʌ'streɪtɪd]	*n* frustration	*frustriert*
nervous	['nɜːvəs]	*n* nervousness	*nervös*
relaxed	[rɪ'lækst]	*n* relaxation	*entspannt, locker*
shocked	[ʃɒkt]	*n* shock	*schockiert*
surprised	[sə'praɪzd]	*n* surprise	*überrascht, erstaunt*
terrified	['terɪfaɪd]	very scared	*erschrocken*
upset	[ˌʌp'set]	unhappy	*bestürzt, entsetzt*

page 66

traffic jam	['træfɪk dʒæm]	*phr* to be stuck in a traffic jam	*(Verkehrs-)Stau*
nursery	['nɜːsəri]	*phr* day nursery, nursery school	*Kindertagesstätte, Kita,*
dry cleaner's	[ˌdraɪ 'kliːnəz]	shop where clothes are cleaned using chemicals	*chemische Reinigung*
fortune	['fɔːtʃuːn]	*phr* to cost a fortune	*Vermögen*
surely	['ʃʊəli]	almost certainly	*sicherlich*
government	['gʌvənmənt]	*v* to govern	*Regierung*
fuel	['fjuːəl]	e.g. petrol, coal, gas	*Kraftstoff*
tax	[tæks]	*phr* tax increases/cuts	*Steuer*
tailback	['teɪlbæk]	long line of still or slow-moving traffic	*Autoschlange*
freedom	['friːdəm]	*adj* free	*Freiheit*
flexibility	[ˌfleksə'bɪləti]	*adj* flexible	*Flexibilität*
privacy	['prɪvəsi]	*adj* private	*Privatsphäre*
campaigner	[kæm'peɪnə]	a person who campaigns for/against sth	*Aktivist/in, Kämpfer/in*
pollution	[pə'luːʃn]	*v* to pollute	*(Umwelt)Verschmutzung*
environmental	[ɪnˌvaɪrən'mentl]	*n* environment	*Umwelt-*
damage	['dæmɪdʒ]	physical harm	*Schaden, Schäden*
exhaust	[ɪg'zɔːst]	pipe in a car through which waste gases pass	*Auspuff(rohr)*
fumes	[fjuːmz]	smoke or gas	*Abgase*
to choke	[tʃəʊk]	to be unable to breathe	*ersticken*
gridlock	['grɪdlɒk]	situation where there are so many cars that none can move	*Verkehrskollaps*
to contain	[kən'teɪn]	to hold, include	*enthalten*
passenger	['pæsɪndʒə]	person in a car who is not the driver	*Fahrgast*
minister	['mɪnɪstə]	government official	*Minister/in*

congestion	[kən'dʒestʃən]	*adj* congested	*Verkehrsstau, Verstopfung*
congested	[kən'dʒestɪd]	full of traffic	*verstopft*
chaos	['keɪɒs]	*adj* chaotic	*Chaos*
to improve	[ɪm'pru:v]	to get better, ↔ to worsen	*verbessern, besser werden*
balance	['bæləns]	of equal weight	*Gleichgewicht*
efficient	[ɪ'fɪʃnt]	*n* efficiency	*effizient, leistungsfähig*
emission	[ɪ'mɪʃn]	*v* to emit	*Emission, Ausstoß*
suburb	['sʌbɜ:b]	*adj* suburban	*Vorort, Außenbezirk*
saving	['seɪvɪŋ]	*v* to save (money)	*Einsparung, Ersparnis*
impact	['ɪmpækt]	*phr* to have an impact on sth	*(Aus-)Wirkung, Einfluss*
colleague	['kɒli:g]	person you work with	*Kollege / Kollegin*
car sharing	['kɑ: ʃeərɪŋ]	sharing a ride to reduce costs/pollution, etc.	*gemeinsame Pkw-Nutzung*

page 67

idiomatic	[ˌɪdiə'mætɪk]	*n* idiom	*idiomatisch*
illegal	[ɪ'li:gl]	↔ legal	*verboten, illegal*
idiom	['ɪdiəm]	*adj* idiomatic	*Idiom, Redewendung*
accident	['æksɪdənt]	*phr* car accident	*Unfall*
mile	[maɪl]	= 1609 metres	*Meile*
motorway	['məʊtəweɪ]	wide road where cars travel long distances	*Autobahn*
to brainstorm	['breɪnstɔ:m]	to write down or think of different ideas quickly	*(Ideen) sammeln*
route	[ru:t]	(in US road names) main road	*Route, Strecke, Weg*
state	[steɪt]	e.g. California, Kentucky	*(Bundes-)Staat*
direction	[də'rekʃn]	*phr* to change direction	*Richtung*
commuter	[kə'mju:tə]	person who travels a long way to get to work every day	*Pendler/in*

page 68

visual	['vɪʒuəl]	*n* vision	*visuell, optisch*
to deliver	[dɪ'lɪvə]	to give or provide	*vermitteln, überbringen*
message	['mesɪdʒ]	written or spoken information	*Botschaft*
memorable	['memərəbl]	easy to remember	*unvergesslich, einprägsam*
vertical	['vɜ:tɪkl]	↔ horizontal	*senkrecht, vertikal*
cliff	[klɪf]	steep edge of a high area of rock	*Klippe, Felsen*
gas	[gæs]	*(AE) BE:* petrol	*Benzin, Treibstoff*
SUV	[ˌes ju: 'vi:]	*(abbrev)* sport utility vehicle	*Geländewagen (mit Vierradantrieb)*
cartoonist	[kɑ:'tu:nɪst]	person who draws cartoons	*Karikaturist/in*
appendix	[ə'pendɪks]	section at the end of a book	*Anhang*

page 69

satellite	['sætəlaɪt]	*phr* satellite television	*Satellit*
zone	[zəʊn]	area	*Zone, Bereich*
rush hour	['rʌʃaʊə]	time when roads are busy	*Hauptverkehrszeit, Berufsverkehr*
unless	[ən'les]	if not	*wenn nicht*
satnav	['sætnæv]	*(abbrev)* satellite navigation	*Satellitennavigation, Navi*
location	[ləʊ'keɪʃn]	*v* to locate	*(Stand-)Ort, Position*
monthly	['mʌnθli]	every month	*monatlich*
haulier	['hɔ:liə]	person who transports goods by road	*Spediteur, Fuhrunternehmen*
to destroy	[dɪ'strɔɪ]	*n* destruction	*zerstören, vernichten*
to estimate	['estɪmeɪt]	*n* estimation	*schätzen*
zero	['zɪərəʊ]	the number 0	*Null*
owner	['əʊnə]	person who owns sth	*Besitzer/in*
environmentalist	[ɪnˌvaɪrən'mentəlɪst]	person who wants to protect the environment	*Umweltschützer/in*
engineer	[ˌendʒɪ'nɪə]	person who designs/builds roads/machines, etc.	*Ingenieur/in, Techniker/in*
to race	[reɪs]	to compete to be the first to do sth	*sich ein Wettrennen liefern*
dweller	['dwelə]	inhabitant	*Bewohner/in*
electricity	[ɪˌlek'trɪsəti]	*adj* electric, electrical	*Elektrizität, Strom*
traditional	[trə'dɪʃənl]	*n* tradition	*traditionell*
power station	['paʊə steɪʃn]	building where electricity is produced	*Kraftwerk*
hybrid	['haɪbrɪd]	using a mixture of fuels	*hybrid*

cleverly	['klevəli]	in a clever way	*klug, intelligent*
movement	['mu:vmənt]	*v* to move	*Bewegung*
motor	['məʊtə]	device that uses fuel to produce movement	*Motor*
to support	[sə'pɔ:t]	to help, back up	*unterstützen*
engine	['endʒɪn]	part of vehicle that produces power to move	*Motor*
hill	[hɪl]	*adj* hilly	*Hügel, Berg*
complicated	['kɒmplɪkeɪtɪd]	complex, intricate	*kompliziert*
development	[dɪ'veləpmənt]	progress	*Entwicklung*
production	[prə'dʌkʃn]	creation, manufacture	*Produktion, Herstellung*
to combine	[kəm'baɪn]	*n* combination	*(sich) verbinden*
hydrogen	['haɪdrədʒən]	chemical element H	*Wasserstoff*
oxygen	['ɒksɪdʒən]	chemical element O	*Sauerstoff*
waste	[weɪst]	*phr* waste product	*Abfall*
to manufacture	[ˌmænju'fæktʃə]	to produce	*herstellen, produzieren*
renewable	[rɪ'nju:əbl]	*phr* renewable energy	*erneuerbar*
source	[sɔ:s]	*phr* energy source	*Quelle*
environmentally friendly	[ɪnˌvaɪrənˌmentəli 'frendli]	not harmful to the environment	*umweltfreundlich*

page 70

to calculate	['kælkjuleɪt]	*n* calculation	*kalkulieren, berechnen*
charge	[tʃɑ:dʒ]	*phr* free of charge	*Kosten*
in common	[ɪn 'kɒmən]	*phr* to have sth in common	*gemeinsam*
eventually	[ɪ'ventʃuəli]	at the end of a period of time	*schließlich, zum Schluss*
to power	['paʊə]	to supply a machine/vehicle with energy	*antreiben, betreiben*
solution	[sə'lu:ʃn]	*v* to solve	*Lösung, Ausweg*
income	['ɪnkʌm]	money earned	*Einkommen*

page 71

congestion charging	[kən'dʒestʃən tʃɑ:dʒɪŋ]	money you have to pay for driving your car in the city centre	*Staugebühr*
to enter	['entə]	to go into	*hineingehen, -fahren*
result	[rɪ'zʌlt]	*phr* as a result of	*Resultat, Ergebnis*
reduction	[rɪ'dʌkʃn]	*v* to reduce	*Verringerung, Senkung*
central	['sentrəl]	in the centre	*zentral*
anger	['æŋgə]	*v* to anger sb	*Zorn, Ärger*
to affect	[ə'fekt]	to have an effect on	*betreffen*
to benefit from	['benɪfɪt frəm]	to be in a better position because of sth	*Nutzen ziehen aus, profitieren von*
businessperson	['bɪznəspɜ:sn]	businessman, businesswoman	*Geschäftsmann/-frau*
official	[ə'fɪʃl]	person in a position of authority	*Beamter/Beamtin*
councillor	['kaʊnsələ]	member of a council	*Ratsmitglied*
to persuade	[pə'sweɪd]	*n* persuasion	*überzeugen, überreden*

page 72

appropriate	[ə'prəʊpriət]	suitable	*angemessen, passend, entsprechend*
old-fashioned	[ˌəʊld 'fæʃənd]	no longer modern or fashionable	*altmodisch, veraltet*
major	['meɪdʒə]	large or important	*groß, größer*
complete	[kəm'pli:t]	total	*völlig*
unavailable	[ˌʌnə'veɪləbl]	<> available	*nicht verfügbar*
extremely	[ɪk'stri:mli]	very	*äußerst, außerordentlich*
personally	['pɜ:sənəli]	individually	*persönlich*

page 73

containerization	[kənˌteɪnəraɪ'zeɪʃn]	using containers to transport goods	*(Umstellung auf) Containerverkehr*
booming	['bu:mɪŋ]	successful, growing rapidly	*blühend*
hold	[həʊld]	storage compartment of a ship	*Lade-, Frachtraum*
deck	[dek]	floor of a ship	*Deck*
cargo	['kɑ:gəʊ]	goods carried by a ship	*Fracht, Ladung*
docker	['dɒkə]	person who loads and unloads ships	*Hafenarbeiter/in*
to load	[ləʊd]	to put in, to fill	*verladen*
on board	[ɒn 'bɔ:d]	on a ship	*an Bord*
carton	['kɑ:tn]	a cardboard or plastic box used to transport goods	*Karton*

crate	[kreɪt]	a wooden box used to transport goods	*(Holz-)Kiste*
barrel	['bærəl]	a container used to transport liquid goods	*Fass*
bale	[beɪl]	bunch, bundle	*Ballen*
to lower	['ləʊə]	to make sth go down	*herablassen*
pallet	['pælət]	a flat wooden board on which goods are stored	*Palette*
crane	[kreɪn]	machinery used to lift heavy weights	*Kran*
procedure	[prə'siːdʒə]	method, way of doing something	*Verfahren*
to break bulk	[breɪk 'bʌlk]	to load a ship	*die Ladung löschen*
labour-intensive	[ˌleɪbər ɪn'tensɪv]	requiring a large number of employees	*arbeitsintensiv*
time-consuming	['taɪm kənsjuːmɪŋ]	requiring a lot of time	*zeitraubend*
damage	['dæmɪdʒ]	physical harm	*Sachschaden*
theft	[θeft]	act of stealing sth	*Diebstahl*
port	[pɔːt]	place where ships load and unload	*Hafen*
ton	[tʌn]	1000 kilograms	*Tonne*
trucking	['trʌkɪŋ]	transporting of goods by truck or lorry	*(Lkw-)Transport*
container ship	[kən'teɪnə ʃɪp]	ship transporting containers of goods	*Containerschiff*
converted	[kən'vɜːtɪd]	changed, transformed	*umgebaut*
tanker	['tæŋkə]	a ship transporting large liquids or gases	*Tanker*
security	[sɪ'kjʊərəti]	safety	*Sicherheit*
to seal	[siːl]	to close completely	*verschließen, versiegeln*
opposition	[ˌɒpə'zɪʃn]	objection, disapproval	*Widerstand*
union	['juːniən]	an organisation of workers	*Gewerkschaft*
revolutionary	[ˌrevə'luːʃənəri]	brand new, innovative	*revolutionär*
mechanically	[mɪ'kænɪkli]	with the help of a machine	*mechanisch*
gantry	['gæntri]	a frame used to support a crane	*Portal(kran)*
warehouse	['weəhaʊs]	a building used to store goods	*Lagerhalle, -haus*
obsolete	['ɒbsəliːt]	old-fashioned, out of date	*veraltet*
terminal	['tɜːmɪnl]	a place where journeys begin and end	*Abfertigungsgebäude*
to source	[sɔːs]	to get sth from somewhere	*beziehen*
virtually	['vɜːtʃuəli]	practically, nearly	*praktisch, nahezu*
practice	['præktɪs]	method, way of doing something	*Methode, Vorgehensweise*
expansion	[ɪk'spænʃn]	making sth bigger	*Ausdehnung*
workforce	['wɜːkfɔːs]	the workers	*Arbeiterschaft*
surrounding	[sə'raʊndɪŋ]	nearby, neighbouring	*umliegend*

page 74

return	[rɪ'tɜːn]	ticket to go to a place and back again	*(hin und) zurück*
election	[ɪ'lekʃn]	a political vote	*(politische) Wahl*

UNIT 5

page 75

disaster	[dɪ'zɑːstə]	a very bad situation or event	*Katastrophe, Unglück*
mixture	['mɪkstʃə]	combination	*Mischung*
brief	['briːf]	quick, for a short time	*kurz*
asteroid	['æstərɔɪd]	a small planet which revolves around the sun	*Asteroid*
catastrophe	[kə'tæstrəfi]	disaster	*Katastrophe*
destruction	[dɪ'strʌkʃn]	*v* to destroy	*Zerstörung, Vernichtung*
epidemic	[ˌepɪ'demɪk]	outbreak of a disease or illness	*Epidemie*
flood	[flʌd]	a place that is filled or covered with water	*Flut, Überschwemmung*
to be set in	[bi 'set ɪn]	the film is set in ..., NOT: ~~the film plays in ...~~	*spielen in*

page 76

report	[rɪ'pɔːt]	*v* to report	*Bericht, Reportage*
fitted	['fɪtɪd]	*v* to fit in place	*eingebaut*
low-energy	[ˌləʊ 'enədʒi]	small or little amount of power	*Niedrigenergie-, Spar-*
bulb	[bʌlb]	*phr* light bulb	*Glühbirne, -lampe*
matter	['mætə]	situation, problem	*Sache, Ding, Angelegenheit*
journalist	['dʒɜːnəlɪst]	a person who collects and writes news stories	*Journalist/in*
progress	['prəʊgres]	⚠ Betonung	*Fortschritt/e*

to turn down	[ˌtɜːn 'daʊn]	*phr* to turn down the temperature	*herunterregeln*
sweater	['swetə]	a piece of clothing for the upper body	*Pullover*
alternative	[ɔːl'tɜːnətɪv]	different option	*alternativ*
turbine	['tɜːbaɪn]	⚠ Aussprache	*Turbine, Rad*
strength	[streŋθ]	*adj* strong	*Kraft, Stärke*
unreliable	[ˌʌnrɪ'laɪəbl]	<> reliable	*unzuverlässig*
solar	['səʊlə]	using the sun's energy to create power	*Sonnen-, Solar-*
to meet needs	[miːt 'niːdz]	to get sth done	*Bedürfnisse decken*
insulation	[ˌɪnsju'leɪʃn]	*phr* wall insulation	*Isolierung*
to face	[feɪs]	*phr* to face a decision	*sich gegenübersehen, vor sich haben*
cycle	['saɪkl]	*n* bicycle	*radfahren*
double-glazing	[ˌdʌbl 'gleɪzɪŋ]	*phr* double-glazed windows	*mit Isolierverglasung versehen*
previous	['priːviəs]	before	*vorher(gehend)*
to run out of	[ˌrʌn 'aʊt əv]	*phr* to run out of money	*ausgehen*
tonne	[tʌn]	1000 kilograms	*Tonne*
amount	[ə'maʊnt]	quantity	*Menge*
average	['ævərɪdʒ]	typical, normal	*durchschnittlich*
lifestyle	['laɪfstaɪl]	how a person lives and works	*Lebensstil*
somehow	['sʌmhaʊ]	in a way which is not clear	*irgendwie*
page 77			
benefit	['benɪfɪt]	advantage	*Nutzen, Vorteil*
page 78			
to rewrite	[ˌriː'raɪt]	to write again	*umschreiben, neu schreiben*
original	[ə'rɪdʒənl]	*phr* the original words from the text	*original, ursprünglich*
to advise	[əd'vaɪz]	to suggest, offer an opinion	*raten, beraten*
to request	[rɪ'kwest]	to ask for	*anfordern, bitten (um)*
junction	['dʒʌŋkʃn]	a place or point where two things come together	*Kreuzung*
bored	[bɔːd]	uninterested	*gelangweilt*
switch	[swɪtʃ]	a device for turning off and on an electrical current	*Schalter*
machinery	[mə'ʃiːnəri]	*n* machine	*Maschine(n), Gerät*
appliance	[ə'plaɪəns]	electronic device	*Gerät*
worried	['wʌrɪd]	*v* to worry	*besorgt*
cloudy	['klaʊdi]	*n* cloud	*bewölkt*
valley	['væli]	the lowest point between two mountains	*Tal*
path	[pɑːθ]	a walkway	*Pfad, Weg*
page 79			
version	['vɜːʃn]	*phr* different versions of the same picture	*Version, Fassung*
page 80			
global	['gləʊbl]	worldwide	*global, weltweit*
desperate	['despərət]	urgent	*verzweifelt*
airwaves	['eəweɪvz]	radio waves used to broadcast radio and TV	*Äther*
atmosphere	['ætməsfɪə]	the mixture of gases that surround the earth	*Atmosphäre*
twice	[twaɪs]	once, twice, three times	*zweimal, doppelt*
level	['levl]	amount	*Niveau, Stand*
industrial	[ɪn'dʌstriəl]	*n* industry	*industriell*
revolution	[ˌrevə'luːʃn]	radical change	*Revolution*
climate	['klaɪmət]	weather	*Klima*
eastern	['iːstən]	<> western, northern, southern	*östlich*
cyclone	['saɪkləʊn]	bad storm with wind and rain	*Zyklon*
desert	['dezət]	dry empty land	*Wüste*
moreover	[mɔːr'əʊvə]	also	*außerdem, zudem*
sheet	[ʃiːt]	*phr* sheet of ice	*Platte, Decke*
to melt	[melt]	<> freeze	*schmelzen*
centimetre	['sentɪmiːtə]	unit for measuring length	*Zentimeter*
low-lying	[ˌləʊ 'laɪɪŋ]	located at a low level	*tief gelegen*
coastal	['kəʊstl]	on the coast	*Küsten-*
to prevent	[prɪ'vent]	to stop sth from happening	*verhindern, verhüten*

champagne	[ʃæm'peɪn]	French sparkling white wine	*Champagner*
to celebrate	['selɪbreɪt]	*phr* to celebrate a birthday	*feiern*
atmospheric	[ˌætməs'ferɪk]	in the atmosphere	*atmosphärisch*
ppm	[ˌpiː piː 'em]	*(abbrev)* parts per million	*Teile pro Million*
economy	[ɪ'kɒnəmi]	*phr* the world economy	*Wirtschaft*
stabilization	[ˌsteɪbəlaɪ'zeɪʃn]	*adj* stable	*Stabilisierung*
coal	[kəʊl]	type of fuel	*Kohle*
fossil fuel	['fɒsl fjuːəl]	type of fuel	*fossiler Brennstoff*
tidal	['taɪdl]	*n* tides	*Gezeiten-*
hydroelectric	[ˌhaɪdrəʊɪ'lektrɪk]	using the power of water to make electricity	*hydroelektrisch*
nuclear	['njuːkliə]	*phr* nuclear weapons	*Atom-*
fusion	['fjuːʒn]	joining things together to make one	*Fusion, Verschmelzung*
thanks to	['θæŋks tə]	because of	*dank*
vision	['vɪʒn]	goal	*Vision, Vorausschau*
to delay	[dɪ'leɪ]	*n* delay	*aufschieben, hinauszögern*
warming	['wɔːmɪŋ]	*adj* warm	*Erwärmung*
severe	[sɪ'vɪə]	very bad	*ernst, schwer, stark*
wise	[waɪz]	smart	*weise, klug*
leader	['liːdə]	*phr* leader of the group	*Führer/in*
to owe	[əʊ]	*phr* to owe money	*verdanken, schulden*
to emerge	[ɪ'mɜːdʒ]	to come out of some place	*heraustreten, hervorkommen*
carbon	['kɑːbən]	a chemical element	*Kohlenstoff*

page 81

century	['sentʃəri]	100 years	*Jahrhundert*
beyond	[bɪ'jɒnd]	further	*darüber hinaus, danach*
fraction	['frækʃn]	a part of a whole	*Bruch(teil)*
percentage	[pə'sentɪdʒ]	%	*Prozentsatz*
a fifth	[fɪfθ]	a third, a fourth, a fifth	*Fünftel*
guest	[gest]	visitor	*Gast*
possibility	[ˌpɒsə'bɪləti]	*adj* possible	*Möglichkeit*
climate change	['klaɪmət tʃeɪndʒ]	alteration of the world's weather patterns	*Klimawandel*
rise	[raɪz]	increase	*Anstieg*
carbon dioxide	[ˌkɑːbən daɪ'ɒksaɪd]	the gas CO_2	*Kohlendioxid*
though	[ðəʊ]	however	*doch, jedoch*
poverty	['pɒvəti]	*adj* poor	*Armut*
standard of living	[ˌstændəd əv 'lɪvɪŋ]	quality of life	*Lebensstandard*
to make up for	[ˌmeɪk 'ʌp fə]	to compensate for	*ausgleichen*
increase	['ɪŋkriːs]	*adj* increasing	*Anstieg*
to hold down	[ˌhəʊld 'daʊn]	to prevent from increasing	*niedrig halten*
cut	[kʌt]	reduction	*Kürzung, Senkung*
figure	['fɪgə]	number or amount	*Zahl*
target	['tɑːgɪt]	goal	*Ziel(vorgaben), Soll(zahlen)*

page 82

chart	[tʃɑːt]	diagram	*Diagramm, Tabelle*
required	[rɪ'kwaɪəd]	necessary	*erforderlich*
per capita	[pə 'kæpɪtə]	average per person	*pro Kopf*
to rephrase	[ˌriː'freɪz]	to say again using different words	*anders ausdrücken, umformulieren*
essential	[ɪ'senʃl]	vital, necessary, important	*notwendig, wesentlich*
anecdote	['ænɪkdəʊt]	a short story	*Anekdote*
simile	['sɪməli]	comparing two things using 'like' or 'as'	*Vergleich*
rhetorical	[rɪ'tɒrɪkl]	*phr* to ask a rhetorical question	*rhetorisch*
repetition	[ˌrepə'tɪʃn]	*adj* repetitive	*Wiederholung*
stormy	['stɔːmi]	*n* storm	*stürmisch*
to respond to	[rɪ'spɒnd tə]	to give an answer	*reagieren auf*
warning	['wɔːnɪŋ]	*v* to warn	*Warnung*

page 83

gone are the days	[ˌgɒn ɑː ðə 'deɪz]	*inf* it is no longer the case	*vergangen ist die Zeit*
plentiful	['plentɪfl]	<> scarce, rare	*reichlich (vorhanden)*
consumption	[kən'sʌmpʃn]	spending, using up	*Verbrauch*
the race is on	[ðə ˌreɪs ɪz 'ɒn]	*inf* doing sth as quickly as possible	*das Rennen ist eröffnet*

to prove	[pru:v]	to turn out	*sich erweisen als*
promising	['prɒmɪsɪŋ]	likely to develop in a desirable way	*vielversprechend*
commercially viable	[kə,mɜ:ʃəli 'vaɪəbl]	not successful in business	*kommerziell lebensfähig*
conventional	[kən'venʃənl]	typical, normal, usual	*herkömmlich, konventionell*
offshore	[,ɒf'ʃɔ:]	in the sea	*vor der Küste*
desert	['dezət]	dry area of land	*Wüste*
wind farm	['wɪnd fɑ:m]	a power plant that uses wind turbines to make electricity	*Windkraftanlage*
solar power	[,səʊlə 'paʊə]	energy from the sun	*Sonnenkraft, -strom*
plant	[plɑ:nt]	factory or place where power is produced	*Anlage*
solar panel	[,səʊlə 'pænl]	board used to change solar energy into electricity	*Sonnenkollektor*
cattle	['kætl]	farm animals	*Rinder, Vieh*
pitch	[pɪtʃ]	sports field	*Platz, (Spiel-)Feld*
waste disposal	['weɪst dɪspəʊzl]	getting rid of rubbish	*Abfallbeseitigung, Müllentsorgung*
liquid	['lɪkwɪd]	<> solid, gas	*flüssig*
manure	[mə'njʊə]	animal waste	*Dung, Dünger*
sugar cane	['ʃʊgə keɪn]	a plant from which sugar is produced	*Zuckerrohr*
sugar beet	['ʃʊgə bi:t]	a white vegetable used to produce sugar	*Zuckerrübe*
wheat	[wi:t]	grain used in bread, pasta, etc.	*Weizen*
natural gas	[,nætʃrəl 'gæs]	a gas found beneath the Earth's surface	*Erdgas*
crust	[krʌst]	surface, skin, edge	*Kruste*
tides	[taɪdz]	rise and fall of the sea	*Gezeiten*
sea level	['si: levl]	height of the sea	*Meeresspiegel*

page 84

dramatic	[drə'mætɪ]	*adv.* dramatically	*dramatisch, drastisch*
issue	['ɪʃu:]	problem	*Frage, Thema, Anliegen*

UNIT 6

page 85

to operate	['ɒpəreɪt]	to run	*betreiben*
seaside	['si:saɪd]	along the ocean	*Bade-, Strand-, See-*
resort	[rɪ'zɔ:t]	a place where people go to on holiday to relax	*Erholungsort*
accountant	[ə'kaʊntənt]	person who looks after and checks financial accounts	*Buchhalter/in*
booking	['bʊkɪŋ]	*v* to book	*Buchung*
clerk	[klɑ:k]	a worker in charge of accounts and records, etc.	*(Bank-)Angestellte/r*
customer relations officer	[,kʌstəmə rɪ'leɪʃnz ɒfɪsə]	person who deals with customers	*Kundendienstmitarbeiter/in, Kundenbetreuer/in*
IT technician	[,aɪ 'ti: tek'nɪʃn]	person who is skilled with information technology	*Informationstechniker/in*
receptionist	[rɪ'sepʃənɪst]	works in a reception	*Empfangsdame, -chef*
publicity	[pʌb'lɪsəti]	*n* public	*Öffentlichkeitsarbeit*
activities officer	[æk'tɪvətiz ɒfɪsə]	person who is in charge of organizing events	*Verantwortliche/r für Aktivitäten und Veranstaltungen*
salesperson	['seɪlzpɜ:sn]	salesman, saleswoman	*Verkaufsmitarbeiter/in, Verkäufer/in*
instructor	[ɪn'strʌktə]	person who gives instructions	*Lehrer/in, Ausbilder/in*
temporary	['temprəri]	<> permanent	*zeitlich befristet*
seasonal	['si:zənl]	*n* season	*Saison-*
paid	[peɪd]	*phr* to get paid money	*bezahlt*
irregular	[ɪ'regjələ]	<> regular	*unregelmäßig*
outdoors	[,aʊt'dɔ:z]	outside	*draußen, im Freien*
independent	[,ɪndɪ'pendənt]	self-reliant	*unabhängig*
office-based	['ɒfɪs beɪst]	to be working within an office	*im Büro, bürogebunden*
routine	[ru:'ti:n]	a regular fixed way of doing things	*Routine, Ablauf*
challenging	['tʃælɪndʒɪŋ]	difficult	*herausfordernd, anstrengend*
reasonable	['ri:znəbl]	okay	*vernünftig*
salary	['sæləri]	amount of money earned	*Gehalt, Lohn*

fringe benefits	['frɪndʒ benəfɪts]	extra things that an employer gives you as well as your salary	*zusätzliche Leistungen, freiwillige Sozialleistungen*
page 86			
workplace	['wɜːkpleɪs]	area where one works	*Arbeitsplatz*
complex	['kɒmpleks]	complicated	*komplex, kompliziert*
diploma	[dɪ'pləʊmə]	graduation certificate	*Diplom*
secretarial course	[ˌsekrə'teəriəl kɔːs]	course on how to become a secretary	*Sekretariatskurs*
CV	[ˌsiː 'viː]	*(abbrev)* Curriculum Vitae	*Lebenslauf*
to drift	[drɪft]	to move slowly and casually	*treiben, zufällig kommen*
stock control	['stɒk kəntrəʊl]	control of supplies	*Lagersteuerung, Lagerkontrolle*
dead-end	[ˌded 'end]	*phr* a dead-end job	*ohne Perspektiven*
redundant	[rɪ'dʌndənt]	made unemployed	*arbeitslos*
to upgrade	[ˌʌp'greɪd]	to make better or to improve	*erweitern, verbessern*
to apply for	[ə'plaɪ fə]	*n* application	*sich bewerben um*
page 87			
vocational	[vəʊ'keɪʃənl]	preparing sb for a specific occupation or trade	*in der beruflichen Ausbildung, beruflich, Berufs-*
to outline	['aʊtlaɪn]	to summarize	*umreißen, skizzieren*
to matter	['mætə]	to be of importance	*von Bedeutung sein*
backwards	['bækwədz]	<> forward(s)	*rückwärts*
oral	['ɔːrəl]	verbal	*mündlich*
page 88			
employment	[ɪm'plɔɪmənt]	job	*Arbeit, Beschäftigung, Beruf*
wages	['weɪdʒɪz]	amount of money earned by or paid to sb	*Lohn, Löhne*
pressure	['preʃə]	stress	*Druck*
responsibility	[rɪˌspɒnsə'bɪləti]	*adj* responsible	*Verantwortung, Verantwortlichkeit*
export sales	['ekspɔːt seɪlz]	things that are being sold to other countries	*Exportverkäufe, Auslandsverkäufe*
IT	[ˌaɪ 'tiː]	*(abbrev)* information technology	*Informationstechnologie*
to mess up	[ˌmes 'ʌp]	*(inf)* to do badly	*es verderben, es verpeilen*
skint	[skɪnt]	*(inf)* having no money	*pleite*
to put down	[ˌpʊt 'daʊn]	to pay up front	*anzahlen*
solar heating	[ˌsəʊlə 'hiːtɪŋ]	system which uses the sun's energy to heat a house	*Solarheizung*
to push up	[ˌpʊʃ 'ʌp]	to increase	*ausbauen, hochtreiben*
to hire	[haɪə]	to recruit, look for new employees	*anstellen*
IT officer	[ˌaɪ 'tiː 'ɒfɪsə]	= IT technician	*EDV-Techniker/in*
support	[sə'pɔːt]	help	*Hilfe, Unterstützung*
pen	[pen]	*phr* ballpoint pen	*Stift*
car seat	['kɑː siːt]	seat in a car	*Autositz*
page 89			
beyond	[bɪ'jɒnd]	apart/aside from	*abgesehen von*
aptitude	['æptɪtjuːd]	ability	*Fähigkeit, Eignung*
prospect	['prɒspekt]	a probable future	*Aussicht*
commitment	[kə'mɪtmənt]	*v* to commit	*Einsatz, Engagement*
retired	[rɪ'taɪəd]	having finished working, usually late in life	*pensioniert, im Ruhestand*
grandad	['grændæd]	grandfather	*Opa*
hardly	['hɑːdli]	barely	*kaum*
terms	[tɜːmz]	conditions	*Bedingungen, Konditionen*
generous	['dʒenərəs]	*n* generosity	*großzügig*
subsidized	['sʌbsɪdaɪzd]	supported financially	*subventioniert*
healthcare	['helθkeə]	service of providing medical care	*medizinische Versorgung*
travel insurance	[ˌtrævl ɪn'ʃʊərəns]	*phr* to take out travel insurance	*Reiseversicherung*
maternity leave	[mə'tɜːnəti liːv]	the amount of paid time soon-to-be mothers have off from work	*Mutterschaftsurlaub*
paternity leave	[pə'tɜːnəti liːv]	the amount of paid time soon-to-be fathers have off from work	*Vaterschaftsurlaub*
creche facilities	[ˌkreʃ fə'sɪlətiz]	a place where babies and small children are taken care of	*Krippeneinrichtungen*
employee	[ɪm'plɔɪiː]	worker	*Arbeitnehmer/in, Beschäftigte/r*
union	['juːniən]	group of working people	*Gewerkschaft*

to invest	[ɪn'vest]	to put money into a business	*investieren*
workforce	['wɜ:kfɔ:s]	the workers	*Belegschaft*
resource	[rɪ'sɔ:s]	reserves	*Reserve, Ressource*
white-collar	[ˌwaɪt 'kɒlə]	working in an office	*Schreibtisch-, Büro-*
clerical	['klerɪkl]	connected with office work	*Schreib-, Büro-*
low-cost	[ˌləʊ'kɒst]	inexpensive	*Niedriglohn-*
page 90			
to illustrate	['ɪləstreɪt]	to visually show	*illustrieren, veranschaulichen*
conclusion	[kən'klu:ʒn]	summary	*(Schluss-)Folgerung*
page 91			
marketing	['mɑ:kɪtɪŋ]		*Marketing, Vertrieb*
ID	[ˌaɪ 'di:]	*(abbrev)* (proof of) identity	*Ausweis*
letter of appointment	[ˌletər əv ə'pɔɪntmənt]	letter sent to a new employee	*Bewerbungsschreiben*
as a matter of fact	[əz ə ˌmætər əv 'fækt]	actually	*um genau zu sein*
to be off to	[bi 'ɒf tə]	to be about to go to	*losgehen*
page 92			
indirectness	[ˌɪndə'rektnəs]	to be indirect	*Indirektheit*
absurd	[əb'sɜ:d]	ridiculous	*absurd*
reply	[rɪ'plaɪ]	*v* to reply	*Antwort, Erwiderung, Reaktion*
freezing	['fri:zɪŋ]	very cold	*eiskalt, sehr kalt*
elderly	['eldəli]	older	*älter*
parcel	['pɑ:sl]	package	*Paket*
to guide	[gaɪd]	to lead	*führen, leiten*
page 93			
headquarters	[ˌhed'kwɔ:təz]	where a company is based	*Hauptsitz, Zentrale*
dialect	['daɪəlekt]	way of speaking in a particular area	*Dialekt, Mundart*
to neutralize	['nju:trəlaɪz]	to reduce the effect of something	*neutralisieren*
car insurance	['kɑ:r ɪnʃʊərəns]	e.g. to take out car insurance	*Kraftfahrzeugversicherung*
headset	['hedset]	earphones, headphones	*Kopfhörer mit Mikrofon*
to deal with	['di:l wɪð]	to take care of, to handle	*bearbeiten, erledigen*
medical support	[ˌmedɪkl sə'pɔ:t]	help with health care	*medizinische Hilfe*
to handle	['hændl]	to deal with	*erledigen, bearbeiten*
shift	[ʃɪft]	e.g. a night shift	*Schicht*
to monitor	['mɒnɪtə]	to supervise, to watch	*überwachen, kontrollieren*
salary	['sæləri]	income, wages	*Gehalt, Lohn*
variable pay	['veəriəbl peɪ]	wages that are dependent on employee success	*variabler Lohn*
to be based on	[bi 'beɪst ɒn]	to use as a basis	*basieren auf*
corporate	['kɔ:pərət]	connected with a corporation	*Firmen-, Konzern-*
job description	[dʒɒb dɪ'skrɪpʃn]	most important responsibilities of a job	*Stellenbeschreibung*
commission	[kə'mɪʃn]	percentage of a sale given to workers to encourage them to sell more	*Provision*
incl	[ɪn'klu:dɪŋ]	*abbrev* including	*einschließlich*
alternate	[ɔ:l'tɜ:nət]	every other	*jede/r zweite*
preferable	['prefərəbl]	more desirable	*vorzuziehen*
graduate	['grædʒʊət]	person who has a university degree	*Hochschulabsolvent/in*
in the daytime	[ɪn ðə 'deɪtaɪm]	during the day	*tagsüber*
page 94			
for ages	[fər 'eɪdʒɪz]	for a very long time	*eine Ewigkeit*
How have you been keeping?	[ˌhaʊ həv ju bi:n 'ki:pɪŋ]	How are you doing?	*Wie geht es dir?*
revision	[rɪ'vɪʒn]	review	*Wiederholung*

UNIT 7

page 95			
directed at	[də'rektɪd ət]	aimed at	*gerichtet auf, abzielend auf*
microchip	['maɪkrəʊtʃɪp]	a chip used in computers	*Mikrochip*
studio	['stju:diəʊ]	the place where art, films or music is created	*Studio*

checklist	['tʃeklɪst]	a list of items	*Checkliste*
equipment	[ɪ'kwɪpmənt]	the things necessary for a particular kind of job	*Ausrüstung*

page 96

globalization	[ˌgləʊbəlaɪ'zeɪʃn]	the expansion of the economy, industry, market or culture	*Globalisierung*
transmission	[træns'mɪʃn]	transfer	*Übertragung*
opportunity	[ˌɒpə'tju:nəti]	a good chance to advance oneself	*Chance, Möglichkeit*
textile	['tekstaɪl]	e.g. weaving, knitting, etc.	*Textil-*
to be required to	[bi rɪ'kwaɪəd tə]	to have to	*müssen*
overtime	['əʊvətaɪm]	working more hours	*Überstunden*
to sack	[sæk]	to fire	*entlassen, feuern*
slave	[sleɪv]	person who is forced to work for no money	*Sklave/Sklavin*
offshore	[ˌɒf'ʃɔ:]	to be relocated in a new country	*ins/im Ausland*
paycheck	['peɪtʃek]	*(AE) BE:* wages, salary, income	*Gehalt(sscheck)*
to rescue	['reskju:]	to save	*retten*
to redevelop	[ˌri:dɪ'veləp]	to restore	*erneuern, neu entwickeln*
reborn	[ˌri:'bɔ:n]	new	*wiedergeboren*
competitive advantage	[kəm'petətɪv ədvɑ:ntɪdʒ]	e.g. lower price, better quality, etc.	*Wettbewerbsvorteil*
cutting-edge	[ˌkʌtɪŋ 'edʒ]	modern	*Spitzen-, Hightech-, modern*

page 97

goods	[gʊdz]	merchandise	*Ware(n), Güter*
explanation	[ˌeksplə'neɪʃn]	*v* to explain	*Erklärung*
disease	[dɪ'zi:z]	illness	*Krankheit, Erkrankung*
infrastructure	['ɪnfrəstrʌktʃə]	the structure of a system or an organization	*Infrastruktur*

page 98

body language	['bɒdi læŋgwɪdʒ]	the signs and gestures we make with our body	*Körpersprache*
personal space	['pɜ:sənl speɪs]	the space around us	*Distanzzone, Abstand zwischen Personen*
acceptable	[ək'septəbl]	approved	*annehmbar, akzeptabel*
sensitive	['sensətɪv]	being easily affected by sth	*empfindlich*
to dominate	['dɒmɪneɪt]	to have command or influence over	*dominieren*
listener	['lɪsnə]	*v* to listen	*Zuhörer/in*
dishonest	[dɪs'ɒnɪst]	<> honest	*unehrlich*
to trust	[trʌst]	to believe or have confidence in sth or sb	*vertrauen*
warmth	[wɔ:mθ]	*adj* warm	*Wärme*
to shake	[ʃeɪk]	*phr* to shake hands	*schütteln*
activist	['æktɪvɪst]	sb who actively stands up for a cause/belief	*Aktivist/in*

page 99

to rely on	[rɪ'laɪ ɒn]	to depend on	*angewiesen sein auf, sich verlassen auf*
supply chain	[sə'plaɪ tʃeɪn]	the chain through which products are distributed from producer to retailer	*Versorgungskette*
casual	['kæʒuəl]	occasional	*Gelegenheits-*
picker	['pɪkə]	*v* to pick	*Pflücker/in*
to despair	[dɪ'speə]	to lose hope	*verzweifeln*
to bury	['berɪ]	*phr* to bury your feelings/hopes/dreams	*begraben*
concern	[kən'sɜ:n]	worry	*Sorge, Interesse, Anliegen*
coordinator	[kəʊ'ɔ:dɪneɪtə]	organizer	*Koordinator/in*
weakness	['wi:knəs]	*adj* weak	*Schwäche*
guaranteed	[ˌgærən'ti:d]	secured	*garantiert*
craft	[krɑ:ft]	handmade art pieces	*(Kunst-)Handwerk*
middlemen	['mɪdlmən]	people in the middle of the supply chain	*Zwischenhändler*
precarious	[prɪ'keəriəs]	risky	*unsicher, prekär*
shareholder	['ʃeəhəʊldə]	sb who owns stocks in a company	*Aktionär/in*
to offload	[ˌɒf'ləʊd]	unload	*weitergeben*
to seek	[si:k]	to look for	*suchen*
sub-contractor	[ˌsʌbkən'træktə]		*Subunternehmer*

page 100

to identify	[aɪ'dentɪfaɪ]	to find	*herausfinden*
to relate to	[rɪ'leɪt tə]	to connect	*sich beziehen auf*

page 101

hectare	['hekteə]	= 10,000 square metres	*Hektar*
co-operative	[kəʊ 'ɒpərətɪv]	workers' group	*Kooperative*
coffee mill	['kɒfi mɪl]	where coffee is produced	*Kaffeemühle*
to install	[ɪn'stɔ:l]	to set up	*installieren*
earnings	['ɜ:nɪŋz]	money made	*Einkünfte*

page 102

security	[sɪ'kjʊərəti]	stability	*Sicherheit*
instability	[ˌɪnstə'bɪləti]	<> stability	*Instabilität*
draft	[drɑ:ft]	a preliminary sketch or idea	*Entwurf*
restatement	[ˌri:'steɪtmənt]	saying sth again	*Neuformulierung*
to weigh up	[ˌweɪ 'ʌp]	to consider everything	*abwägen*
neat	[ni:t]	tidy	*ordentlich, sauber*

page 103

branch	[brɑ:ntʃ]	local part of a larger business	*Filiale, Niederlassung*
fair trade	[ˌfeə 'treɪd]	paying fair prices so that workers get a share of the profit	*fairer Handel*
to source	[sɔ:s]	to get sth from somewhere	*beziehen*
ingredient	[ɪn'gri:diənt]	component, element	*Bestandteil, Zutat*
values	['vælju:z]	beliefs, convictions	*Werte*
to found	[faʊnd]	to establish, to create	*gründen*
campaign	[kæm'peɪn]	*phr* to campaign for	*Kampagne*
injustice	[ɪn'dʒʌstɪs]	unfairness, wrong	*Ungerechtigkeit, Unrecht*
vulnerable	['vʌlnərəbl]	<> safe, secure	*wehrlos*
to speak out for	[ˌspi:k 'aʊt fə]	to stand up for	*sprechen für*
charity	['tʃærəti]	*phr* an act of charity	*Wohltätigkeit(sorganisation)*
public good	[ˌpʌblɪk 'gʊd]	benefit to society	*das öffentliche Wohl*
greed	[gri:d]	<> generosity	*Gier, Habsucht*
foundation	[faʊn'deɪʃn]	an institution paid for by charity	*Stiftung*
violence	['vaɪələns]	physical fighting	*Gewalt*
trafficking	['træfɪkɪŋ]	illegal transportation of goods	*illegaler (Rauschgift-)Handel*
torture	['tɔ:tʃə]	abuse, ill treatment	*Folter*
working conditions	[ˌwɜ:kɪŋ kən'dɪʃnz]	circumstances in which people work	*Arbeitsbedingungen*

page 104

dryer	['draɪə]	a machine that dries	*Trockner*
dried	[draɪd]	when sth lacks water	*Trocken-*
basket	['bɑ:skɪt]	an object used to hold things	*Korb*
specialist	['speʃəlɪst]	expert	*speziell, Fach-*
payment	['peɪmənt]	*v* to pay (for)	*Bezahlung*
receipt	[rɪ'si:t]	written statement that money has been received	*Eingang, Erhalt*

UNIT 8

page 105

treaty	['tri:ti]	an agreement between countries	*Vertrag*
headquarters	[ˌhed'kwɔ:təz]	main office	*Hauptsitz, Zentrale*
commission	[kə'mɪʃn]	an official group of people who control sth	*Kommission*
voter	['vəʊtə]	*v* to vote	*Wähler/in*
to reject	[rɪ'dʒekt]	to refuse	*ablehnen*
constitution	[ˌkɒnstɪ'tju:ʃn]	an established arrangement	*Verfassung*
anthem	['ænθəm]	*phr* national anthem	*Hymne*
peace	[pi:s]	a state of mutual harmony	*Frieden*
prosperity	[prɒ'sperəti]	success	*Wohlstand*

page 106

internship	['ɪntɜ:nʃɪp]	work providing experience in firm	*Volontariat*
to involve	[ɪn'vɒlv]	to include	*einschließen, beinhalten*

tourism	['tʊərɪzəm]	*n* tourist	*Tourismus, Fremdenverkehr*
practical	['præktɪkl]	basic	*praktisch*
intern	['ɪntɜːn]	person doing an internship	*Praktikant/in, Volontär/in*
to contact	['kɒntækt]	to get in touch with sb	*Kontakt aufnehmen zu, sich wenden an*
to specialize in	['speʃəlaɪz ɪn]	to be good at sth specific	*sich spezialisieren auf*
sector	['sektə]	section	*Sektor, Bereich*
duty	['djuːti]	task	*Pflicht, Aufgabe*
enquiry	[ɪn'kwaɪəri]	question	*Anfrage*
accommodation	[əˌkɒmə'deɪʃn]	food and lodging	*Unterkunft*
fluent	['fluːənt]	*phr* to be fluent in a language	*fließend, gewandt, flüssig*
licence	['laɪsns]	*phr* driving licence	*Führerschein*
outgoing	['aʊtgəʊɪŋ]	confident and friendly	*kontaktfreudig*
contribution	[ˌkɒntrɪ'bjuːʃn]	*v* to contribute	*Beitrag, Beihilfe*
expenses	[ɪk'spensɪz]	costs	*Kosten, Ausgaben*
negotiation	[nɪˌgəʊʃi'eɪʃn]	discussion	*Verhandlung*
attachment	[ə'tætʃmənt]	*v* to attach	*Anlage*
reference	['refrəns]	written statement about character and skills	*Zeugnis*
to provide	[prə'vaɪd]	to supply	*(an)bieten, sorgen für, zur Verfügung stellen*
fee	[fiː]	*phr* admission fee	*Gebühr*
council	['kaʊnsl]	an assembly of people	*Rat, Gemeinderat*
to gain	[geɪn]	to receive	*sammeln, erlangen*
to attach	[ə'tætʃ]	to join onto sth	*beilegen, -fügen*
query	['kwɪəri]	question	*Frage, Rückfrage*
Yours faithfully	[jɔːz 'feɪθfʊli]	phrase used to end formal letters	*Mit freundlichen Grüßen*

page 107

unpaid	[ˌʌn'peɪd]	<> paid	*unbezahlt*
enthusiasm	[ɪn'θjuːziæzəm]	excitement	*Begeisterung (-sfähigkeit)*
agreement	[ə'griːmənt]	*v* to agree	*Vertrag, Abkommen, Zusage*
department	[dɪ'pɑːtmənt]	a section of a business	*Abteilung*
theoretical	[ˌθɪə'retɪkl]	<> practical	*theoretisch*
request	[rɪ'kwest]	*v* to request	*Bitte, Aufforderung, Wunsch*

page 108

referee	[ˌrefə'riː]	person who writes a job reference	*Referenzgeber/in*
regarding	[rɪ'gɑːdɪŋ]	concerning	*bezüglich, betreffend*
marital status	[ˌmærɪtl 'steɪtəs]	whether or not you are married	*Familienstand*
operator	['ɒpəreɪtə]	*v* to operate	*Veranstalter/in*

page 109

landline	['lændlaɪn]	home phone	*Festnetz(leitung)*
Do you mind if ...?	[də ju 'maɪnd ɪf]	Is it all right if ...?	*Haben Sie etwas dagegen, wenn ...?*
cyclist	['saɪklɪst]	bike rider	*Fahrradfahrer/in*
outdoor clothing	['aʊtdɔː kləʊðɪŋ]	clothes for hiking, camping, etc.	*Wanderbekleidung*
prompt	['prɒmpt]	immediate	*unverzüglich, zügig*
typical	['tɪpɪkl]	ordinary	*typisch*

page 110

corruption	[kə'rʌpʃn]	*v* to corrupt	*Korruption*
bureaucracy	[bjʊə'rɒkrəsi]		*Bürokratie*
interference	[ˌɪntə'fɪərəns]	*v* to interfere	*Einmischung*
affair	[ə'feə]	event or happening	*Angelegenheit*
undemocratic	[ˌʌndemə'krætɪk]	not practising social equality	*undemokratisch*
bunch	[bʌntʃ]	a lot of	*Gruppe, Haufen*
unelected	[ˌʌnɪ'lektɪd]	people who were not chosen	*nicht gewählt*
bang	[bæŋ]	expression used when sth starts dramatically	*Paukenschlag*
misleading	[ˌmɪs'liːdɪŋ]	leading in the wrong direction	*irreführend*
frank	['fræŋk]	honest	*offen, ehrlich*
legislative	['ledʒɪslətɪv]	legal	*gesetzgebend*
to recommend	[ˌrekə'mend]	to suggest	*empfehlen*
to defend	[dɪ'fend]	to ward off attack from sb or sth	*verteidigen*

take on	['teɪk ɒn]	opinion on	*Einstellung zu*
relatively	['relətɪvli]	quite, somewhat	*verhältnismäßig*
wrongdoing	['rɒŋduːɪŋ]	to do sth wrong	*Fehlverhalten*
frontier	['frʌntɪə]	boundary	*Grenze*

page 111

currency	['kʌrənsi]	system of money that a country uses	*Währung*
stability	[stə'bɪləti]	*adj* stable	*Stabilität*
sovereignty	['sɒvrənti]	independent power/authority	*Souveränität, Unabhängigkeit*
anyhow	['enihaʊ]	in any case	*sowieso*
threat	[θret]	sth that is a source of danger	*Bedrohung, Drohung*
scarcity	['skeəsəti]	*adj* scarce	*Knappheit*
migration	[maɪ'greɪʃn]	to move from one part of the world to another	*Wanderung(sbewegung)*
border	['bɔːdə]	boundary	*Grenze, Grenz-*
to integrate	['ɪntɪgreɪt]	to become part of sth	*sich integrieren*
recommendation		*v* to recommend	*Empfehlung*
widening	['waɪdnɪŋ]	increase in size	*Erweiterung*

page 112

lawyer	['lɔːjə]	person who has studied law	*(Rechts-)Anwalt/Anwältin*
to evaluate	[ɪ'væljueɪt]	to assess	*einschätzen, bewerten*
federal	['fedərəl]	*phr* federal government of the USA	*föderal(istisch)*
to unite	[ju'naɪt]	to bring together	*vereinigen*
diverse	[daɪ'vɜːs]	differing from one another	*verschieden, unterschiedlich*

page 113

currency	['kʌrənsi]	e.g. the euro currency	*Währung*
physical	['fɪzɪkl]	real, material	*physisch*
note	[nəʊt]	paper money	*(Bank-)Note, (Geld-)Schein*
coin	[kɔɪn]	piece of metal money	*Münze*
sole	[səʊl]	only	*alleinig*
to adopt	[ə'dɒpt]	to accept, to take	*einführen*
trading bloc	['treɪdɪŋ blɒk]	free trade area agreed by several countries which allows them to trade more easily	*Handelsblock*
to manage	['mænɪdʒ]	to be in charge, to run	*verwalten*
to establish	[ɪ'stæblɪʃ]	to create, to set up	*(be)gründen, einrichten*
cross-border	['krɒs bɔːdə]	from one country to another	*grenzüberschreitend*
direct debit	[dəˌrekt 'debɪt]	*phr* to pay by direct debit	*Lastschrift-, Einzugsverfahren*
pound	[paʊnd]	UK currency	*Pfund (Sterling)*
whisky distillery	[ˌwɪski dɪ'stɪləri]	place where whisky is made	*Whisky-Brennerei*
foreign exchange	[ˌfɒrən ɪks'tʃeɪndʒ]	changing of one currency into another	*Fremdwährung, Devisen*
benefit	['benɪfɪt]	advantage	*Vorteil*
drawback	['drɔːbæk]	<> advantage, benefit	*Nachteil*

page 114

pound	[paʊnd]	currency of the United Kingdom	*Pfund (Sterling)*
to adopt	[ə'dɒpt]	to vote to accept	*einführen*
to opt out	[ˌɒpt 'aʊt]	to choose not to participate in sth	*austreten, aussteigen*
isolated	['aɪsəleɪtɪd]	being separated from	*isoliert*
referendum	[ˌrefə'rendəm]	when everyone in a country votes on an important issue	*Volksentscheid*
gigantic	[dʒaɪ'gæntɪk]	huge	*gigantisch, riesig*
office block	['ɒfɪs blɒk]	tall building containing offices	*Bürogebäude, -hochhaus*
nonsense	['nɒnsns]	not making sense	*Unsinn*
luck	[lʌk]	*adj* lucky	*Glück*

UNIT 9

page 115

heritage	['herɪtɪdʒ]	sth that is passed on through generations	*Erbe, Herkunft*
musician	[mju'zɪʃn]	a person who writes or performs music	*Musiker/in*
peer group	['pɪə gruːp]	people who have equal standing in age, class or rank	*Gleichaltrige, Clique*
role model	['rəʊl mɒdl]	sb whose actions other people follow	*Vorbild*

page 116

to bring up	[ˌbrɪŋ 'ʌp]	to raise	*großziehen*
washing powder	['wɒʃɪŋ paʊdə]	clothes detergent	*Waschpulver*
to polish	['pɒlɪʃ]	to make clean	*polieren, putzen*
emotional	[ɪ'məʊʃənl]	sad, happy, in love, angry, fearful, etc.	*emotional*
childcare	['tʃaɪldkeə]	taking care of children	*(Kinder-)Erziehung*
abandoned	[ə'bændənd]	deserted	*verlassen*
rejected	[rɪ'dʒektɪd]	*v* to reject	*abgelehnt*
to care for sb	['keə fə]	to raise or nurture sb	*jdn pflegen, sich um jdn kümmern*

page 117

upbringing	['ʌpbrɪŋɪŋ]	*v* to bring up	*Erziehung*
childminder	['tʃaɪldmaɪndə]	babysitter	*Kinderbetreuer/in, Tagesmutter/-vater*
nervous breakdown	[ˌnɜ:vəs 'breɪkdaʊn]	illness when you are mentally not be able to deal with life	*Nervenzusammenbruch*
social services	[ˌsəʊʃl 'sɜ:vɪsɪz]	a service that ensures child safety within the household	*Sozialamt, Sozialdienste*
to retire	[rɪ'taɪə]	to go into retirement	*in Rente/Pension gehen*

page 118

custom	['kʌstəm]	practices, habits, norms, traditions	*Brauch*
psychiatric	[ˌsaɪki'ætrɪk]	*n* psychiatrist	*psychiatrisch*
to come to terms with	[kʌm tə 'tɜ:mz]	to accept	*zurechtkommen mit*
board game	['bɔ:d geɪm]	e.g. monopoly, backgammon, etc.	*Brettspiel*
to catch sb off guard	[kætʃ ˌɒf 'gɑ:d]	to surprise	*jdn überraschen, ertappen*
braid	[breɪd]	small tight plait	*(geflochtener) Zopf*
input	['ɪnpʊt]	contribution	*hier: Aufwendung, Hingabe*
schoolyard	['sku:ljɑ:d]	*(AE) BE:* (school) playground	*Schulhof*
myth	[mɪθ]	rumour	*Legende*
literally	['lɪtərəli]	honestly	*buchstäblich*
to fail sb	[feɪl]	to not give sb what they need	*jdn enttäuschen, jdm etw nicht geben können*
ultimate	['ʌltɪmət]	definitive example of	*ultimativ*
baggage	['bægɪdʒ]	*phr* emotional baggage	*Gepäck, Last*
to miss out on	[ˌmɪs 'aʊt ɒn]	to not get to do	*verpassen*
nail polish	['neɪl pɒlɪʃ]	paint for fingernails	*Nagellack*
to lean on	['li:n ɒn]	to support oneself against	*sich lehnen an*
once in a while	[ˌwʌns ɪn ə 'waɪl]	now and then, from time to time	*dann und wann*
overly	['əʊvəli]	excessively	*übermäßig*
minor	['maɪnə]	very small	*geringfügig*
wound	[wu:nd]	injury	*Wunde*
to rub	[rʌb]	*phr* to rub salt into the wound	*reiben*
to carry on	[ˌkæri 'ɒn]	to keep going	*weitermachen*
motherly	['mʌðəli]	maternal	*mütterlich*
you bet	[ju 'bet]	of course	*ganz bestimmt, und ob*
doll	[dɒl]	*phr* Barbie doll	*Puppe*
hairstyle	['heəstaɪl]	the way hair is styled	*Frisur*
inability	[ˌɪnə'bɪləti]	<> ability	*Unfähigkeit*
effort	['efət]	attempt	*Bemühung, Anstrengung*
depressing	[dɪ'presɪŋ]	very sad	*bedrückend, deprimierend*
tiring	['taɪərɪŋ]	exhausting	*anstrengend, ermüdend*

page 119

nurse	[nɜ:s]	sb who looks after sick people	*Krankenschwester, -pfleger/in*
priest	[pri:st]	a minister of any religion	*Priester/in, Geistliche/r*
solicitor	[sə'lɪsɪtə]	legal advisor	*(Rechts-)Anwalt/Anwältin*
powerful	['paʊəfl]	*n* power	*mächtig, stark*
shade	[ʃeɪd]		*Schattierung*
march	[mɑ:tʃ]	*phr* peace march	*(Protest-)Marsch*
disobedience	[ˌdɪsə'bi:diəns]	misbehaving, breaking rules	*Ungehorsam*
demonstration	[ˌdemən'streɪʃn]	a public display of discontent	*Demonstration*
arrest	[ə'rest]	*v* to arrest	*Verhaftung, Festnahme*

violence	['vaɪələns]	physical fighting	*Gewalt*
sympathy	['sɪmpəθi]	feeling sorry for	*Mitgefühl, Mitleid*
suffragette	[ˌsʌfrə'dʒet]	female supporter of votes for women	*Frauenrechtlerin*
battle	['bætl]	a conflict or struggle	*Kampf*
logging	['lɒgɪŋ]	cutting down and removing trees	*Abholzung*
rope	[rəʊp]	cord	*Seil, Tau*
mainstream	['meɪnstriːm]	dominant, popular	*vorherrschend(e Meinung)*
page 120			
to achieve	[ə'tʃiːv]	to accomplish sth	*erreichen*
demo	['deməʊ]	*(abbrev)* demonstration	*Demo(nstration)*
foot	[fʊt]	measurement: 30.48cm	*Fuß*
height	[haɪt]	distance from ground upwards	*Höhe, Größe*
to be concerned with	[bi kən'sɜːnd wɪð]	to be worried about	*sich befassen mit, sich kümmern um*
page 121			
broad	[brɔːd]	wide	*breit*
proportion	[prə'pɔːʃn]	dimensions or size	*Teil, Verhältnis*
registered	['redʒɪstəd]	*v* to register	*registriert, eingetragen*
runner-up	[ˌrʌnər 'ʌp]	person or team that finished second	*Zweite/r*
to extend	[ɪk'stend]	to make bigger	*ausweiten, ausbauen*
extension	[ɪk'stenʃn]	development	*Ausbau*
to recap	['riːkæp]	to repeat the main facts	*rekapitulieren, zusammenfassen*
runway	['rʌnweɪ]	landing strip	*Landebahn*
to knock down	[ˌnɒk 'daʊn]	to demolish	*abreißen*
to crash	[kræʃ]	to have an accident	*(ab)stürzen*
air pollution	[eə pə'luːʃn]	*v* to pollute	*Luftverschmutzung*
to go ahead	[ˌgəʊ ə'hed]	to continue as planned	*vorangehen, vonstatten gehen*
to summarize	['sʌməraɪz]	*n* summary	*zusammenfassen*
estuary	['estʃuəri]	where a river meets the sea	*Mündung*
page 122			
delivery	[dɪ'lɪvəri]	*v* to deliver	*Darbietung*
inclusion	[in'kluːʒn]	*v* to include	*Einbeziehung*
single-issue	[ˌsɪŋgl 'iʃuː]	*phr* a single-issue campaign	*Ein-Themen-, auf ein Thema beschränkt*
agenda	[əˌdʒendə]		*Tagesordnung*
page 123			
silver market	[ˌsɪlvə 'mɑːkɪt]	market segment of people over 50	*Silbermarkt*
to host	[həʊst]	to present, to introduce	*moderieren*
to have no use for	[həv nəʊ 'juːs fə]	to not need	*keine Verwendung haben für*
robotics	[rəʊ'bɒtɪks]	design and use of robots	*Robotik, Automatisierung*
large print	[lɑːdʒ 'prɪnt]	with big letters	*Großdruck*
chores	[tʃɔːz]	everyday work around the house	*Hausarbeit(en)*
humanoid	['hjuːmənɔɪd]	looking like a human being	*menschenähnlich(e Figur)*
companion	[kəm'pæniən]	friend, helper	*Begleiter/in*
disabled	[dɪs'eɪbld]	e.g. physically disabled	*Behinderte/r*
mobility	[məʊ'bɪləti]	ability to move easily	*Beweglichkeit, Mobilität*
hi-tech	[ˌhaɪ'tek]	involving advanced technology	*technisch hoch entwickelt*
device	[dɪ'vaɪs]	machine, appliance	*Gerät, Apparat*
emotion	[ɪ'məʊʃn]	feelings	*Gefühl, Emotion*
LED	[ˌel iː 'diː]	*abbrev* light-emitting diode	*LED-Anzeige*
widow	['wɪdəʊ]	a woman whose husband has died	*Witwe*
life expectancy	['laɪf ɪkspektənsi]	how long a person is likely to live	*Lebenserwartung*
page 124			
high	[haɪ]	effect experienced when taking drugs	*high, auf Drogen*
to snort	[snɔːt]	to inhale power through the nose	*sniffen, schnupfen*
needle	['niːdl]	medical instrument used to insert liquid into the body	*Nadel*
to break	[breɪk]	to give up addiction to sth	*abbrechen*
overdose	['əʊvədəʊs]	consuming too much of sth	*Überdosis*
to get clear of	[get 'klɪər əv]	*phr* to get clear of sth bad	*wegkommen von*

enemy	['enəmi]	sb you hate	*Feind*
experienced	[ɪk'spɪəriənst]	having a lot of experience	*erfahren*
social worker	['səʊʃl wɜːkə]	sb whose job is social work	*Sozialarbeiter/in*
broken	['brəʊkən]	used for a family where the parents are divorced or separated	*getrennt, kaputt*
foster family	[ˌfɒstə 'fæməli]	foster mother/father, foster parents	*Pflegefamilie*

UNIT 10

page 125

multiculturalism	[ˌmʌlti-'kʌltʃərəlɪzəm]	different cultures coexisting in a society	*Multikulturalismus*
Afro-Caribbean	[ˌæfrəʊ ˌkærə'biːən]	African and Caribbean	*afro-karibisch*
headscarf	['hedskɑːf]	worn by Muslim women to cover their heads	*Kopftuch*
sari	['sɑːri]	a garment worn by Hindu women	*Sari (Kleidungsstück)*

page 126

fanatic	[fə'nætɪk]	*n* fanatic, fanaticism	*Fanatiker/in*
to tremble	['trembl]	to shake with fear, nerves or cold	*zittern*
to loosen	['luːsn]	to make less tight	*lockern*
tie	[taɪ]	garment worn around the neck	*Krawatte, Schlips*
harsh	[hɑːʃ]	unpleasant	*scharf, harsch*
forbidden	[fə'bɪdn]	not allowed	*verboten*
gambling	['gæmblɪŋ]	betting money in a game	*Glücksspiel*
accompaniment	[ə'kʌmpənimənt]	*v* to accompany	*Begleitung*
disgust	[dɪs'gʌst]	repulsion, horror	*Ekel*
censure	['senʃə]	disapproval	*Tadel, Missbilligung*
temper	['tempə]	*phr* to lose one's temper	*Beherrschung*
to stare	[steə]	to look directly and fixedly at sth	*starren*
conscience	['kɒnʃəns]	inner sense of what is right and wrong	*Gewissen*
monotonous	[mə'nɒtənəs]	to speak using one tone of voice	*monoton*
countless	['kaʊntləs]	so many that they cannot be counted	*zahllos*
for instance	[fə'rɪnstəns]	for example	*zum Beispiel*
to demand	[dɪ'mɑːnd]	to ask in a bold, authoritative way	*(nach)fragen*

page 127

to deny	[dɪ'naɪ]	to state that sth is not true	*bestreiten*
mushroom	['mʌʃrʊm]	*phr* fried mushrooms	*Pilz*
fried	[fraɪd]	cooked in oil	*gebraten, geröstet*
perplexed	[pə'plekst]	confused	*perplex, verblüfft*
civilisation	[ˌsɪvəlaɪ'zeɪʃn]	an advanced state of human society	*Zivilisation*
materialist	[mə'tɪəriəlɪst]	person only concerned with material things	*Materialist/in*
miserable	['mɪzrəbl]	unhappy	*kläglich*
rowdy	['raʊdi]	disorderly	*laut, randalierend*
to convince	[kən'vɪns]	to persuade	*überzeugen*
homosexual	[ˌhəʊmə'sekʃuəl]	person sexually attracted to people of the same sex	*Homosexuelle/r*
prostitute	['prɒstɪtjuːt]	person who engages in sexual acts for money	*Prostituierte/r*
paradise	['pærədaɪs]	a state of supreme happiness	*Paradies*
to swallow	['swɒləʊ]	muscle movement used when eating and drinking	*(ver)schlucken*

page 128

setting	['setɪŋ]	scene	*Szenerie, Schauplatz*
incident	['ɪnsɪdənt]	event	*Vorfall, Ereignis*
conflicting	[kɒn'flɪktɪŋ]	different	*gegensätzlich*
gesture	['dʒestʃə]	body movement	*Geste(n), Gestik*
to mediate	['miːdieɪt]	to settle an argument	*vermitteln*
to work oneself up	[ˌwɜːk 'ʌp]	to get excited	*sich aufregen*
rage	[reɪdʒ]	extreme anger	*Wut, Zorn*

page 129

cheekbones	['tʃi:kbəʊnz]	bones at the top of the cheeks, below the eyes	*Wangenknochen*
jet-colored	[ˌdʒet 'kʌləd]	*(AE) BE:* jet-coloured	*pechschwarz*
ancestry	['ænsestri]	lineage, parentage	*Abstammung, Herkunft*
to define	[di'faɪn]	to describe sth accurately	*(sich) definieren*
to apply to	[ə'plaɪ tə]	to count for	*gelten für, zutreffen auf*
neutral	['nju:trəl]	indifferent	*neutral*
unclear	[ˌʌn'klɪə]	<> clear	*unklar*
tremendous	[trɪ'mendəs]	huge	*gewaltig*
appeal	[ə'pi:l]	attraction	*Anziehungskraft, Anreiz*
census	['sensəs]	periodic count of population	*(Volks-)Zählung*
to tick	[tɪk]	to mark an option with a tick	*ankreuzen*
multiracial	[ˌmʌlti'reɪʃl]	of many races, mixed-race	*ethnisch gemischt*
demographer	[dɪ'mɒgrəfi]	person who studies population data	*Demograph*
intermarriage	[ˌɪntə'mærɪdʒ]	the marriage of two people of different races	*Mischehe*
segregation	[ˌsegrɪ'geɪʃn]	the separation of different races	*Rassentrennung*
casting agent	['kɑ:stɪŋ eɪdʒənt]	person who chooses models and actors for events/films	*Besetzungsagent/in*
Nordic	['nɔ:dɪk]	connected with the countries of Scandinavia	*nordisch*
asset	['æset]	a valuable thing to own or have	*Wert, Vorteil*
to enable	[ɪ'neɪbl]	to help to make possible	*(es) ermöglichen, in die Lage versetzen*
ethnicity	[eθ'nɪsəti]	race	*ethnische Zugehörigkeit*
to pose	[pəʊz]	to take on the role of sb	*posieren, darstellen*
to reflect	[rɪ'flekt]	to show	*widerspiegeln*
fascination	[ˌfæsɪ'neɪʃn]	strong interest	*Faszination*
uniformity	[ˌju:nɪ'fɔ:məti]	quality or state of being alike	*Gleichmäßigkeit*
badge	[bædʒ]	trademark	*Abzeichen*

page 130

respondent	[rɪ'spɒndənt]	person who responds	*Befragte/r*
out-dated	[ˌaʊt 'deɪtɪd]	old-fashioned	*überholt, veraltet*
minority	[maɪ'nɒrəti]	<> majority	*Minderheit*
to outnumber	[ˌaʊt'nʌmbə]	to exceed in amount	*übertreffen*
to shrink	[ʃrɪŋk]	to get smaller	*schrumpfen, zurückgehen*

page 131

Caucasian	[kɔ:'keɪziən]	person of European descent	*Weiße/r, Hellhäutige/r*
Native American	[ˌneɪtɪv ə'merɪkən]	person descended from the original inhabitants of America	*Indianer/in, indianisch*
to tolerate	['tɒləreɪt]	*adj* tolerant	*tolerieren, ertragen*
entire	[ɪn'taɪə]	complete	*vollkommen, gänzlich*
selfish	['selfɪʃ]	only interested in oneself	*egoistisch*
limitless	['lɪmɪtləs]	boundless	*grenzenlos, uneingeschränkt*
cooperative	[kəʊ'ɒpərətɪv]	willing to help	*kooperativ*
to be to blame	[bi tə 'bleɪm]	he's to blame = it's his fault	*an etwas schuld sein*
law-abiding	['lɔ: əbaɪdɪŋ]	non-criminal	*gesetzestreu*
domestic	[də'mestɪk]	in the household	*in der Familie, häuslich*
nanny	['næni]	child-minder	*Kindermädchen*
citizenship	['sɪtɪznʃɪp]	membership of a country	*Staatsbürgerschaft*
humane	[hju:'meɪn]	kind to humans and animals	*human*
civil rights	[ˌsɪvl 'raɪts]	democratic rights	*bürgerliche Rechte*
to reward	[rɪ'wɔ:d]	to give a prize to	*belohnen*
to break a law	[breɪk ə 'lɔ:]	to commit a crime	*das Gesetz brechen/übertreten*
to deport	[dɪ'pɔ:t]	to remove sb from a country	*ausweisen, abschieben*
to ship	[ʃɪp]	to send by boat	*verschiffen, transportieren*
for sb's sake	[fə 'seɪk]	for the good of sb (used as an exclamation of annoyance)	*um jds willen*
wage	[weɪdʒ]	salary	*Lohn*
to flood	[flʌd]	to fill to overflowing	*überschwemmen*
to claim	[kleɪm]	to state sth as true	*behaupten, erklären*

humanitarian	[hju,mænɪ'teəriən]	having concern for the welfare of other people	*humanitär*
domestic service	[də,mestɪk 'sɜ:vɪs]	paid help with household chores	*Hausangestellte*
to be willing	[bi 'wɪlɪŋ]	to be inclined/open to	*bereit/gewillt sein*

page 132

foreground	['fɔ:graʊund]	front	*Vordergrund*
to cart sth away	[,kɑ:t ə'weɪ]	to transport sth in a cart	*wegkarren*
barbed wire	[,bɑ:bd 'waɪə]	twisted strands of wire with sharp points	*Stacheldraht(zaun)*
fence	[fens]	barrier to confine or prevent entrance	*Zaun*
spade	[speɪd]	tool used for digging	*Spaten*
contradictory	[,kɒntrə'dɪktəri]	opposite	*widersprüchlich*
canyon	['kænjən]	a deep valley with steep sides	*Canyon, tiefes/enges Tal*
to wander	['wɒndə]	to walk aimlessly	*(ziellos) herumlaufen*
to crawl	[krɔ:l]	to move on your hands and knees	*kriechen, krabbeln*
wreck	[rek]	mess left after car crash	*(Auto-)Wrack*
confused	[kən'fju:zd]	unclear, difficult to understand	*verwirrt*
temperature	['temprətʃə]	e.g. Fahrenheit, Celsius	*Temperatur*
hunter	['hʌntə]	person who hunts animals	*Jäger/in*
to light	[laɪt]	*phr* to light a fire	*anzünden*
unhurt	[ʌn'hɜ:t]	<> hurt	*unverletzt*

page 133

to marinate	['mærɪneɪt]	to leave food in a sauce before cooking	*marinieren*
to serve	[sɜ:v]	to give sb food	*servieren*
delicious	[dɪ'lɪʃəs]	tasty	*köstlich, lecker*
curry house	['kʌri haʊs]	Indian restaurant	*indisches Restaurant*
taste	[teɪst]	liking, preference	*Geschmack*
to go for	['gəʊ fə]	to choose, to select	*sich entscheiden für*
mild	[maɪld]	<> spicy, hot	*mild*
immigrant	['ɪmɪgrənt]	*v* to immigrate	*Einwanderer/-rin*
occupation	[,ɒkju'peɪʃn]	job, profession	*Beruf, Tätigkeit*
to make a living	[meɪk ə 'lɪvɪŋ]	to earn money	*den Lebensunterhalt verdienen*
to stand at	['stænd ət]	to be at a certain level	*liegen bei*
to estimate	['estɪmeɪt]	*n* estimation	*schätzen*
shortage of	['ʃɔ:tɪdʒ əv]	not having enough	*Mangel an*
to recruit	[rɪ'kru:t]	to hire	*einstellen, rekrutieren*
to set its sights on	[set ɪts 'saɪt ɒn]	to decide you want sth	*den Blick richten auf*
to be reliant on	[bi rɪ'laɪənt ɒn]	to depend on	*angewiesen sein auf*

page 134

governor	['gʌvənə]	the executive head of a state in the US	*Gouverneur/in*
crossing point	['krɒsɪŋ pɔɪnt]	place where people cross a border	*Übergang(sstelle)*
guard	[gɑ:d]	person who protects a place or people	*Wache*
valid	['vælɪd]	relevant	*gültig*
to inquire	[ɪn'kwaɪə]	to ask	*fragen, sich erkundigen*
vehicle papers	['vi:əkl peɪpəz]	car registration documents	*Wagenpapiere*
to seal off	[,si:l 'ɒf]	to close	*absperren, abriegeln*
virtually	['vɜ:tʃuəli]	entirely	*praktisch, nahezu*
feasible	['fi:zəbl]	capable of being done	*(praktisch) durchführbar, machbar*
amnesty	['æmnəsti]	a general pardon for offences	*Amnestie*
quota system	['kwəʊtə sɪstəm]	a proportional share assigned to each person	*Quotensystem*
to go bust	[gəʊ 'bʌst]	to fall apart or lose money	*Pleite gehen*

UNIT 11

page 135

patience	['peɪʃns]	*adj* patient	*Geduld*
ransom	['rænsəm]	money paid to kidnappers	*Lösegeld*
diet	['daɪət]	*phr* to be on a strict diet	*Ernährung, Diät*
to deceive	[dɪ'si:v]	to lie to, trick	*betrügen*
to trick	[trɪk]	to deceive or create an illusion	*betrügen, hereinlegen*
victim	['vɪktɪm]	someone who suffers injury, loss or death	*Opfer*

burglary	['bɜːgləri]	breaking into a building with the intention of stealing something	*Einbruch*
prison	['prɪzn]	a place where criminals are locked up	*Gefängnis*
drink driving	['drɪŋk draɪvɪŋ]	driving after drinking too much alcohol	*Trunkenheit am Steuer*
fraud	[frɔːd]	using lies and deceit to get access to money	*Betrug, Unterschlagung*
armed robbery	[ˌɑːmd 'rɒbəri]	a robbery with weapons involved	*bewaffneter Raubüberfall*
trivial	['trɪviəl]	not important	*trivial, geringfügig*
property	['prɒpəti]	what sb owns	*Eigentum*
page 136			
cruel	[kruːəl]	unfeeling and harsh	*grausam*
Supreme Court	[suˌpriːm 'kɔːt]	highest judicial body in the US	*Oberster Gerichtshof*
to rule	[ruːl]	to decide (legally)	*entscheiden*
death penalty	['deθ penlti]	execution of a person by the state as punishment for a crime	*Todesstrafe*
constitutional	[ˌkɒnstɪ-'tjuːʃənl]	acceptable to the US Constitution	*verfassungsgemäß*
execution	[ˌeksɪ'kjuːʃn]	the act of killing by law as a punishment	*Hinrichtung*
murder	['mɜːdə]	the crime of killing sb	*Mord*
convention	[kən'venʃn]	socially accepted way of doing sth	*Konvention*
lethal	['liːθl]	deadly	*tödlich*
injection	[ɪn'dʒekʃn]	fluid introduced into body using a needle	*Spritze, Injektion*
painless	['peɪnləs]	without pain	*schmerzlos*
massive	['mæsɪv]	very large	*massiv, enorm*
dose	[dəʊs]	amount	*Dosis*
fast-acting	[ˌfɑːst 'æktɪŋ]	taking effect quickly	*schnell wirkend*
anaesthetic	[ˌænəs'θetɪk]	a substance that causes no physical pain and in large amounts is deadly	*Narkosemittel*
routinely	[ruː'tiːnli]	*n* routine	*routinemäßig*
to be troubled	[bi 'trʌbld]	to be concerned	*beunruhigt sein*
to subject	[səb'dʒekt]	to force sb to suffer sth	*unterwerfen, aussetzen*
attempt	[ə'tempt]	try	*Versuch*
feminist	['femənɪst]	person who supports women's rights	*Feministin*
awkward	['ɔːkwəd]	uncomfortable	*unangenehm, lästig, peinlich*
victory	['vɪktəri]	win	*Sieg*
capital punishment	[ˌkæpɪtl 'pʌnɪʃmənt]	execution as punishment	*Todesstrafe*
corporal punishment	[ˌkɔːpərəl 'pʌnɪʃmənt]	physical injury as punishment	*körperliche Züchtigung*
alliance	[ə'laɪəns]	union, agreement	*Allianz, Bündnis*
fundamentalist	[ˌfʌndə-'mentəlɪst]	believing strongly in one idea	*fundamentalistisch*
conservative	[kən'sɜːvətɪv]	favouring traditional views and values	*Konservative/r*
to be opposed to sth	[bi ə'pəʊzd tə]	to be against sth	*gegen etw sein*
principle	['prɪnsəpl]	personal rule for correct conduct	*Prinzip*
hence	[hens]	therefore	*daher*
apparent	[ə'pærənt]	visible	*offensichtlich, deutlich*
bias	['baɪəs]	supporting sth more due to external factors	*Vorurteil*
repugnant	[rɪ'pʌgnənt]	offensive, unpleasant	*widerlich*
page 137			
remorse	[rɪ'mɔːs]	regret	*Reue*
devout	[dɪ'vaʊt]	committed (religious)	*fromm*
clemency	['klemənsi]	mercy	*Milde, Nachsicht*
insane	[ɪn'seɪn]	mentally ill, crazy	*geisteskrank*
liberal	['lɪbərəl]	sb who supports progress and change	*Liberale/r*
passion	['pæʃn]	powerful emotion	*Leidenschaft, Emotion*
reformed	[rɪ'fɔːmd]	made better, altered	*gebessert*
repentant	[rɪ'pentənt]	feeling guilty for committing a sin	*reuig, reumütig*
uncanny	[ʌn'kæni]	extraordinary, strange	*ungeheuer, unheimlich*
bedfellow	['bedfeləʊ]	companion	*Bettgenosse, Schlafkamerad*
to strap	[stræp]	to tie down	*anschnallen, festbinden*
to deserve	[dɪ'zɜːv]	to be worthy of receiving sth	*verdienen*
axe	[æks]	tool used to chop wood	*Axt*

microphone	['maɪkrəfəʊn]	device used to record/emit sound	*Mikrophon*
page 138			
to abolish	[ə'bɒlɪʃ]	to get rid off	*abschaffen*
to reintroduce	[ˌriːˌɪntrə'djuːs]	to introduce again	*wieder einführen*
abolition	[ˌæbə'lɪʃn]	*v* to abolish	*Abschaffung*
even	['iːvn]	smooth	*gleichmäßig*
imprisonment	[ɪm'prɪznmənt]	being kept in prison	*Haft, Gefängnis(strafe)*
retribution	[ˌretrɪ'bjuːʃn]	punishment which was deserved	*Vergeltung*
deterrent	[dɪ'terənt]	making people not want to do sth	*abschreckend*
rehabilitation	[ˌriːəˌbɪlɪ'teɪʃn]	sth giving people a fresh start in life	*Rehabilitation*
page 139			
to associate	[ə'səʊʃieɪt]	to connect with, be in the company of	*assoziieren, verbinden*
justice	['dʒʌstɪs]	fair outcome	*Gerechtigkeit*
stitch	[stɪtʃ]	A stitch in time saves nine = *Vorsicht ist besser als Nachsicht*	*Stich*
to slide	[slaɪd]	to glide smoothly downwards	*(ab)rutschen, (ab)sacken*
heavily-armed	[ˌhevɪli 'ɑːmd]	protected using weapons	*schwer bewaffnet*
to register	['redʒɪstə]	to record	*registrieren*
rape	[reɪp]	unwanted sexual assault	*Vergewaltigung*
robbery	['rɒbəri]	*v* to rob	*Raub, Überfall*
to dare	[deə]	to try sth risky	*(es) wagen*
turnaround	['tɜːnəraʊnd]	big change/improvement	*Kehrtwendung, Umschwung*
decent	['diːsnt]	respectable	*anständig*
tolerant	['tɒlərənt]	able to endure/accept sth	*tolerant*
rotten	['rɒtn]	corrupt	*korrupt*
drug abuse	[ˌdrʌg ə'bjuːs]	excessive use of drugs	*Drogenmissbrauch*
bribery	['braɪbəri]	*v* to bribe	*Bestechung*
nepotism	['nepətɪzəm]	when people hire relatives	*Vetternwirtschaft*
merciless	['mɜːsiləs]	*n* mercy	*unbarmherzig*
to weed out	[ˌwiːd 'aʊt]	weed = *Unkraut*	*aussondern, -merzen*
tolerance	['tɒlərəns]	*adj* tolerant	*Toleranz*
pension	['penʃn]	payment made by the government to those not in work due to age/illness	*Rente, Pension*
to prosecute	['prɒsɪkjuːt]	to accuse sb of a crime and question them	*anklagen, strafrechtlich verfolgen*
policy	['pɒləsi]	rule	*Politik, Linie*
seed	[siːd]	thing from which a plant grows, starting point	*Samen(korn)*
to focus on	['fəʊkəs ɒn]	to concentrate on sth	*sich konzentrieren auf*
dealing	['diːlɪŋ]	*phr* drug dealing	*Handel*
incidence	['ɪnsɪdəns]	recorded number of sth	*Vorkommen, Häufigkeitsrate*
page 140			
radical	['rædɪkl]	extreme	*radikal*
diametrically opposed	[ˌdaɪə'metrɪkli əpəʊzd]	completely different	*diametral entgegengesetzt*
nickname	['nɪkneɪm]	an informal name for a person	*Spitzname*
offence	[ə'fens]	sth done against the law	*Delikt, Straftat*
warehouse	['weəhaʊs]	a building that stores supplies	*Lager(halle)*
flick knife	['flɪk naɪf]	a folding pocket knife	*Springmesser*
to resist	[rɪˌzɪst]	to refuse	*Widerstand leisten gegen, sich etw widersetzen*
appointment	[ə'pɔɪntmənt]	an arranged meeting	*Termin, Verabredung*
page 141			
verdict	['vɜːdɪkt]	a decision (legal)	*Urteil, Beurteilung*
probation	[prə'beɪʃn]	test period to monitor good behaviour	*Bewährung*
suspended sentence	[səˌspendɪd 'sentəns]	a possible punishment used as a threat	*(Freiheits-)Strafe auf Bewährung*
to impose	[ɪm'pəʊz]	to force	*auferlegen, erlassen*
nationwide	['neɪʃnwaɪd]	across the country	*landesweit*
to speculate	['spekjuleɪt]	to think about, wonder	*spekulieren, Vermutungen anstellen*
policing	[pə'liːsɪŋ]	police control/surveillance	*Kontrolle, Überwachung*
homicide	['hɒmɪsaɪd]	murder	*Tötung, Mord*

involvement	[ɪn'vɒlvmənt]	being involved in sth	*Beteiligung*

page 142

speeding	['spi:dɪŋ]	driving above the speed limit	*Geschwindigkeitsüberschreitung*
deputy	['depjuti]	officer ranked just below the head of a police department	*Hilfs-, Vertretungs-*
drunk driving	['drʌŋk draɪvɪŋ]	*(AE) BE:* drink driving	*Trunkenheit am Steuer*
registration papers	[ˌredʒɪ'streɪʃn peɪpəz]	official documents (for a car)	*Papiere, Zulassung*
to hack up	[ˌhæk 'ʌp]	to roughly cut up into pieces	*zerstückeln*
trunk	[trʌŋk]	*(AE) BE:* boot (of car)	*Kofferraum*
to back away	['bæk ə'weɪ]	to retreat	*zurückgehen*
backup	['bækʌp]	help	*Hilfe, Unterstützung*
to approach	[ə'prəʊtʃ]	to go towards	*sich nähern, zugehen auf*
to dig into	['dɪg ɪntə]	to rummage in	*wühlen in*
puzzled	['pʌzld]	confused	*verdutzt*
liar	['laɪə]	*v* to lie	*Lügner/in*
to arrest	[ə'rest]	to hold sb by law as a potential criminal	*festnehmen, verhaften*
punch line	['pʌntʃ laɪn]	funny conclusion of a joke	*Pointe*

page 143

shoplifting	['ʃɒplɪftɪŋ]	stealing from shops	*Ladendiebstahl*
nail varnish	['neɪl vɑ:nɪʃ]	paint for nails	*Nagellack*
eyeliner	['aɪlaɪnə]	make-up used to emphasize the eyes	*Eyeliner, Lidstrich*
store detective	[ˌstɔ: dɪ'tektɪv]	sb who watches customers in a shop so they cannot steal anything	*Warenhausdetektiv*
to ban	[bæn]	to forbid	*Hausverbot erhalten*
constable	['kʌnstəbl]	a police officer	*Wachtmeister/in*
motive	['məʊtɪv]	reason for doing sth	*Motiv, Beweggrund*
greed	[gri:d]	*adj* greedy	*Gier, Habsucht*
peer group pressure	[ˌpɪə gru:p 'preʃə]	being persuaded to do sth by friends	*Gruppendruck*
mental illness	[ˌmentl 'ɪlnəs]	disease of the mind	*Geisteskrankheit*
to pass on	[ˌpɑ:s 'ɒn]	to give to sb else	*weitergeben*
plain clothes	[pleɪn 'kləʊðz]	not wearing a uniform	*Zivilkleidung*
uniformed	['ju:nɪfɔ:md]	wearing a uniform	*uniformiert*
guard	[gɑ:d]	person who protects or looks after sth	*Wachleute, -dienst*
closed-circuit television	[ˌkləʊzd ˌsɜ:kɪt 'telɪvɪʒn]	*abbrev* CCTV	*Überwachungskameras*
staff	[stɑ:f]	group of employees	*Angestellte, Personal*
to a lesser extent	[tu ə ˌlesər ɪk'stent]	not as much, not as frequently	*in geringerem Umfang*
store card	['stɔ: kɑ:d]	a credit card for a specific shop	*Kundenkreditkarte*

page 144

cell	[sel]	room in a prison where inmates live	*(Gefängnis-)Zelle*
scandalous	['skændələs]	socially inappropriate, shocking	*skandalös*

UNIT 12

page 145

hereditary	[hə'redɪtri]	sth that passes from parent to offspring	*erblich*
cloning	['kləʊnɪŋ]	to make a genetic replica of sth	*Klonen*
conservation	[ˌkɒnsə'veɪʃn]	preservation, protection	*Schutz, Erhaltung*

page 146

boycott	['bɔɪkɒt]	refusing to buy or use a product	*Boykott*
genetically modified	[dʊəˌnetɪkli 'mɒdɪfaɪd]	when genes have been altered in food	*genmanipuliert*
to announce	[ə'naʊns]	to declare	*ankündigen*
offspring	['ɒfsprɪŋ]	children	*Nachkommen*
revelation	[ˌrevə'leɪʃn]	to reveal information	*Enthüllung*
separate	['seprət]	<> together	*getrennt*
loophole	['lu:phəʊl]	when a law can be disobeyed due to ambiguous word use	*Schlupfloch*
to stock	[stɒk]	to have sth in a shop, warehouse, etc.	*führen, anbieten*

to derive	[dɪ'raɪv]	to come from, originate	*abstammen*
ban	[bæn]	an official rule that says sth is not allowed	*Verbot*
ingredient	[ɪn'gri:diənt]	one of the foods that make up a dish	*Zutat, Bestandteil*
astonishing	[ə'stɒnɪʃɪŋ]	unexpected or amazing	*erstaunlich*

page 147

nucleus	['nju:kliəs]	the centre of a cell where DNA is located	*Kern*
dairy	['deəri]	e.g. the dairy industry	*hier: Milchvieh*
herd	[hɜ:d]	a group of grazing animals	*Herde*
to be capable of	[bi 'keɪpəbl əv]	to be able to	*können, fähig sein*
vast	[vɑ:st]	immense	*riesig, ungeheuer*
mammal	['mæml]	animal that gives birth to live young and feeds them on milk	*Säugetier*
premature	['premətʃə]	unexpectedly early	*vorzeitig, frühzeitig*
lung	[lʌŋ]	organ used to breathe	*Lunge*
infection	[ɪn'fekʃn]	*adj* infectious	*Entzündung*
to diagnose	['daɪəgnəʊz]	to identify a disease or an illness	*diagnostizieren*
arthritis	[ɑ:'θraɪtɪs]	painful inflammation of the joints	*Arthritis, Gelenkentzündung*
miscarriage	[ˌmɪs'kærɪdʒ]	failed pregnancy	*Fehlgeburt*
abnormal	[æb'nɔ:ml]	<> normal	*abnorm, anomal, ungewöhnlich*
organ	['ɔ:gən]	body part with specific function	*Organ*
labelling	['leɪblɪŋ]	system of labels on products	*Kennzeichnung*
omission	[ə'mɪʃn]	leaving sth out	*Lücke*
doubt	[daʊt]	uncertainty	*Zweifel*
alteration	[ˌɔ:ltə'reɪʃn]	change	*Veränderung*
exceptional	[ɪk'sepʃənl]	unusually (positive)	*außergewöhnlich*
supervision	[ˌsu:pə'vɪʒn]	watching/observing sb	*Überwachung*

page 148

supporter	[sə'pɔ:tə(r)]	*v* to support	*Anhänger/in*
to introduce	[ˌɪntrə'dju:s]	to make sth available for use	*einführen*
outline	['aʊtlaɪn]	*v* to outline	*Umriss*

page 149

gene	[dʒi:n]	*adj* genetic	*Gen*
to maintain	[meɪn'teɪn]	to support	*aufrechterhalten*
to alter	['ɔ:ltə]	to change	*(ver)ändern*
organism	['ɔ:gənɪzəm]	a living thing	*Organismus*
yield	[ji:ld]	e.g. crop yield, milk yield	*Ertrag*
tendency	['tendənsi]	inclination, trend	*Tendenz*
dementia	[dɪ'menʃə]	mental illness	*Demenz*
diabetes	[ˌdaɪə'bi:ti:z]	metabolic disorder	*Zuckerkrankheit, Diabetes*
transplant	['trænsplɑ:nt]	operation to replace damaged organ	*Transplantation*
breeding	['bri:dɪŋ]	producing offspring	*Zucht, Züchtung*
crop	[krɒp]	agricultural plant	*(Anbau)Pflanze*
to cross-breed	['krɒs bri:d]	to breed from two different species	*kreuzen*
species	['spi:ʃi:z]	animal type, e.g. monkeys, dogs, birds, etc.	*Art(en)*
mule	[mju:l]	male donkey used for farm labour	*Maultier, -esel*
time-consuming	['taɪm kənsju:mɪŋ]	taking up a lot of time	*zeitraubend*
predictable	[prɪ'dɪktəbl]	*n* prediction	*voraussagbar*
to interact	[ˌɪntər'ækt]	to work with one another	*sich gegenseitig beeinflussen*
manipulation	[məˌnɪpju'leɪʃn]	*v* to manipulate	*Manipulation, Veränderung*
accidental	[ˌæksɪ'dentə]	unintentional	*zufällig, versehentlich*
substance	['sʌbstəns]	matter	*Substanz, Stoff*
poisonous	['pɔɪzənəs]	toxic	*giftig*
to trigger	['trɪgə]	to make sth active	*auslösen*
allergy	['ælədʒi]	*adj* allergic	*Allergie*
antibiotic-resistant	[ˌæntibaɪˌɒtɪk rɪ'zɪstənt]	not affected by antibiotic drugs	*resistent gegen Antibiotika*
micro-organism	[ˌmaɪkrəʊ 'ɔ:gənɪzəm]	very small organism	*Mikroorganismus*
flavour	['fleɪvə]	taste	*Geschmack*
shelf life	['ʃelf laɪf]	date when a product expires	*Haltbarkeit*

nutritional	[nju'trɪʃənl]	to do with food and health	*Nähr-*
page 150			
consumption	[kən'sʌmpʃn]	when sb uses/eats sth	*Verzehr*
to obey	[ə'beɪ]	to follow a rule	*befolgen*
to store	[stɔː]	to keep sth somewhere	*lagern, aufbewahren*
lobby	['lɒbi]	e.g. gun lobby	*Lobby, Interessengruppe*
harmful	['hɑːmfl]	bad, dangerous	*schädlich*
herbicide	['hɜːbɪsaɪd]	chemical substance used to inhibit the growth of unwanted plants	*Unkrautvernichtungsmittel*
contaminated	[kən'tæmɪneɪtɪd]	polluted	*verunreinigt, verseucht*
to play havoc	[pleɪ 'hævək]	to ruin, to mess sth up	*verheerende Schäden anrichten*
contrary	['kɒntrəri]	*phr* on the contrary	*Gegenteil*
bioengineer	[ˌbaɪəʊ-ˌendʒɪ'nɪə]	a person who has studied genetic engineering	*Gentechniker/in*
fertilizer	['fɜːtəlaɪzə]	a substance added to soil which improves plant growth	*Dünger*
pesticide	['pestɪsaɪd]	chemical used to kill pests on plants	*Schädlingsbekämpfungsmittel*
uncultivated	[ʌn'kʌltɪveɪtɪd]	untidy, not looked after carefully	*brachliegend*
habitat	['hæbɪtæt]	the natural home and environment of an organism	*Lebensraum*
convincing	[kən'vɪnsɪŋ]	persuasive	*überzeugend*
toxic	['tɒksɪk]	poisonous	*giftig, toxisch*
page 151			
blueprint	['bluːprɪnt]	prototype, plan	*Blaupause, Bauplan*
to imply	[ɪm'plaɪ]	to suggest	*andeuten, implizieren*
unintentional	[ˌʌnɪn'tenʃənl]	not on purpose	*unabsichtlich*
to halve	[hɑːv]	to split sth into two, make half of a whole	*(sich) halbieren*
by-product	['baɪ prɒdʌkt]	side effect, unintentional outcome	*Nebenprodukt*
pollination	[ˌpɒlə'neɪʃn]	fertilization of plants causing production of seeds	*Bestäubung*
radiation	[ˌreɪdi'eɪʃn]	energy transmitted as electromagnetic waves	*Strahlung*
mast	[mɑːst]	pole, tower	*Mast*
page 152			
spare part	[ˌspeə 'pɑːt]	replacement	*Ersatzteil*
potential	[pə'tenʃl]	possibilities	*Potenzial*
cure	[kjʊə]	remedy	*Heilung, Heilmittel*
downside	['daʊnsaɪd]	disadvantage	*Nachteil*
to abuse	[ə'bjuːz]	to use for a bad purpose	*missbrauchen*
clone	[kləʊn]	exact genetic copy	*Klon*
media hype	['miːdiə haɪp]	over-the-top journalism	*Medienrummel*
to feed	[fiːd]	*n* food	*ernähren*
conventional	[kən'venʃənl]	traditional	*konventionell, herkömmlich*
field trial	['fiːld traɪəl]	test in natural conditions	*Freilandversuch*
superweed	['suːpəwiːd]	weed which is hard to kill	*hoch resistentes Unkraut*
bee	[biː]		*Biene*
cross-breeding	['krɒsbriːdɪŋ]	*v* to cross-breed	*Kreuzung*
shortage	['ʃɔːtɪdʒ]	not having enough of sth	*Knappheit, Mangel*
page 153			
to queue	[kjuː]	to stand in a line	*anstehen, sich anstellen*
to jump the queue	[dʒʌmp ðə 'kjuː]	to go to the front of the line	*sich vordrängeln*
checkout	['tʃekaʊt]	place where customers pay in a shop	*Kasse*
trolley	['trɒli]	a wheeled container used to carry goods in a supermarket	*(Einkaufs-)Wagen*
cart	[kɑːt]	*(AE) BE:* trolley	*(Einkaufs-)Wagen*
to scan in	['skæn ɪn]	to enter information into a computer	*einscannen*
radio frequency	[ˌreɪdiəʊ 'friːkwənsi]	radio signal	*Funkfrequenz*
buying history	['baɪɪŋ hɪstri]	list of things that sb has bought previously	*Kaufverhalten*
to upload	[ˌʌp'ləʊd]	to transfer information to a central computer	*senden, hinaufladen*

recipe	['resəpi]	instructions for how to cook sth	*(Koch-)Rezept*
running total	[ˌrʌnɪŋ 'təʊtl]	*phr* to keep a running total	*(End-)Summe, Gesamtpreis*
fingerprint	['fɪŋgəprɪnt]	pattern of lines on a finger	*Fingerabdruck*
by electronic means	[baɪ ˌɪlek'trɒnɪk mi:nz]	electronically	*elektronisch*
free of charge	[fri: əv 'tʃɑ:dʒ]	costing nothing	*kostenlos, gebührenfrei*

page 154

to publish	['pʌblɪʃ]	to make e.g. a book public	*veröffentlichen, herausgeben*
stamp	[stæmp]	mark of payment on an envelope	*Briefmarke*

BUSINESS TOPICS

TOPIC 1

page 156

stock exchange ['stɒk ɪkstʃeɪndʒ]	*(Wertpapier-)Börse*
stock market ['stɒk mɑ:kɪt]	*(Wertpapier-)Börse*
sum [sʌm]	*Summe, Betrag*
to raise [reɪz]	*aufbringen*
stocks [stɒks]	*Anleihen, Aktien*
corporation [ˌkɔ:pə'reɪʃn]	*(Aktien-)Gesellschaft, Kapitalgesellschaft*
expansion [ɪk'spænʃn]	*Expansion, Ausweitung*
research and development (R&D) [rɪˌsɜ:tʃ ən dɪ'veləpmənt]	*Forschung und Entwicklung*
venture ['ventʃə]	*Unternehmen, Wagnis*
stockholder ['stɒkhəʊldə]	*Aktionär/in*
liable ['laɪəbl]	*haftbar*
separate ['sepərət]	*getrennt*
legal entity [ˌli:gl 'entəti]	*juristische Einheit*
legal action [ˌli:gl 'ækʃn]	*rechtliche Schritte*
trading floor [ˌtreɪdɪŋ 'flɔ:]	*Börsensaal*
face-to-face [ˌfeɪs tə 'feɪs]	*von Angesicht zu Angesicht, persönlich*
dealer ['di:lə]	*Händler/in*
share [ʃeə]	*Anteil*
joint [dʒɔɪnt]	*gemeinsam*
to entitle [ɪn'taɪtl]	*berechtigen*
profit ['prɒfɪt]	*Profit, Gewinn*
in the form of [ɪn ðə 'fɔ:m əv]	*in Form von*
dividend ['dɪvɪdend]	*Dividende*
supply and demand [səˌplaɪ ən dɪ'mɑ:nd]	*Angebot und Nachfrage*
annual ['ænjuəl]	*Jahres-*
voting rights ['vəʊtɪŋ raɪts]	*Stimmrechte*
speculation [ˌspekju'leɪʃn]	*Spekulation*
preferred stock [prɪˌfɜ:d 'stɒk]	*Vorzugsaktie*
common stock [ˌkɒmən 'stɒk]	*Stammaktie*
to be second in line [bi 'sekənd ɪn laɪn]	*nachgeordnet sein*

page 157

to enable [ɪ'neɪbl]	*(es) ermöglichen, in die Lage versetzen*
loss [lɒs]	*Verlust*
capital ['kæpɪtl]	*Kapital; Großbuchstabe*
enormous [ɪ'nɔ:məs]	*riesig*
to compile [kəm'paɪl]	*zusammenstellen*
turnover ['tɜ:nəʊvə]	*Umsatz*

page 158

entrepreneur [ˌɒntrəprə'nɜ:]	*Unternehmer/in*
penniless ['peniləs]	*mittellos*
refugee [ˌrefju'dʒi:]	*Flüchtling*
timeline ['taɪmlaɪn]	*Zeitachse, -rahmen*
loan [ləʊn]	*Kredit, Darlehen*
delighted [dɪ'laɪtɪd]	*(sehr) erfreut*
opportunity [ˌɒpə'tju:nəti]	*Gelegenheit, Chance*
direction [də'rekʃn]	*Richtung*
to gain [geɪn]	*gewinnen, erlangen*
to set up [ˌset 'ʌp]	*einrichten, gründen*
to open up [ˌəʊpən 'ʌp]	*eröffnen*
debt [det]	*Schuld(en)*
partnership ['pɑ:tnəʃɪp]	*Partnerschaft*
stake [steɪk]	*Anteil*
runway ['rʌnweɪ]	*Laufsteg*
to exhibit [ɪg'zɪbɪt]	*ausstellen*
to retail ['ri:teɪl]	*verkaufen*
market segment [ˌmɑ:kɪt 'segmənt]	*Marktsegment*
to target ['tɑ:gɪt]	*zielen auf*
to premiere ['premieə]	*uraufführen, vorstellen*
collection [kə'lekʃn]	*Sammlung, Kollektion*
to sell out [ˌsel 'aʊt]	*ausverkaufen*
broadcast ['brɔ:dkɑ:st]	*Sendung*
to expand [ɪk'spænd]	*expandieren, erweitern*
to introduce [ˌɪntrə'dju:s]	*einführen*
menswear ['menzweə]	*Herrenbekleidung*
to float [fləʊt]	*an die Börse bringen*
attention [ə'tenʃn]	*Aufmerksamkeit*
holiday resort ['hɒlədeɪ rɪzɔ:t]	*Urlaubsort*
equipment [ɪ'kwɪpmənt]	*Ausstattung, Einrichtung*
fee [fi:]	*Gebühr*
target group ['tɑ:gɪt gru:p]	*Zielgruppe*

TOPIC 2

page 159

to set a trend [set ə 'trend]	*einen Trend starten*
rise [raɪz]	*An-, Aufstieg*
to view [vjuː]	*ansehen, betrachten*
manual worker ['mænjuəl wɜːkə]	*Handwerker, körperliche/r Arbeiter/in*
mass-produced [ˌmæs prə'djuːst]	*in Massenproduktion hergestellt*
a pair of jeans [ə peər əv 'dʒiːnz]	*eine Jeans*
low-wage [ˌləʊ 'weɪdʒ]	*Niedriglohn-, Billiglohn-*
dress code ['dres kəʊd]	*Kleiderordnung*
court case ['kɔːt keɪs]	*Gerichtsverhandlung*
employee [ɪm'plɔɪiː]	*Angestellte/r, Beschäftigte/r*
suit [suːt]	*Anzug*
matching ['mætʃɪŋ]	*(zueinander) passend*
unthinkable [ʌn'θɪŋkəbl]	*unvorstellbar, undenkbar*
universally [ˌjuːnɪ'vɜːsəli]	*allgemein, universell*
strategy ['strætədʒi]	*Strategie, Taktik*
loose [luːs]	*weit (geschnitten), lose*
fit [fɪt]	*Passform, Sitz*
celebrity [sə'lebrəti]	*Prominente/r*
brand [brænd]	*Marke*
to emerge [ɪ'mɜːdʒ]	*entstehen*
mankind [mæn'kaɪnd]	*Menschheit*
household name ['haʊshəʊld neɪm]	*bekannter Begriff, Markenname*
distressed [dɪ'strest]	*auf alt getrimmt*
to rip [rɪp]	*(zer)reißen*
manufacturer [ˌmænju'fæktʃərə]	*Hersteller/in, Produzent/in, Fabrikant/in*

page 160

striking ['straɪkɪŋ]	*bemerkenswert, auffallend*
brand name ['brænd neɪm]	*Markenzeichen, -name*
to influence ['ɪnfluəns]	*beeinflussen*
promotion [prə'məʊʃn]	*Werbung, Marketing*
price tag ['praɪs tæg]	*Preisschild*

page 161

percentage [pə'sentɪdʒ]	*Prozentsatz*
breakdown ['breɪkdaʊn]	*Auflistung, -teilung*
storage ['stɔːrɪdʒ]	*Lager(haltung)*
to convert [kən'vɜːt]	*umwandeln*
profitable ['prɒfɪtəbl]	*gewinnbringend*
trial ['traɪəl]	*Probe(bestellung)*
unit price [ˌjuːnɪt 'praɪs]	*Stück-, Einzelpreis*
terms of delivery [ˌtɜːmz əv dɪ'lɪvəri]	*Lieferbedingungen*
enquiry [ɪn'kwaɪəri]	*Anfrage*
shipping ['ʃɪpɪŋ]	*Versand, Fracht*
door-to-door [ˌdɔː tə 'dɔː]	*von Tür zu Tür*
valid ['vælɪd]	*gültig*
discount ['dɪskaʊnt]	*Rabatt, Skonto*
to sb's liking [tə 'laɪkɪŋ]	*nach jds Geschmack*
query ['kwɪəri]	*Frage, Rückfrage*
bank transfer ['bæŋk trænsfɜː]	*Banküberweisung*
letter of credit [ˌletər əv 'kredɪt]	*Akkreditiv, Kreditbrief*
warehouse ['weəhaʊs]	*Lager(halle)*

TOPIC 3

page 162

county ['kaʊnti]	*Grafschaft, Bezirk*
keen [kiːn]	*(sehr) interessiert*
debit card ['debɪt kɑːd]	*Scheck-, Bankkarte*
to draw out [ˌdrɔː 'aʊt]	*abheben*
current account ['kʌrənt əkaʊnt]	*Girokonto*
bank statement ['bæŋk steɪtmənt]	*Kontoauszug*
debit ['debɪt]	*Soll, Lastschrift*
transaction [træn'zækʃn]	*Überweisung, Vorgang*
stroke of luck [strəʊk əv 'lʌk]	*glücklicher Zufall*
by mistake [baɪ mɪ'steɪk]	*aus Versehen, irrtümlich*
customer service representative [ˌkʌstəmə ˌsɜːvɪs ˌreprɪ'zentətɪv]	*Kundendienstmitarbeiter/in*
to trace [treɪs]	*zurückverfolgen*
search engine ['sɜːtʃ endʒɪn]	*Suchmaschine*
fraudster ['frɔːdstə]	*Betrüger/in*
website development expert [ˌwebsaɪt dɪ'veləpmənt ekspɜːt]	*Webseite-Entwickler/in*
to abuse [ə'bjuːz]	*missbrauchen*
to break the law [ˌbreɪk ðə 'lɔː]	*gegen das Gesetz verstoßen*
hacker ['hækə]	*Hacker/in*
to clean out [ˌkliːn 'aʊt]	*räumen, leeren*
to freeze an account [friːz ən ə'kaʊnt]	*ein Konto blockieren*
to refund [rɪ'fʌnd]	*zurückzahlen, erstatten*
guidelines ['gaɪdlaɪnz]	*Richtlinien*
directory information [də'rektəri infə'meiʃn]	*Telefonauskunft*
confirmation [ˌkɒnfə'meɪʃn]	*Bestätigung*

page 163

thief [θiːf]	*Dieb/in*
to access ['ækses]	*zugreifen auf*
acknowledgement [ək'nɒlɪdʒmənt]	*Bestätigung*
to proceed [prə'siːd]	*vorgehen*
checkout ['tʃekaʊt]	*Kasse*
button ['bʌtn]	*Taste*

page 164

downside ['daʊnsaɪd]	*Nachteil, Kehrseite*
to queue [kjuː]	*anstehen, sich anstellen*
shift [ʃɪft]	*Schicht*
bargain hunting ['bɑːgɪn hʌntɪŋ]	*Schnäppchenjagd*
habit ['hæbɪt]	*Gewohnheit*
safety measure ['seɪfti meʒə]	*Sicherheitsmaßnahme*

TOPIC 4

page 165

freight [freɪt]	*Fracht, Güter*
forwarding ['fɔːwədɪŋ]	*Versand, Transport*
plant [plɑːnt]	*Anlage, Werk, Betrieb*
raw materials [ˌrɔː mə'tɪəriəlz]	*Rohstoffe*
consumer durables [kənˌsjuːmə 'djʊərəblz]	*Gebrauchsgüter, langlebige Konsumgüter*
containerization [kənˌteɪnəraɪ'zeɪʃn]	*Verpackung in Container*
to outsource ['aʊtsɔːs]	*auslagern*
virtually ['vɜːtʃuəli]	*praktisch, nahezu*
consequently ['kɒnsɪkwəntli]	*infolgedessen*
supply chain [sə'plaɪ tʃeɪn]	*Versorgungskette*
division [dɪ'vɪʒn]	*Abteilung*
carrier ['kæriə]	*Transportunternehmen, Spediteur*
definite ['defɪnət]	*bestimmt*
delivery [dɪ'lɪvəri]	*Zustellung, (Aus-)Lieferung*
consignment [kən'saɪnmənt]	*(Waren-)Sendung, Lieferung*
sophisticated [sə'fɪstɪkeɪtɪd]	*differenziert, erfahren*
logistics [lə'dʒɪstɪks]	*Logistik, Auslieferung*
means of transport [miːnz əf 'trænspɔːt]	*Beförderungs-, Verkehrsmittel*
to combat ['kɒmbæt]	*bekämpfen*
global warming [ˌgləʊbl 'wɔːmɪŋ]	*Erderwärmung*
customs clearance [ˌkʌstəmz 'klɪərəns]	*Zollabfertigung*
to track [træk]	*(zurück)verfolgen*
to trace [treɪs]	*zurückverfolgen*
groupage consignment [ˌgruːpɪdʒ kən'saɪnmənt]	*Gruppenlieferung*
consolidated shipment [kənˌsɒlɪdeɪtɪd 'ʃɪpmənt]	*gemeinsame Beförderung*
procurement [prə'kjʊəmənt]	*Beschaffung*
assembly [ə'sembli]	*Zusammenbau, Montage*
warehousing ['weəhaʊzɪŋ]	*Lagerhaltung*
distribution [ˌdɪstrɪ'bjuːʃn]	*(Aus-)Lieferung*
installation [ˌɪnstə'leɪʃn]	*Installation, Auf-, Einbau*
carbon footprint ['kɑːbən fʊtprɪnt]	*Kohlendioxidausstoß*
to coordinate [kəʊ'ɔːdɪneɪt]	*aufeinander abstimmen, koordinieren*
origin ['ɒrɪdʒɪn]	*Ursprung, Herkunft*
deadline ['dedlaɪn]	*Liefertermin, Frist*
permission [pə'mɪʃn]	*Erlaubnis, Genehmigung*
formality [fɔː'mæləti]	*Formalität*

page 166

coal [kəʊl]	*Kohle*
ore [ɔː]	*Erz*
household appliance [ˌhaʊshəʊld ə'plaɪəns]	*Haushaltsgerät*
technically-advanced [ˌteknɪkli əd'vɑːnst]	*technisch fortgeschritten*
industrialized country [ɪnˌdʌstriəlaɪzd 'kʌntri]	*Industriestaat*
production facility [prəˌdʌkʃn fə'sɪləti]	*Produktionsstätte*
retail outlet ['riːteɪl aʊtlet]	*Einzelhandelsgeschäft*

page 167

spare part [ˌspeə 'pɑːt]	*Ersatzteil*
existing [ɪg'zɪstɪŋ]	*bestehend, vorhanden*
to transfer [træns'fɜː]	*weiterleiten*
records ['rekɔːdz]	*Unterlagen, Akten*
premises ['premɪsɪz]	*Gelände, Räumlichkeiten*
to log on [ˌlɒg 'ɒn]	*einloggen*
signature ['sɪgnətʃə]	*Unterschrift*
to schedule ['ʃedjuːl]	*einplanen*
bad line [bæd 'laɪn]	*schlechte Verbindung*
to get on to [ˌget 'ɒn tə]	*sich in Verbindung setzen mit*
to dispatch [dɪ'spætʃ]	*(aus)liefern, abschicken, aufgeben*
incorporated [ɪn'kɔːpəreɪtɪd]	*(als Kapitalgesellschaft) eingetragen*
decoration [ˌdekə'reɪʃn]	*Schmuck*

TOPIC 5

page 168

CEO (chief executive officer) [ˌtʃiːf ɪg'zekjətɪv ɒfɪsə]	*Vorstandsvorsitzende/r*
the way forward [ðə weɪ 'fɔːwəd]	*die Zukunft, der Fortschritt*
revolutionary [ˌrevə'luːʃənəri]	*revolutionär*
approach [ə'prəʊtʃ]	*Ansatz, Herangehen(sweise)*
mobility [məʊ'bɪləti]	*Beweglichkeit, Mobilität*
recharging [ˌriː'tʃɑːdʒɪŋ]	*Lade-*
range [reɪndʒ]	*Reichweite*
to pioneer [ˌpaɪə'nɪə]	*entwickeln*
in view of [ɪn 'vjuː əv]	*angesichts*
incentive [ɪn'sentɪv]	*Anreiz*
subscription-based [səb'skrɪpʃn beɪst]	*Abonnements-*
van [væn]	*Lieferwagen, Transporter*
SUV (sports utility vehicle) [ˌes juː 'viː]	*Geländewagen (mit Vierradantrieb)*
pickup ['pɪkʌp]	*Pritschenwagen*

page 169

to predict [prɪ'dɪkt]	*vorhersagen*
to rocket ['rɒkɪt]	*kräftig (an)steigen*
to soar [sɔː]	*stark ansteigen*
to afford [ə'fɔːd]	*(es) sich leisten (können)*
convenience [kən'viːniəns]	*Komfort, Bequemlichkeit*
biofuel [ˌbaɪəʊ'fjuːəl]	*Biokraftstoff*
fuel cell ['fjuːəl sel]	*Brennstoffzelle*
compressed air [kəm'prest eə]	*Druckluft*

page 170

saloon [sə'luːn]	*Limousine*
spacious ['speɪʃəs]	*geräumig*

state-of-the-art [ˌsteɪt əv ði 'ɑːt]	*letzter Stand der Technik, hochmodern*
fuel-efficient [ˌfjuːəl ɪ'fɪʃnt]	*Treibstoff sparend, mit geringem Treibstoffverbrauch*
fuel consumption ['fjuːəl kənsʌmpʃn]	*Kraftstoffverbrauch*
hybrid ['haɪbrɪd]	*Hybrid(fahrzeug)*
suitable ['suːtəbl]	*geeignet*
traffic lights ['træfɪk laɪts]	*(Verkehrs-)Ampel*
to power ['paʊə]	*antreiben*
to kick in [ˌkɪk 'ɪn]	*(sich) einschalten*
economical [ˌiːkə'nɒmɪkl]	*sparsam, wirtschaftlich*
braking system ['breɪkɪŋ sɪstəm]	*Bremssystem*
repair [rɪ'peə]	*Reparatur*
maintenance ['meɪntənəns]	*Wartung*
to rate [reɪt]	*einstufen*
mph [ˌem piː 'eɪtʃ]	*m/h (Meilen pro Stunde)*
carbon emission [ˌkɑːbən ɪ'mɪʃn]	*Kohlendioxid-Ausstoß*
battery charger ['bætəri tʃɑːdʒə]	*Batterieladegerät*

TOPIC 6

page 171

to get sth off one's chest [ˌget 'ɒf wʌnz tʃest]	*etw loswerden wollen*
makeover ['meɪkəʊvə]	*Neugestaltung*
line manager ['laɪn mænɪdʒə]	*Vorgesetzte/r, Chef/in*
to appreciate [ə'priːʃieɪt]	*würdigen, schätzen*
to boost [buːst]	*steigern*
teleworking ['teliwɜːkɪŋ]	*Heimarbeit (am Computer)*
spreadsheet ['spredʃiːt]	*Tabellenprogramm, -kalkulation*
in the comfort of your own home [ɪn ðə ˌkʌmfət əv jɔːr 'əʊn həʊm]	*bequem zu Hause*
to have seen better days [həv siːn 'betə deɪz]	*bessere Tage gesehen haben*
to upgrade [ˌʌp'greɪd]	*aufrüsten*
dedicated ['dedɪkeɪtɪd]	*fest zugeordnet*
paycheck ['peɪtʃek]	*Gehaltszahlung*
to be in shock [bi ɪn 'ʃɒk]	*schockiert sein*
the writing's on the wall [ðə ˌraɪtɪŋz ɒn ðə 'wɔːl]	*das ist ein Warnsignal*
to grab [græb]	*(er)greifen*
to be out on your ear [bi ˌaʊt ɒn jɔːr 'ɪə]	*rausfliegen*
to be plain sailing [bi pleɪn 'seɪlɪŋ]	*ganz einfach sein*
to pull one's weight [pʊl wʌnz 'weɪt]	*sich voll einsetzen*
telework ['teliwɜːk]	*Heimarbeit (am Computer)*
to log [lɒg]	*registrieren, aufzeichnnen*
accordingly [ə'kɔːdɪŋli]	*entsprechend*
team-building ['tiːm bɪldɪŋ]	*Teamentwicklung*
seminar ['semɪnɑː]	*Seminar, Fachtagung*
demo ['deməʊ]	*Demonstration, Vorführung*
tool [tuːl]	*Werkzeug*
to regret [rɪ'gret]	*bedauern, bereuen*

page 172

overtime ['əʊvətaɪm]	*Überstunden*
to plot a graph [plɒt ə 'grɑːf]	*eine Grafik anlegen/ aufzeichnen*
agenda [ə'dʒendə]	*Tagesordnung*
to get through [ˌget 'θruː]	*durchnehmen*
to hand over [ˌhænd 'əʊvə]	*übergeben*
to review [rɪ'vjuː]	*zusammenfassen*
handout ['hændaʊt]	*Merkblatt*
to leap [liːp]	*springen; sprunghafter Anstieg*
in the space of [ɪn ðə 'speɪs əv]	*im Zeitraum von*
Hold your horses! [həʊld jɔː 'hɔːsɪz]	*Immer sachte mit den jungen Pferden!*
prime time ['praɪm taɪm]	*Hauptsendezeit*
coverage ['kʌvərɪdʒ]	*Berichterstattung, Präsenz*
to make a point [meɪk ə 'pɔɪnt]	*etw dazu sagen*
go ahead [ˌgəʊ ə'hed]	*fortfahren*
expenditure [ɪk'spendɪtʃə]	*Ausgabe(n), Kosten*
to level out [ˌlevl 'aʊt]	*abflachen*

page 173

clarification [ˌklærɪfɪ'keɪʃn]	*Erklärung, Klarstellung*
to return to [rɪ'tɜːn tə]	*zurückkehren zu*
to delay [dɪ'leɪ]	*aufschieben*
to sum up [ˌsʌm 'ʌp]	*zusammenfassen*
participant [pɑː'tɪsɪpənt]	*Teilnehmer/in*
to make a contribution [meɪk ə ˌkɒntrɪ'bjuːʃn]	*einen Beitrag leisten*
joke [dʒəʊk]	*Witz, Scherz*
body language ['bɒdi læŋgwɪdʒ]	*Körpersprache*
to sense [sens]	*wahrnehmen*
to get stuck in traffic [get ˌstʌk ɪn 'træfɪk]	*im Stau stecken*

TOPIC 7

page 174

giant ['dʒaɪənt]	*Riese, Gigant*
chairman ['tʃeəmən]	*Vorsitzende(r)*
to dominate ['dɒmɪneɪt]	*beherrschen*
emerging market [ɪˌmɜːdʒɪŋ 'mɑːkɪt]	*Schwellenmarkt*
petrochemicals [ˌpetrəʊ'kemɪklz]	*Petrochemikalien*
billionaire [ˌbɪljə'neə]	*Milliardär/in*
advance [əd'vɑːns]	*Fortschritt*
natural resources [ˌnætʃrəl rɪ'sɔːsɪz]	*Bodenschätze, natürliche Ressourcen*
infrastructure ['ɪnfrəstrʌktʃə]	*Infrastruktur*

page 175

weather report ['weðə rɪpɔ:t]	*Wetterbericht*
quarter ['kwɔ:tə]	*Vierteljahr, Quartal*
wireless ['waɪələs]	*drahtlos, Funk-*
to rank [ræŋk]	*einstufen*
to jam [dʒæm]	*verstopfen*
to graduate ['grædʒʊeɪt]	*einen (Hochschul-)Abschluss machen*
anecdotal [,ænɪk'dəʊtl]	*anekdotisch*
labour force ['leɪbə fɔ:s]	*Arbeitskräfte*
to deploy [dɪ'plɔɪ]	*einsetzen*
to hold back [,həʊld 'bæk]	*zurückhalten*
crop [krɒp]	*Ernte*
weather forecast ['weðə fɔ:kɑ:st]	*Wettervorhersage*
illiterate [ɪ'lɪtərət]	*ungebildet, des Lesens unkundig*

page 176

backbone ['bækbəʊn]	*Rückgrat*
skilled [skɪld]	*ausgebildet, Fach-*
job security [,dʒɒb sɪ'kjʊərəti]	*Arbeitsplatzsicherheit*
to sack [sæk]	*entlassen*
works council [,wɜ:ks 'kaʊnsl]	*Betriebsrat*
to be comprised of [bi kəm'praɪzd əv]	*umfassen*
high-end [,haɪ'end]	*für gehobene Ansprüche*
core competence [kɔ: 'kɒmpɪtəns]	*Kernkompetenz*
job loss ['dʒɒb lɒs]	*Arbeitsplatzverlust*

TOPIC 8

page 177

labour market ['leɪbə mɑ:kɪt]	*Arbeitsmarkt*
tear [tɪə]	*Träne*
papers ['peɪpəz]	*(Ausweis-)Papiere*
vibrant ['vaɪbrənt]	*vibrierend, aufregend*
in search of [ɪn 'sɜ:tʃ əv]	*auf der Suche nach*
migrant worker ['maɪgrənt wɜ:kə]	*Wanderarbeiter/in*
to stream [stri:m]	*strömen*
to be dependent on [bi dɪ'pendənt ɒn]	*abhängig sein von*
to be out of the question [bi ,aʊt əv ðə 'kwestʃən]	*nicht in Frage kommen*
rent [rent]	*Miete*
astronomical [,æstrə'nɒmɪkl]	*astronomisch*
radio station ['reɪdiəʊ steɪʃn]	*Radiosender*
to stock [stɒk]	*führen, auf Lager haben*
minimum wage [,mɪnɪməm 'weɪdʒ]	*Mindestlohn*
counterpart ['kaʊntəpɑ:t]	*Gegenstück, Gegenüber*
inflation [ɪn'fleɪʃn]	*Inflation*
reputation [,repju'teɪʃn]	*Ruf*

page 178

native ['neɪtɪv]	*Heimat-*
overseas workers [,əʊvə'si:z wɜ:kəz]	*ausländische Arbeiter*
maid [meɪd]	*Dienstmädchen*
attendant [ə'tendənt]	*Betreuer/in*
packer ['pækə]	*Packer/in*
restriction [rɪ'strɪkʃn]	*Einschränkung*
to draw up [,drɔ: 'ʌp]	*aufstellen, formulieren*

page 179

tragic ['trædʒɪk]	*tragisch*
to concern [kən'sɜ:n]	*betreffen*
hardship ['hɑ:dʃɪp]	*Not, Mühsal*
poverty line ['pɒvəti laɪn]	*Armutsgrenze*
outdoor ['aʊtdɔ:]	*im Freien*
running water [,rʌnɪŋ 'wɔ:tə]	*fließendes Wasser*
closure ['kləʊʒə]	*Schließung*
to conduct [kən'dʌkt]	*abhalten, (durch)führen*
convincing [kən'vɪnsɪŋ]	*überzeugend-*

TOPIC 9

page 180

to smash [smæʃ]	*zertrümmern, durchbrechen*
glass ceiling [,glɑ:s 'si:lɪŋ]	*unsichtbare Beförderungssperre*
to shock bomb ['ʃɒk bɒm]	*schockieren*
board of directors [,bɔ:d əv də'rektəz]	*Aufsichtsrat, Vorstand*
board member ['bɔ:d membə]	*Vorstandsmitglied*
to account for [ə'kaʊnt fə]	*ausmachen, betragen*
affirmative [ə'fɜ:mətɪv]	*positiv*
to name and shame [neɪm ənd 'ʃeɪm]	*namentlich verurteilen*
high-flying [,haɪ'flaɪɪŋ]	*erfolgreich*
executive [ɪg'zekjətɪv]	*leitende/r Angestellte/r, Manager/in*
gorgeous ['gɔ:dʒəs]	*prächtig, großartig*
lecture ['lektʃə]	*Vortrag*
to be close to my heart [bi ,kləʊs tə maɪ 'hɑ:t]	*liegt mir am Herzen*
to pearl dive ['pɜ:l daɪv]	*gezielt suchen*
rising ['raɪzɪŋ]	*aufsteigend*
scheme [ski:m]	*Plan, Projekt*
mentor ['mentɔ:]	*Mentor/in*
hierarchy ['haɪərɑ:ki]	*Hierarchie*
to handle sth ['hændl]	*mit etw umgehen*
old boy's club [əʊld 'bɔɪz klʌb]	*Altherrenklub*
maternity leave [mə'tɜ:nəti li:v]	*Mutterschaftsurlaub*
to breast feed ['brest fi:d]	*stillen*

page 181

to fire ['faɪə]	*entlassen*
to appoint [ə'pɔɪnt]	*einstellen*

workaholic [ˌwɜːkəˈhɒlɪk]	*Arbeitssüchtige/r*
housewife [ˈhaʊswaɪf]	*Hausfrau*
domination [ˌdɒmɪˈneɪʃn]	*Vorherrschaft*
company director [ˌkʌmpəni dəˈrektə]	*Firmenchef/in*
literally [ˈlɪtərəli]	*(wort)wörtlich*
athletic [æθˈletɪk]	*sportlich*
invisible [ɪnˈvɪzəbl]	*unsichtbar*
barrier [ˈbæriə]	*Schranke, Barriere*
hidden [ˈhɪdn]	*verborgen*
capable [ˈkeɪpəbl]	*fähig, kompetent*

page 182

mommy track [ˈmɒmi træk]	*Mutterschaftsschiene*
middle management [ˌmɪdl ˈmænɪdʒmənt]	*mittleres Management*
insulted [ɪnˈsʌltɪd]	*beleidigt, empört*
to award [əˈwɔːd]	*vergeben*
on the basis of [ɒn ðə ˈbeɪsɪs əv]	*auf der Basis von, aufgrund*
gender [ˈdʒendə]	*Geschlecht*
merit [ˈmerɪt]	*Verdienst(e)*
quota [ˈkwəʊtə]	*Quote*
gender gap [ˈdʒendə gæp]	*Geschlechterfalle*
to ensure [ɪnˈʃʊə]	*sicherstellen, gewährleisten*

TOPIC 10

page 183

diary [ˈdaɪəri]	*Tagebuch*
to fork out [ˌfɔːk ˈaʊt]	*blechen, berappen*
crammed [kræmd]	*gepfercht, vollgestopft*
jetliner [ˈdʒetlaɪnə]	*Düsenflugzeug*
courtesy of [ˈkɜːtəsi əv]	*dank*
to pronounce [prəˈnaʊns]	*aussprechen*
carbon offsetting [ˌkɑːbən ˈɒfsetɪŋ]	*Umweltabgabe*
princely sum [ˈprɪnsli sʌm]	*fürstlicher Betrag*
my heart was in my mouth [maɪ ˌhɑːt wəz ɪn maɪ ˈmaʊθ]	*das Herz schlug mir bis zum Hals*
residence [ˈrezɪdəns]	*Wohnsitz*
daddy's boy syndrome [ˌdædiz bɔɪ ˈsɪndrəʊm]	*Vaters-Sohn-Syndrom*
price elastic [praɪs ɪˈlæstɪk]	*preislich variabel*
to have mass appeal [həv ˈmæs əpiːl]	*den Massengeschmack treffen*
marital status [ˌmærɪtl ˈsteɪtəs]	*Familienstand*
scholarship [ˈskɒləʃɪp]	*Stipendium*
proverb [ˈprɒvɜːb]	*Sprichwort*

page 184

the man in the street [ðə ˌmæn ɪn ðə ˈstriːt]	*der Mann auf der Straße*
scheduled flight [ˈʃedjuːld flaɪt]	*Linienflug*
narrow [ˈnærəʊ]	*eng, schmal*
inch [ɪntʃ]	*Zoll*
amenity [əˈmiːnəti]	*Annehmlichkeit*
centrally heated [ˌsentrəli ˈhiːtɪd]	*zentral beheizt*
facilities [fəˈsɪlətiz]	*Möglichkeiten, Einrichtungen*
sheet [ʃiːt]	*(Bett-)Laken*
duvet [ˈduːveɪ]	*Tagesdecke*
pillow [ˈpɪləʊ]	*Kopfkissen*
washbasin [ˈwɒʃbeɪsn]	*Waschbecken*
remote control [rɪˌməʊt kənˈtrəʊl]	*Fernbedienung*
air conditioning [ˈeə kəndɪʃnɪŋ]	*Klimaanlage*

page 185

kettle [ˈketl]	*(Wasser-)Kessel*
saucer [ˈsɔːsə]	*Untertasse*
parking space [ˈpɑːkɪŋ speɪs]	*Parkplatz*

TOPIC 11

page 186

fake [feɪk]	*Fälschung*
imitation [ˌɪmɪˈteɪʃn]	*Nachahmung*
counterfeit [ˈkaʊntəfɪt]	*gefälscht, nachgemacht*
black market [ˌblæk ˈmɑːkɪt]	*Schwarzmarkt*
to pirate [ˈpaɪrət]	*raubkopieren, unerlaubt nachmachen*
must-have [mʌst ˈhæv]	*was man unbedingt haben muss*
genuine [ˈdʒenjuɪn]	*echt*
to be short of cash [bi ˈʃɔːt əv kæʃ]	*knapp bei Kasse sein*

page 187

in agony [ɪn ˈægəni]	*unter heftigen Schmerzen*
heart attack [ˈhɑːt ətæk]	*Herzinfarkt, -anfall*
cough medicine [ˌkɒf ˈmedsɪn]	*Hustensaft*
in one respect [ɪn wʌn rɪˈspekt]	*in einer Hinsicht*
poisonous [ˈpɔɪzənəs]	*giftig*
cough syrup [ˌkɒf ˈsɪrəp]	*Hustensaft*
unwitting [ʌnˈwɪtɪŋ]	*unwissentlich*
health care [ˈhelθ keə]	*Gesundheitsfürsorge*
diethylene glycol [daɪˌeθɪliːn ˈglaɪkɒl]	*Diäthylenglykol*
glycerine [ˈglɪsəriːn]	*Glyzerin*
antifreeze [ˈæntifriːz]	*Frostschutzmittel*
futuristic-looking [ˌfjuːtʃəˈrɪstɪk lʊkɪŋ]	*futuristisch aussehend*
storey [ˈstɔːri]	*Stockwerk, Geschoss*
free trade zone [ˌfriː ˈtreɪd zəʊn]	*Freihandelszone*
death toll [ˈdeθ təʊl]	*Todesrate*
aircraft [ˈeəkrɑːft]	*Flugzeug*
lining [ˈlaɪnɪŋ]	*Innenfutter*
regulation [ˌregjuˈleɪʃn]	*Verordnung, Vorschrift*
host country [həʊst ˈkʌntri]	*Gastland*
to transship [trænsˈʃɪp]	*versenden*

to substitute ['sʌbstɪtjuːt]	*ersetzen*

page 188

to enforce [ɪn'fɔːs]	*durchsetzen*
tempting ['temptɪŋ]	*verlockend*
to get your hands on [get jɔː 'hændz ɒn]	*erwerben*
to beware [bɪ'weə]	*aufpassen*
vendor ['vendə]	*(Straßen-)Händler/in*

TOPIC 12

page 189

stem cell ['stem sel]	*Stammzelle*
self-repair [ˌself rɪ'peə]	*Selbstheilung*
kit [kɪt]	*Ausstattung*
cure [kjʊə]	*Heilmittel*
cancer ['kænsə]	*Krebs(krankheit)*
master cell ['mɑːstə sel]	*Grundzelle*
building block ['bɪldɪŋ blɒk]	*Bauklotz*
regeneration [rɪˌdʒenə'reɪʃn]	*Regeneration*
embryo ['embriəʊ]	*Embryo*
to fertilize ['fɜːtəlaɪz]	*befruchten*
to regenerate [rɪ'dʒenəreɪt]	*erneuern*
embryonic [ˌembri'ɒnɪk]	*embryonal*
on moral grounds [ɒn ˌmɒrəl 'graʊndz]	*aus moralischen Gründen*
abortion [ə'bɔːʃn]	*Abtreibung, Schwangerschafts-abbruch*
federal government [ˌfedərəl 'gʌvənmənt]	*Bundesregierung*
funding ['fʌndɪŋ]	*Finanzierung*
government-backed ['gʌvənmənt bækt]	*staatlich subventioniert*
backdrop ['bækdrɒp]	*Hintergrund*
to launch [lɔːntʃ]	*starten*
to pump [pʌmp]	*pumpen*
taxpayer ['tækspeɪə]	*Steuerzahler/in*
to flock [flɒk]	*strömen*
to donate [dəʊ'neɪt]	*spenden*

page 190

pharmaceutical [ˌfɑːmə'suːtɪkl]	*pharmazeutisch*
resident ['rezɪdənt]	*Bewohner/in*

page 191

retirement [rɪ'taɪəmənt]	*Ruhestand, Pensionierung*
short of breath [ˌʃɔːt əv 'breθ]	*außer Atem*
physician [fɪ'zɪʃn]	*(praktische/r) Arzt/Ärztin*
to diagnose ['daɪəgnəʊz]	*diagnostizieren*
heart failure ['hɑːt feɪljə]	*Herzversagen*
heart transplant [hɑːt 'trænsplɑːnt]	*Herztransplantation*
to come across [ˌkʌm ə'krɒs]	*zufällig finden, stoßen auf*
to entail [ɪn'teɪl]	*mit sich bringen*
to culture ['kʌltʃə]	*kultivieren, züchten*
to inject [ɪn'dʒekt]	*(ein)spritzen*
to drive [draɪv]	*treiben, schlagen*
new lease on life [njuː ˌliːs ɒn 'laɪf]	*neue Lebensqualität*
symptom ['sɪmptəm]	*Symptom*
dental ['dentl]	*Zahn-, zahnärztlich*
surgery ['sɜːdʒəri]	*chirurgischer Eingriff, Operation*
sacred ['seɪkrɪd]	*heilig*
will [wɪl]	*Wille*
success rate [sək'ses reɪt]	*Erfolgsrate*
mortality [mɔː'tæləti]	*Todesfall*
niche [nɪtʃ]	*Nische*

A–Z word list

Dieses Wörterverzeichnis enthält alle Wörter aus **Focus on Success – The new edition: Ausgabe Wirtschaft** in alphabetischer Reihenfolge. Nicht aufgeführt sind die Wörter aus der *Basic word list* sowie internationale Wörter wie *hotel, email* usw.
Wörter, die in den Hörverständnistexten vorkommen, sind mit einem ***t*** hinter der Seitenzahl gekennzeichnet.

A

abandoned *116* verlassen
abbreviation *52* Abkürzung
ability *7* Fähigkeit
abnormal *147* abnorm, anomal, ungewöhnlich
to abolish *138* abschaffen
abolition *138* Abschaffung
abortion *189* Abtreibung, Schwangerschaftsabbruch
to abridge *59* (ab)kürzen
absolutely *22* absolut
absurd *92* absurd
abuse *56* Anpöbelung, Beschimpfung(en)
to abuse *152t* missbrauchen
abusive *57* beleidigend, ausfallend
to accept *13* akzeptieren
acceptable *98* annehmbar, akzeptabel
to access *163* zugreifen auf
accessible *43* zugänglich
accessory *95* Zubehör, Accessoire
accident *67* Unfall
accidental *149* zufällig, versehentlich
accommodation *43* Unterkunft, Wohnraum
accompaniment *126* Begleitung
according to *7* nach, gemäß
accordingly *171* entsprechend
account executive *54* Kunden-berater/in, -betreuer/in
to account for *180* ausmachen, betragen
account manager *46* Kunden-betreuer/in
accountant *85* Buchhalter/in
accurate *57* genau
to achieve *120* erreichen
acknowledgement *163* Bestätigung
acronym *51t* Akronym, Initialwort
action *56* Aktion, Handlung
activist *98* Aktivist/in
activities officer *85* Verantwortliche/r für Aktivitäten und Veranstaltungen
actress *56* Schauspielerin
actually *29* tatsächlich, eigentlich
ad *18* Anzeige
to adapt *59* adaptieren
addicted *56* süchtig nach
addiction *16* Sucht, Abhängigkeit
to adjust *153* anpassen, abstimmen
to admit *49* zugeben, gestehen
to adopt *113* einführen
advance *174* Fortschritt
advertisement *45* Anzeige, Werbespot
advertiser *49* Werbefirma
advertising *40* Werbung
advice *19* Rat(schlag)
to advise *78* raten, beraten
affair *110* Angelegenheit
to affect *71* betreffen
affirmative *180* positiv
to afford *169* (es) sich leisten (können)
affordable *43* erschwinglich
afraid: I'm afraid *7* leider
Afro-Caribbean *125* afro-karibisch
agency *46* Agentur
agenda *122, 172t* Tagesordnung
ages: for ages *94* eine Ewigkeit
agreement *107* Vertrag, Abkommen, Zusage
aim *45* Ziel
aimed at *51t* abgezielt auf, gerichtet an
air conditioning *184* Klimaanlage
air pollution *121t* Luftverschmutzung
aircraft *187* Flugzeug
airfare *43* Flugkosten, -preis
airwaves *80* Äther
all over the place *7* überall
allergy *149* Allergie
alliance *136* Allianz, Bündnis
all-star *58t* Star-, mit vielen Stars
to alter *149* (ver)ändern
alteration *147* Veränderung
alternate *93* jede/r zweite
alternative *76* alternativ
although *14* obwohl
altogether *59* alles in allem
amazed *65* erstaunt
amenity *184* Annehmlichkeit
amnesty *134* Amnestie
amount *76* Menge
anaesthetic *136* Narkosemittel
to analyze *51t* analysieren
ancestry *129* Abstammung, Herkunft
anecdotal *175* anekdotisch
anecdote *82* Anekdote
anger *71* Zorn, Ärger
to announce *146* ankündigen
annoyed *65* verärgert
annoying *45* lästig, ärgerlich
annual *156* Jahres-
anorexia *16* Magersucht
anthem *105* Hymne
antibiotic-resistant *149* resistent gegen Antibiotika
antifreeze *187* Frostschutzmittel
anti-theft pad *28* Diebstahl-sicherung
anxious *65* besorgt, beunruhigt
anyhow *111* sowieso
apparent *136* offensichtlich, deutlich
appeal *129* Anziehungskraft, Anreiz
to appear *56* erscheinen
appendix *68* Anhang
appliance *78* Gerät
applicant *59* Bewerber/in
application *48* Bewerbung
to apply for *86* sich bewerben um
to apply to *129* gelten für, zutreffen auf
to appoint *181* einstellen
appointment *63* Termin, Verabredung
to appreciate *171* würdigen, schätzen
to approach *142t* sich nähern, zugehen auf
approach *168* Ansatz, Herangehen(sweise)
appropriate *72* angemessen, passend, entsprechend
approx. *44* ungefähr, etwa, zirka
aptitude *89* Fähigkeit, Eignung
area *40* Gebiet, Bereich
armed robbery *135* bewaffneter Raubüberfall
arrest *119* Verhaftung, Festnahme
to arrest *142* festnehmen, verhaften
arrival *34* Ankunft

arthritis *147* Arthritis, Gelenkentzündung
ashamed *17* beschämt
aspect *41* Aspekt, Seite
assembly *165* Zusammenbau, Montage
asset *129* Wert, Vorteil
to associate *139* assoziieren, verbinden
association *16* Verband, Verein
asteroid *75* Asteroid
astonishing *146* erstaunlich
astronomical *177* astronomisch
athletic *181* sportlich
atmosphere *80* Atmosphäre
atmospheric *80* atmosphärisch
to attach *106* beilegen, -fügen
attachment *106* Anlage
attack *40* Angriff
attempt *136* Versuch
to attend *48* teilnehmen (an)
attendant *178* Betreuer/in
attention *51t* Aufmerksamkeit
attitude *17* Haltung, Einstellung
to attract *18* anziehen, anlocken
attraction *41* Anziehung
attractive *16* attraktiv
auction *27* Auktion, Versteigerung
audience *56* Zuschauer
average *76* durchschnittlich
to avoid *62* (ver)meiden
award *52* Auszeichnung
to award *182* vergeben
awesome *12* überwältigend
awkward *136* unangenehm, lästig, peinlich
axe *137* Axt

B

to back away *142t* zurückgehen
to back off *12* zurücktreten
backbone *176* Rückgrat
backdrop *189* Hintergrund
background *55* Hintergrund, Herkunft
backup *142t* Hilfe, Unterstützung
backwards *87* rückwärts
bad line *167t* schlechte Verbindung
badge *129* Abzeichen
baggage *118t* Gepäck, Last
balance *66* Gleichgewicht
bale *73* Ballen
to ban *12* verbieten; Hausverbot erhalten
ban *146* Verbot
bang *110* Paukenschlag
bank statement *162* Kontoauszug
bank transfer *161* Banküberweisung
bank: to not break the bank *54* nicht die Welt kosten
bankrupt *40* bankrott, pleite
banner ad *45* Bannerwerbung
barbecue *20* Grillparty
barbed wire *132* Stacheldraht(zaun)
bargain *26* Sonderangebot
bargain hunting *164* Schnäppchenjagd
barrel *73* Fass
barrier *181* Schranke, Barriere
bartender *33* Barmann, -frau
to be based on *93* basieren auf
basket *104* Korb
battery charger *170* Batterieladegerät
battle *119* Kampf
to beat *12* schlagen
bedfellow *137* Bettgenosse, Schlafkamerad
bee *152t* Biene
beggar *43* Bettler/in
to behave *56* sich benehmen, sich verhalten
behaviour *57* Verhalten, Benehmen
below *10* unten
to bend *16* (sich) beugen
benefit *77* Nutzen, Vorteil
to benefit from *71* Nutzen ziehen aus, profitieren von
to bet *61* wetten; **you bet** *118t* ganz bestimmt, und ob
to beware *188* aufpassen
beyond *81, 89* darüber hinaus, danach; abgesehen von
bias *136* Vorurteil
bid *53* (An-)Gebot
billionaire *174* Milliardär/in
bioengineer *150* Gentechniker/in
biofuel *169* Biokraftstoff
birth *41* Geburt
bite *39* Bissen, Happen
black market *186* Schwarzmarkt
blame: to be to blame *131t* an etwas schuld sein
to blame sb *56* die Schuld geben, verantwortlich machen
blog *55* Blog
blouse *26* Bluse
to blow sb away *37* jdn überwältigen
blueprint *151* Blaupause, Bauplan
board game *118t* Brettspiel
board member *180* Vorstandsmitglied
board of directors *180* Aufsichtsrat, Vorstand
body language *98* Körpersprache
bold *62* fett
booker *47* Besteller/in
booking *85* Buchung
booming *73* blühend
to boost *171* steigern
border *111* Grenze, Grenz-
bored *78* gelangweilt
borough *40* (Stadt-)Bezirk
bother *56* Ärger
to bottom out *43* die Talsohle erreichen
bouncy castle *64* Hüpfburg
box: the box *7* die Kiste
boycott *146* Boykott
braid *118t* (geflochtener) Zopf
to brainstorm *67* (Ideen) sammeln
braking system *170t* Bremssystem
branch *103* Filiale, Niederlassung
brand *45* Marke
brand name *160* Markenzeichen, -name
branded *49* Marken-
brave *58t* tapfer
to break *124* abbrechen
to break a law *131t* das Gesetz brechen/übertreten
to break bulk *73* die Ladung löschen
to break into *23* einbrechen
to break the law *162* gegen das Gesetz verstoßen
breakdown *161* Auflistung, -teilung
to breast feed *180* stillen
breath: to take sb's breath away *40* jdm den Atem rauben
breeding *149* Zucht, Züchtung
bribery *139* Bestechung
brief *75* kurz
bright *22* hell; glänzend, schlau
to bring up *116* großziehen
broad *121* breit
broadcast *158t* Sendung
brochure *32* Broschüre, Prospekt
broken *124* getrennt, kaputt
budget *53* Etat, Budget; Billig-
building block *189* Bauklotz
bulb *76* Glühbirne, -lampe
bulimia *16* Bulimie, Ess-Brech-Sucht
bunch *110* Gruppe, Haufen
bureaucracy *110* Bürokratie
burglary *135* Einbruch
to bury *99* begraben
business person *71* Geschäftsmann/-frau
bust: to go bust *134* Pleite gehen
butterfly *59* Schmetterling
button *163* Taste
to buy sth on credit *29* etw auf Kredit kaufen
buying history *153* Kaufverhalten
by electronic means *153* elektronisch
by mistake *162* aus Versehen, irrtümlich
by-product *151* Nebenprodukt

C

to calculate *70* kalkulieren, berechnen
calm *36* ruhig
campaign *46* (Werbe-)Feldzug, Kampagne
campaigner *66* Aktivist/in, Kämpfer/in
camping: to go camping *15* campen
can *19* Dose
cancer *189* Krebs(krankheit)
candidate *48* Kandidat/in, Bewerber/in
canyon *132* Canyon, tiefes/enges Tal
capable *181* fähig, kompetent
to be capable of *147* können, fähig sein
capital *18, 157* Hauptstadt; Kapital
capital (letter) *62* Groß(buchstabe)
capital punishment *136* Todesstrafe
car insurance *93* Kraftfahrzeugversicherung
car seat *88t* Autositz
car sharing *66* gemeinsame Pkw-Nutzung
caramel *16* Karamel
carbon *80* Kohlenstoff
carbon dioxide *81t* Kohlendioxid
carbon emission *170* Kohlendioxid-Ausstoß
carbon footprint *165* Kohlendioxidausstoß
carbon offsetting *183* Umweltabgabe
to care for sb *116* jdn pflegen, sich um jdn kümmern
careers adviser *31* Berufsberater/in
careless *32* sorglos, nachlässig
cargo *73* Fracht, Ladung
carrier *165* Transportunternehmen, Spediteur
carrot *21* Karotte
to carry on *118t* weitermachen
to carry out *6* ausführen
cart *153* (Einkaufs-)Wagen
to cart sth away *132* wegkarren
carton *73* Karton
cartoon *32* Karikatur
cartoonist *68* Karikaturist/in
case study *16* Fallstudie
cash machine *11* Geldautomat
cashier *33* Kassierer/in
casting agent *129* Besetzungsagent/in
casual *99* Gelegenheits-
catastrophe *75* Katastrophe
to catch sb off guard *118t* jemanden überraschen, ertappen
cattle *83* Rinder, Vieh
Caucasian *131* Weiße/r, Hellhäutige/r
to celebrate *80* feiern
celebrity *55* Prominente/r
cell *144* (Gefängnis-)Zelle
censure *126* Tadel, Missbilligung
census *129* (Volks-)Zählung
centimetre *80* Zentimeter
central *71* zentral
centrally heated *184* zentral beheizt
century *81* Jahrhundert
CEO (chief executive officer) *168* Vorstandsvorsitzende/r
certain *7* gewiss, sicher
chairman *174* Vorsitzende(r)
challenge *12* Herausforderung
to challenge *13* herausfordern
challenging *85* herausfordernd, anstrengend
champagne *80* Champagner
channel *49* Kanal
chaos *66* Chaos
characteristic *40* Eigenschaft, Merkmal
to charge *53* berechnen
charge *70* Kosten
charity *55* wohltätiger Verein, Wohltätigkeit(sorganisation)
charming *16* charmant, bezaubernd
chart *82* Diagramm, Tabelle
chatroom *6* Chatroom, Diskussionsforum
to check out *37* herausfinden
checklist *95* Checkliste
checkout *153* Kasse
cheekbones *129* Wangenknochen
cheeky *16* frech, kess
chief *43* Chef
childcare *116* (Kinder-)Erziehung
childminder *117* Kinderbetreuer/in, Tagesmutter/-vater
to chill out *6* sich entspannen
choice *17* Wahl
to choke *66* ersticken
chores *123* Hausarbeit(en)
cinema *8* Kino
circle *60* Kreis
citizenship *131t* Staatsbürgerschaft
civil rights *131t* bürgerliche Rechte
civilisation *127* Zivilisation
to claim *131* behaupten, erklären
clarification *173* Erklärung, Klarstellung
clash *56* Konflikt, Zusammenstoß
classified *45* nach Rubriken geordnet
to clean out *162* räumen, leeren
to clean up the streets *43* die Straßen säubern
clemency *137* Milde, Nachsicht
clerical *89* Schreib-, Büro-
clerk *85* (Bank-)Angestellte/r
cleverly *69* klug, intelligent
click-through *53* Anklicken
client *46* Kunde/Kundin
cliff *68* Klippe, Felsen
climate *80* Klima
climate change *81t* Klimawandel
to climb *43* klettern, steigen
clone *152t* Klon
cloning *145* Klonen
to be close to my heart *180* liegt mir am Herzen
closed-circuit television *143* Überwachungskameras
closeness *48* Vertrautheit
closure *179* Schließung
cloudy *78* bewölkt
clubbing: to go clubbing *6* in Discos gehen
clue *44* Schlüssel
coach *7* Trainer/in
coal *80* Kohle
coastal *80* Küsten-
coffee mill *101t* Kaffeemühle
coin *113* Münze
to collapse *49* zusammenbrechen
colleague *66* Kollege/Kollegin
to collect *41* sammeln
collection *158t* Sammlung, Kollektion
college of further education *51t* Fachoberschule, Weiterbildungskolleg
column *19* Spalte
to combat *165* bekämpfen
to combine *69* (sich) verbinden
to come across *191t* zufällig finden, stoßen auf
come on *22* komm (schon)
comedy *58* Komödie, Comedy
comment *44* Kommentar
commercial *45* Anzeige, Werbespot
commercial break *49* Werbepause
commercially viable *83* kommerziell lebensfähig
commission *93, 105* Provision, Gebühr; Kommission
commitment *89* (Selbst-)Verpflichtung, Einsatz, Engagement
common stock *156* Stammaktie
common: in common *70* gemeinsam
communication *55* Kommunikation, Mitteilung, Benachrichtigung
community *16* Gemeinde
commuter *67* Pendler/in
companion *123* Begleiter/in
company director *181* Firmenchef/in
to compare *17* vergleichen

comparison *44* Vergleich, Steigerung
to compete *12* konkurrieren
competing *49* konkurrierend
competition *13* Wettkampf
competitive *7* Wettkampf-
competitive advantage *96* Wettbewerbsvorteil
to compile *157* zusammenstellen
to complain *32* reklamieren, sich beklagen, beschweren
to complete *93* vervollständigen, abschließen
complex *86* komplex, kompliziert
complicated *69* kompliziert
component *61* Bestandteil
comprehension *42* Verständnis
compressed air *169* Druckluft
to be comprised of *176* umfassen
to concentrate *31* sich konzentrieren
to concern *179* betreffen
concern *99* Sorge, Interesse, Anliegen
to be concerned with *120* sich befassen mit, sich kümmern um
conclusion *90* (Schluss-)Folgerung
to conduct *179* abhalten, (durch) führen
to confirm *48* bestätigen
confirmation *162* Bestätigung
conflicting *128* gegensätzlich
confused *132* verwirrt
congested *66* verstopft
congestion *66* Verkehrsstau, Verstopfung
congestion charging *71* Staugebühr
congratulations *29* Glückwunsch
conscience *126* Gewissen
consequently *165* infolgedessen
conservation *145* Schutz, Erhaltung
conservative *136* Konservative/r
to consider *53* berücksichtigen
considered: to be considered *62* berücksichtigt werden
consignment *165* (Waren-) Sendung, Lieferung
consolidated shipment *165* gemeinsame Beförderung
constable *143* Wachtmeister/in
constitution *105* Verfassung
constitutional *136* verfassungsgemäß
construction *40* Bau, Bauweise
consumer durables *165* Gebrauchsgüter, langlebige Konsumgüter
consumption *83* Verbrauch, Verzehr
contact *55* Kontakt, Verbindung
to contact *106* Kontakt aufnehmen zu, sich wenden an
to contain *66* enthalten
container ship *73* Containerschiff
containerization *73* (Umstellung auf) Containerverkehr, Verpackung in Container
contaminated *150* verunreinigt, verseucht
contestant *56* Kandidat/in
context *38* Kontext, Zusammenhang
context-sensitive *53* kontextbezogen
continuously *63* ständig
contract *46* (Arbeits-)Vertrag
contradictory *132* widersprüchlich
contrary *150* Gegenteil
to contrast *36* gegenüberstellen
to contribute *43* beitragen
contribution *106* Beitrag, Beihilfe
controversial *43* kontrovers, umstritten
convenience *169* Komfort, Bequemlichkeit
convenient *28* bequem
convention *136* Konvention
conventional *83* herkömmlich, konventionell
to convert *161* umwandeln
converted *73* umgebaut
to convince *127* überzeugen
convincing *150* überzeugend
cookbook *20* Kochbuch
cooperative *131t* kooperativ
co-operative *101t* Kooperative
to coordinate *165* aufeinander abstimmen, koordinieren
coordinator *99* Koordinator/in
core competence *176* Kernkompetenz
corporal punishment *136* körperliche Züchtigung
corporate *93* Firmen-, Konzern-
corporation *156* (Aktien-)Gesellschaft, Kapitalgesellschaft
correspondence *48* Korrespondenz
corruption *110* Korruption
cough medicine *187* Hustensaft
cough syrup *187* Hustensaft
council *106* Rat, Gemeinderat
councillor *71* Ratsmitglied
countable *19* zählbar
counter *16* Tresen, Ladentisch
counterfeit *186* gefälscht, nachgemacht
counterpart *177* Gegenstück, Gegenüber
countless *126* zahllos
county *162* Grafschaft, Bezirk
court case *159* Gerichtsverhandlung
courtesy of *183* dank
coverage *172t* Berichterstattung, Präsenz
craft *99* (Kunst-)Handwerk
crammed *183* gepfercht, vollgestopft
crane *73* Kran
crash *52* Zusammenbruch
to crash *121t* (ab)stürzen
crate *73* (Holz-)Kiste
to crawl *132* kriechen, krabbeln
to create *51t* hervorrufen, erzeugen, wecken
crèche facilities *89* Krippeneinrichtungen
creditor *28* Gläubiger/in
crime rate *43* Kriminalitätsrate
criticism *17* Kritik
crop *149, 175* (Anbau)Pflanze; Ernte
to cross out *38* durchstreichen
cross-border *113* grenzüberschreitend
to cross-breed *149* kreuzen
cross-breeding *152t* Kreuzung
crossing point *134* Übergang(sstelle)
crowded *40* überfüllt
cruel *136* grausam
crust *83* Kruste
cubicle *16* Kabine
cultural *40* kulturell
to culture *191t* kultivieren, züchten
curable *18* heilbar
cure *152t* Heilung, Heilmittel
currency *111* Währung
current account *162* Girokonto
currently *10* zurzeit
curry house *133* indisches Restaurant
custom *118* Brauch
customer relations officer *85* Kundendienstmitarbeiter/in, Kundenbetreuer/in
customer service representative *162* Kundendienstmitarbeiter/in
customs *154* Zoll
customs clearance *165* Zollabfertigung
to cut *49* ausblenden
cut *81t* Kürzung, Senkung
cutting-edge *96* Spitzen-, High-tech-, modern
CV *86* Lebenslauf
to cycle *76* radfahren
cyclist *109t* Fahrradfahrer/in
cyclone *80* Zyklon

D

daddy's boy syndrome *183* Vaters-Sohn-Syndrom
dairy *147* hier: Milchvieh

damage *66* Schaden, Schäden, Sachschaden
to dare *139* (es) wagen
database *53* Datenbank
date: to go on a date *15* eine Verabredung haben
day off *34* freier Tag
dead-end *86* ohne Perspektiven
deadline *165* Liefertermin, Frist
to deal with *32, 93* sich beschäftigen mit, mit jdm zu tun haben; bearbeiten, erledigen
dealer *156* Händler/in
dealing *139* Handel
death penalty *136* Todesstrafe
death toll *187* Todesrate
debit *162* Soll, Lastschrift
debit card *162* Scheck-, Bankkarte
debt *63* Schuld(en)
to deceive *135* betrügen
decent *139* anständig
deck *73* Deck
to decline *47* abnehmen, sinken, zurückgehen
decline *51* Rückgang
decoration *167* Schmuck
to decrease *51* fallen, sinken
dedicated *171* fest zugeordnet
to defend *110* verteidigen
to define *129* (sich) definieren
definite *165* bestimmt
definitely *25* bestimmt, definitiv
definition *7* Definition
to delay *80* aufschieben, hinauszögern
delicious *133* köstlich, lecker
delighted *65* (sehr) erfreut, entzückt
to deliver *68* vermitteln, überbringen
delivery *122* Darbietung; *165* Zustellung, (Aus-)Lieferung
to demand *126* (nach)fragen
dementia *149* Demenz
demo *120* Demo(nstration), Vorführung
demographer *129* Demograph
demonstration *119* Demonstration
dental *191* Zahn-, zahnärztlich
to deny *127* bestreiten
department *107* Abteilung
department store *26* Kauf-, Warenhaus
departure *44* Abfahrt
to depend on *30* abhängen von
to be dependent on *177* abhängig sein von
to deploy *175* einsetzen
to deport *131t* ausweisen, abschieben
depressed *65* deprimiert, niedergeschlagen
depressing *118* bedrückend, deprimierend
deputy *142t* Hilfs-, Vertretungs-
to derive *146* abstammen
desert *80* Wüste
to deserve *137* verdienen
to design *46* entwerfen
desire *51t* Begehren, Verlangen
to despair *99* verzweifeln
desperate *80* verzweifelt
despite *43* trotz
dessert *16* Nachspeise, -tisch
destination *22* (Fahrt-)Ziel
to destroy *69* zerstören, vernichten
destruction *75* Zerstörung, Vernichtung
deterrent *138* abschreckend
developer *46* Entwickler/in
development *69* Entwicklung
device *123* Gerät, Apparat
devout *137* fromm
diabetes *149* Zuckerkrankheit, Diabetes
to diagnose *147* diagnostizieren
dialect *93* Dialekt, Mundart
diametrically opposed *140* diametral entgegengesetzt
diary *183* Tagebuch
diet *135* Ernährung, Diät
diethylene glycol *187* Diäthylenglykol
to differ *41* sich unterscheiden
to dig into *142t* wühlen in
diploma *86* Diplom
direct debit *113* Lastschrift-, Einzugsverfahren
directed at *95* gerichtet auf, abzielend auf
direction *67* Richtung
directory information *162* Telefonauskunft
dirty *16* schmutzig
disabled *123* Behinderte/r
disadvantage: at a disadvantage *31* benachteiligt
to disagree (with) *17* widersprechen, nicht zustimmen
disagreement *50* Widerspruch, Uneinigkeit
disappointed *65* enttäuscht
disaster *75* Katastrophe, Unglück
discount *161* Rabatt, Skonto
to discover *6* entdecken
to discriminate *13* unterscheiden, diskriminieren
discrimination *12* Diskriminierung
discussion *49* Diskussion
disease *97* Krankheit, Erkrankung
disgust *126* Ekel
disgusting *18* ekelhaft
dish *40* Gericht
dishonest *98* unehrlich
disobedience *119* Ungehorsam
to dispatch *167* (aus)liefern, abschicken, aufgeben
display *28* Ausstellung
distant *40* fern
distressed *159* auf alt getrimmt
distribution *165* Vertrieb, (Waren-) Verteilung, (Aus-)Lieferung
diverse *112* verschieden, unterschiedlich
dividend *156* Dividende
division *165* Abteilung
docker *73* Hafenarbeiter/in
documentary *58* Dokumentarbericht, -film
doll *118* Puppe
domestic *131t* in der Familie, häuslich
domestic service *131* Hausangestellte
to dominate *98* dominieren, beherrschen
domination *181* Vorherrschaft
to donate *189* spenden
donut *16* Pfannkuchen, Krapfen
door-to-door *161* von Tür zu Tür
dose *136* Dosis
double life *16* Doppelleben
double-decker *16* Doppeldecker
double-glazing *76* mit Isolierverglasung versehen
doubt *147* Zweifel
downside *152t* Nachteil, Kehrseite
downtown *37* im Stadtzentrum
draft *102* Entwurf
dramatic *84* dramatisch, drastisch
to draw out *162* abheben
to draw up *178* aufstellen, formulieren
drawback *113* Nachteil
dress code *159* Kleiderordnung
dried *104* Trocken-
to drift *86* treiben, zufällig kommen
drink driving *135* Trunkenheit am Steuer
to drive *191t* treiben, schlagen
to drop *49* fallen
to drown in *49* ertränken in
drug abuse *139* Drogenmissbrauch
drum *9* Trommel
drunk driving *(AE) 142t* Trunkenheit am Steuer
dry cleaner's *66* chemische Reinigung
dryer *104* Trockner
due: to be due to *47* darauf zurückzuführen sein
duty *106* Pflicht, Aufgabe
duvet *184* Tagesdecke
dweller *69* Bewohner/in

E

earth: Why on earth? *21* Warum um Himmels willen?
eastern *80* östlich
eating disorder *16* Essstörung
economical *170t* sparsam, wirtschaftlich
economy *80* Wirtschaft
effect *40* Auswirkung
efficient *66* effizient, leistungsfähig
effort *118* Bemühung, Anstrengung
either *58t* hier: beides
elderly *92* älter
to elect *43* wählen
election *74* (politische) Wahl
electricity *69* Elektrizität, Strom
elevator ***(AE)*** *37* Lift
embarrassed *17* verlegen
embarrassing *56* peinlich
embryo *189* Embryo
embryonic *189* embryonal
to emerge *80* heraustreten, hervorkommen, entstehen
emerging market *174* Schwellenmarkt
emission *66* Emission, Ausstoß
emotion *123* Gefühl, Emotion
emotional *116* emotional
to emphasize *62* betonen, hervorheben
employee *89* Arbeitnehmer/in, Beschäftigte/r
employer *8* Unternehmer, Arbeitgeber
employment *88* Arbeit, Beschäftigung, Beruf
to enable *129* (es) ermöglichen, in die Lage versetzen
to encourage *51t* anregen
encyclopedia *39* Lexikon, Enzyklopädie
enemy *124* Feind
energy *40* Energie
to enforce *188* durchsetzen
engine *69* Motor
engineer *69* Ingenieur/in, Techniker/in
enjoyable *36* angenehm
enormous *157* riesig
enquiry *106* Anfrage
to ensure *182* sicherstellen, gewährleisten
to entail *191t* mit sich bringen
to enter *71* hineingehen, -fahren
entertaining *56* unterhaltsam
entertainment *49* Unterhaltung
enthusiasm *107* Begeisterung (-sfähigkeit)
entire *131t* vollkommen, gänzlich
to entitle *156* berechtigen
entrepreneur *158* Unternehmer/in
entry *39* Eintrag
environmental *66* Umwelt-
environmentalist *69* Umweltschützer/in
environmentally friendly *69* umweltfreundlich
epidemic *75* Epidemie
equal *12* Gleichberechtigte/r, Ebenbürtige/r
equipment *95* Ausrüstung, Ausstattung, Einrichtung
equivalent (of) *18* Entsprechung
to escape *49* flüchten
especially *22* besonders, insbesondere
essential *82* notwendig, wesentlich
to establish *113* (be)gründen, einrichten
to estimate *69* schätzen
estuary *121t* Mündung
ethnic *40* ethnisch
ethnicity *129* ethnische Zugehörigkeit
to evaluate *112* einschätzen, bewerten
even *138* gleichmäßig
event *36* Ereignis, Veranstaltung
eventually *70* schließlich, zum Schluss
evidence *17* Beweis, Beleg
to exaggerate *50* übertreiben
exam results *64* Examensnoten
exceptional *147* außergewöhnlich
exchange *64* (Kurz-)Dialog, Austausch
excited *65* aufgeregt, erregt
exclusive *26* exklusiv
execution *136* Hinrichtung
executive *180* leitende/r Angestellte/r, Manager/in
exercise bike *11* Heimtrainer
exhaust *66* Auspuff(rohr)
exhausted *65* erschöpft
to exhibit *158t* ausstellen
exhibition *38* Ausstellung
existing *167t* bestehend, vorhanden
exotic *22* exotisch
to expand *46* expandieren, (sich) ausdehnen, erweitern
expansion *52* Erweiterung, Ausdehnung, Ausweitung
to expect *7* erwarten
expenditure *172t* Ausgabe(n), Kosten
expenses *106* Kosten, Ausgaben
experience *61* Erfahrung
experienced *124* erfahren
experiment *53* Versuch, Experiment
explanation *97* Erklärung
to exploit *56* be-, ausnutzen
to explore *40* erkunden
export sales *88* Exportverkäufe, Auslandsverkäufe
expression *7* Ausdruck
to extend *121t* ausweiten, ausbauen
extended *49* verlängert
extension *121t* Ausbau
extent *65* (Aus-)Maß, Umfang, Grad
extremely *72* äußerst, außerordentlich
eyeliner *143* Eyeliner, Lidstrich

F

fabulous *26* fabelhaft
to face *76* sich gegenübersehen, vor sich haben
face-to-face *156* von Angesicht zu Angesicht, persönlich
facilities *184* Möglichkeiten, Einrichtungen
to fail *49* versagen, scheitern; **to fail sb** *118t* jdn enttäuschen, jdn etwas nicht geben können
failure *40* Versagen
fair trade *103* fairer Handel
fairly *47* ziemlich
fake *186* Fälschung
to fall *43* fallen
fame *56* Ruhm
familiar *16* bekannt
fanatic *126* Fanatiker/in
farewell *25* Abschied
farther *44* weiter
fascination *129* Faszination
fashion-conscious *26* modebewusst
fast-acting *136* schnell wirkend
fatty *18* fetthaltig, fettig
fear *12* Furcht
feasible *134* (praktisch) durchführbar, machbar
feature *28* Eigenschaft
to feature *35* eine Rolle spielen
federal *112* föderal(istisch)
federal government *189* Bundesregierung
fee *106* Gebühr
to feed *152t* ernähren
to feel lost *63* sich verloren fühlen
feminine *13* weiblich
feminist *136* Feministin
fence *132* Zaun
ferry *38* Fähre
to fertilize *189* befruchten
fertilizer *150* Dünger
field trial *152t* Freilandversuch
fifth: a fifth *81* Fünftel
figure *81t* Zahl
filling station *33* Tankstelle
finance *40* Finanzen
financial *22* finanziell
to find the way *63* den Weg finden

fingerprint *153* Fingerabdruck
to fire *181* entlassen
first aider *13* Sanitäter
to fit *30* passen
fit *159* Passform, Sitz
fitted *76* eingebaut
fixed *28* befestigt
flashing banner *53* blinkende Bannerwerbung
flavour *149* Geschmack
flexibility *66* Flexibilität
flick knife *140* Springmesser
to float *158t* an die Börse bringen
to flock *43* strömen
flood *75* Flut, Überschwemmung
to flood *131t* überschwemmen
flow chart *47* Flussdiagramm
fluent *106* fließend, gewandt, flüssig
focus *35* Blickpunkt
to focus on *139* sich konzentrieren auf
foot *120* Fuß
football *14* American Football (*BE:* Fußball)
forbidden *126* verboten
to force *57* zwingen
foreground *132* Vordergrund
foreign exchange *113* Fremdwährung, Devisen
forest *37* Wald
to fork out *183* blechen, berappen
formality *165* Formalität
former *40* früher
formula *51t* Formel
fortunately *29* glücklicherweise
fortune *66* Vermögen
forum *49* Forum
forwarding *165* Versand, Transport
fossil fuel *80* fossiler Brennstoff
foster family *124* Pflegefamilie
to found *103* gründen
foundation *103* Stiftung
founder *53* Gründer/in
fraction *81* Bruch(teil)
frank *110* offen, ehrlich
fraud *135* Betrug, Unterschlagung
fraudster *162* Betrüger/in
free of charge *153* kostenlos, gebührenfrei
free trade zone *187* Freihandelszone
freedom *66* Freiheit
freelance *46* freiberuflich
freely *59* freimütig
to freeze an account *162* ein Konto blockieren
freezer *20* Gefrierschrank
freezing *92* eiskalt, sehr kalt
freight *165* Fracht, Güter
frequency *29* Häufigkeit
frequent *44* häufig
fridge *21* Kühlschrank
fried *127* gebraten, geröstet
frightening *13* beängstigend, erschreckend
fringe benefits *85* zusätzliche Leistungen, freiwillige Sozialleistungen
frontier *110* Grenze
frustrated *65* frustriert
fuel *66* Kraftstoff
fuel cell *169* Brennstoffzelle
fuel consumption *170t* Kraftstoffverbrauch
fuel-efficient *170t* Treibstoff sparend, mit geringem Treibstoffverbrauch
fumes *66* Abgase
fundamentalist *136* fundamentalistisch
funding *189* Finanzierung
fundraising *64* Wohltätigkeitsveranstaltung, Spendensammeln
further *15* weiter
fusion *80* Fusion, Verschmelzung
futuristic-looking *187* futuristisch aussehend

G

to gain *106* sammeln, erlangen, gewinnen
gambling *126* Glücksspiel
gantry *73* Portal(kran)
gas *68* Benzin, Treibstoff
gateway *38t* Tor, Pforte
gender *182* Geschlecht
gender gap *182* Geschlechterfalle
gene *149* Gen
general *9* allgemein
to generate *53* aufbringen, erzielen
generation *31* Generation
generous *89* großzügig
genetically-modified *146* genmanipuliert
genre *58* Genre
gentle *36* freundlich
genuine *16* echt
geography *38t* Lage, Geographie
gesture *128* Geste(n), Gestik
to get a lot out of sth *7* viel davon haben
to get by *31* durchkommen
to get clear of *124* wegkommen von
to get drunk *18* sich betrinken
to get on to *167t* sich in Verbindung setzen mit
to get real *17* die Realität anerkennen
to get sth off one's chest *171* etw loswerden wollen
to get stuck in traffic *173* im Stau stecken
to get the green light *46* grünes Licht erhalten
to get through *172t* durchnehmen
to get used to *37* sich gewöhnen an
to get your hands on *188* erwerben
giant *174* Riese, Gigant
gigantic *114* gigantisch, riesig
glad *13* froh
glamorous *45* glamourös
glass ceiling *180* unsichtbare Beförderungssperre
global *80* global, weltweit
global warming *165* Erderwärmung
globalization *96* Globalisierung
to glow *28* leuchten
glycerine *187* Glyzerin
to go ahead *121t, 172t* vorangehen, vonstatten gehen; fortfahren
to go bankrupt *52* in Konkurs gehen, Pleite gehen
to go for *133* sich entscheiden für
gone are the days *83* vergangen ist die Zeit
good-looking *18* gut aussehend
goods *97* Ware(n), Güter
gorgeous *180* prächtig, großartig
government *66* Regierung
government-backed *189* staatlich subventioniert
governor *134* Gouverneur/in
to grab *171* (er)greifen
grade *14* Note
gradual *51* allmählich, nach und nach
graduate *93* Hochschulabsolvent/in
to graduate *175* einen (Hochschul-) Abschluss machen
gran *63* Oma
grandad *89* Opa
greed *103* Gier, Habsucht
greedy *16* gierig
greeting *38* Begrüßung
gridlock *66* Verkehrskollaps
to grin *16* lächeln, grinsen
grotesque *56* grotesk
groupage consignment *165* Gruppenlieferung
guaranteed *99* garantiert
guard *134* Wache, Wachdienst
to guess *44* raten
guest *81* Gast
to guide *92* führen, leiten
guidebook *39* Reiseführer
guidelines *162* Richtlinien
guilty *16* schuldig
guy *12* Kerl, Typ

H

habit *164* Gewohnheit
habitat *150* Lebensraum
to hack up *142t* zerstückeln
hacker *162* Hacker/in
hairdresser *15* Friseur/in
hairstyle *118* Frisur
to halve *151* (sich) halbieren
ham *19* Schinken
to hand in *30* abgeben
to hand over *172t* übergeben
to handle *93* erledigen, bearbeiten, umgehen mit
to handle sth *180* mit etw umgehen
handout *172t* Merkblatt
to hang around *6* rumhängen
hard sell *50* aggressive Verkaufstechnik
hardly *89* kaum
hardship *179* Not, Mühsal
hardware *19* Hardware, Geräte
harmful *150* schädlich
harsh *126* scharf, harsch
haulier *69* Spediteur, Fuhrunternehmen
to have mass appeal *183* den Massengeschmack treffen
to have no use for *123* keine Verwendung haben für
to have seen better days *171* bessere Tage gesehen haben
havoc: to play havoc *150* verheerende Schäden anrichten
heading *49* Überschrift
headquarters *93* Zentrale, Hauptsitz
headscarf *125* Kopftuch
headset *93* Kopfhörer mit Mikrofon
health care *89* medizinische Versorgung
heart attack *187* Herzinfarkt, -anfall
heart failure *191t* Herzversagen
heart transplant *191t* Herztransplantation
heating *73* Heizung
heavily-armed *139* schwer bewaffnet
hectare *101t* Hektar
height *120* Höhe, Größe
hence *136* daher
herbicide *150* Unkrautvernichtungsmittel
herd *147* Herde
hereditary *145* erblich
heritage *115* Erbe, Herkunft
hidden *181* verborgen
hierarchy *180* Hierarchie
high *124* high, auf Drogen
high-end *176* für gehobene Ansprüche
high-flying *180* erfolgreich
hill *69* Hügel, Berg
to hire sb/sth *52* ein-/anstellen, mieten, anheuern
hi-tech *123* technisch hochentwickelt
hold *12* Griff
hold *73* Lade-, Frachtraum
to hold back *175* zurückhalten
to hold down *81t* niedrig halten
Hold your horses! *172t* Immer sachte mit den jungen Pferden!
holiday resort *158* Urlaubsort
homeless: the homeless *7* die Obdachlosen
homicide *141* Tötung, Mord
homosexual *127* Homosexuelle/r
honest *28* ehrlich
to host *123* moderieren
host country *187* Gastland
household appliance *166* Haushaltsgerät
household name *159* bekannter Begriff, Markenname
housemate *57* Mitbewohner/in
housewife *181* Hausfrau
huge *37* gewaltig
hulk *12* Kerl wie ein Baum
Human Resources *48* Personal(abteilung)
humane *131t* human
humanitarian *131* humanitär
humanoid *123* menschenähnlich(e Figur)
hunter *132* Jäger/in
hurricane *55* Orkan, Wirbelsturm
hybrid *69, 170t* hybrid; Hybrid(fahrzeug)
hydroelectric *80* hydroelektrisch
hydrogen *69* Wasserstoff

I

ice-hockey *13* Eishockey
ID *91t* Ausweis
ideal *65* ideal
to identify *100* herausfinden
identity *59* Identität
idiom *67* Idiom, Redewendung
idiomatic *67* idiomatisch
illegal *67* verboten, illegal
illiterate *175* ungebildet, des Lesens unkundig
to illustrate *90* illustrieren, veranschaulichen
imitation *186* Nachahmung
immediate *51t* umgehend, sofort
immigrant *39* Einwanderer/ Einwanderin
to immigrate *41* einwandern
impact *43* (Aus-)Wirkung, Einfluss
to imply *151* andeuten, implizieren
to impose *141* auferlegen, erlassen
to impress *12* imponieren
impression *13* Eindruck
imprisonment *138* Haft, Gefängnis(strafe)
to improve *66* verbessern, besser werden
in agony *187* unter heftigen Schmerzen
in instalments *63* ratenweise
in one respect *187* in einer Hinsicht
in search of *177* auf der Suche nach
in the comfort of your own home *171* bequem zu Hause
in the daytime *93* tagsüber
in the form of *156* in Form von
in the space of *172t* im Zeitraum von
in view of *168* angesichts
inability *118* Unfähigkeit
incentive *168* Anreiz
inch *184* Zoll
incidence *139* Vorkommen, Häufigkeitsrate
incident *128* Vorfall, Ereignis
incl *93* einschließlich
including *40* einschließlich, inbegriffen, darunter
inclusion *122* Einbeziehung
income *70* Einkommen
incorporated *167* (als Kapital-gesellschaft) eingetragen
to increase *31* ansteigen, zunehmen
increase *81t* Anstieg
increasing *13* zunehmend, steigend
independent *85* unabhängig
indirectness *92* Indirektheit
industrial *80* industriell
industrialized country *166* Industriestaat
industry *41* Industrie
infamous *43* berüchtigt
infection *147* Entzündung
inflation *177* Inflation
to influence *50* beinflussen
informative *41* informativ
infrastructure *97* Infrastruktur
ingredient *103* Bestandteil, Zutat
to inject *191t* (ein)spritzen
injection *136* Spritze, Injektion
to injure *12* verletzen
injury *13* Verletzung
injustice *103* Ungerechtigkeit, Unrecht
innovative *47* innovativ
input *53, 118t* Eingabe; hier: Aufwendung, Hingabe
to inquire *134* fragen, sich erkundigen
insane *137* geisteskrank
instability *102* Instabilität

to install *101t* installieren
installation *165* Installation, Auf-, Einbau
instance: for instance *126* zum Beispiel
instead of *8* statt, anstatt (von)
instructor *85* Lehrer/in, Ausbilder/in
insulation *76* Isolierung
insulted *182* beleidigt,empört
to integrate *111* sich integrieren
intense *36* intensiv
to interact *149* sich gegenseitig beeinflussen
interactive *55* interaktiv
interference *110* Einmischung
intermarriage *129* Mischehe
intern *106* Praktikant/in, Volontär/in
internet connection *53* Internetanschluss, -verbindung
internship *106* Volontariat
to interview *31* interviewen
to introduce *148* einführen
to invent *40* erfinden
invention *43* Erfindung
to invest *89* investieren
invisible *181* unsichtbar
to involve *106* einschließen, beinhalten
involvement *141* Beteiligung
ironing *15* Bügeln
irregular *85* unregelmäßig
irresponsible *29* unverantwortlich
island *40* Insel
isolated *114* isoliert
issue *84* Frage, Thema, Anliegen
IT *88t* Informationstechnologie
IT officer *88t* EDV-Techniker/in
IT technician *85* Informationstechniker/in

J

to jam *175* verstopfen
jar *19* (Einmach)Glas
jet-colored *129* pechschwarz
jetliner *183* Düsenflugzeug
job description *93* Stellenbeschreibung
job loss *176* Arbeitsplatzverlust
job security *176* Arbeitsplatzsicherheit
job-related *31* beruflich
to join *51t* beitreten, sich anmelden
joint *156* gemeinsam
joke *173* Witz, Scherz
to joke: Are you joking? *7* Ist das dein Ernst?
journalist *76* Journalist/in
journey *46* Reise, Fahrt
to jump the queue *153* sich vordrängeln
junction *78* Kreuzung
junior *44* untergeordnet
justice *139* Gerechtigkeit

K

keen *162* (sehr) interessiert
to keep: How have you been keeping? *94* Wie geht es dir?
to keep in touch with *28* in Verbindung bleiben
kettle *185* (Wasser-)Kessel
keyboard *61* Tastatur
to kick in *170t* (sich) einschalten
kid *62* Kind
kit *189* Ausstattung
to knock down *121t* abreißen
knowledge *19* Wissen

L

label *26* Label, Marke
labelling *147* Kennzeichnung
labour force *177* Arbeitskräfte
labour market *133* Arbeitsmarkt
labour-intensive *73* arbeitsintensiv
lake *38t* (Binnen-)See
landline *109* Festnetz(leitung)
large print *123* Großdruck
large-scale *42* in großer Zahl
latest *55* neueste, letzte
to launch *46* einführen, starten
law-abiding *131t* gesetzestreu
lawyer *112* (Rechts-)Anwalt/ Anwältin
leader *80* Führer/in
leading *51t* führend
leaflet *45* Broschüre, Flugblatt
to lean on *118t* sich lehnen an
to leap *172t* springen; sprunghafter Anstieg
least: at least *15* mindestens
lecture *180* Vortrag
LED *123* LED-Anzeige
legal *57* legal
legal action *156* rechtliche Schritte
legal entity *156* juristischeeinheit
legible *57* leserlich
legislative *110* gesetzgebend
leisure centre *15* Freizeitzentrum
length *44* Länge, Dauer
lesson: to teach sb a lesson *13* jdm eine Lektion erteilen
lethal *136* tödlich
letter of appointment *91t* Bewerbungsschreiben
letter of credit *161* Akkreditiv, Kreditbrief
level *80* Niveau, Stand
to level out *172t* abflachen
liable *156* haftbar
liar *142t* Lügner/in
liberal *137* Liberale/r
library *55* Bücherei, Bibliothek
licence *106* Führerschein
to lie *60* lügen
life expectancy *123* Lebenserwartung
lifestyle *76* Lebensstil
lift: to give a lift *24* mit dem Auto mitnehmen
to light *132* anzünden
to lighten up *49* aufheitern
limitless *131t* grenzenlos, uneingeschränkt
line manager *171* Vorgesetzte/r, Chef/in
lining *187* Innenfutter
to link *27* verbinden
liquid *83* flüssig
listener *98* Zuhörer/in
literally *118t* buchstäblich, (wort)wörtlich
lively *49* lebhaft
living expenses *22* Lebenshaltungskosten
to load *73* verladen
loads *30* eine Menge
loaf *19* (Laib) Brot
loan *158* Kredit, Darlehen
lobby *150* Lobby, Interessengruppe
to locate *63* orten
location *43* (Stand-)Ort, Lage
to log *171* registrieren, aufzeichnen
to log on *167t* einloggen
logging *119* Abholzung
logical *57* logisch
logistics *165* Logistik, Auslieferung
long-running *56* mit langer Laufzeit
to look round *7* sich umsehen
loophole *146* Schlupfloch
loose *159* weit (geschnitten), lose
to loosen *126* lockern
to lose control over *16* die Beherrschung verlieren
loss *157* Verlust
lovely *26* hübsch
low-cost *89* Niedriglohn-
low-energy *76* Niedrigenergie-, Spar-
to lower *73* herablassen
low-lying *80* tief gelegen
low-wage *159* Niedriglohn-, Billiglohn-
luck *114* Glück
lucky: to be lucky *8* Glück haben
luggage *19* Gepäck
lunchtime *15* Mittagspause
lung *147* Lunge

M

machinery *78* Maschine(n), Gerät
madness *55* Wahnsinn
magical *40* magisch
maid *178* Dienstmädchen

mailbox *63* Anrufbeantworter
mail-order catalogue *26* Versandhauskatalog
mainstream *119* vorherrschend(e Meinung)
to maintain *149* aufrechterhalten
maintenance *170t* Wartung
major *72* groß, größer
to make a contribution *173* einen Beitrag leisten
to make a living *133* den Lebensunterhalt verdienen
to make a point *172t* etw dazu sagen
to make up *12* bilden
to make up for *81t* ausgleichen
makeover *171* Neugestaltung
mammal *147* Säugetier
to manage *11, 113* zurechtkommen, (es) schaffen; verwalten
manipulation *149* Manipulation, Veränderung
mankind *159* Menschheit
man-made *41* von Menschenhand
manual worker *159* Handwerker, körperliche/r Arbeiter/in
to manufacture *69* herstellen, produzieren
manufacturer *159* Hersteller/in, Produzent/in, Fabrikant/in
manure *83* Dung, Dünger
march *119* (Protest-)Marsch
to marinate *133* marinieren
marital status *108* Familienstand
mark *9* Note
market segment *158t* Marktsegment
marketing *91* Marketing, Vertrieb
mass tourism *43* Massentourismus
massive *136* massiv, enorm
mass-produced *159* in Massenproduktion hergestellt
mast *151* Mast
master cell *189* Grundzelle
mat *12* Matte
matching *159* (zueinander) passend
mate *10* Kumpel
materialist *127* Materialist/in
maternity leave *89* Mutterschaftsurlaub
matter *76* Sache, Ding, Angelegenheit
to matter *87* von Bedeutung sein
matter: as a matter of fact *91t* um genau zu sein
matter: What's the matter with ...? *18* Was ist los mit ...?
mayor *43* Bürgermeister/in
means of transport *165* Beförderungs-, Verkehrsmittel
meantime: in the meantime *26* inzwischen

mechanically *73* mechanisch
media hype *152t* Medienrummel
to mediate *128* vermitteln
medical *17* medizinisch
medical support *93* medizinische Hilfe
medium *59* Medium
to meet needs *76* Bedürfnisse decken
to melt *80* schmelzen
melting pot *40* Schmelztiegel
membership *51t* Mitgliedschaft
memorable *68* unvergesslich, einprägsam
menswear *158t* Herrenbekleidung
mental *17* mental
mental illness *143* Geisteskrankheit
to mention *50* erwähnen; **don't mention it** *31* gern geschehen
mentor *180* Mentor/in
merciless *139* unbarmherzig
merit *182* Verdienst(e)
to mess up *88t* es verderben, es verpeilen
message *68* Botschaft
microchip *95* Mikrochip
micro-organism *149* Mikroorganismus
microphone *137* Mikrophon
microwave *54* Mikrowelle
Middle Ages *49* Mittelalter
middle management *182* mittleres Management
middlemen *99* Zwischenhändler
migrant worker *177* Wanderarbeiter/in
migration *111* Wanderung(sbewegung)
mild *133* mild
mile *67* Meile
to mind: Do you mind if ...? *109t* Haben Sie etwas dagegen, wenn ...?
minimum wage *177* Mindestlohn
minister *66* Minister/in
minor *118t* geringfügig
minority *130* Minderheit
miscarriage *147* Fehlgeburt
miserable *127* kläglich
misleading *110* irreführend
to miss out on *118t* verpassen
missing *13* fehlend
misunderstanding *32* Missverständnis
mixture *75* Mischung
MMS *63* multimediale Nachricht per Mobiltelefon
mobile *63* Handy, Mobiltelefon
mobility *123* Beweglichkeit, Mobilität
mommy track *182* Mutterschaftsschiene

to monitor *93* überwachen, kontrollieren
monotonous *126* monoton
monthly *69* monatlich
moral *57* moralisch
moreover *80* außerdem, zudem
mortality *191* Todesfall
motherly *118t* mütterlich
motive *143* Motiv, Beweggrund
motor *69* Motor
motorway *67* Autobahn
move: on the move *65* unterwegs
movement *69* Bewegung
movies *6* Kino
mph *170* m/h (Meilen pro Stunde)
mule *149* Maultier, -esel
multiculturalism *125* Multikulturalismus
multiracial *129* ethnisch gemischt
murder *136* Mord
muscle *12* Muskel
mushroom *127* Pilz
musician *115* Musiker/in
mustard *19* Senf
must-have item *63* was man unbedingt haben muss
my heart was in my mouth *183* das Herz schlug mir bis zum Hals
myth *118t* Legende

N

nail polish *118t* Nagellack
nail varnish *143* Nagellack
to name and shame *180* namentlich verurteilen
nanny *131t* Kindermädchen
narrow *184* eng, schmal
nasty *12* gemein
nationwide *141* landesweit
native *178* Heimat-
Native American *131* Indianer/in, indianisch
natural gas *83* Erdgas
natural resources *174* Bodenschätze, natürliche Ressourcen
neat *102* ordentlich, sauber
necessarily: not necessarily *8* nicht unbedingt
need: in need *55* bedürftig
needle *124* Nadel
negotiation *106* Verhandlung
nepotism *139* Vetternwirtschaft
nervous *65* nervös
nervous breakdown *117* Nervenzusammenbruch
net *6* Internet
netiquette *62* Netiquette, Umgangsformen (im Internet)
to network *7* vernetzen
neutral *129* neutral
to neutralize *93* neutralisieren

new lease on life *191t* neue Lebensqualität
newly *40* kürzlich
newsletter *55* Rundschreiben, (Info-)Blatt
next door *12* nebenan
niche *191* Nische
nickname *140* Spitzname
nightmare *37* Albtraum
nonsense *114* Unsinn
Nordic *129* nordisch
not ... either *21* auch nicht
to not be able to help *16* nicht umhin können
note *113* (Bank-)Note, (Geld-)Schein
novel *39* Roman
now and then *29* ab und zu
nuclear *80* Atom-
nucleus *147* Kern
nurse *119* Krankenschwester, -pfleger/in
nursery *66* Kindertagesstätte, Kita
nutritional *149* Nähr-

O

to obey *150* befolgen
objection to *32* Ablehnung gegenüber
obsolete *73* veraltet
obviously *29* offensichtlich
occasional *28* gelegentlich
occupation *133* Beruf, Tätigkeit
off: to be off *91t* losgehen
offence *140* Straftat, Vergehen, Delikt
office block *114* Bürogebäude, -hochhaus
office-based *85* im Büro, bürogebunden
official *71* Beamter/Beamtin
offline *59* offline, nicht im Internet
to offload *99* weitergeben
offshore *83* vor der Küste; ins/im Ausland
offspring *146* Nachkommen
old boy's club *180* Altherrenklub
old people's home *33* Seniorenheim
old-fashioned *72* altmodisch, veraltet
omission *147* Lücke
on board *73* an Bord
on moral grounds *189* aus moralischen Gründen
on the basis of *182* auf der Basis von, aufgrund
once in a while *118t* dann und wann
one-sided *50* einseitig
to open up *158t* eröffnen
to operate *85* betreiben
operator *108* Veranstalter/in
opponent *13* Gegner/in
opportunity *96* Chance, Möglichkeit, Gelegenheit
opposed: to be opposed to sth *136* gegen etw sein
opposition *73* Widerstand
to opt out *114* austreten, aussteigen
oral *87* mündlich
order *8* Reihenfolge
ordinary *11* gewöhnlich, normal
ore *166* Erz
organ *147* Organ
organism *149* Organismus
organized crime *43* organisierte Kriminalität
organizer *63* elektronischer Kalender
origin *165* Ursprung, Herkunft
original *78* original, ursprünglich
otherwise *17* sonst, ansonsten
ought to *58* sollte/n
to be out on your ear *171* rausfliegen
out-dated *130* überholt, veraltet
outdoor *179* im Freien
outdoor clothing *109t* Wanderbekleidung
outdoors *85* draußen, im Freien
outgoing *106* kontaktfreudig
outline *148* Umriss
to outline *87* umreißen, skizzieren
to outnumber *130* übertreffen
to outsource *165* auslagern
to overcome *18* überwinden
overdose *124* Überdosis
overly *118t* übermäßig
overseas workers *178* ausländische Arbeiter
overtime *96* Überstunden
to owe *80* verdanken, schulden
owner *69* Besitzer/in
oxygen *69* Sauerstoff

P

PA *47* persönliche/r Assistent/in
packer *178* Packer/in
packet *16* Schachtel, Packung, Tüte
paid *85* bezahlt
painless *136* schmerzlos
paint *19* Farbe
pallet *73* Palette
panel *45* hier: Spalte, Fläche
to panic *21* in Panik geraten
papers *177* (Ausweis-)Papiere
paradise *127* Paradies
parcel *92* Paket
parking space *185* Parkplatz, Parklücke
participant *173* Teilnehmer/in
particular *36* bestimmt, speziell, besonders
partnership *158t* Partnerschaft
part-time job *7* Teilzeitjob
part-timer *34* Teilzeitarbeiter/in
to pass *49* weitergegeben werden
to pass on *143* weitergeben
passenger *66* Fahrgast
passion *137* Leidenschaft, Emotion
paternity leave *89* Vaterschaftsurlaub
path *78* Pfad, Weg
patience *135* Geduld
to pay attention to *60* beachten, achten auf
pay-as-you-go *63* mit Karte, vorausbezahlt
paycheck *96* Gehalt(sscheck), Gehaltszahlung
payment *104* Bezahlung
peace *105* Frieden
to peak *43* den Höhepunkt erreichen, gipfeln
to pearl dive *180* gezielt suchen
peer group *115* Gleichaltrige, Clique
peer group pressure *143* Gruppendruck
pen *88t* Stift
penalty *11* Strafstoß
penniless *158* mittellos
pension *139* Rente, Pension
per capita *82* pro Kopf
percentage *81* Prozentsatz
perfect *57* vollkommen
permanent *7* ständig, dauerhaft
permission *165* Erlaubnis, Genehmigung
perplexed *127* perplex, verblüfft
personal space *98* Distanzzone, Abstand zwischen Personen
personality *56* Persönlichkeit
personally *72* persönlich
perspective *36* Perspektive, Ansicht
to persuade *71* überzeugen, überreden
pesticide *150* Schädlingsbekämpfungsmittel
petrochemicals *147* Petrochemikalien
petrol *8* Benzin
pharmaceutical *190* pharmazeutisch
phenomenal *14* phänomenal
phrase *17* Wendung, Ausdruck
physical *113* physisch
physician *191t* (praktische/r) Arzt/Ärztin
to pick fruit *22* Obst pflücken
to pick up *58t* abholen
picker *99* Pflücker/in
pickup *168* Pritschenwagen
pillow *184* Kopfkissen
to pioneer *168* entwickeln

pirate *58* Pirat
to pirate *186* raubkopieren, unerlaubt nachmachen
pitch *46* anbieten, anpreisen
pitch *83* Platz, (Spiel-)Feld
pity: it's a pity *58* es ist schade
pix (pictures) *63* Bilder
to place *53* aufgeben
placement *49* (Produkt-)Werbung
to plague *43* plagen
plain clothes *143* Zivilkleidung
to be plain sailing *171* ganz einfach sein
planner *15* (Termin-)Kalender
plant *83* Anlage, Werk, Betrieb
play on words *51t* Wortspiel
pleasant *13* angenehm
plentiful *83* reichlich (vorhanden)
plenty of *20* viel(e)
to plot a graph *172* eine Grafik anlegen/aufzeichnen
point of view *58* Standpunkt, Ansicht
poisonous *149* giftig
police officer *19* Polizeibeamter/beamtin
policing *141* Kontrolle, Überwachung
policy *43* (praktische) Politik, Linie
to polish *116* polieren, putzen
polite *62* höflich
pollination *151* Bestäubung
pollution *66* (Umwelt)Verschmutzung
popular press *56* Boulevardpresse
pop-up ad *45* Internet-Anzeige
port *73* Hafen
to pose *129* posieren, darstellen
position *29* Stellung
possibility *81* Möglichkeit
posting *63* Posting, Leserbrief im Internet
potential *46, 152t* potentiell; Potenzial
pound *113* Pfund (Sterling)
poverty *81t* Armut
poverty line *179* Armutsgrenze
to power *70* antreiben, betreiben
power station *69* Kraftwerk
powerful *119* mächtig, stark
ppm *80* Teile pro Million
practical *106* praktisch
practice *73* Methode, Vorgehensweise
to practise *11* üben
precarious *99* unsicher, prekär
precisely *13* genau
to predict *169* vorhersagen
predictable *149* voraussagbar
preferable *93* vorzuziehen
preferred stock *156* Vorzugsaktie
premature *147* vorzeitig, frühzeitig
to premiere *158t* uraufführen, vorstellen
premises *167t* Gelände, Räumlichkeiten
present: at present *10* gegenwärtig
presentation *51* Vorstellung, Präsentation
presenter *38* Moderator/in
pressure *88* Druck
pretty soon *37* sehr bald
to prevent *80* verhindern, verhüten
previous *76* vorher(gehend)
price elastic *183* preislich variabel
price tag *160* Preisschild
priest *119* Priester/in, Geistliche/r
prime time *172t* Hauptsendezeit
princely sum *183* fürstlicher Betrag
princess *12* Prinzessin
principle *136* Prinzip
prison *135* Gefängnis
privacy *66* Privatsphäre
private *13* privat, persönlich
probation *141* Bewährung
procedure *73* Verfahren
to proceed *163* vorgehen
process *47* Prozess, Vorgang
procurement *165* Beschaffung
producer *56* Produzent/in, Erzeuger
product placement *45* Schleichwerbung
production *69* Produktion, Herstellung
production facility *166* Produktionsstätte
profile *53* Profil, Ansicht, Herkunft, Berufsbild
profit *56* Profit, Gewinn
profitable *43* gewinnbringend, rentabel
progress *76* Fortschritt/e
promising *83* vielversprechend
to promote *45* fördern
promotion *160* Werbung, Marketing
prompt *109* unverzüglich, zügig
to pronounce *183* aussprechen
proper *22* richtig, geeignet, korrekt, ordentlich
property *135* Eigentum
proportion *121* Teil, Verhältnis
to prosecute *139* anklagen, strafrechtlich verfolgen
prospect *89* Aussicht
prosperity *105* Wohlstand
prostitute *127* Prostituierte/r
proud *13* stolz
to prove *83* sicherweisen als
proverb *183* Sprichwort
to provide *106* (an)bieten, sorgen für, zur Verfügung stellen
provider *59* Anbieter
psychiatric *118* psychiatrisch
psychological *56* psychologisch
psychology *56* Psychologie
pub *10* Kneipe
public *55* öffentlich
public good *103* das öffentliche Wohl
public school *12* staatliche Schule
publicity *85* Öffentlichkeitsarbeit
to publish *154* veröffentlichen, herausgeben
to pull one's weight *171* sich voll einsetzen
to pull oneself together *17* sich zusammenreißen
to pump *189* pumpen
punch line *142* Pointe
punctuation *62* Zeichensetzung, Interpunktion
punishment *29* Strafe, Bestrafung
purchase *26* (Ein-)Kauf
pure *26* rein
to push up *88t* ausbauen, hochtreiben
pushy *26* aufdringlich
to put down *88t* anzahlen
to put forward *58* vorbringen, zur Diskussion stellen
to put on weight *16* zunehmen
puzzled *142t* verdutzt

Q

qualification *8* Qualifikation, Ausbildung
quality *26* Qualität
quantity *20* Menge, Quantität
quarter *175* Vierteljahr, Quartal
query *106* Frage, Rückfrage
question: to be out of the question *177* nicht in Frage kommen
questionnaire *30* Fragebogen
queue *19* (Warte-)Schlange
to queue *153* anstehen, sich anstellen
quota *182* Quote
quota system *134* Quotensystem
quotation *35* Zitat

R

to race *69* sich ein Wettrennen liefern
rack *32* Ständer
radiation *151* Strahlung
radical *140* radikal
radio frequency *153* Funkfrequenz
radio station *177* Radiosender
rage *128* Wut, Zorn
to raise *51t, 55, 156* wecken; sammeln; aufbringen
range *62, 168* Reihe, Spektrum; Reichweite
to rank *175* einstufen, -ordnen

ransom *135* Lösegeld
rape *139* Vergewaltigung
rapid *51* rapide, schnell
rare *9* selten
to rate *170t* einstufen
rather *42* lieber, eher
raw material *50* Rohstoff
to react *55* reagieren
reality *65* Wirklichkeit
reality TV *56* Reality TV
to realize one's potential *43* seine Möglichkeiten verwirklichen
really something *37* toll, beeindruckend
reasonable *85* vernünftig
reborn *96* wiedergeboren
to recap *121t* rekapitulieren, zusammenfassen
receipt *104* Eingang, Erhalt
to receive *38* empfangen
recently *33* kürzlich, neulich
receptionist *85* Empfangsdame, -chef
recharging *168* Lade-
recipe *153* (Koch-)Rezept
to recognize *49* erkennen
to recommend *110* empfehlen
recommendation *111* Empfehlung
to record *15* aufzeichnen
records *167t* Unterlagen, Akten
recovery *40* Erholung
to recruit *133* einstellen, rekrutieren
Red Cross *7* Rotes Kreuz
to redevelop *96* erneuern, neu entwickeln
to reduce *61* reduzieren, verringern
reduction *71* Verringerung, Senkung
redundant *86* arbeitslos
to refer to *8* sich beziehen auf
referee *108* Referenzgeber/in
reference *106* Zeugnis
referendum *114* Volksentscheid
to reflect *129* widerspiegeln
reformed *137* gebessert
refugee *55* Flüchtling
to refund *162* zurückzahlen, erstatten
to refuse *16* ablehnen, sich weigern, widerstehen
regarding *108* bezüglich, betreffend
to regenerate *189* erneuern
regeneration *189* Regeneration
to register *139* registrieren
registered *121* registriert, eingetragen
registration papers *142t* Papiere, Zulassung
to regret *171* bedauern, bereuen
regulation *187* Verordnung, Vorschrift
rehabilitation *138* Rehabilitation
to reintroduce *138* wiedereinführen
to reject *105* ablehnen
rejected *116* abgelehnt
to relate to *100* sich beziehen auf
relationship *38* Verhältnis
relatively *110* verhältnismäßig
relaxed *65* entspannt, locker
relevant *57* relevant, wichtig
reliable *28* zuverlässig
to be reliant on *133* angewiesen sein auf
to rely on *99* angewiesen sein auf, sich verlassen auf
to remain *51* bleiben
remark *57* Bemerkung
reminder function *63* Erinnerungsfunktion
remorse *137* Reue
remote control *184* Fernbedienung
renewable *69* erneuerbar
to rent *38t* mieten
rent *177* Miete
repair *170t* Reparatur
to repay *28* zurückzahlen
repentant *137* reuig, reumütig
repetition *82* Wiederholung
to rephrase *82* anders ausdrücken, umformulieren
to replace *8* ersetzen
reply *92* Antwort, Erwiderung, Reaktion
report *76* Bericht, Reportage
repugnant *136* widerlich
reputation *177* Ruf
to request *78* anfordern, bitten (um)
request *107* Bitte, Aufforderung, Wunsch
to require *13* erfordern
required *82* erforderlich
to be required to *96* müssen
requirement *12* Erfordernis
to rescue *96* retten
research *19* Forschung
research and development (R&D) *156* Forschung und Entwicklung
researcher *59* Forscher/in
residence *183* Wohnsitz
resident *190* Bewohner/in
to resist *140* Widerstand leisten gegen, sich etw widersetzen
resort *85* Erholungsort
resource *89* Reserve, Ressource
to respond to *82* reagieren auf
respondent *130* Befragte/r
responsibility *88* Verantwortung, Verantwortlichkeit
restatement *102* Neuformulierung
restriction *178* Einschränkung
result *71* Resultat, Ergebnis
to retail *158t* verkaufen
retail outlet *166* Einzelhandelsgeschäft
retailer *29* Einzelhändler/in
to retire *117* in Rente/Pension gehen
retired *89* pensioniert, im Ruhestand
retirement *191t* Ruhestand, Pensionierung
retribution *138* Vergeltung
return *74* (hin und) zurück
to return to *173* zurückkehren zu
reunion *59* Treffen, Wiedersehen
revelation *146* Enthüllung
revenue *53* Einkünfte, Einnahmen, Gewinn
to review *172t* zusammenfassen
revision *94* Wiederholung
revolution *80* Revolution
revolutionary *73* revolutionär
to reward *131t* belohnen
to rewrite *78* umschreiben, neu schreiben
rhetorical *82* rhetorisch
ride *38t* Tour, Fahrt, Flug
ring tone *63* Klingelton
to rip *159* (zer)reißen
to rise *43* (an)steigen
rise *81t* An-, Aufstieg
rising *180* aufsteigend
risk: at risk *59* gefährdet
rival *12* Gegner/in, Rivale, -lin
to rival *13* konkurrieren
road: to go down a road *16* etwas erleben
robbery *139* Raub, Überfall
robotics *123* Robotik, Automatisierung
to rocket *169* kräftig (an)steigen
role *15* Rolle
role model *115* Vorbild
Roman *56* Römer/in
room: to have room *20* Platz haben
rope *119* Seil, Tau
rotten *139* korrupt
roughly *36* ungefähr
route *67* Route, Strecke, Weg
routine *85* Routine, Ablauf
routinely *136* routinemäßig
row *28* Reihe
rowdy *127* laut, randalierend
to rub *118t* reiben
to rule *136* entscheiden
to run out of *76* ausgehen
to run up debts *26* sich verschulden, Schulden anhäufen
runner-up *121* Zweite/r
running total *153* (End-)Summe, Gesamtpreis
running water *179* fließendes Wasser

runway *121t, 158t* Landebahn; Laufsteg
rural *36* ländlich
rush hour *69* Hauptverkehrszeit, Berufsverkehr

S

to sack *96* entlassen, feuern
sacred *191* heilig
safety measure *164* Sicherheitsmaßnahme
sake: for sb's sake *131t* um jds willen
salary *85* Gehalt, Lohn
sale *29* Schlussverkauf
sales *26* Verkaufs-
sales figures *54* Verkaufszahlen
salesman *65* Verkäufer
salesperson *85* Verkaufs-mitarbeiter/in, Verkäufer/in
saloon *170t* Limousine
sari *125* Sari (Kleidungsstück)
satellite *69* Satellit
satire *58* Satire
satnav *69* Satellitennavigation, Navi
saucer *185* Untertasse
saving *66* Einsparung, Ersparnis
to scan *36* überfliegen, absuchen
to scan in *153* einscannen
scandalous *144* skandalös
scarcity *111* Knappheit
scary *37* unheimlich, beängstigend
sceptical *28* skeptisch
to schedule *167t* einplanen
scheduled flight *184* Linienflug
scheme *180* Plan, Projekt
scholarship *183* Stipendium
school-leaver *25* Schulabgänger/in
schoolwork *7* Hausaufgaben
schoolyard *118t* Schulhof
sci-fi *58* Science-Fiction, wissenschaftlich-utopisch
to score a goal *8* ein Tor erzielen
to scream *16* schreien
screen *53* Bildschirm
to screen *56* ausstrahlen
sea level *83* Meeresspiegel
to seal *73* verschließen, versiegeln
to seal off *134* absperren, abriegeln
search engine *53* Suchmaschine
seaside *85* Bade-, Strand-, See-
seasonal *85* Saison-
second-hand *27* gebraucht
to be second in line *156* nachgeordnet sein
secret *16* geheim
secretarial course *86* Sekretariatskurs
sector *106* Sektor, Bereich
secure *64* sicher
security *73* Sicherheit
security check *38t* Sicherheitskontrolle
seed *139* Samen(korn)
to seek *99* suchen
to be seen as *63* gesehen werden als
segregation *129* Rassentrennung
seldom *9* selten
selfish *131t* egoistisch
self-repair *189* Selbstheilung
to sell out *158t* ausverkaufen
seminar *171* Seminar, Fachtagung
senior *37* Schüler/in im letzten Schuljahr
sense *40* Sinn, Gefühl
to sense *173* wahrnehmen
sense: to make no sense *59* nicht sinnvoll sein
sensible *31* vernünftig
sensitive *98* empfindlich
separate *146* getrennt
sequence *35* Episode, Sequenz
series *56* Serie
to serve *11* servieren
service *44* (Bus-/Zug-)Verbindung
session *12* Treffen, Termin
to set a trend *159* einen Trend starten
to set foot in *35* betreten
to set its sights on *133* den Blick richten auf
to set to work *12* ans Werk gehen
to set up *47* begründen, einrichten, gründen
set: to be set in *75* spielen in
setting *128* Szenerie, Schauplatz
several *25* mehrere, einige
severe *80* ernst, schwer, stark
shade *119* Schattierung
to shake *98* schütteln
share *156* Anteil
shareholder *99* Aktionär/in
sharp *51* rasch, schnell, stark
sheet *80, 184* Platte, Decke; (Bett-) Laken
shelf *31* Regal
shelf life *149* Haltbarkeit
shelf-stacker *33* Regalauffüller/in
shift *93* Schicht
to shine *40* glänzen
to ship *131t* verschiffen, transportieren
shipping *161* Versand, Fracht
shiver *12* Zittern
shock: to be in shock *171* schockiert sein
to shock bomb *180* schockieren
shocked *65* schockiert
shoplifter *29* Ladendieb/in
shoplifting *29* Ladendiebstahl
shopping mall *38* Einkaufszentrum
shopping trolley *26* Einkaufswagen
shore *40* Ufer
short of breath *191t* außer Atem
to be short of cash *186* knapp bei Kasse sein
shortage *152* Knappheit, Mangel
shortage of *133* Mangel an
to shorten *61* (ver)kürzen
shortlisted *48* in der engeren Wahl
to shrink *130* schrumpfen, zurückgehen
to shut up *62* den Mund halten
signature *167t* Unterschrift
silk *26* Seide
silver market *123* Silbermarkt
simile *82* Vergleich
since *31* seit
single-issue agenda *122* Ein-Themen-, auf ein Thema beschränkte Tagesordnung
to sink *16* sinken
to sit back *30* sich zurückhalten, sich zurücklehnen
site *26* Website
skill *7* Fähigkeit, Geschick
skilled *176* ausgebildet, Fach-
skint *88t* pleite
skyline *37* Silhouette
skyscraper *37* Wolkenkratzer
slave *96* Sklave/Sklavin
sleepy *41* müde
to slide *139* (ab)rutschen, (ab)sacken
slight *47* leicht
slot *47* Termin
to smash *180* zertrümmern, durchbrechen
to snort *124* sniffen, schnupfen
to soar *53* steil/stark ansteigen
social life *30* Sozialkontakte
social services *117* Sozialamt, Sozialdienste
social worker *124* Sozialarbeiter/in
soft drink *64* alkoholfreies Getränk
soft sell *50* zurückhaltende Verkaufstechnik
software *19* Software, Programme
solar *76* Sonnen-, Solar-
solar heating *88t* Solarheizung
solar panel *83* Sonnenkollektor
solar power *83* Sonnenkraft, -strom
sole *113* alleinig
solicitor *119* (Rechts-)Anwalt/ Anwältin
solution *70* Lösung, Ausweg
somehow *76* irgendwie
sophisticated *165* differenziert, erfahren
to sort *32* sortieren
source *53* Quelle

to source *73* beziehen
sovereignty *111* Souveränität, Unabhängigkeit
spacious *170t* geräumig
spade *132* Spaten
spare part *152t* Ersatzteil
to speak out for *103* sprechen für
specialist *104* speziell, Fach-
to specialize in *106* sich spezialisieren auf
special offer *18* Sonderangebot
species *149* Art(en)
to speculate *141* spekulieren, Vermutungen anstellen
speculation *156* Spekulation
speech bubble *6* Sprechblase
speeding *142* Geschwindigkeitsüberschreitung
spelling *62* Rechtschreibung
sponsor *46* Sponsor/in
to sponsor *48* finanziell unterstützen
sponsorship *45* finanzielle Unterstützung
to spread *49* (sich) verbreiten
spreadsheet *171* Tabellenprogramm, -kalkulation
spy *58* Spion/in, Spionage-
stability *111* Stabilität
stabilization *80* Stabilisierung
stable *47* fest
staff *26* Personal, Angestellte, Mitarbeiter/innen
stake *158t* Anteil
stamp *154* Briefmarke
to stand at *133* liegen bei
to stand for sth *51* für etw stehen
standard of living *81t* Lebensstandard
to stare *126* starren
to start up *53* starten, gründen
to starve yourself *17* hungern
state *67* (Bundes-)Staat
statement *13* Aussage
state-of-the-art *170t* letzter Stand der Technik, hochmodern
statistical *51* statistisch
to stay up *30* aufbleiben
steady *51* stetig, fest, regelmäßig
steel-frame *40* Stahlträger
stem cell *189* Stammzelle
stereotype *12* Klischee
stitch *139* Stich
to stock *146* führen, anbieten, auf Lager haben
stock control *86* Lagersteuerung, Lagerkontrolle
stock exchange *156* (Wertpapier-) Börse
stock market *156* (Wertpapier-) Börse
stockholder *156* Aktionär/in
stocks *156* Anleihen, Aktien
storage *161* Lager(haltung)
to store *150* lagern, aufbewahren
store card *143* Kundenkreditkarte
store detective *143* Warenhausdetektiv
storey *187* Stockwerk, Geschoss
stormy *82* stürmisch
stranger *59* Fremde/r
to strap *137* anschnallen, festbinden
strategy *159* Strategie, Taktik
to stream *177* strömen
strength *76* Kraft, Stärke
to strengthen *41* stärken
stressful *47* stressig, anstrengend
stretcher *12* Trage
striking *160* bemerkenswert, auffallend
stroke of luck *162* glücklicher Zufall
structure *41* Gebäude, Struktur, Aufbau
stuck: to be stuck *37* feststecken
studio *95* Studio
stuff *7* Zeug
to stuff *16* stopfen
sub-contractor *99* Subunternehmer/in
sub-heading *39* Untertitel
to subject *136* unterwerfen, aussetzen
subscription-based *168* Abonnements-
subsidized *89* subventioniert
substance *149* Substanz, Stoff
to substitute *187* ersetzen
suburb *66* Vorort, Außenbezirk
success rate *191* Erfolgsrate
to suffer *7* leiden
sufferer *17* Leidende/r
suffragette *119* Frauenrechtlerin
sugar beet *83* Zuckerrübe
sugar cane *83* Zuckerrohr
to suggest *48* vorschlagen, andeuten
suggestion *38* Vorschlag
suit *159* Anzug
suitable *8* passend, geeignet
sum *156* Summe, Betrag
to sum up *173* zusammenfassen
to summarize *121t* zusammenfassen
supervision *147* Überwachung
superweed *152t* hoch resistentes Unkraut
to supply *48* liefern
supply *48* Lieferung
supply and demand *156* Angebot und Nachfrage
supply chain *99* Versorgungskette
to support *69* unterstützen
support *88t* Hilfe, Unterstützung
supporter *148* Anhänger/in
Supreme Court *136* Oberster Gerichtshof
surely *66* sicherlich
to surf *9* surfen
surgery *191* chirurgischer Eingriff, Operation
surprised *65* überrascht, erstaunt
surrounding *73* umliegend
surveillance *134* Überwachung
survey *6* Umfrage
to survive *56* überleben
suspended sentence *141* (Freiheits-)Strafe auf Bewährung
SUV (sports utility vehicle) *68* Geländewagen (mit Vierradantrieb)
to swallow *127* (ver)schlucken
to swap *15* tauschen
sweater *76* Pullover
sweetie *12* Liebling, Schatz
switch *78* Schalter
to switch off *28* abschalten
sympathetic *17* mitfühlend, verständnisvoll
sympathy *119* Mitgefühl, Mitleid
symptom *191* Symptom

T

tailback *66* Autoschlange
to take off *24* starten
take on *110* Einstellung zu
to take over *40* übernehmen
talent *14* Talent
tanker *73* Tanker
target *81t* Ziel(vorgaben), Soll(zahlen)
to target *158t* zielen auf
target group *158* Zielgruppe
targeted *53* gezielt
task *17* Aufgabe
taste *133* Geschmack
tax *66* Steuer
taxpayer *40* Steuerzahler/in
team-building *171* Teamentwicklung
teammate *12* Mannschaftskamerad/in
tear *177* Träne
technically-advanced *166* technisch fortgeschritten
technique *51t* Methode, (Arbeits-) Technik
telework *171* Heimarbeit (am Computer)
teleworking *171* Heimarbeit (am Computer)
temper *126* Beherrschung
temperature *132* Temperatur
temporary *43* vorübergehend, zeitweilig, zeitlich befristet
tempting *188* verlockend
tendency *149* Tendenz
term *43* Amtszeit

terminal *73* Abfertigungsgebäude
terms *89* Bedingungen, Konditionen
terms of delivery *161* Lieferbedingungen
terms: to come to terms with *118t* zurechtkommen mit
terrible *49* schrecklich, furchtbar
terrified *65* erschrocken
terrorist *40* Terrorist/in
to test *7* prüfen
to text *30* SMS schicken, simsen
text message *6* SMS
textile *96* Textil-
thanks to *80* dank
the man in the street *184* der Mann auf der Straße
the race is on *83* das Rennen ist eröffnet
the way forward *168* die Zukunft, der Fortschritt
the writing's on the wall *171* das ist ein Warnsignal
theft *73* Diebstahl
theme *31* Thema
theoretical *107* theoretisch
thief *59* Dieb/in
though *81t* doch, jedoch
threat *111* Bedrohung, Drohung
thrill *26* Spannung
to throw out *56* hinauswerfen
to throw up *16* (sich) erbrechen
to tick *129* ankreuzen
tidal *80* Gezeiten-
tides *83* Gezeiten
tie *126* Krawatte, Schlips
tight *38t* knapp, eng
time off *21* Freizeit
time out *22* Freizeit
time: from time to time *29* von Zeit zu Zeit
time: in no time *16* im Handumdrehen
time-consuming *73* zeitraubend
timeline *52* Zeitachse, -rahmen
times *8* mal
timetable *42* Zeitplan, Fahrplan
tingling *16* kribbelnd, prickelnd
tiring *118* anstrengend, ermüdend
to a lesser extent *143* in geringerem Umfang
to sb's liking *161* nach jds Geschmack
toilet pan *16* Kloschüssel
tolerance *139* Toleranz
tolerant *139* tolerant
to tolerate *131t* tolerieren
ton *73* Tonne
tonne *76* Tonne
tool *171* Werkzeug
top: over the top *61* übertrieben
torture *103* Folter
tough *43* hart, streng
tourism *106* Tourismus, Fremdenverkehr
tourist guide *38* Reiseführer/in
toxic *150* giftig, toxisch
to trace *63* (zurück)verfolgen
to track *165* (zurück)verfolgen
trading bloc *113* Handelsblock
trading floor *156* Börsensaal
tradition *40* Tradition
traditional *69* traditionell
traffic jam *66* (Verkehrs-)Stau
traffic lights *170t* (Verkehrs-)Ampel
trafficking *103* illegaler (Rauschgift-)Handel
tragic *179* tragisch
transaction *162* Überweisung, Vorgang
to transfer *167t* weiterleiten
transmission *96* Übertragung
transplant *149* Transplantation
transport *65* Verkehr(smittel)
to transship *187* versenden
travel agency *32* Reisebüro
travel insurance *89* Reiseversicherung
treatment *17* Behandlung
treaty *105* Vertrag
to tremble *126* zittern
tremendous *129* gewaltig
trend *52* Trend
trial *161* Probe(bestellung)
to trick *135* betrügen, hereinlegen
to trigger *149* auslösen
trivial *135* trivial, geringfügig
trolley *153* (Einkaufs-)Wagen
trouble *56* Schwierigkeiten, Ärger
troubled: to be troubled *136* beunruhigt sein
trucking *73* (Lkw-)Transport
trunk *(AE)* *142t* Kofferraum
to trust *98* vertrauen
to try on *11* anprobieren
tub *16* Becher
tube *19* Tube
tuition *33* Unterricht
turbine *76* Turbine, Rad
to turn down *76* herunterregeln
turn: to take it in turns *33* sich abwechseln
turnaround *139* Kehrtwendung, Umschwung
turnover *157* Umsatz
twice *80* zweimal, doppelt
to twist *12* (ver)drehen
typical *109* typisch

U

ultimate *118t* ultimativ
unavailable *72* nicht verfügbar
unblinking *12* unbewegt
uncanny *137* ungeheuer, unheimlich
unclear *129* unklar
uncool *22* uncool
uncountable *19* nicht zählbar
uncultivated *150* brachliegend
undemocratic *110* undemokratisch
to underline *62* unterstreichen
underlined *8* unterstrichen
understandable *21* verständlich
unelected *110* nicht gewählt
unemployment *40* Arbeitslosigkeit
unhurt *132* unverletzt
uniformed *143* uniformiert
uniformity *129* Gleichmäßigkeit
unintentional *151* unabsichtlich
union *73* Gewerkschaft
unit price *161* Stück-, Einzelpreis
to unite *112* vereinigen
universally *159* allgemein, universell
unless *69* wenn nicht
unluckily *29* unglücklicherweise
unnecessary *62* unnötig
unpaid *107* unbezahlt
unreliable *76* unzuverlässig
unspecified *20* unbestimmt
unthinkable *159* unvorstellbar, undenkbar
unusual *59* ungewöhnlich
unwitting *187* unwissentlich
up: to be up for *58t* bereit sein für, Lust haben auf
upbringing *117* Erziehung
to upgrade *86* erweitern, verbessern, aufrüsten
to upload *153* senden, hinaufladen
up-market *43* im oberen Marktsegment
upset *65* bestürzt, entsetzt
urban *36* städtisch
urgent *48* dringend,eilig
user *59* Anwender/in, Benutzer/in

V

valid *134* gültig
valley *78* Tal
valuable *7* wertvoll
value *28* Wert
values *103* Werte
van *168* Lieferwagen, Transporter
vandal *43* Vandale
variable pay *93* variabler Lohn
variety *40* Vielfalt
various *65* verschieden
to vary *45* variieren
vast *147* riesig, ungeheuer
vehicle papers *134* Wagenpapiere
vendor *188* (Straßen-)Händler/in
venture *156* Unternehmen, Wagnis
verdict *141* Urteil, Beurteilung
version *79* Version, Fassung
vertical *68* senkrecht, vertikal
vibrant *177* vibrierend, aufregend

victim *135* Opfer
victory *136* Sieg
to view *159* ansehen, betrachten
violence *103* Gewalt
violent *7* gewalttätig
viral *49* viral, Virus-
virtual *26* virtuell
virtually *73* praktisch, nahezu
visa *24* Visum
vision *80* Vision, Vorausschau
visual *68* visuell, optisch
vocational *87* beruflich, Berufs-
voluntary *7* freiwillig
to vomit *16* erbrechen
to vote *56* abstimmen, wählen
voter *105* Wähler/in
voting rights *156* Stimmrechte
vulnerable *103* wehrlos

W

wage *131t* Lohn
wages *88* Lohn, Löhne
waiter *17* Kellner, Ober
to wander *132* (ziellos) herumlaufen
wardrobe *26* Kleiderschrank, Garderobe
warehouse *73* Lagerhalle, -haus
warehousing *165* Lagerhaltung
warming *80* Erwärmung
warmth *98* Wärme
warning *82* Warnung
warrior *12* Krieger
washbasin *184* Waschbecken
washing powder *116* Waschpulver
waste *69* Abfall
waste disposal *83* Abfallbeseitigung, Müllentsorgung
wasteful *49* verschwenderisch
to watch out *24* aufpassen
waterfall *37* Wasserfall
wave *40* Welle
weakness *99* Schwäche
weather forecast *175* Wettervorhersage
weather report *175* Wetterbericht
weatherman *24* Meteorologe
website development expert *162* Webseite-Entwickler/in
to weed out *139* aussondern, -merzen
weekday *9* Wochentag
to weigh up *102* abwägen
whatever *58* was (auch) immer
wheat *83* Weizen
whisky distillery *113* Whisky-Brennerei
white-collar *89* Schreibtisch-, Büro-
wide range *43* breite Palette
widening *111* Erweiterung
widow *123* Witwe
will *191* Wille
willing: to be willing *131* bereit/gewillt sein
wind farm *83* Windkraftanlage
wireless *175* drahtlos, Funk-
wise *80* weise, klug
within *40* innerhalb
to wonder *56* sich fragen, sich wundern
word of mouth *49* Mundpropaganda
to work oneself up *128* sich aufregen
to work out *51t* trainieren
workaholic *181* Arbeitssüchtige/r
workforce *73* Arbeiterschaft, Belegschaft
working conditions *103* Arbeitsbedingungen
workplace *86* Arbeitsplatz
works council *176* Betriebsrat
worried: to be worried *59* befürchten; besorgt sein
worthwhile *7* der Mühe wert
wound *118t* Wunde
wreck *132* (Auto-)Wrack
to wrestle *12* ringen
wrestler *13* Ringer/in
wrongdoing *110* Fehlverhalten

XYZ

to yell *37* schreien
yield *149* Ertrag
Yours faithfully *106* Mit freundlichen Grüßen
zero *69* Null
zone *69* Zone, Bereich

Geographical names

Abilene ['æbəli:n] *Abilene*
Africa ['afrɪkə] *Afrika*
Alexandria [ˌælɪg'zɑ:ndriə] *Alexandria*
America [ə'merɪkə] *Amerika*
Antarctic [ænt'ɑ:ktɪk] *die Antarktis*
Arizona [ærɪ'zəʊnə] *Arizona*
Asia ['eɪʃə] *Asien*
Atlanta [ət'læntə] *Atlanta*
Austin [ˌtɪm 'ɒstɪn] *Austin*
Australia [ɒ'streɪliə] *Australien*
Austria ['ɒstriə] *Österreich*
Bangalore [ˌbæŋgə'lɔ:] *Bangalore*
Belgium ['beldʒəm] *Belgien*
Bengal [ˌben'gɔ:l] *Bengalen*
Big Apple [ˌbɪd 'æpl] *Spitzname für New York*
Brazil [brə'zɪl] *Brasilien*
Bristol ['brɪstl] *Bristol*
Britain ['brɪtn] *Großbritannien*
Broadway ['brɔ:dweɪ] *Broadway (Straßenname)*
Bronx [brɒŋks] *Bronx*
Brooklyn ['brʊklɪn] *Brooklyn*
Brussels ['brʌslz] *Brüssel*
Bulgaria [bʌl'geəriə] *Bulgarien*
California [ˌkælə'fɔ:niə] *Kalifornien*
Canada ['kænədə] *Kanada*
Cape Town ['keɪptaʊn] *Kapstadt*
(the) Caribbean [ðə ˌkærə'bi:ən] *(die) Karibik*
Central America [ˌsentrəl ə'merɪkə] *Mittelamerika*
Chicago [ʃɪ'kɑ:gəʊ] *Chicago*
China ['tʃaɪnə] *China*
Cologne [kə'ləʊn] *Köln*
Colorado [ˌkɒlə'rɑ:dəʊ] *Colorado*
Dublin ['dʌblɪn] *Dublin*
East Asia [ˌi:st 'eɪʃə] *Ostasien*
East River [ˌi:st 'rɪvə] *East River*
eastern Europe [ˌi:stən 'jʊərəp] *Osteuropa*
Eighth Ave [ˌeɪtθ 'ævənju:] *Eighth Ave (Straßenname)*
England ['ɪŋglənd] *England*
Europe ['jʊərəp] *Europa*
Finland ['fɪnlənd] *Finnland*
Florida ['flɒrɪdə] *Florida*
France [frɑ:ns] *Frankreich*
Galax ['gæləks] *Galax*
Georgia ['dʒɔ:dʒə] *Georgia*
Germany ['dʒɜ:məni] *Deutschland*
Greenland ['gri:nlənd] *Grönland*
Guatemala [ˌgwɑ:tə'mɑ:lə] *Guatemala*
Harlem ['hɑ:ləm] *Harlem*
Holland ['hɒlənd] *Holland*
Houston ['hju:stən] *Houston*
Hudson River [ˌhʌdsn 'rɪvə] *Hudson River*
Hull [hʌl] *Hull*
Illinois [ˌɪlə'nɔɪ] *Illinois*
India ['ɪndiə] *Indien*
Indonesia [ˌɪndəʊ'ni:ziə] *Indonesien*
Iran [ɪ'rɑ:n] *Iran*
Ireland ['aɪələnd] *Irland*
Italy ['ɪtəli] *Italien*
Kings Street [ˌkɪŋz 'stri:t] *Kings Street (Straßenname)*
Latin America [ˌlætɪn ə'merɪkə] *Lateinamerika*
Littleton ['lɪtltən] *Littleton*
London ['lʌndən] *London*
Los Angeles [lɒs 'ændʒəli:z] *Los Angeles*
Luxemburg ['lʌksəmbɜ:g] *Luxemburg*
Manchester ['mæntʃɪstə] *Manchester*
Manhattan [mæn'hætn] *Manhattan*
(the) Mediterranean [ðə ˌmedɪtə'reɪniən] *Mittelmeer*
Miami [maɪ'æmi] *Miami*
Morocco [mə'rɒkəʊ] *Marokko*
(the) Netherlands [ðə 'neðələndz] *die Niederlande*
New Orleans [ˌnju: ɔ:'li:əns] *New Orleans*
New York (NY) [ˌnju: 'jɔ:k] *New York*
New York Bay [ˌnju: jɔ:k 'beɪ] *New Yorker Bucht*
New York City [ˌnju: jɔ:k 'sɪti] *New York City*
New Zealand [ˌnju: 'zi:lənd] *Neuseeland*
Norfolk ['nɔ:fək] *Norfolk*
North America [ˌnɔ:θ ə'merɪkə] *Nordamerika*
Norway ['nɔ:weɪ] *Norwegen*
Norwich ['nɒrɪdʒ] *Norwich*
Oak Street [ˌəʊk 'stri:t] *Oak Street (Straßenname)*
Oregon ['ɒrɪgən] *Oregon*
Oxford ['ɒksfəd] *Oxford*
Paris ['pærɪs] *Paris*
Perryton ['perɪtən] *Perryton*
(the) Philippines [ðə 'fɪləpi:nz] *die Philippinen*
Phoenix ['fi:nɪks] *Phoenix*
Queens [kwi:nz] *Queens*
Richmond ['rɪtʃmənd] *Richmond*
Rio Grande [ˌri:əʊ 'grænd] *Rio Grande*
Rome [rəʊm] *Rom*
Route 66 [ˌru:t ˌsɪksti 'sɪks] *Route 66 (Straßenverbindung zur US-amerikanischen Westküste)*
Russia ['rʌʃə] *Russland*

San Bernando [sæn bə'nændəʊ] *San Bernando*
San Diego [ˌsæn di'eɪgəʊ] *San Diego*
San Francisco [ˌsæn frən'sɪskəʊ] *San Francisco*
Seattle [si'ætl] *Seattle*
Shanghai [ˌʃæŋ'haɪ] *Shanghai*
Shropshire ['ʃrɒpʃə] *Shropshire*
Silver Creek [ˌsɪlvə 'kri:k] *Silver Creek*
South Africa [saʊθ 'æfrɪkə] *Südafrika*
South America [ˌsaʊθ ə'merɪkə] *Südamerika*
Stafford ['stæfəd] *Stafford*
Staten Island [ˌstætn 'aɪlənd] *Staten Island*
Strasbourg ['stræzbɜ:g] *Straßburg*
Sweden ['swi:dn] *Schweden*
Swindon ['swɪndən] *Swindon*
Texas ['teksəs] *Texas*
Tokyo ['təʊkiəʊ] *Tokio*
Tucson ['tu:sɒn] *Tucson*
Turkey ['tɜ:ki] *Türkei*
Tuusula ['tu:sulɑ] *Tuusula*
(the) UK [ðə ˌju: 'keɪ] *(das) Vereinigte Königreich*
(the) USA [ðə ˌju: es 'eɪ] *(die) Vereinigten Staaten von Amerika*
Vermont [və'mɒnt] *Vermont*
Virginia [və'dʒɪniə] *Virginia*
Wales [weɪlz] *Wales*
Washington D.C. ['wɒʃɪŋtən ˌdi: 'si:] *Washington D.C.*

Irregular verbs

be	was/were	been	*sein*
beat	beat	beaten	*schlagen, besiegen*
become	became	become	*werden*
begin	began	begun	*anfangen, beginnen*
bend	bent	bent	*(sich) beugen*
blow	blew	blown	*wehen, blasen, ziehen*
break	broke	broken	*brechen*
breed	bred	bred	*sich vermehren, sich ausbreiten*
bring	brought	brought	*(mit)bringen*
build	built	built	*bauen*
burn	burnt/ burned	burnt/ burned	*(ver)brennen*
buy	bought	bought	*kaufen*
catch	caught	caught	*fangen, fassen, erreichen*
choose	chose	chosen	*(aus)wählen*
come	came	come	*kommen*
cost	cost	cost	*kosten*
cross-breed	cross-bred	cross-bred	*kreuzen*
cut	cut	cut	*schneiden*
deal	dealt	dealt	*versetzen, verteilen*
dig	dug	dug	*graben*
do	did	done	*tun, machen*
draw	drew	drawn	*zeichnen*
dream	dreamt/ dreamed	dreamt/ dreamed	*träumen*
drink	drank	drunk	*trinken*
drive	drove	driven	*fahren*
eat	ate	eaten	*essen*
fall	fell	fallen	*fallen*
feed	fed	fed	*füttern, ernähren*
feel	felt	felt	*(sich) fühlen, empfinden*
fight	fought	fought	*kämpfen*
find	found	found	*finden*
fit	fit/fitted	fit/fitted	*passen, entsprechen, anbringen*
fly	flew	flown	*fliegen*
forbid	forbade	forbidden	*verbieten*
forget	forgot	forgotten	*vergessen*
get	got	got (*AE* gotten)	*bekommen*
give	gave	given	*geben*
go	went	gone	*gehen, fahren*
grow	grew	grown	*wachsen*
hang	hung	hung	*hängen*
have	had	had	*haben*
hear	heard	heard	*hören*
hide	hid	hidden	*(sich) verstecken*
hit	hit	hit	*schlagen*
hold	held	held	*halten, festhalten*

hurt	hurt	hurt	*verletzen*
keep	kept	kept	*behalten*
know	knew	known	*kennen, wissen*
lay	laid	laid	*legen*
lead	led	led	*führen*
lean	leant/ leaned	leant/ leaned	*sich lehnen, sich beugen*
learn	learnt/ learned	learnt/ learned	*lernen*
leave	left	left	*abfahren, verlassen, weggehen*
let	let	let	*lassen*
lie	lay	lain	*liegen*
light	lit	lit	*anzünden, beleuchten*
lose	lost	lost	*verlieren*
make	made	made	*machen*
mean	meant	meant	*meinen, bedeuten*
meet	met	met	*treffen*
overcome	overcame	overcome	*überwinden, überwältigen*
override	overrode	overridden	*sich hinwegsetzen über*
panic	panicked	panicked	*in Panik geraten*
pay	paid	paid	*bezahlen*
put	put	put	*setzen, stellen, legen*
quit	quit/ quitted	quit/ quitted	*verlassen, aufhören*
read	read	read	*lesen*
repay	repaid	repaid	*zurückzahlen*
rewrite	rewrote	rewritten	*umschreiben*
ride	rode	ridden	*reiten, fahren*
ring	rang	rung	*anrufen, läuten*
rise	rose	risen	*(an)steigen*
run	ran	run	*laufen, rennen*
say	said	said	*sagen*
see	saw	seen	*sehen*
seek	sought	sought	*suchen*
sell	sold	sold	*verkaufen*
send	sent	sent	*senden, schicken*
set	set	set	*setzen, stellen*
shake	shook	shaken	*schütteln*
shine	shone	shone	*scheinen, glänzen*
show	showed	shown	*zeigen*
shrink	shrank	shrunk	*schrumpfen, zurückgehen*
shut	shut	shut	*schließen*
sing	sang	sung	*singen*
sink	sank	sunk	*sinken*
sit	sat	sat	*sitzen*
sleep	slept	slept	*schlafen*
slide	slid	slid	*(ab)rutschen, (ab)sacken*
smell	smelt/ smelled	smelt/ smelled	*riechen*
speak	spoke	spoken	*sprechen*

spell	spelt/ spelled	spelt/ spelled	*buchstabieren*	tell	told	told	*sagen, erzählen*
spend	spent	spent	*ausgeben, verbringen*	think	thought	thought	*denken*
spread	spread	spread	*(sich) verbreiten*	throw	threw	thrown	*werfen*
stand	stood	stood	*stehen*	understand	understood	understood	*verstehen*
steal	stole	stolen	*stehlen*	wake	woke	woken	*aufwachen, aufwecken*
swim	swam	swum	*schwimmen*	wear	wore	worn	*tragen*
take	took	taken	*nehmen*	win	won	won	*gewinnen*
teach	taught	taught	*unterrichten, beibringen*	write	wrote	written	*schreiben*

Quellenverzeichnis

Titel: Corbis/J. Fuste Raga; Alamy/K-Photos, Getty RF; istockphoto

RF photos:
Alamy: S. 6/2/E.Audras, S/3/Itani, S. 7/4/IS503; S. 16/T. Kroeger, S. 46/moodboard, S. 52/K. Brofsky, S. 77/2/J. Pelaez, S. 85/2/BananaStock, S. 85/4/EV107, S. 85/5/R. McVay, S. 85/6/IS147, S. 89/2/J. Hollingsworth, S. 89/3/Bananastock, S. 93/2/C. Anderson, S. 103/A. King, S. 95/3/WidStock, S. 105/3/BigCheeseSpecial, S. 96/1/J. Woodhouse, S. 96/5/SomosGroup1, S. 106/Niehoff, S. 110/K. Glubish, S. 111/1/IS945, S. 111/2/rubberball, S. 111/3Radius images, S. 111/4/J. Hollingsworth, S. 116/2/BananaStock, S. 116/3/IS732, S. 120/1/Shoosh, S. 123/indykb, S. 140/2/Photodisc, S. 140/3/S. Marcus;
Corbis: S. 14/moodboard, S. 17/1, S. 141/5/R. Meinychuk;
Comstock: S. 17/2;
istock: S. 6/1/3; S7/1/2, S. 37/2;
Maly, V.: S. 95/2, S99/1/2;
Masterfile: S. 72/1/2, S. 114;
Shutterstock: S. 22/1/2, S. 26/1/2, S. 35/2/3/4/6, S. 50/1-5, S. 63, S. 66/1/3/4/5, S. 73, S. 77/1, S. 95/1, S. 96/1/3, S99/3, S. 103/1-4, S. 105/1, S. 115/2-8, S. 143/1/3, S. 145/4/6;
istockphoto: S. 164/1/2, S. 165, S. 171, S. 177/1, S. 180/1-3, S. 183/1;

RM photos:
Actionpress: S. 145/7;
Advertising Archives: S. 45/1/2/3/5, S. 53;
Alamy: S. 30/1/P. Cutler, S. 30/2/J. West, S. 35/5/BLimages, S. 37/1/D. Frates, S. 40/P. Bennett, S. 66/2/Travelshots, S. 71/Kiedrowski, S. 76/1/G. Williams, S. 76/3/J. Moers, S. 76/4/Caro, S. 89/4/zoonar.com, S. 93/1/F.Waldhaeus, S. 94/Pixland0907, S. 113/E. Parker, S. 116/1/ClassicStock, S. 123/J. Sutton-Hibbert, S. 133/J. Blackler, S. 124/acestock, S. 127/1/dbtravel, S. 139/1/H. Threlfall, S. 139/2/D. Grossman, S. 140/1/T. McGuire, S. 141/4/H. Westheim, S. 145/2/acestock, S. 143/2/D. Hoffman, S. 146/A. Segre, S. 150/R. Rivett, S. 160/A. Segre, S. 162/D. Hurst;
Cinetext: S. 58, S. 75/1;
Corbis: S. 12/1/Emely, S. 12/2/Duomo, S. 89/1, S. 96/3/E. Jansson, S. 153/R.Friedman;
Fotofinder: S. 16/2/Andreas Buck, S. 26/Fotoagentur Magics/P. Schatz, S. 30/Weisflog, S. 73/mediacolors, S. 76/2/ImageSource, S. 85/1/A1Pix, S. 85/3/Matthias Stolt, S. 86/Mediacolors, S. 105/2/F1online, S. 189/fab-pics/F. Ricci; S. 115/tranistArchiv/T. Roetting, S. 120/2/Caro/Teschner;
PictureAlliance: S. 35/7, S. 56/1/GMTV, S. 56/2/J. Ryan, S. 75/2/3/4, S. 105/4/R. Hirschberger, S. 105/5/dpa, S. 119/1/PA, S. 119/2/L. Ruymen, S. 121/EPA, S. 127/2, S. 129/2/A. Teich, S. 129/3/I. West, S. 131/1/L. Stringer, S. 131/2/G. Caddick, S136/P. Buck, S. 143/1/AFP, S. 143/3/DBThüringer Allgemeine, S143/3/PA-5322625, S. 145/1/EPA, S. 145/5/P. Kneffel, S. 158/A.M. Parks, S. 175/W. Wisniewski; S. 177/2/B. Settnik, S. 179/F. Tschauner, S. 183/2/PA Hanson, S. 185/photoshot, S. 188/1/T. Dashuber, S. 188/2/epa/Y. Cortez;
Ullstein-Bild: S. 137; S. 156/Momentphoto;;

Cartoons: cartoonStock.com: S. 62, 65, 68, 122; Martyn Ford, LGP, Brighton: S. 92; Julie Brown, Tribune Media Service Inc.: S. 132; The Cartoonist Group: S. 132; Punch Ltd: S. 135

Textquellen: S. 59: Adapted and abridged from *Things you wouldn't tell your mother* by Alison George, New Scientist 16/09/06, p. 50; S. 126/127: Hanif Kureishi, *Love in a Blue Time*, Faber and Faber, 1997 S. 136: Based on *http://en.wikipedia.org/wiki/Karla_Faye_Tucker;* S. 146: abridged from *British supermarkets call for a boycott of 'cloned' meat and milk*, Daily Mail 10.01.07; S. 175: Adapted and abridged from *Reuters ploughs into Indian farming*, Sunday Times, 30th March 2008; S. 183: Adapted and abridged from *Stelios Haji-Ioannou: The serial entrepreneur*, The Prague Tribune, February 2005; S. 187: Adapted and abridged from *From China to Panama, a Trail of Poisoned Medicine,* The New York Times, 6th May 2007

European Union